HOW THE EXPERTS HELP YOU PA

- **PROVEN TEACHING METHODOLOGY** Text based on thousands of hours of classroom experience—Global gets people trained and certified. (200,000 professionals can't be wrong!)

- **MORE PRACTICE TESTS** Test Yourself Practice exam software with hundreds of challenging questions—including in-depth answers and detailed score analysis.

- **AUTHORITATIVE INFORMATION** Developed and reviewed by master MCSE and MCT professionals.

- **EXAM WATCH** Warnings based on post-exam research identifying troublesome exam questions.

MCDBA	MCSE	MCSE+Internet	CERTIFICATION PRESS STUDY GUIDES
EACH CORE REQUIRED, CHOOSE 1 ELECTIVE	CHOOSE 4 CORE & 2 ELECTIVE	CHOOSE 7 CORE & 2 ELECTIVE	
CORE	ELECTIVE	ELECTIVE	MCDBA SQL Server 7.0 Administration Study Guide (Exam 70-28) 0-07-211904-7
CORE	ELECTIVE		MCDBA SQL Server 7.0 Design Study Guide (Exam 70-29) 0-07-212078-9
CORE	CORE	CORE	MCSE Windows NT Server 4.0 Study Guide (Exam 70-67) 0-07-882491-5
CORE	CORE	CORE	MCSE Windows NT Server 4.0 in the Enterprise Study Guide (Exam 70-68) 0-07-882490-7
	CORE (CHOOSE ONE)	CORE (CHOOSE ONE)	MCSE Windows NT Workstation 4.0 Study Guide (Exam 70-73) 0-07-882492-3
	CORE	CORE	MCSE Windows 98 Study Guide (Exam 70-98) 0-07-882532-6
	CORE	CORE	MCSE Networking Essentials Study Guide (Exam 70-58) 0-07-882493-1
ELECTIVE	CORE	CORE	MCSE Microsoft TCP/IP on Windows NT 4.0 Study Guide (Exam 70-59) 0-07-882489-3
	ELECTIVE	CORE	MCSE Internet Explorer Administration Kit Study Guide (Exam 70-79) 0-07-211931-4
	ELECTIVE	CORE	MCSE Internet Information Server 4.0 Study Guide (Exams 70-87, 70-79, 70-88) 0-07-882560-1
	ELECTIVE	ELECTIVE	MCSE Exchange Server 5.5 Study Guide (Exam 70-81) 0-07-882488-5
	ELECTIVE	ELECTIVE	
	ELECTIVE		
ELECTIVE	ELECTIVE		
ELECTIVE	ELECTIVE	ELECTIVE	
ELECTIVE	ELECTIVE	ELECTIVE	
ELECTIVE	ELECTIVE	ELECTIVE	

MCSE Networking Essentials
MCSE Windows NT Workstation 4.0
MCSE Windows NT Server 4.0
MCSE Windows NT Server 4.0

MICROSOFT CERTIFIED DATABASE ADMINISTRATOR

MCDBA SQL Server 7.0 Database Design Study Guide

(Exam 70-29)

Syngress Media, Inc.

Osborne McGraw-Hill

Berkeley New York St. Louis San Francisco Auckland Bogotá Hamburg London Madrid Mexico City
Milan Montreal New Delhi Panama City Paris São Paulo Singapore Sydney Tokyo Toronto

Osborne/**McGraw-Hill**
2600 Tenth Street
Berkeley, California 94710
U.S.A.

For information on translations or book distributors outside the U.S.A., or to arrange bulk purchase discounts for sales promotions, premiums, or fund-raisers, please contact Osborne/**McGraw-Hill** at the above address.

MCDBA SQL Server 7.0 Database Design Study Guide (Exam 70-29)

1234567890 AGM AGM 90198765432109

ISBN 0-07-212078-9

Publisher
Brandon A. Nordin

**Associate Publisher and
Editor-in-Chief**
Scott Rogers

Acquisitions Editor
Gareth Hancock

Project Editor
Mark Karmendy

Editorial Assistant
Tara Davis

Technical Editors
Michael Lane Thomas
Robert Aschermann

Technical Consultant
George Pandapas

Copy Editor
Lynette Crane

Proofreaders
Linda and Paul Medoff

Indexer
Richard Shrout

Computer Designers
Mickey Galicia
Roberta Steele
Ann Sellers

Illustrators
Brian Wells
Robert Hansen
Beth Young

Series Design
Roberta Steele

Cover Design
Regan Honda

FOREWORD

From Global Knowledge

At Global Knowledge we strive to support the multiplicity of learning styles required by our students to achieve success as technical professionals. In this series of books, it is our intention to offer the reader a valuable tool for successful completion of the MCDBA and MCSE Certification Exams.

As the world's largest IT training company, Global Knowledge is uniquely positioned to offer these books. The expertise gained each year from providing instructor-led training to hundreds of thousands of students worldwide has been captured in book form to enhance your learning experience. We hope that the quality of these books demonstrates our commitment to your lifelong learning success. Whether you choose to learn through the written word, computer-based training, Web delivery, or instructor-led training, Global Knowledge is committed to providing you the very best in each of those categories. For those of you who know Global Knowledge, or those of you who have just found us for the first time, our goal is to be your lifelong competency partner.

Thank you for the opportunity to serve you. We look forward to serving your needs again in the future.

Warmest regards,

Duncan Anderson
President and Chief Executive Officer, Global Knowledge

The Global Knowledge Advantage

Global Knowledge has a global delivery system for its products and services. The company has 28 subsidiaries, and offers its programs through a total of 60+ locations. No other vendor can provide consistent services across a geographic area this large. Global Knowledge is the largest independent information technology education provider, offering programs on a variety of platforms. This enables our multi-platform and multi-national customers to obtain all of their programs from a single vendor. The company has developed the unique CompetusTM Framework software tool and methodology which can quickly reconfigure courseware to the proficiency level of a student on an interactive basis. Combined with self-paced and on-line programs, this technology can reduce the time required for training by prescribing content in only the deficient skills areas. The company has fully automated every aspect of the education process, from registration and follow-up, to "just-in-time" production of courseware. Global Knowledge, through its Enterprise Services Consultancy, can customize programs and products to suit the needs of an individual customer.

Global Knowledge Classroom Education Programs

The backbone of our delivery options is classroom-based education. Our modern, well-equipped facilities staffed with the finest instructors offer programs in a wide variety of information technology topics, many of which lead to professional certifications.

Custom Learning Solutions

This delivery option has been created for companies and governments that value customized learning solutions. For them, our consultancy-based approach of developing targeted education solutions is most effective at helping them meet specific objectives.

Self-Paced and Multimedia Products

This delivery option offers self-paced program titles in interactive CD-ROM, videotape and audio tape programs. In addition, we offer custom development of interactive multimedia courseware to customers and partners. Call us at 1 (888) 427-4228.

Electronic Delivery of Training

Our network-based training service delivers efficient competency-based, interactive training via the World Wide Web and organizational intranets. This leading-edge delivery option provides a custom learning path and "just-in-time" training for maximum convenience to students.

ARG

American Research Group (ARG), a wholly-owned subsidiary of Global Knowledge, one of the largest worldwide training partners of Cisco Systems, offers a wide range of internetworking, LAN/WAN, Bay Networks, FORE Systems, IBM, and UNIX courses. ARG offers hands on network training in both instructor-led classes and self-paced PC-based training.

Global Knowledge Courses Available

Network Fundamentals
- Understanding Computer Networks
- Telecommunications Fundamentals I
- Telecommunications Fundamentals II
- Understanding Networking Fundamentals
- Implementing Computer Telephony Integration
- Introduction to Voice Over IP
- Introduction to Wide Area Networking
- Cabling Voice and Data Networks
- Introduction to LAN/WAN protocols
- Virtual Private Networks
- ATM Essentials

Network Security & Management
- Troubleshooting TCP/IP Networks
- Network Management
- Network Troubleshooting
- IP Address Management
- Network Security Administration
- Web Security
- Implementing UNIX Security
- Managing Cisco Network Security
- Windows NT 4.0 Security

IT Professional Skills
- Project Management for IT Professionals
- Advanced Project Management for IT Professionals
- Survival Skills for the New IT Manager
- Making IT Teams Work

LAN/WAN Internetworking
- Frame Relay Internetworking
- Implementing T1/T3 Services
- Understanding Digital Subscriber Line (xDSL)
- Internetworking with Routers and Switches
- Advanced Routing and Switching
- Multi-Layer Switching and Wire-Speed Routing
- Internetworking with TCP/IP
- ATM Internetworking
- OSPF Design and Configuration
- Border Gateway Protocol (BGP) Configuration

Authorized Vendor Training
Cisco Systems
- Introduction to Cisco Router Configuration
- Advanced Cisco Router Configuration
- Installation and Maintenance of Cisco Routers
- Cisco Internetwork Troubleshooting
- Cisco Internetwork Design
- Cisco Routers and LAN Switches
- Catalyst 5000 Series Configuration
- Cisco LAN Switch Configuration
- Managing Cisco Switched Internetworks
- Configuring, Monitoring, and Troubleshooting Dial-Up Services
- Cisco AS5200 Installation and Configuration
- Cisco Campus ATM Solutions

Bay Networks
- Bay Networks Accelerated Router Configuration
- Bay Networks Advanced IP Routing
- Bay Networks Hub Connectivity
- Bay Networks Accelar 1xxx Installation and Basic Configuration
- Bay Networks Centillion Switching

FORE Systems
- FORE ATM Enterprise Core Products
- FORE ATM Enterprise Edge Products
- FORE ATM Theory
- FORE LAN Certification

Operating Systems & Programming
Microsoft
- Introduction to Windows NT
- Microsoft Networking Essentials
- Windows NT 4.0 Workstation
- Windows NT 4.0 Server
- Advanced Windows NT 4.0 Server
- Windows NT Networking with TCP/IP
- Introduction to Microsoft Web Tools
- Windows NT Troubleshooting
- Windows Registry Configuration

UNIX
- UNIX Level I
- UNIX Level II
- Essentials of UNIX and NT Integration

Programming
- Introduction to JavaScript
- Java Programming
- PERL Programming
- Advanced PERL with CGI for the Web

Web Site Management & Development
- Building a Web Site
- Web Site Management and Performance
- Web Development Fundamentals

High Speed Networking
- Essentials of Wide Area Networking
- Integrating ISDN
- Fiber Optic Network Design
- Fiber Optic Network Installation
- Migrating to High Performance Ethernet

DIGITAL UNIX
- UNIX Utilities and Commands
- DIGITAL UNIX v4.0 System Administration
- DIGITAL UNIX v4.0 (TCP/IP) Network Management
- AdvFS, LSM, and RAID Configuration and Management
- DIGITAL UNIX TruCluster Software Configuration and Management
- UNIX Shell Programming Featuring Kornshell
- DIGITAL UNIX v4.0 Security Management
- DIGITAL UNIX v4.0 Performance Management
- DIGITAL UNIX v4.0 Intervals Overview

DIGITAL OpenVMS
- OpenVMS Skills for Users
- OpenVMS System and Network Node Management I
- OpenVMS System and Network Node Management II
- OpenVMS System and Network Node Management III
- OpenVMS System and Network Node Operations
- OpenVMS for Programmers
- OpenVMS System Troubleshooting for Systems Managers
- Configuring and Managing Complex VMScluster Systems
- Utilizing OpenVMS Features from C
- OpenVMS Performance Management
- Managing DEC TCP/IP Services for OpenVMS
- Programming in C

Hardware Courses
- AlphaServer 1000/1000A Installation, Configuration and Maintenance
- AlphaServer 2100 Server Maintenance
- AlphaServer 4100, Troubleshooting Techniques and Problem Solving

January 12, 1998

Dear Osborne/McGraw-Hill Customer:

Microsoft is pleased to inform you that Osborne/McGraw-Hill is a participant in the Microsoft® Independent Courseware Vendor (ICV) program. Microsoft ICVs design, develop, and market self-paced courseware, books, and other products that support Microsoft software and the Microsoft Certified Professional (MCP) program.

To be accepted into the Microsoft ICV program, an ICV must meet set criteria. In addition, Microsoft reviews and approves each ICV training product before permission is granted to use the Microsoft Certified Professional Approved Study Guide logo on that product. This logo assures the consumer that the product has passed the following Microsoft standards:

- The course contains accurate product information.
- The course includes labs and activities during which the student can apply knowledge and skills learned from the course.
- The course teaches skills that help prepare the student to take corresponding MCP exams.

Microsoft ICVs continually develop and release new MCP Approved Study Guides. To prepare for a particular Microsoft certification exam, a student may choose one or more single, self-paced training courses or a series of training courses.

You will be pleased with the quality and effectiveness of the MCP Approved Study Guides available from Osborne/McGraw-Hill.

Sincerely,

Becky Kirsininkas

Becky Kirsininkas
ICV Program Manager
Microsoft Training & Certification

About Syngress Media

Syngress Media creates books and software for Information Technology professionals seeking skill enhancement and career advancement. Its products are designed to comply with vendor and industry standard course curricula, and are optimized for certification exam preparation. Visit the Syngress Web site at www.syngress.com.

Contributors

Kerry Sutton (MCSE+I, MCT, MCSD) is a Managing Consultant with Metamor Consulting Solutions, the 1997 Microsoft Solution Provider Partner of the Year Worldwide. Kerry has been fortunate enough to work on several mission-critical SQL Server implementations to which he owes a great deal of his knowledge. Kerry currently splits his time between working with Fortune 500 customers who are implementing Microsoft Backoffice (especially SQL Server) and expanding a new office for Metamor Consulting Solutions in Jacksonville, Florida. Kerry especially enjoys helping others to understand this technology—both in the formal classroom setting and during consulting assignments. He is a Microsoft Certified System Engineer + Internet, a Microsoft Certified Trainer, and a Microsoft Certified Solution Developer. Kerry was also a contributor for MCDBA SQL Server 7.0 Administration Study Guide (Exam 70-028). You may contact Kerry via email at KERRY.SUTTON@METAMOR.COM.

Derrick Woo (MCSD, MCSE, MCP+I, A+) is a networking and solution development specialist. He is president and co-founder of Obelisk Software. Prior to founding his own company, he worked as a network engineer at IBM, consulted for numerous Southern California firms, and was part of the support team for the world's largest fully switched Ethernet network. He works primarily with Windows NT and BackOffice solutions.

Derrick was also a contributor for MCDBA SQL Server 7.0 Administration Study Guide (Exam 70-028).

Mike Martone (MCSD, MCSE, MCP+Internet, LCNAD) is a senior software engineer and consultant for Berish & Associates (http://www.berish.com), a Cleveland-based Microsoft Certified Solutions Provider – Partner Level. In 1995, Mike became one of the first thousand MCSDs, and is certified in VB 3, 4, and 5. Since graduating from Bowling Green State University with degrees in Computer Science and Psychology, he has specialized in developing Visual Basic, Internet, and Office applications for corporations and government institutions. In a previous life, Mike worked as a software developer in the court of Caesar Augustus, where he attempted to fix the Year Zero bug, caused by the inability of early Roman computers to handle positive numbers. Mike lives in Lakewood, Ohio, and can be reached at martone@berish.com.

Todd Meadors (CNE, MCSE) teaches full-time computer classes for DeKalb Technical Institute, outside Atlanta, Georgia. He holds CNE and MCSE certifications, and he has an MBA and MS in Computer Information Systems (CIS). He credits LANOP The Computer Lab for assisting him in obtaining the MCSE. He would like to dedicate his sections of the book to his family: Micki, Zac, and Jessie.

Lauri M. Bryant (MCT, MCSD, NCI) is the principal owner of LM Bryant and Associates, a small consulting firm located in Chicago, Illinois. Her firm focuses on providing support and training for Microsoft's visual tools. She has been programming for the past 15 years. Lauri's training career began 10 years ago providing end-user training for the Fortune 100. Five years ago she became certified to deliver Microsoft training. Lauri attended Rutgers University and has a background in English and graphical design.

Thomas Huff (MCSD) has over a decade of experience in the field. Thomas hails from Silver Spring, Maryland, where he works at PowerVision Corporation (www.powervision.com) as a Systems Engineer. He graduated magna cum laude from the University of Maryland, Baltimore County, with a degree in Computer Science, and is currently pursuing a master's degree at Johns Hopkins University. In his spare time he enjoys science fiction, ice hockey, heavy metal, and skydiving.

Technical Review and From the Classroom Sidebars

Michael Lane Thomas (MCP, MCP+I, MCSE, MCSE+I, MCT, MCSD, MCP+SB, MSS, A+) is a computer industry consultant analyst, and technical trainer, and President/CEO of theFastLane.com Inc.. He has spoken publicly on some of the hottest technologies to hit the industry, such as XML, SQL, and Y2K issues, and has been heard at Microsoft-sponsored national technical conferences, special interest groups, and on Kansas City's airwaves on 980KMBZ radio.

Michael teaches Microsoft Official Curriculum (MOC) courses, ranging from BackOffice products such as Proxy, SQL Server, and IIS, to development technologies such as Visual InterDev, Visual Basic, COM, and Visual Studio. Michael is certified to teach over 40 Microsoft courses, with more on the horizon, but he prefers to focus on the most recent development courses because "that's where the fun stuff is!"

When not writing, Michael spends his time consulting and training, although he prefers the challenge of designing, building, and developing complex intranet, three-tier Web applications, and advanced Web-based solutions using the full range of available Microsoft technologies. He is currently waiting on beta scores for the SQL 7.0 Administration and Implementation exams to secure his MCDBA charter certification, to go with status as a charter MCSE+I and MCP+SB professional. Michael has successfully passed 30 Microsoft exams.

After graduating from the University of Kansas with a B.A. and B.S. in Mathematics, Michael has continued his traditional academic pursuits with a slow but steady climb towards his M.S. in Engineering Management from the University of Kansas. Michael is a former contributor and technical editor for the *Microsoft Certified Professional Magazine,* and author, contributor, and/or technical editor for nine books to date. Michael can be reached at michael@thefastlane.com.

Robert Aschermann (MCP, MCSE, MCT, MBA) has been involved with information systems as an IS professional for nearly 10 years. During his career he has worked in technical support, systems design, consulting, and training. Robert has been an MCSE for almost five years now and has passed more than 15 Microsoft certification exams. Currently Robert works for a large computer manufacturer based in Austin, Texas. His job responsibilities include systems engineering, project management, and business analysis. As a project manager he has lead large Windows NT and Windows 95 operating system migrations and many small to medium size client/server development projects. As a systems engineer and architect his responsibilities include identifying business processes that need improvement, drafting design specifications for solutions, and building systems that meet those design specifications. He routinely works with Microsoft development tools such as SQL Server 7.0, Access, IIS 4.0, Visual InterDev, Visual Basic, and the Microsoft Solutions Framework.

ACKNOWLEDGMENTS

We would like to thank the following people:

- Richard Kristof of Global Knowledge for championing the series and providing us access to some great people and information.

- All the incredibly hard-working folks at Osborne/McGraw-Hill: Brandon Nordin, Scott Rogers, and Gareth Hancock for their help in launching a great series and being solid team players. In addition, Tara Davis and Mark Karmendy for their help in fine-tuning the book.

- Becky Kirsininkas and Karen Croner at Microsoft Corp., for being patient and diligent in answering all our questions.

CONTENTS AT A GLANCE

XV

CONTENTS

PREFACE

This book's primary objective is to help you prepare for and pass the required MCDBA/MCSE exam so you can begin to reap the career benefits of certification. We believe that the only way to do this is to help you increase your knowledge and build your skills. After completing this book, you should feel confident that you have thoroughly reviewed all of the objectives that Microsoft has established for the exam.

In This Book

This book is organized around the actual structure of the Microsoft exams administered at Sylvan Testing Centers. Most of the MCDBA and MCSE exams have six parts to them: Planning, Installation and Configuration, Managing Resources, Connectivity, Monitoring and Optimization, and Troubleshooting. Microsoft has let us know all the topics we need to cover for the exam. We've followed their list carefully, so you can be assured you're not missing anything.

In Every Chapter

We've created a set of chapter components that call your attention to important items, reinforce important points, and provide helpful exam-taking hints. Take a look at what you'll find in every chapter:

- Every chapter begins with the **Certification Objectives**—what you need to know in order to pass the section on the exam dealing with the chapter topic. The Certification Objective headings identify the objectives within the chapter, so you'll always know an objective when you see it!

- **Exam Watch** notes call attention to information about, and potential pitfalls in, the exam. These helpful hints are written by MCSEs who have taken the exams and received their

EXERCISES

certification—who better to tell you what to worry about? They know what you're about to go through!

- ■ **On the Job** notes point out procedures and techniques important for coding actual applications for employers or contract jobs.

- ■ **Certification Exercises** are interspersed throughout the chapters. These are step-by-step exercises that mirror vendor-recommended labs. They help you master skills that are likely to be an area of focus on the exam. Don't just read through the exercises; they are hands-on practice that you should be comfortable completing. Learning by doing is an effective way to increase your competency with a product.

- ■ **From the Classroom** sidebars describe the issues that come up most often in the training classroom setting. These sidebars give you a valuable perspective into certification- and product-related topics. They point out common mistakes and address questions that have arisen from classroom discussions.

- ■ **Q & A** sections lay out problems and solutions in a quick-read format:

QUESTIONS AND ANSWERS

We need to have quick access to our data and maintain data integrity...	Implement one of the RAID levels.
What if I need SQL Server to run on multiple processors?	On NT, SQL can support SMP with up to four CPUs. On Windows 95/98, there is no SMP support.

- ■ The **Certification Summary** is a succinct review of the chapter and a re-statement of salient points regarding the exam.

- ■ The **Two-Minute Drill** at the end of every chapter is a checklist of the main points of the chapter. It can be used for last-minute review.

■ The **Self Test** offers questions similar to those found on the certification exams, including multiple choice, true/false questions, and fill-in-the-blank. The answers to these questions, as well as explanations of the answers, can be found in Appendix A. By taking the Self Test after completing each chapter, you'll reinforce what you've learned from that chapter, while becoming familiar with the structure of the exam questions.

Some Pointers

Once you've finished reading this book, set aside some time to do a thorough review. You might want to return to the book several times and make use of all the methods it offers for reviewing the material:

1. *Re-read all the Two-Minute Drills*, or have someone quiz you. You also can use the drills as a way to do a quick cram before the exam.

2. *Re-read all the Exam Watch notes.* Remember that these are written by MCSEs who have taken Microsoft exams and passed. They know what you should expect—and what you should be careful about.

3. *Review all the Q & A scenarios* for quick problem solving.

4. *Re-take the Self Tests.* Taking the tests right after you've read the chapter is a good idea, because it helps reinforce what you've just learned. However, it's an even better idea to go back later and do all the questions in the book in one sitting. Pretend you're taking the exam. (For this reason, you should mark your answers on a separate piece of paper when you go through the questions the first time.)

5. *Complete the exercises.* Did you do the exercises when you read through each chapter? If not, do them! These exercises are designed to cover exam topics, and there's no better way to get to know this material than by practicing.

6. *Check out the Web site.* Global Knowledge invites you to become an active member of the Access Global Web site. This site is an online mall and an information repository that you'll find invaluable. You can access many types of products to assist you in your preparation

for the exams, and you'll be able to participate in forums, on-line discussions, and threaded discussions. No other book brings you unlimited access to such a resource. You'll find more information about this site in Appendix C.

MCDBA and MCSE Certification

Although you've obviously picked up this book to study for a specific exam, we'd like to spend some time covering what you need to complete in order to attain MCDBA or MCSE status. Because this information can be found on the Microsoft Web site, www.microsoft.com/train_cert, we've repeated only some of the more important information. You should review the train_cert site and check out Microsoft's information, along with their list of reasons to become an MCDBA or MCSE, including job advancement.

As you probably know, to attain MCSE status, you must pass a total of six exams—four requirements and two electives. For MCDBA status, one elective is required. One required exam is on networking basics, one on NT Server, one on NT Server in the Enterprise, and one on a client (either Windows NT Workstation or Windows 95 or 98). There are several electives from which to choose—and many of these electives also count toward Microsoft's MCSE+Internet (MCSE+I) certification. The following table lists the exam names, their corresponding course numbers, and whether they are required or elective. We're showing you the NT 4.0 track.

Exam Number	Exam Name	Required or Elective
70-58	Networking Essentials	Required for MCSE
70-64 or 70-98	Implementing and Supporting Microsoft Windows 95 or 98	Required for MCSE (either 70-63, 70-64, 70-98, or 70-73)
70-67	Implementing and Supporting Microsoft Windows NT Server 4.0	Required for MCDBA and MCSE
70-68	Implementing and Supporting Microsoft Windows NT Server 4.0 in the Enterprise	Required for MCDBA and MCSE

Exam Number	Exam Name	Required or Elective
70-73	Implementing and Supporting Microsoft Windows NT Workstation 4.0	Required for MCSE (either 70-73, 70-64 or 70-98)
70-13	Implementing and Supporting Microsoft SNA Server 3.0	Elective for MCSE (either 70-13 or 70-85)
70-14	Supporting Microsoft System Management Server 1.2	Elective for MCSE
70-15	Designing and Implementing Distributed Applications with Microsoft Visual C++ 6.0	Elective for MCDBA
70-18	Implementing and Supporting Microsoft Systems Management Server 1.2	Elective for MCSE (either 70-18 or 70-86)
70-19	Designing and Implementing Data Warehouses with Microsoft SQL Server 7.0	Elective for MCDBA and MCSE
70-59	Internetworking with Microsoft TCP/IP on Windows NT 4.0	Elective for MCDBA and MCSE
70-81	Implementing and Supporting Microsoft Exchange Server 5.5	Elective for MCSE (either 70-81 of 70-76)
70-85	Implementing and Supporting Microsoft SNA Server 4.0	Elective for MCSE (either 70-85 or 70-13)
70-86	Implementing and Supporting Microsoft Systems Management Server 2.0	Elective for MCSE (either 70-86 or 70-18)
70-87	Implementing and Supporting Microsoft Internet Information Server 4.0	Elective for MCDBA and MCSE and Required for MCSE+I
70-88	Implementing and Supporting Microsoft Proxy Server 2.0	Elective for MCSE
70-28	Administering Microsoft SQL Server 7.0	Required for MCDBA and Elective for MCSE
70-29	Designing and Implementing Databases with Microsoft SQL Server 7.0	Required for MCDBA and Elective for MCSE

Exam Number	Exam Name	Required or Elective
70-76	Implementing and Supporting Microsoft Exchange Server 5	Elective for MCSE (either 70-76 or 70-81)
70-79	Implementing and Supporting Microsoft Internet Explorer 4.0 by Using the Internet Explorer Administration Kit	Elective for MCSE and Required for MCSE+I
70-175	Designing and Implementing Distributed Applications with Microsoft Visual Basic 6.0	Elective for MCDBA

The CD-ROM Resource

This book comes with a CD-ROM full of supplementary material you can use while preparing for the MCDBA and MCSE exams. You'll find an electronic version of the book, where you can look up items easily and search on specific terms. You'll find more information about the CD-ROM in Appendix B.

How to Take a Microsoft Certification Examination

If you are new to Microsoft certification, we have some good news and some bad news. The good news, of course, is that Microsoft certification is one of the most valuable credentials you can earn. It sets you apart from the crowd, and marks you as a valuable asset to your employer. You will gain the respect of your peers, and Microsoft certification can have a wonderful effect on your income.

The bad news is that Microsoft certification tests are not easy. You may think you will read through some study material, memorize a few facts, and pass the Microsoft examinations. After all, these certification exams are just computer-based, multiple-choice tests, so they must be easy. If you believe this, you are wrong. Unlike many "multiple guess" tests you have been exposed to in school, the questions on Microsoft certification examinations go beyond simple factual knowledge. The purpose of this introduction is to teach you how to take a Microsoft certification examination. To be successful, you need to know something about the purpose and structure of these tests. We will also look at the latest innovations in Microsoft testing. Using *simulations* and *adaptive testing*, Microsoft is enhancing both the validity and security of the certification process. These factors have some important effects on how you should prepare for an exam, as well as your approach to each question during the test.

We will begin by looking at the purpose, focus, and structure of Microsoft certification tests, and examine the effect these factors have on the kinds of questions you will face on your certification exams. We will define the structure of examination questions and investigate some common formats. Next, we will present a strategy for answering these questions. Finally, we will give some specific guidelines on what you should do on the day of your test.

Why Vendor Certification?

The Microsoft Certified Professional program, like the certification programs from Lotus, Novell, Oracle, and other software vendors, is maintained for the ultimate purpose of increasing the corporation's profits. A successful vendor certification program accomplishes this goal by helping to create a pool of experts in a company's software and by "branding" these experts so that companies using the software can identify them.

We know that vendor certification has become increasingly popular in the last few years because it helps employers find qualified workers, and because it helps software vendors like Microsoft sell their products. But why vendor certification rather than a more traditional approach like a college degree in computer science? A college education is a broadening and enriching experience, but a degree in computer science does not prepare students for most jobs in the IT industry.

A common truism in our business states, "If you are out of the IT industry for three years and want to return, you have to start over." The problem, of course, is *timeliness*; if a first-year student learns about a specific computer program, it probably will no longer be in wide use when he or she graduates. Although some colleges are trying to integrate Microsoft certification into their curriculum, the problem is not really a flaw in higher education, but a characteristic of the IT industry. Computer software is changing so rapidly that a four-year college just can't keep up.

A marked characteristic of the Microsoft certification program is an emphasis on performing specific job tasks rather than merely gathering knowledge. It may come as a shock, but most potential employers do not care how much you know about the theory of operating systems, networking, or database design. As one IT manager put it, "I don't really care what my employees know about the theory of our network. We don't need someone to sit at a desk and think about it. We need people who can actually do something to make it work better."

You should not think that this attitude is some kind of anti-intellectual revolt against "book learning." Knowledge is a necessary prerequisite, but it is not enough. More than one company has hired a computer science graduate as a network administrator, only to learn that the new employee has no idea how to add users, assign permissions, or perform the other day-to-day tasks necessary to maintain a network. This brings us to the second major characteristic of Microsoft certification that affects the questions you must be prepared to answer. In addition to timeliness, Microsoft certification is also job task oriented.

The timeliness of Microsoft's certification program is obvious, and is inherent in the fact that you will be tested on current versions of software in wide use today. The job task orientation of Microsoft certification is almost as obvious, but testing real-world job skills using a computer-based test is not easy.

Computerized Testing

Considering the popularity of Microsoft certification, and the fact that certification candidates are spread around the world, the only practical way to administer tests for the certification program is through Sylvan Prometric testing centers. Sylvan Prometric provides proctored testing services for Microsoft, Oracle, Novell, Lotus, and the A+ computer technician certification. Although the IT industry accounts for much of Sylvan's revenue, the company provides services for a number of other businesses and organizations, such as FAA pre-flight pilot tests. In fact, most companies that need secure test delivery over a wide geographic area use the services of Sylvan Prometric. In addition to delivery, Sylvan Prometric also scores the tests and provides statistical feedback on the performance of each test question to the companies and organizations that use their services.

Typically, several hundred questions are developed for a new Microsoft certification examination. The questions are first reviewed by a number of subject matter experts for technical accuracy, and then are presented in a beta test. The beta test may last for several hours, due to the large number of questions. After a few weeks, Microsoft Certification uses the statistical feedback from Sylvan to check the performance of the beta questions.

Questions are discarded if most test takers get them right (too easy) or wrong (too difficult), and a number of other statistical measures are taken of each question. Although the scope of our discussion precludes a rigorous treatment of question analysis, you should be aware that Microsoft and other vendors spend a great deal of time and effort making sure their examination questions are valid. In addition to the obvious desire for quality, the fairness of a vendor's certification program must be legally defensible.

The questions that survive statistical analysis form the pool of questions for the final certification examination.

Test Structure

The kind of test we are most familiar with is known as a *form* test. For Microsoft certification, a form usually consists of 50–70 questions and takes 60–90 minutes to complete. If there are 240 questions in the final pool for an examination, then four forms can be created. Thus, candidates who retake the test probably will not see the same questions.

Other variations are possible. From the same pool of 240 questions, *five* forms can be created, each containing 40 unique questions (200 questions) and 20 questions selected at random from the remaining 40.

The questions in a Microsoft form test are equally weighted. This means they all count the same when the test is scored. An interesting and useful characteristic of a form test is that you can mark a question you have doubts about as you take the test. Assuming you have time left when you finish all the questions, you can return and spend more time on the questions you have marked as doubtful.

Microsoft may soon implement *adaptive* testing. To use this interactive technique, a form test is first created and administered to several thousand certification candidates. The statistics generated are used to assign a weight, or difficulty level, for each question. For example, the questions in a form might be divided into levels one through five, with level one questions being the easiest and level five the hardest.

When an adaptive test begins, the candidate is first given a level three question. If it is answered correctly, a question from the next higher level is presented, and an incorrect response results in a question from the next lower level. When 15–20 questions have been answered in this manner, the scoring algorithm is able to predict, with a high degree of statistical certainty, whether the candidate would pass or fail if all the questions in the form were answered. When the required degree of certainty is attained, the test ends and the candidate receives a pass/fail grade.

Adaptive testing has some definite advantages for everyone involved in the certification process. Adaptive tests allow Sylvan Prometric to deliver more tests with the same resources, as certification candidates often are in and out in 30 minutes or less. For Microsoft, adaptive testing means that fewer test questions are exposed to each candidate, and this can enhance the security, and therefore the validity, of certification tests.

One possible problem you may have with adaptive testing is that you are not allowed to mark and revisit questions. Since the adaptive algorithm is interactive, and all questions but the first are selected on the basis of your response to the previous question, it is not possible to skip a particular question or change an answer.

Question Types

Computerized test questions can be presented in a number of ways. Some of the possible formats are used on Microsoft certification examinations, and some are not.

True/False

We are all familiar with True/False questions, but because of the inherent 50 percent chance of guessing the correct answer, you will not see questions of this type on Microsoft certification exams.

Multiple Choice

The majority of Microsoft certification questions are in the multiple-choice format, with either a single correct answer or multiple correct answers. One interesting variation on multiple-choice questions with multiple correct answers is whether or not the candidate is told how many answers are correct.

EXAMPLE:

Which two files can be altered to configure the MS-DOS environment? (Choose two.)
or
Which files can be altered to configure the MS-DOS environment? (Choose all that apply.)

You may see both variations on Microsoft certification examinations, but the trend seems to be toward the first type, where candidates are told explicitly how many answers are correct. Questions of the "choose all that apply" variety are more difficult, and can be merely confusing.

Graphical Questions

One or more graphical elements are sometimes used as exhibits to help present or clarify an exam question. These elements may take the form of a network diagram, pictures of networking components, or screen shots from the software on which you are being tested. It is often easier to present the concepts required for a complex performance-based scenario with a graphic than with words.

Test questions known as *hotspots* actually incorporate graphics as part of the answer. These questions ask the certification candidate to click on a location or graphical element to answer the question. As an example, you might be shown the diagram of a network and asked to click on an appropriate location for a router. The answer is correct if the candidate clicks within the *hotspot* that defines the correct location.

Free Response Questions

Another kind of question you sometimes see on Microsoft certification examinations requires a *free response* or type-in answer. An example of this type of question might present a TCP/IP network scenario and ask the candidate to calculate and enter the correct subnet mask in dotted decimal notation.

Knowledge-Based and Performance-Based Questions

Microsoft Certification develops a blueprint for each Microsoft certification examination with input from subject matter experts. This blueprint defines the content areas and objectives for each test, and each test question is created to test a specific objective. The basic information from the examination blueprint can be found on Microsoft's Web site in the Exam Prep Guide for each test.

Psychometricians (psychologists who specialize in designing and analyzing tests) categorize test questions as knowledge-based or performance-based. As the names imply, knowledge-based questions are designed to test knowledge, while performance-based questions are designed to test performance.

Some objectives demand a knowledge-based question. For example, objectives that use verbs like *list* and *identify* tend to test only what you know, not what you can do.

EXAMPLE:

Objective: Identify the MS-DOS configuration files.
  Which two files can be altered to configure the MS-DOS environment? (Choose two.)

    A. COMMAND.COM

    B. AUTOEXEC.BAT

    C. IO.SYS

    D. CONFIG.SYS
    Correct answers: B, D

Other objectives use action verbs like *install, configure,* and *troubleshoot* to define job tasks. These objectives can often be tested with either a knowledge-based question or a performance-based question.

EXAMPLE:

Objective: Configure an MS-DOS installation appropriately using the PATH statement in AUTOEXEX.BAT.
Knowledge-based question: What is the correct syntax to set a path to the D:directory in AUTOEXEC.BAT?

    A. SET PATH EQUAL TO D:

    B. PATH D:

    C. SETPATH D:

    D. D:EQUALS PATH
    Correct answer: B

Performance-based question: Your company uses several DOS accounting applications that access a group of common utility programs. What is the best strategy for configuring the computers in the accounting department so that the accounting applications will always be able to access the utility programs?

A. Store all the utilities on a single floppy disk, and make a copy of the disk for each computer in the accounting department.

B. Copy all the utilities to a directory on the C: drive of each computer in the accounting department, and add a PATH statement pointing to this directory in the AUTOEXEC.BAT files.

C. Copy all the utilities to all application directories on each computer in the accounting department.

D. Place all the utilities in the C: directory on each computer, because the C: directory is automatically included in the PATH statement when AUTOEXEC.BAT is executed.

Correct answer: B

Even in this simple example, the superiority of the performance-based question is obvious. Whereas the knowledge-based question asks for a single fact, the performance-based question presents a real-life situation and requires that you make a decision based on this scenario. Thus, performance-based questions give more bang (validity) for the test author's buck (individual question).

Testing Job Performance

We have said that Microsoft certification focuses on timeliness and the ability to perform job tasks. We have also introduced the concept of performance- based questions, but even performance-based multiple-choice questions do not really measure performance. Another strategy is needed to test job skills.

Given unlimited resources, it is not difficult to test job skills. In an ideal world, Microsoft would fly MCP candidates to Redmond, place them in a controlled environment with a team of experts, and ask them to plan, install, maintain, and troubleshoot a Windows network. In a few days at most, the experts could reach a valid decision as to whether each candidate should or should not be granted MCDBA or MCSE status. Needless to say, this is not likely to happen.

Closer to reality, another way to test performance is by using the actual software, and creating a testing program to present tasks and automatically grade a candidate's performance when the tasks are completed. This *cooperative* approach would be practical in some testing situations, but the same test that is presented to MCP candidates in Boston must also be available in Bahrain and Botswana. Many Sylvan Prometric testing locations around the world cannot run 32-bit applications, much less provide the complex networked solutions required by cooperative testing applications.

The most workable solution for measuring performance in today's testing environment is a *simulation* program. When the program is launched during a test, the candidate sees a simulation of the actual software that looks, and behaves, just like the real thing. When the testing software presents a task, the simulation program is launched and the candidate performs the required task. The testing software then grades the candidate's performance on the required task and moves to the next question. In this way, a 16-bit simulation program can mimic the look and feel of 32-bit operating systems, a complicated network, or even the entire Internet.

Microsoft has introduced simulation questions on the certification examination for Internet Information Server 4.0. Simulation questions provide many advantages over other testing methodologies, and simulations are expected to become increasingly important in the Microsoft certification program. For example, studies have shown that there is a very high correlation between the ability to perform simulated tasks on a computer-based test and the ability to perform the actual job tasks. Thus, simulations enhance the validity of the certification process.

Another truly wonderful benefit of simulations is in the area of test security. It is just not possible to cheat on a simulation question. In fact, you will be told exactly what tasks you are expected to perform on the test. How can a certification candidate cheat? By learning to perform the tasks? What a concept!

Study Strategies

There are appropriate ways to study for the different types of questions you will see on a Microsoft certification examination.

Knowledge-Based Questions

Knowledge-based questions require that you memorize facts. There are hundreds of facts inherent in every content area of every Microsoft certification examination. There are several keys to memorizing facts:

- **Repetition**   The more times your brain is exposed to a fact, the more likely you are to remember it.

- **Association**   Connecting facts within a logical framework makes them easier to remember.

- **Motor Association**   It is often easier to remember something if you write it down or perform some other physical act, like clicking on a practice test answer.

We have said that the emphasis of Microsoft certification is job performance, and that there are very few knowledge-based questions on Microsoft certification exams. Why should you waste a lot of time learning filenames, IP address formulas, and other minutiae? Read on.

Performance-Based Questions

Most of the questions you will face on a Microsoft certification exam are performance-based scenario questions. We have discussed the superiority of these questions over simple knowledge-based questions, but you should remember that the job task orientation of Microsoft certification extends the knowledge you need to pass the exams; it does not replace this knowledge. Therefore, the first step in preparing for scenario questions is to absorb as many facts relating to the exam content areas as you can. In other words, go back to the previous section and follow the steps to prepare for an exam composed of knowledge-based questions.

The second step is to familiarize yourself with the format of the questions you are likely to see on the exam. You can do this by answering the questions in this study guide, by using Microsoft assessment tests, or by using practice tests. The day of your test is not the time to be surprised by the convoluted construction of Microsoft exam questions.

For example, one of Microsoft Certification's favorite formats of late takes the following form:

Scenario: You have a network with...
Primary Objective: You want to...
Secondary Objective: You also want to...
Proposed Solution: Do this...
What does the proposed solution accomplish?

    A. Satisfies the primary and the secondary objective

    B. Satisfies the primary but not the secondary objective

    C. Satisfies the secondary but not the primary objective

    D. Satisfies neither the primary nor the secondary objective

This kind of question, with some variation, is seen on many Microsoft Certification examinations.

At best, these performance-based scenario questions really do test certification candidates at a higher cognitive level than knowledge-based questions. At worst, these questions can test your reading comprehension and test-taking ability rather than your ability to use Microsoft products. Be sure to get in the habit of reading the question carefully to determine what is being asked.

The third step in preparing for Microsoft scenario questions is to adopt the following attitude: Multiple-choice questions aren't really performance-based. It is all a cruel lie. These scenario questions are just knowledge-based questions with a little story wrapped around them.

To answer a scenario question, you have to sift through the story to the underlying facts of the situation, and apply your knowledge to determine the correct answer. This may sound silly at first, but the process we go through in solving real-life problems is quite similar. The key concept is that every scenario question (and every real-life problem) has a fact at its center, and if we can identify that fact, we can answer the question.

Simulations

Simulation questions really do measure your ability to perform job tasks. You must be able to perform the specified tasks. There are two ways to prepare for simulation questions:

1. Get experience with the actual software. If you have the resources, this is a great way to prepare for simulation questions.

2. Use official Microsoft practice tests. Practice tests are available that provide practice with the same simulation engine used on Microsoft certification exams. This approach has the added advantage of grading your efforts.

Signing Up

Signing up to take a Microsoft certification examination is easy. Sylvan operators in each country can schedule tests at any testing center. You can reach Sylvan at (800) 755-EXAM. There are, however, a few things you should know:

1. If you call Sylvan during a busy time period, get a cup of coffee first, because you may be in for a long wait. Sylvan does an excellent job, but everyone in the world seems to want to sign up for a test on Monday morning.

2. You will need your social security number or some other unique identifier to sign up for a Sylvan test, so have it at hand.

3. Pay for your test by credit card if at all possible. This makes things easier, and you can even schedule tests for the same day you call, if space is available at your local testing center.

4. Know the number and title of the test you want to take before you call. This is not essential, and the Sylvan operators will help you if they can. Having this information in advance, however, speeds up the registration process.

Taking the Test

Teachers have always told you not to try to cram for examinations because it does no good. Sometimes they lied. If you are faced with a knowledge-based test requiring only that you regurgitate facts, cramming can mean the difference between passing and failing. This is not the case, however, with Microsoft certification exams. If you don't know it the night before, don't bother to stay up and cram.

Instead, create a schedule and stick to it. Plan your study time carefully, and do not schedule your test until you think you are ready to succeed. Follow these guidelines on the day of your exam:

1. Get a good night's sleep. The scenario questions you will face on a Microsoft certification examination require a clear head.

2. Remember to take two forms of identification—at least one with a picture. A driver's license with your picture and social security or credit cards are acceptable.

3. Leave home in time to arrive at your testing center a few minutes early. It is not a good idea to feel rushed as you begin your exam.

4. Do not spend too much time on any one question. If you are taking a form test, take your best guess and mark the question so you can come back to it if you have time. You cannot mark and revisit questions on an adaptive test, so you must do your best on each question as you go.

5. If you do not know the answer to a question, try to eliminate the obviously wrong answers and guess from the rest. If you can eliminate two out of four options, you have a 50 percent chance of guessing the correct answer.

6. For scenario questions, follow the steps we outlined earlier. Read the question carefully and try to identify the facts at the center of the story.

Finally, we would advise anyone attempting to earn Microsoft MCDBA and MCSE certification to adopt a philosophical attitude. Even if you are the kind of person who never fails a test, you are likely to fail at least one Microsoft certification test somewhere along the way. Do not get discouraged. If Microsoft certification were easy to obtain, more people would have it, and it would not be so respected and so valuable to your future in the IT industry.

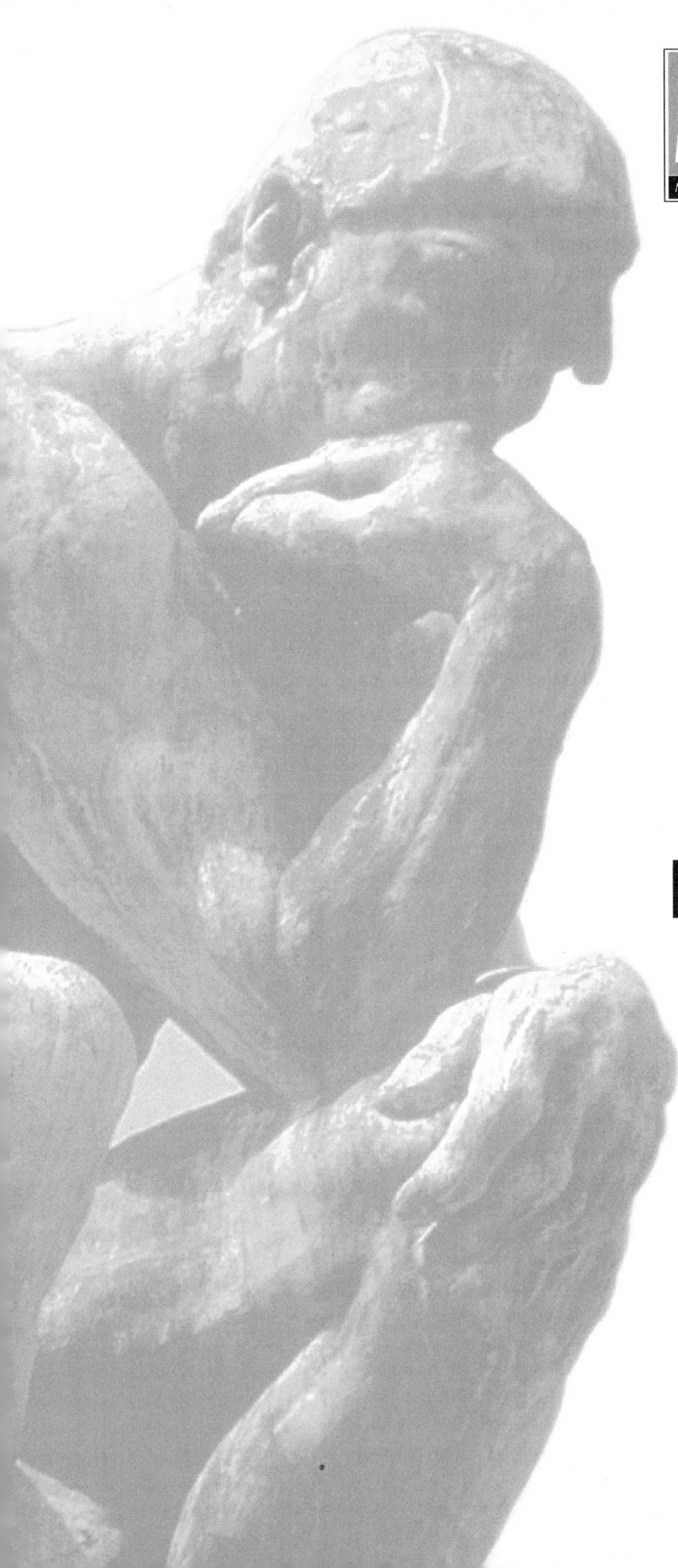

MCDBA
MICROSOFT CERTIFIED DATABASE ADMINISTRATOR

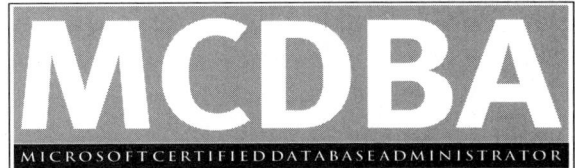

1

Microsoft SQL Server 7.0 Overview

CERTIFICATION OBJECTIVES

- 1.01 Defining Microsoft SQL Server
- 1.02 SQL Server Architecture
- 1.03 SQL Server Databases
- 1.04 SQL Server Security

This introductory chapter gives some historical background on SQL and defines Microsoft SQL Server. It also explores the SQL Server architecture, SQL Server security, and SQL Server databases. Finally, we will see just how to use Microsoft SQL Server.

Historical Perspective

The database system design has rapidly replaced the older file design of mainframe systems. With traditional files, termed *flat* files, several problems exist about how the data is managed. The problems are data redundancy, inconsistency, and lack of central control and security. In the early days of computing, data was not centrally managed or controlled. For example, an organization may have multiple departments that maintain data separately. The organization may run different applications that have some of the same data in different files within each application. This redundancy can cause serious problems because the data is inconsistent among various applications. Just because the data within one application is changed to reflect an update, does not necessarily mean the duplicate data within the second application is updated. In a database system, redundancy can be reduced since the organization can centrally manage the activities of the data. Nowadays, the data is considered an asset of the company, and in some cases, it is the company.

This data redundancy also led to increased use of disk storage. The data had to be stored multiple times in various applications. This resulted in less efficient use of disk space. Although a database design uses disk space for maintaining indexes and logging, it reduces the need to repetitively store the same data on disk multiple times.

Another benefit that these flat file designs did not provide was the ability for the data to grow and be changed very easily. On these application systems, the programming language is strictly tied to the data layout. If the length of a data field changes, the program must be changed and recompiled. In order to add four digits to the ZIP code, for instance, you would have to change all the programs and data files that referenced the ZIP code. In a database system, the programs and the data are independent. To increase the ZIP code by four, it would mean merely changing the data and not necessarily the programs themselves. Incidentally, the infamous Y2K (Year 2000) problem is a direct result of some of these same issues.

The security of the data is at risk in a more traditional flat file design. Because the data is managed on a decentralized basis, there are more places where intruders could gain access to the data. Access to the data in a database system is controlled centrally, so there is one point of entry to the data instead of many.

In short, the database design was a natural solution to the traditional file design. It has overcome the shortcomings of the file design used in the early days of computing. In the next section, we examine the history behind SQL.

A Brief History of SQL

There are three types of database designs: hierarchical, network, and relational. Both the hierarchical and network designs represent the data in a tree-like fashion, similar to the MS-DOS file system. The data is stored in records, and address pointers link multiple occurrences of different records. In a relational database system, there are no address pointers linking the next data. Instead, data in a relational database is accessed by the contents of the data using language statements such as WHERE, GROUP BY, and JOIN. These SQL statements are explored in subsequent chapters.

The relational database is the most popular of the database types and is the foundation of SQL (Structured Query Language). IBM developed SQL, pronounced *sequel*, in the 1970s in San Jose, California. Over the years, the American National Standards Institute (ANSI) and the International Standards Organization (ISO) have developed standards. There is an ANSI-92 standard that Microsoft SQL Server 7.0 is based on. Microsoft SQL Server 7.0 uses Transact-SQL, or T-SQL, with language extensions to the ANSI-92 standard.

Defining Microsoft SQL Server

When Microsoft and Sybase teamed up in the late 1980s to create SQL Server, it only ran on IBM's OS/2 operating-system platform. It was not until about a decade later, with the release of SQL 6.5, and after Microsoft and Sybase went their separate ways, that SQL Server made headway into the competitive database market. Although Microsoft had great success with operating systems such as MS-DOS and Windows 95, it was competing in a slightly different software arena that was dominated by names such as Oracle, Informix, Progress, and Ingres, not to mention IBM's DB2 and IMS mainframe databases.

Let's look at an interesting point about SQL Server 7.0. When a company writes software, the company typically gives it an internal code name. This is done to minimize competitive efforts to discover what an organization is developing. Microsoft's internal code name for SQL Server 7.0 was *Sphinx*. At release, of course, this name was changed to the official marketing product name, Microsoft SQL Server 7.0.

Microsoft SQL Server 7.0 enables a database administrator (DBA) to develop and manage an organization's data up to the enterprise level. The enterprise level encompasses all of the organization's internal and external data interfaces. This would include, for example, handling data that is transferred internally from a sales order entry to the accounts receivable function on an intra-organizational level. On an enterprise level, SQL could be deployed to handle transactions over the Internet utilizing Microsoft's Internet Information Server (IIS).

FROM THE CLASSROOM

The Sequel That Keeps Getting Better, Microsoft SQL Server!

With the latest release of their flagship database product, Microsoft SQL Server 7.0, Microsoft has continued the trend of providing a reliable and stable database management system (DBMS) in an affordable package. Far beyond that, though, Microsoft has provided a DBMS that scales from laptops to large multiprocessor systems, with everything from small business needs to large data warehousing concerns in mind.

The Structured Query Language (SQL), upon which all data retrieval, modification, and manipulations are based, is a relatively simple language to learn. It provides language elements designed to make efficient data retrieval requests or modifications possible. SQL also provides conditional logic keywords that can be used to provide basic levels of logical processing to assist in providing intelligent processing procedures.

The lastest release of SQL Server is squarely positioned to be the best DBMS choice for most of the business and corporate needs in today's business environment. SQL Server will become even more important as a server product as the wave of Internet-based businesses and activities continues to swell. SQL Server can be used as the data services tier for a database-integrated Web site or application, allowing incredible scalability and flexibility. The use of automated tasks and assorted stored procedures within Microsoft SQL Server provides a platform allowing incredible levels of automated maintenance and support.

The administration of Microsoft SQL Server is accomplished through the Microsoft Management Console (MMC) application. The MMC allows applications or server products to provide a software "plug-in" to be added to the application framework provided by the MMC. Through this framework, a centralized method of administration of server products, like SQL server, can be easily accomplished.

—Michael Lane Thomas, MCSE+I, MCSD,
MCP+SB, MSS, MCT, A+

Major SQL Features

The following are the major SQL features, which are discussed in detail subsequently.

- Support for the client/server model
- Operating-system compatibility
- Multiple-platform support
- Multiple-protocol compatibility
- Symmetric multiprocessing (SMP) compatibility
- Data warehousing
- ANSI SQL-92 compatibility
- Data replication
- Windows appearance
- Full-Text Search
- Books Online

Support for the Client/Server Model

Microsoft SQL Server 7.0 is designed to be a client/server model. In this model, the client and server take part in a request-response dialog. An application runs on the client and requests data from the SQL Server. The SQL Server executes code in the application and sends back only the data needed; this is usually based on queries. So, the workload is split between the client and the server. The client's job is to request the data via language statements, whereas the server's job is to process the data and send the results back to the client.

For example, in determining whether or not a student makes the Dean's list, a query such as the following will cause the server to send back only the name, major, and degree_type data for a student who has a GPA over 3.5

and carries more than 12.0 quarter hours. However, there is probably more data stored about the student in the database.

```
SELECT name, major, degree_type
FROM students
WHERE gpa > = 3.5
AND credit_hours > = 12.0
```

Operating-System Compatibility

Of course, Microsoft would not create a product that would not run on its major operating systems. Microsoft's operating systems have been its "bread and butter" for more than two decades. Therefore, SQL Server 7.0 runs on Windows 95/98 and Windows NT Server 4.0. Although Windows 2000 is not on the market currently, you can bet that SQL Server 7.0 will be supported under those operating systems. You need to know that SQL Server must have Service Pack 4 (SP4) to run on Windows NT 4.0. It also requires the post-Beta 1 builds for Windows 2000—on Alpha and Intel processors. Windows 95/98 do *not* support some of the same features that Microsoft Windows NT 4.0 does. The following features are supported by Windows NT 4.0, but not by Windows 95/98:

- **Symmetric multiprocessing (SMP)**   Windows NT 4.0 provides support for up to four CPUs (32 with vendor support).

- **Redundant Array of Inexpensive Disks (RAID)**   Windows NT 4.0 enables RAID levels 0, 1, and 5, which offer varying degrees of disk performance and ensure data integrity through parity.

- **Multiplatform support**   Windows NT 4.0 runs on both Reduced Instruction Set Computing (RISC) and Complex Instruction Set Computing (CISC) processors. These processors are discussed in a later section.

- **Security**   Windows NT 4.0 is C2-level compliant. C2 is a government standard.

exam
ⓌatchMake sure you know the operating systems and which service packs
are required in order for SQL to run.*

Along with Microsoft's proprietary operating systems, SQL Server is
supported as a client under the following nonproprietary operating systems:

- Novell NetWare
- UNIX
- AppleTalk
- OS/2
- Banyan VINES

Multiple-Platform Support

Microsoft has developed SQL Server using a highly portable language; it can
be *carried* to different processor architectures and run successfully. It can
run on Intel CISC processors and also on the faster, and costlier, Alpha
RISC processors. A CISC processor has a larger instruction set for its CPU
than does a RISC processor. Think of the instruction set as the number of
words in the processor's vocabulary. Examples are ADD, SUBTRACT,
MULTIPLY, DIVIDE, COPY, and MOVE. A CISC processor is slower
because it has to translate each instruction into its binary, or machine-level,
equivalent. A RISC processor, on the other hand, has fewer instructions in
its instruction set. To accommodate for the lack of an instruction, the RISC
processor executes the "missing" instruction in multiple machine cycles or
steps. Intuitively, this would seem longer; however, the RISC processors are
optimized to execute extremely quickly. RISC processors cost more due to
the technology that makes them run faster.

Take, for example, a CISC processor with both an ADD and a
MULTIPLY instruction. A RISC processor may only have the ADD
instruction and not the MULTIPLY instruction. Nobody would buy a
processor that could not even compute its payroll (HOURS * RATE).
In fact, the RISC processor performs several iterations of the ADD
instruction. It is faster because this is done at the CPU level and the
MULTIPLY instruction does not have to be decoded into binary format.

Therefore, the DBA or the management team must decide what is more important—speed or reducing expenses.

Now, review what we have learned so far regarding SQL requirements with the following Q&A scenarios:

QUESTIONS AND ANSWERS

I have NT Server 4.0 with no Service Packs. Will SQL Server install?	No, install SP 4.
I need several CPUs installed in my SQL Server...	Install SQL on an NT Server with SMP support.
We don't have NT and need to run SQL on Windows 95/98...	SQL will run on these operating systems.
My boss demands our data be secure...	Run SQL on an NT system since it is C2 compliant; Windows 95 will not provide the same security.
I support UNIX and Novell clients. Can I still use SQL Server?	Yes! SQL supports these clients.
We need to have quick access to our data and maintain data integrity...	Implement one of the RAID levels.
What if I need SQL Server to run on multiple processors?	On NT, SQL can support SMP with up to four CPUs. On Windows 95/98, there is no SMP support.

Multiple-Protocol Compatibility

A *protocol* is a set of standardized rules that multiple entities agree to abide by. Protocols exist throughout the languages we, as people, speak and the customs we have. The same idea is used in networking. Computers need a standard set of procedures in order to manage the data packets that they send and receive. They must use the same compatible protocol or the communication will not work. There are numerous protocols in existence in networking. Microsoft SQL Server 7.0 supports the popular protocols. You may ask yourself why there are so many different networking protocols. Well, each company tries to carve out a market niche with its operating system and several companies have developed their own protocol to network their proprietary computers.

Refer to Table 1-1 for a list of supported protocols and a brief description of each.

exam
Ⓦatch

Understand the protocols supported by SQL Server. The protocol of choice will eventually be TCP/IP, due to the popularity of the Internet.

SMP Compatibility (Scalability)

SMP, or Symmetrical Multi Processing, is the concept that a computer system can support multiple processors and the processors can balance the load between themselves. If your computer has four CPUs, then they would share the processing work load and each one could participate in executing parts of a single program. This would be much faster, about four times as fast, compared to a system with a single processor. Having SMP leads to *scalability*.

Scalability means the system can operate with one or more processors. This term is sometimes confusing, so let's look at a short analogy. Think of a toy model airplane. It is a scale smaller in size than the real airplane. So,

TABLE 1-1	Protocol	Description
Descriptions of SQL Server-Supported Protocols	NWLink	Microsoft wrote NWLink (NetWareLink) for compatibility with Novell's native protocol, Internetwork Packet Exchange/Sequenced Packet Exchange (IPX/SPX). IPX/SPX is a routable protocol—meaning data packets can cross subnets.
	TCP/IP	Transmission Control Protocol/Internet Protocol (TCP/IP) is the protocol of the Internet. That's where the term came from. TCP/IP was developed by ARPA, a branch of the government, and has been around for decades. It is a routable protocol.
	NetBEUI	Originally written by IBM, NetBEUI runs on all Microsoft operating systems. It is a very fast, yet nonroutable protocol. It is ideally suited to an organization with few computers.
	AppleTalk	AppleTalk is Apple's protocol that runs on Apple MacIntosh computers.
	Banyan VINES	Banyan VINES clients running the Sequenced Packet Protocol (SPP).

when someone says that SQL Server 7.0 is scalable, they mean it runs on hardware that can have processors that are smaller in size, larger in size, or come in greater or lesser numbers. SQL Server 7.0 can support a maximum of four processors. However, with vendor support, it can support up to 32 CPUs. Windows 95/98 cannot support more than one CPU, so Windows NT 4.0 would have to be the operating system used with SQL Server if your business needs dictate SMP support.

Because Windows NT 4.0 supports SMP, load balancing can occur among the processors. This provides tremendous processor efficiency and speed. Applications written to take advantage of SMP support are termed *multithreaded.* A *thread* is an instance of an application executing in the processor. SQL Server is written as a multithreaded program and each thread of execution can process independently of another. In SQL terms, a program accessing the data in the database is called a *query.* For design considerations, running SQL Server on Windows NT 4.0, with several processors, would make the queries run faster than on Windows 95/98. However, the cost is also greater because you would need to purchase the additional processors.

Data Warehousing

There are basically two types of data designs: transaction-oriented and Decision Support Systems (DSS). Transaction-oriented systems are systems on which users change customer data on a daily basis. Users may add a new customer order to the database, delete another one, and update sales orders. On a DSS system, managers may ask a question, or query the database, searching for data based on certain criteria. In the following T-SQL query, a manager may be looking at which products sold over a certain dollar amount. This might help a store manager decide what products to stock up on. You could help the manager by writing the following query that displays the product name, the product in inventory, and the product price from the products database if the quantity sold is over 1,000 units:

```
SELECT prod_name, prod_on_hand, prod_price
FROM products
WHERE prod_quantity_sold >= 1000
```

The data in a transaction-based model is dynamic—it is always being added, changed, and deleted. All this changing could cause record locking Record locking could cause results and performance to vary when running a query.

Imagine what could happen if the preceding query were relying on static data. This would lead to data being locked by another process, which would increase processing time. It also leads to queries yielding inconsistent results because they are retrieving data that is constantly changing.

The solution to this problem is data warehousing. Microsoft uses a repository where the data is copied to a database—hence the data warehouse—where it will not be affected by the transactions. A data warehousing solution often keeps a "nonupdating" copy of the data for people like managers to query against. This makes results more consistent and performance more predictable.

The data in the data warehouse is static data; it does not change like the dynamic data in a transaction-oriented environment. Thus, managers can query the database and not have to worry about whether the data is up-to-date or not.

ANSI/ISO SQL-92 Compliant

Microsoft SQL Server 7.0 is compliant with the standards set by ANSI/ISO SQL-92. Microsoft has also added some language extensions called Transact-SQL.

Data Replication Support

SQL Server 7.0 supports data replication. This means that the data will be automatically replicated, or duplicated, to another SQL Server. Replication follows a *publish and subscribe* approach. The *publisher* is a server that enables its data to be accessible for replication to other servers, known as *subscribers*. The publisher identifies the data to be replicated and checks for data that has been updated since the last replication. Data integrity is maintained since data can be replicated from only one publisher. A subscriber is a server that receives the replicated data from the publisher and keeps the replicated data stored on its database.

There are three major types of replication available for SQL Server. They are described in the following table.

Type of Replication	Description
Snapshot	This technique takes a snapshot of the current data on the publisher and replaces all of the data on the subscriber periodically.
Merge	This form of replication enables sites to make independent changes to replicated data. Later, changes are merged at all sites. However, this does not ensure data consistency at each site.
Transactional	This replication technique replicates from publisher to subscriber as changes occur to the data.

Windows Appearance

Microsoft has developed Microsoft SQL Server 7.0 to have the appearance that other Windows products have. Look at Windows 3.1, Windows 95/98, and Windows NT 4.0. They all have a very similar orientation. Also, other Microsoft products such as Visual Basic have this same appearance. This provides consistency in what the user sees. Microsoft may not have initially developed the windows concept—actually Xerox did—but it has definitely helped in encouraging other vendors to be consistent. Gone are the days when we must put a paper or plastic template on top of our keyboard because the procedure to save in one application is different in another application. Refer to Figure 1-1 for a sample screen of the initial SQL Server product and tools.

Full-Text Search

The Full-Text Search feature enables you to search character data. Examples include searches for whole words and phrases in the data. These are extensions to the T-SQL language. An index is created of all the data necessary to locate the word in a given table. There is an Indexing Wizard to help you with the task of creating a full-text index. Refer to Figure 1-2 for a display of the Create Index Wizard. In order to get to the wizard, click Start | Programs | Microsoft SQL Server 7.0 | Enterprise Manager | Tools | Wizards | Databases | Create Index Wizard.

FIGURE 1-1

Windows screen shot
of SQL Server products
and tools

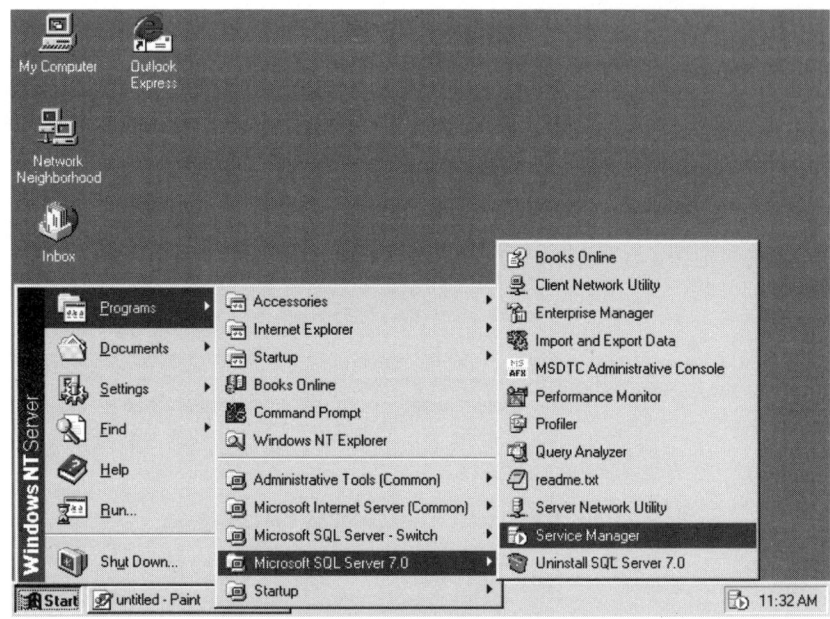

FIGURE 1-2

The Create Index Wizard

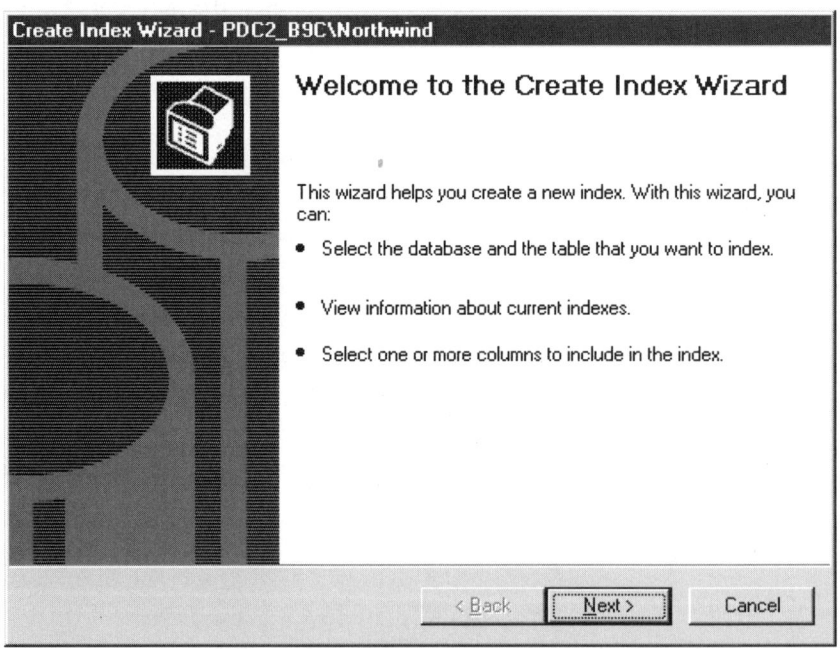

FIGURE 1-3

SQL Server Books Online

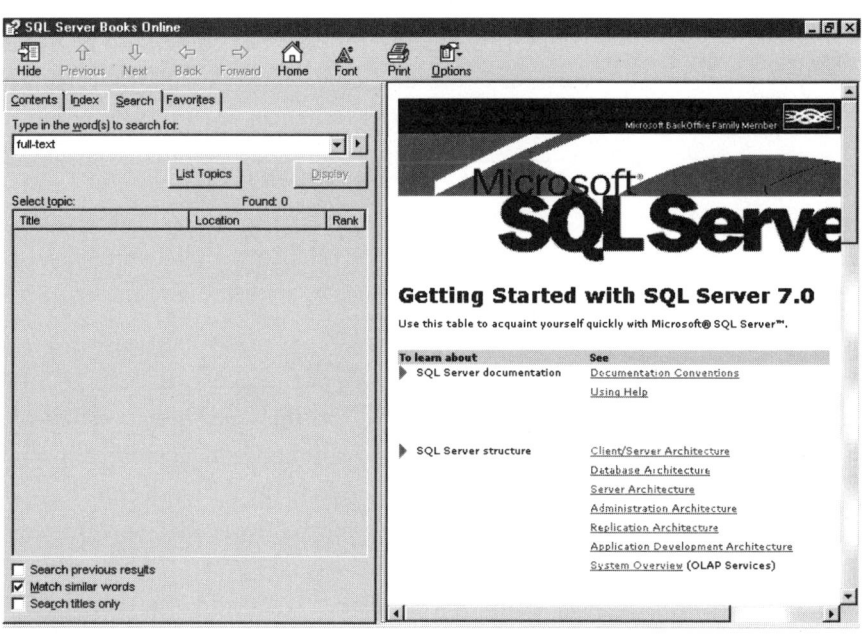

Books Online

Although Books Online, shown in Figure 1-3, is an add-on component and takes up more room on the server, it is a valuable reference tool to install.

CERTIFICATION OBJECTIVE 1.02

SQL Server Architecture

The SQL Server architecture is based on the client/server concept and is comprised of three main elements. They are

- Client software
- SQL Server software
- Network connection software using interprocess communications (IPC)

The client software resides on a client workstation. Programmers must write this software; it does not come with SQL Server 7.0. These clients cannot communicate directly with SQL Server; they communicate via *application program interfaces* (API). SQL Server supports the following client APIs:

■ OLE DB

■ ODBC

■ DB-Library

On the server side of the house, there is an API just like there is on the client side. The API on the server side is called *Open Data Services (ODS)* and it acts as the liaison between the server applications and the network connection. The server ODS API and the client APIs communicate over the network through a mechanism called *interprocess communications,* or IPCs for short. There are several known IPCs in use. These are contained as *dynamic link libraries* (DLLs) and are termed *Net-Libraries.* SQL Server supports several IPCs:

■ Named Pipes

■ TCP/IP

■ Multiprotocol

■ NWLink IPX/SPX

■ AppleTalk

■ Banyan VINES

Let's take a look at an example of how this client/server process works. A user sits at a client computer and requests data within an application. The client and server are connected over the network and TCP/IP is the protocol installed. Note that the programmer has already written the appropriate code using a compatible API, for example, ODBC on the client and ODS on the server.

The request passes through the client layer as ODBC, then the request is sent to the network connection, or Net-Library layer, and the appropriate

DLL is pulled out of the Net-Library. In this case, it is TCP/IP. Then, this request is sent out on the network card and over the physical wire as a TCP/IP packet. Next, the SQL Server receives the request. At the server, the TCP/IP DLL is pulled out of the Net-Library. The packet is then passed to the server layer, implemented through ODS. ODS understands the ODBC request and responds with the appropriate data sent back through the same layers.

See Figure 1-4 for an overview of the different components.

The flow from a client request to the server response

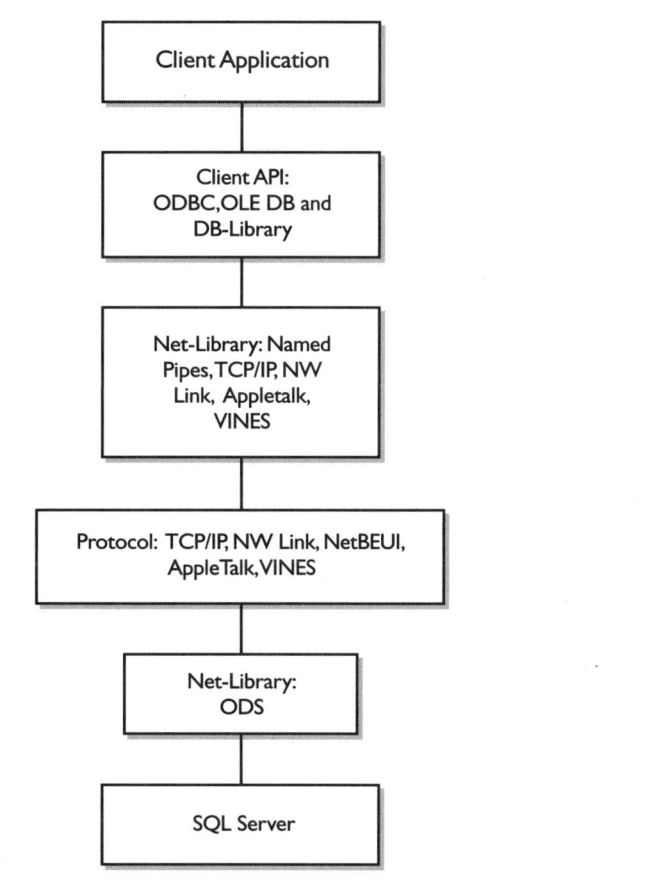

on the
Job

You can use the MAKEPIPE and READPIPE diagnostic programs to test the SQL Server connection. Follow the steps outlined below:

At the command prompt of one window, enter

C:\>MAKEPIPE

At the command prompt of another window enter

C:\>READPIPE /sBDC1_B9C /d"Testing 1, 2, 3"

The READPIPE command has the syntax READPIPE /sserver /dstring with no spaces after the /s nor after the /d. The text "Testing 1, 2, 3" will appear in both windows. You can try this on a client system or on the same system.

The following illustration shows a sample of the MAKEPIPE diagnostic utility:

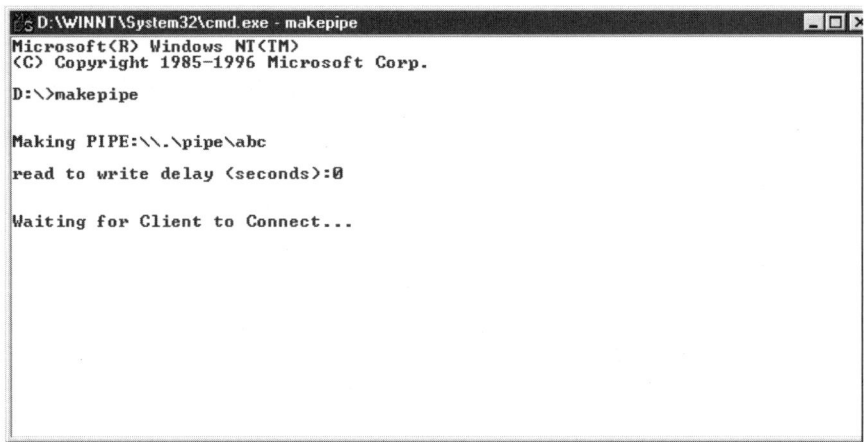

Refer to the following illustration for a sample of the READPIPE commands to test the SQL Server connection:

```
D:\WINNT\System32\cmd.exe                                          _ □ ×
Microsoft(R) Windows NT(TM)
(C) Copyright 1985-1996 Microsoft Corp.

D:\>readpipe /sbdc1_b9c /d"Testing, 1, 2, 3"

SvrName:\\bdc1_b9c
PIPE   :\\bdc1_b9c\pipe\abc
DATA   :Testing, 1, 2, 3
Data Sent: 1 :Testing, 1, 2, 3
Data Read: 1 :Testing, 1, 2, 3

D:\>
```

e x a m
 ⓦ a t c h   ***The same IPC mechanism must be installed on both the client and
server or else the two will not be able to communicate.***

See the following three illustrations for screen shots of the Named Pipes,
Net-Libraries, and DB-Library options, respectively.

The General tab shown here shows the Named Pipes network library.

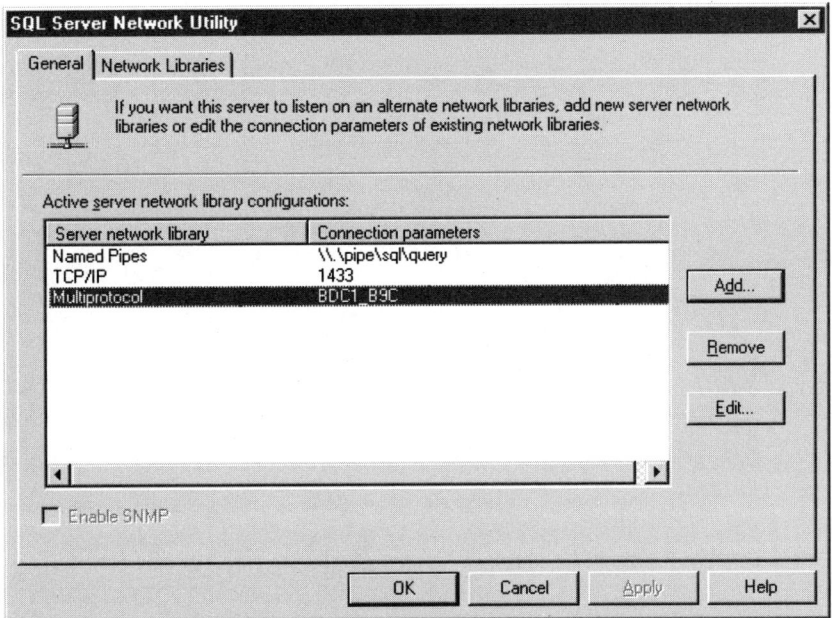

The Network Libraries tab shown here shows the currenly installed modules.

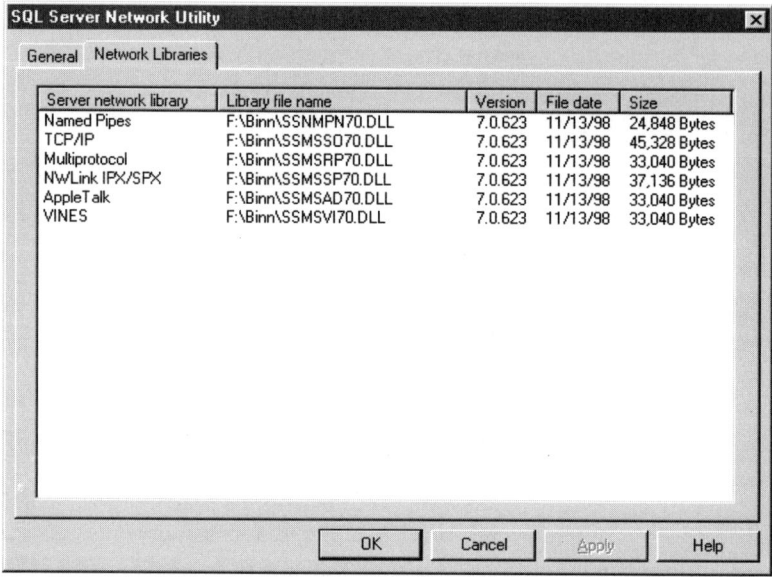

The DB-Library tab, shown here, lets you select two options.

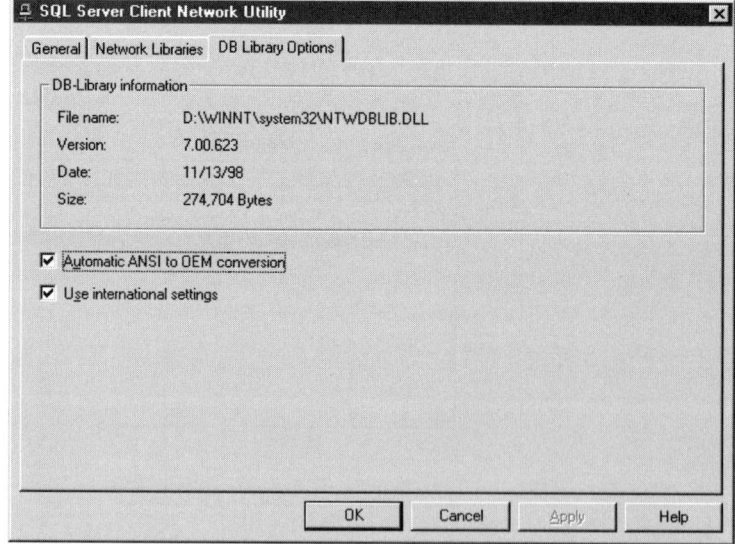

Now that you have studied the architecture of SQL server, here are some possible scenario questions and answers regarding the client/server architecture.

QUESTIONS AND ANSWERS

My programmers need to write client-side software. What API can they use?	Use OLE DB, ODBC, and DB-Library.
I am running the Novell Client 32 on my Windows 95 system...	Install NWLink on the client. NWLink is Microsoft's version of Novell's IPX/SPX.
I am unable to connect to SQL Server. What can I do?	Run the MAKEPIPE and READPIPE commands to test the connection.
Why do my client and server need to use the same Net-Library DLL?	They must use the same IPC DLL from the Net-Library in order to communicate.

SQL Server Installation Requirements

Refer to the following table for a summary of the hardware requirements for SQL Server:

Hardware Component	Requirement
Processor	Intel compatible 32-bit CPU (200 MHz or higher) or a DEC Alpha AXP.
Disk space	Anywhere from 80 to 85MB for a minimum install to around 215 to 225MB for a full install.
Network interface card	Necessary if clients are connected to the SQL Server. Suggested is a PCI bus network interface card (NIC).
RAM	32MB
CD-ROM	Necessary for CD installation; otherwise, you'll need to map a network share.

on the **Job**

Refer to the Hardware Compatibility List (HCL) at the Microsoft Web site for the latest changes to the HCL at http://www.microsoft.com.

CERTIFICATION OBJECTIVE 1.03

SQL Server Databases

Now, we need to discuss database terms. A database is just a logical collection of data stored in a file on a disk. A physical database is a collection of physical files that comprise the database. A physical database has a data file for holding actual data and a transaction log file to recover data in case of database problems. Users do not necessarily see the physical files. They will see a part of the actual database file logically.

SQL Fundamentals

You need to understand some fundamental database terminology, as described in the following list:

- **Table** A collection of data made up of rows and columns, looking much like a spreadsheet.

- **Column** An individual data item; they are called *fields* in traditional programming. An example is *Student_Name*.

- **Row** A set of related columns; they are called *records* in traditional programming. Some examples are *Student_Name*, *Student_Address*, and *Student_City*.

- **View** A view is a subset of one or more than one table. A user might see, or view, only a few columns from one table instead of the whole table.

- **Data type** These define the type of data that you can enter in the columns. Sample data types include Char, Real, and Float.

- **Rule**   Validate user input into a column. You can use this to force a user to put numeric data in a certain column.

- **Stored procedures**   A precompiled statement in T-SQL.

- **Triggers**   These are stored procedures that are triggered to execute when an event such as data being inserted, deleted or updated occurs.

- **Default**   These set predefined values in a column.

- **Index**   An index is a method of accessing the data quickly using key fields. Queries can retrieve data based on the key field instead of searching sequentially. There are two types of indexes: clustered, which sort rows in a table, and nonclustered, which sort pointers to the data instead of the actual rows.

The Databases in SQL Server

The following databases are set up by SQL Server:

- **Master**   Used to track all other databases and store configuration information.

- **Msdb**   Used by SQL Server Agent to manage alerts.

- **Model**   Used to create all other databases.

- **TempDB**   Used to hold temporary tables.

Refer to Figure 1-5 for a screen picture of the databases.

Administration Tools

Administration tools enable you to administer SQL Server. These tools include the following:

- **SQL Server Agent**   Enables you to schedule tasks and alerts.

- **SQL Server Profiler**   Enables you to monitor SQL Server network traffic between client and server.

Screen display showing the
SQL Server 7.0 databases

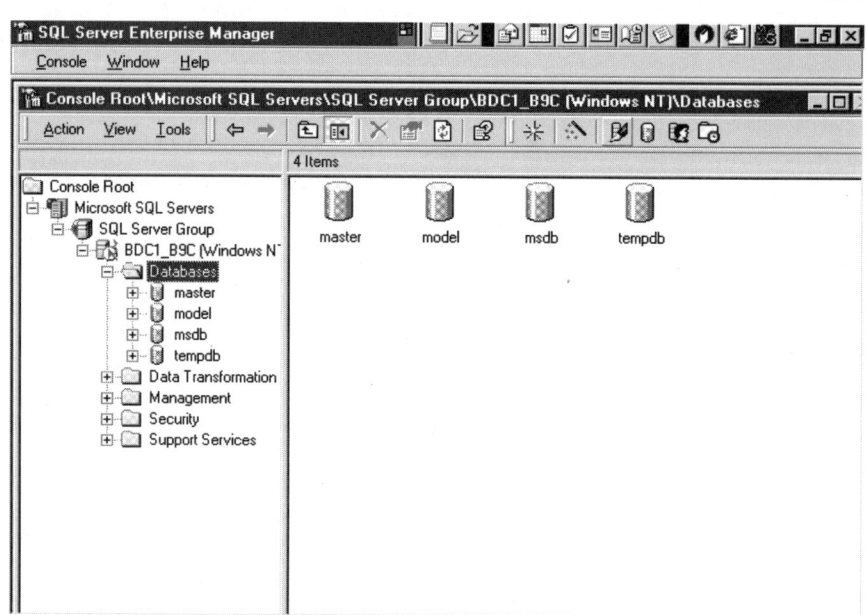

- **SQL Server Performance Monitor** Enables you to monitor and graph SQL Server activity.

- **SQL Server Enterprise Manager** The main tool used to manage the SQL Server enterprise.

- **Wizards** These enable you to easily perform tasks such as create databases and perform index tuning.

  The following list describes some of SQL Server's wizards:

  - **Create Login Wizard** Used to create SQL Server login accounts.

  - **Create Index Wizard** Used to create a Full-Text index.

  - **Create View Wizard** Used to create a view or subset of a table.

  - **Create Stored Procedure** Used to create a query that can be executed multiple times.

SQL Server Security

SQL Server must authenticate a user before he or she can access any of the data in the database. There are two modes of user authentication. They are as follows:

■ SQL Server and Windows NT 4.0

■ Windows NT 4.0 only

You must decide which mode of authentication to employ in your organization. Under SQL Server and Windows NT 4.0 mode, either SQL Server or Windows NT 4.0 can authenticate a user. Under the Windows NT 4.0–only mode, a user can only be validated in Windows NT 4.0. Since the first method is a bit more flexible, it is the default. Changing to the Windows NT 4.0–only authentication mode means the user must have a valid Windows NT 4.0 username.

See Figure 1-6 for a look at SQL Server authentication.

After a user gets logged on with a username under Windows NT 4.0, he or she has to pass a few more security checkpoints. The user must have a valid username to access the database; he or she needs a database username. Typically, the Windows NT 4.0 and SQL Server usernames are identical; users do not have to remember multiple usernames. Another level of security is the permission. If a user gets logged in with a Windows NT 4.0 username and a SQL Server username, he or she must have the appropriate permission to access the data in the database. Users can get permissions by either being given explicit access or by being a member of a group that has access. In SQL Server, the term group is an NT Global Group created on the primary domain controller (PDC) in a domain.

exam
Watch

If using Windows NT 4.0–only mode, the user does not have to enter in a separate database username since the usernames are the same in Windows NT 4.0 and SQL Server.

Options under the SQL
Server authentication
Security tab

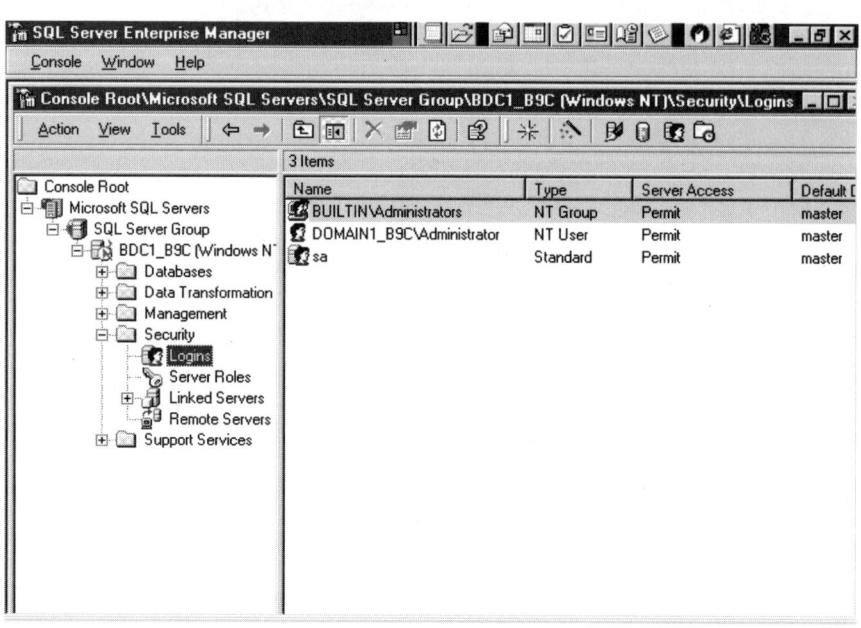

There are three types of permissions: statement, object, and implied.
Statement permissions are those that affect what a user can do in T-SQL and
are typically assigned to administrators of SQL Server. They are listed below:

- **CREATE DATABASE**   Enables a user to create a database.

- **CREATE TABLE**   Enables a user to create a table in a database.

- **CREATE PROCEDURE**   Gives a user the permission to make a
  stored procedure.

- **CREATE DEFAULT**   Enables a user to set default values in a table.

- **CREATE RULE**   Enables a user to create a validation rule to
  create data.

- **CREATE VIEW**   Enables a user to create a subset of a table.

- **DUMP DATABASE**   A user with this permission can back up
  the database.

- **DUMP TRANSACTION**   A user with this permission can back
  up a transaction log.

SQL Server has combined these permissions into what Microsoft calls a *role*. A role is assigned to a user. An example of a role is the *sysadmin* role. This is a SQL Server–based role that is the most powerful user. It is analogous to the Administrator user on Windows NT 4.0, the Admin user on Novell NetWare, or the *root* user on UNIX systems. Do not assign this role to ordinary users! Other server roles are db_creator, diskadmin, processadmin, securityadmin, serveradmin, and setupadmin. These roles have various levels of permissions that they can use.

Object permissions are usually given to users, groups, and roles. The following is a list of object permissions:

- **DELETE**   With this permission, a user can delete a view or table of a database.
- **EXECUTE**   Enables the user to run a stored procedure.
- **UPDATE**   Enables the user to change data in a table, column, or view.
- **SELECT**   A user can do a search on data in a view, column, or table.
- **REFERENCES**   Enables users to JOIN multiple databases.
- **INSERT**   A user can add a new row in a table or in a view.

Given that there are object permissions regarding what a user can do, there is also a set of roles, similar to server roles, called *database roles*. The db_owner role can do anything to the database. Other database roles include db_accessadmin, db_datareader, db_datawriter, db_ddladmin, db_securityadmin, db_dumpoperator, db_denydatawriter, and db_denyreader.

The *implied* permission is automatically assigned to a user by the user being a member of a server or database role. Implied permissions cannot be explicitly assigned. This relates to a concept of database object owner. When a user has the appropriate statement permission, if the user creates a table, he or she becomes a database object owner, meaning the user has total control over that table or object.

See Figure 1-7 for a look at the server roles. They are described on the right side of the figure.

Server roles and their
descriptions

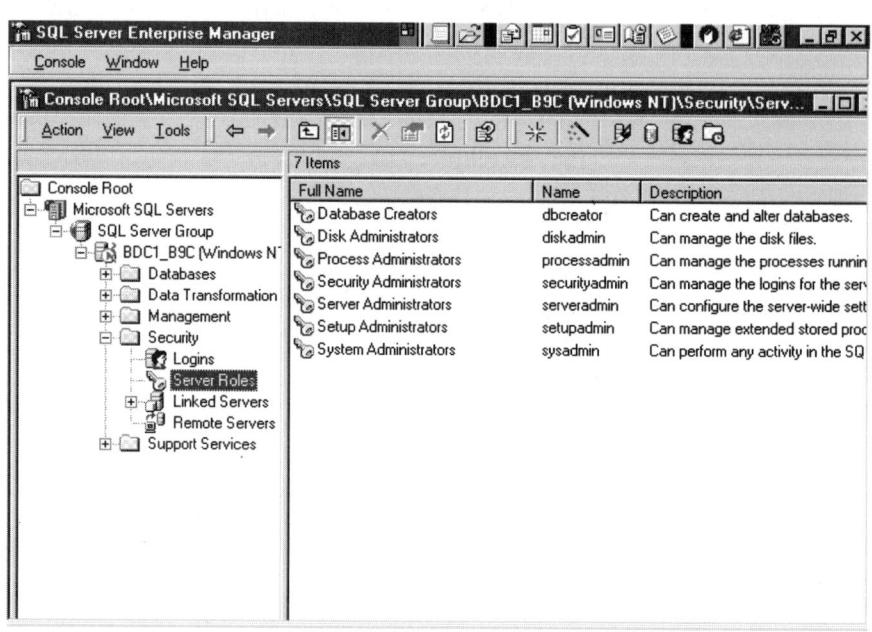

Fault Tolerance, Performance, and SQL Server

Microsoft SQL Server 7.0 running on Microsoft Windows NT 4.0 supports
fault tolerance by using Redundant Array of Inexpensive Disks (RAID).
Fault tolerance is the degree of hardware failure that a system can have and
still recover from it. RAID comes in three levels. Although there are actually
five levels, Microsoft implements RAID 0, RAID 1, and RAID 5.

RAID 0　RAID 0, also known as striping, takes the data and spreads it
across at least two disks. The data is written to successive disks. This is good
for SQL Server because the data can be read for multiple disks concurrently.
This speeds up data access. However, there is no data integrity provided
with RAID 0. So, you should make sure the data is backed up to tape, for
instance.

RAID 1   RAID 1 is implemented by using two disks and mirroring the data on both disks. RAID 1 can be implemented with a disk controller going to each disk, which is called *disk duplexing*. Mirroring is slow when it comes to writing disks because the data must be written twice—once for each disk. Duplexing is faster because the data can be read from both controller cards concurrently. They both provide data integrity because the data is on two disks. If one disk fails, the mirror can be broken and the disk can be replaced. Then, two disks can be remirrored. The data on the good disk is still intact. See Figure 1-8 for a view of disk mirroring and disk duplexing.

FIGURE 1-8

A diagram of disk mirroring and disk duplexing

Disk mirroring with one disk controller card

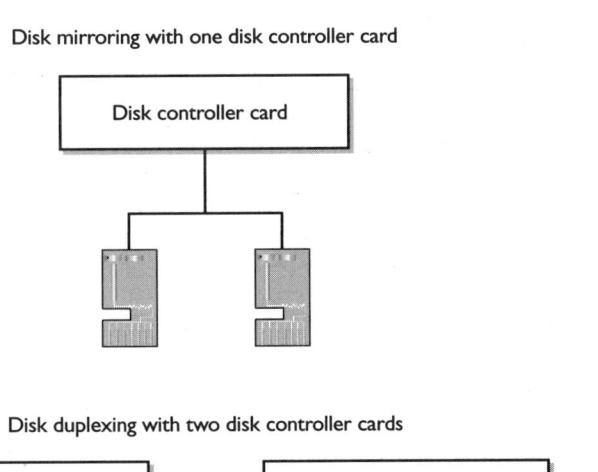

Disk controller card

Disk duplexing with two disk controller cards

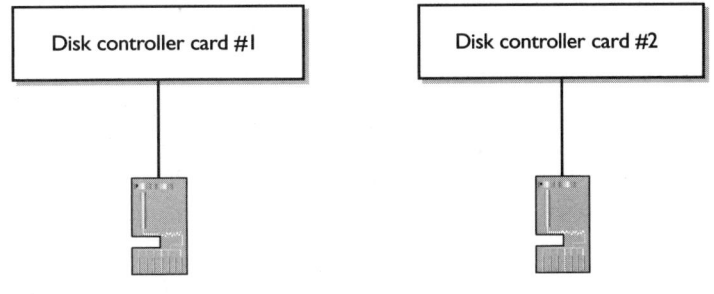

Disk controller card #1   Disk controller card #2

RAID 5   RAID 5 provides the highest level of data integrity. You will need at least three disks to implement RAID 5. Like RAID 0, the data is spread evenly across the disks; however, the parity data is written on one of the stripes. *Parity* is a computation performed on the data and is used to preserve the data in case one of the disks fails. RAID 5 is a little slow when it comes to writing the data since it must calculate the parity.

In summary, you must decide which, if any, level of RAID to implement. They each have various advantages and disadvantages. RAID 0 is the fastest, but offers no parity. RAID 1 is slower, but offers the advantage of data integrity through an online copy. RAID 5 is a good combination of the two.

CERTIFICATION SUMMARY

SQL was developed by IBM in order to alleviate some of the problems associated with traditional *flat* file designs. The problems were data redundancy and data dependency. Transact-SQL is Microsoft's enhanced version of the ANSI SQL-92 standard.

We explored the major features of SQL Server. Some of the highlights we discussed were operating-system compatibility, support for multiple-hardware platforms, and multiple-protocol support. In terms of data, we investigated the ideas of data warehousing and replication. The Windows appearance gives it an easy interface to the Transact-SQL commands.

We also defined SQL Server terms. Remember, a database consists of multiple tables. A table is a collection of data defined as rows and columns. A column (field) is a single piece of data, while a row (record) is a group of related columns. Stored procedures are programs that Microsoft has developed to make a DBA's job easier. A query is a set of T-SQL statements that perform a certain task; think of a query as a miniprogram. There are two types of indexes: clustered and nonclustered. Basically, an index is a method to quickly retrieve data based on a unique column (the primary key). Typically, a Social Security Number or account number is a primary key field. We also saw the four major databases in SQL Server: master, model, Msdb, and TempDB.

Security in a database is of prime importance. SQL has different roles and permissions that can be assigned to individual users based on the needs of the organization. The sysadmin role is the most powerful role in SQL Server and has complete control over the database.

In conclusion, SQL Server provides many useful tools for a DBA to administer the database for an organization's enterprise. The DBA must decide with the management the best way to configure the system. A DBA must be aware of the levels of fault tolerance and which ones provide speed over data integrity. The DBA must also be aware of the security concerns of the organization.

 # TWO-MINUTE DRILL

❑ With traditional files, termed *flat* files, several problems exist with how the data is managed. The problems are data redundancy, inconsistency, and lack of central control and security.

❑ The security of the data is at risk in a more traditional flat file design. Because the data is managed on a decentralized basis, there are more places where intruders could gain access to the data. Access to the data in a database system is controlled centrally, so there is one point of entry to the data instead of many.

❑ There are three types of database designs: hierarchical, network, and relational.

❑ The relational database is the most popular of the database types and is the foundation of SQL (Structured Query Language).

❑ IBM developed SQL, pronounced *sequel*, in the 1970s in San Jose, California.

❑ Microsoft SQL Server 7.0 uses Transact-SQL, or T-SQL, with language extensions to the ANSI-92 standard.

❑ Microsoft SQL Server 7.0 enables a database administrator (DBA) to develop and manage an organization's data up to the enterprise level. The enterprise level encompasses all of the organization's internal and external data interfaces.

❑ The administration of Microsoft SQL Server is accomplished through the Microsoft Management Console (MMC) application. The MMC allows applications or server products to provide a software "plug-in" to be added to the application framework provided by the MMC.

❑ Microsoft SQL Server 7.0 is designed to be a client/server model. In this model, the client and server take part in a request-response dialog.

❑ SQL Server 7.0 runs on Windows 95/ 98 and Windows NT Server 4.0.

❑ SQL Server must have Service Pack 4 (SP4) to run on Windows NT 4.0. It also requires the post-Beta 1 builds for Windows 2000—on Alpha and Intel processors.

❑ Microsoft has developed SQL Server using a highly portable language; it can be *carried* to different processor architectures and run successfully.

❑ Understand the protocols supported by SQL Server. The protocol of choice will eventually be TCP/IP, due to the popularity of the Internet.

❑ SMP, or Symmetrical Multi Processing, is the concept that a computer system can support multiple processors and the processors can balance the load between themselves.

❑ SQL Server 7.0 can support a maximum of four processors. However, with vendor support, it can support up to 32 CPUs.

❑ Because Windows NT 4.0 supports SMP, load balancing can occur among the processors. This provides tremendous processor efficiency and speed. Applications written to take advantage of SMP support are termed *multithreaded*.

❑ There are basically two types of data designs: transaction-oriented and Decision Support Systems (DSS). Transaction-oriented systems are systems on which users change customer data on a daily basis.

❑ The data in a transaction-based model is dynamic—it is always being added, changed, and deleted.

❑ A data warehousing solution often keeps a "nonupdating" copy of the data for people like managers to query against. This makes results more consistent and performance more predictable.

❑ Microsoft SQL Server 7.0 is compliant with the standards set by ANSI/ISO SQL-92. Microsoft has also added some language extensions called Transact-SQL.

❑ SQL Server 7.0 supports data replication. This means that the data will be automatically replicated, or duplicated, to another SQL Server. Replication follows a *publish and subscribe* approach. The *publisher* is a server that enables its data to be accessible for replication to other servers, known as *subscribers*.

❑ The SQL Server architecture is based on the client/server concept and is comprised of three main elements. They are Client software, SQL Server software, and Network connection software using interprocess communications (IPC).

❑ You can use the MAKEPIPE and READPIPE diagnostic programs to test the SQL Server connection.

❑ The same IPC mechanism must be installed on both the client and server or else the two will not be able to communicate.

❑ A database is just a logical collection of data stored in a file on a disk. A physical database is a collection of physical files that comprise the database. A physical database has a data file for holding actual data and a transaction log file to recover data in case of database problems.

❑ SQL Server must authenticate a user before he or she can access any of the data in the database. There are two modes of user authentication. They are SQL Server and Windows NT 4.0, or Windows NT 4.0 only.

❑ If using Windows NT 4.0, only mode, the user does not have to enter a separate database username, since the usernames are the same in Windows NT 4.0 and SQL Server.

❑ Microsoft SQL Server 7.0 running on Microsoft Windows NT 4.0 supports fault tolerance by using Redundant Array of Inexpensive Disks (RAID). *Fault tolerance* is the degree of hardware failure that a system can have and still recover from it.

❑ You must decide which, if any, level of RAID to implement. They each have various advantages and disadvantages. RAID 0 is the fastest, but offers no parity. RAID 1 is slower, but offers the advantage of data integrity through an online copy. RAID 5 is a good combination of the two.

SELF TEST

The following Self Test questions will help you measure your understanding of the material presented in this chapter. Read all the choices carefully, as there may be more than one correct answer. Choose all correct answers for each question.

1. What company first developed SQL?

    A. Microsoft

    B. Oracle

    C. Ingres

    D. IBM

    E. Sybase

2. With which operating systems is Microsoft SQL Server 7.0 compatible? (Choose all that apply.)

    A. Windows 95

    B. Windows 98

    C. Windows NT Workstation 4.0

    D. Windows NT Server 4.0

    E. TCP/IP

3. How many CPUs can Microsoft SQL Server 7.0 run on without any vendor-added support?

    A. 1

    B. 2

    C. 4

    D. 8

    E. 32

4. With which protocols is SQL Server 7.0 compatible? (Choose all that apply.)

    A. NW Link

    B. Windows 95/98

    C. NetBEUI

    D. UNIX

    E. TCP/IP

5. The term used to describe the ability of SQL Server to support additional processors is

    A. Multiprotocol support

    B. RAID

    C. SMP

    D. NW Link

    E. C2-level compliant

6. Which form of data replication allows each site to change replicated data?

    A. Transactional

    B. Snapshot

    C. Picture

    D. Merge

    E. Duplicated Transactional Replication (DTR)

7. What is the minimum CPU required to install SQL Server? (Choose all that apply.)

    A. Intel 16 bit

    B. Intel 32 bit

    C. DEC Alpha AXP

    D. Intel 80386

    E. DEC Beta BXP with 32-bit enhanced mode

8. How can you test the SQL Server connection between a client and a server?

   A. Use RAID 3.

   B. Add additional CPUs.

   C. Run MAKEPIPE and READPIPE commands.

   D. Run Windows Diagnostics.

9. In order to execute a T-SQL command, what type of permissions are used?

   A. REFERENCES

   B. Statement

   C. Implied

   D. Object

10. What type of permission enables you to view data in a table?

    A. DELETE

    B. EXECUTE

    C. CREATE VIEW

    D. SELECT

11. What role allows complete control over SQL Server?

    A. Syscreator

    B. Sysadmin

    C. Administrator

    D. Domain admins

12. What role gives the user the ability to create a database?

    A. Db_creator

    B. Db_owner

    C. Administrator

    D. Domain admins

13. A single data element, such as Social Security Number, is considered a

    A. Row

    B. Column

    C. Rule

    D. Cluster

14. The type of index that sorts pointers to the columns in a table is called

    A. Clustered

    B. Nonclustered

    C. Triggers

    D. Sorted

15. A set of precompiled programs that can be executed to make a DBA's job easier is called a

    A. Trigger

    B. Clustered index

    C. Stored procedure

    D. Rule

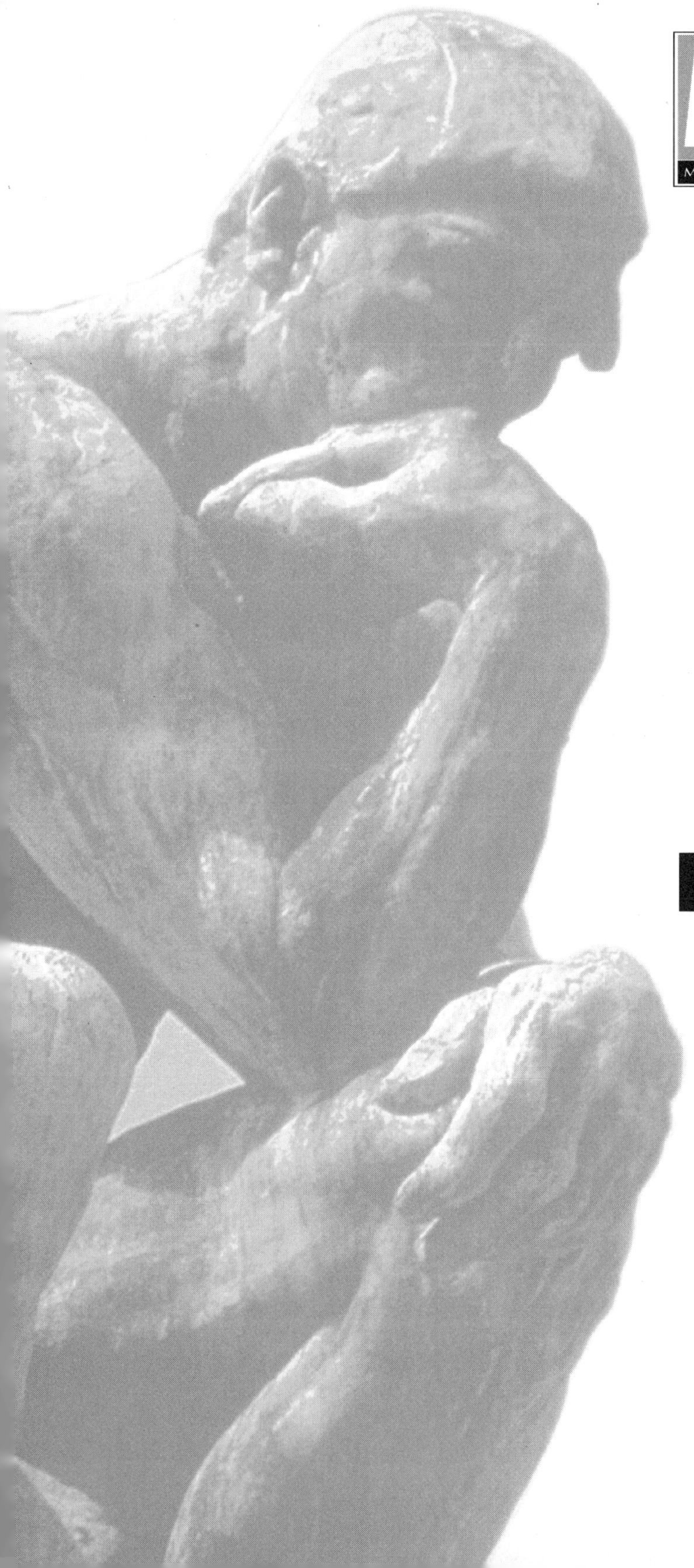

MCDBA
MICROSOFT CERTIFIED DATABASE ADMINISTRATOR

2

Transact-SQL Overview

CERTIFICATION OBJECTIVES

2.01	Microsoft SQL Server Programming Tools
2.02	Transact-SQL Programming Language
2.03	Elements of Transact-SQL
2.04	Dynamic SQL Statements

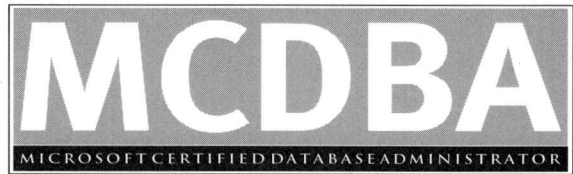

T here are many demands placed on the database administrator (DBA) in an organization. The DBA must be able to handle issues concerning creating and managing the database, regulating security, and determining whether the database is performing as it should. The DBA also needs to be aware of the SQL programming environment. Although the DBA may not be a programmer, he or she does need to be aware of the major aspects of the programming tools and techniques available in SQL.

This chapter introduces the Microsoft SQL Server 7.0 programming environment, Transact-SQL. Transact-SQL encompasses the ANSI SQL-92 standard with enhancements. We will look at Transact-SQL, compare the traditional and SQL programming environments, explore queries and scripts, and perform some hands-on exercises.

CERTIFICATION OBJECTIVE 2.01

Microsoft SQL Server Programming Tools

In this section, we will briefly discuss the programming tools available to SQL Server DBAs. The following is a brief list of some of the tools:

- Enterprise Manager
- Query Analyzer
- Bulk copy program (bcp)
- Data Transformation Services (DTS)

Enterprise Manager

The Enterprise Manager allows you to create the following through a graphical interface:

- **Diagrams**   Create a graphical view of the tables.
- **Tables**   Create and delete tables.
- **Views**   Create a subset of a table or tables.

FROM THE CLASSROOM

Programming Microsoft SQL Server

What would a database management system (DBMS) be without its own programming language for data manipulation and retrieval? With Microsoft SQL Server, that language is Transact-SQL. T-SQL has been the variation of SQL utilized by Microsoft's flagship DBMS since its inception. This version of Structured Query Language, or SQL, is used exclusively within the functionality of Microsoft SQL Server 7.0. You should keep certain points in mind when using T-SQL and Microsoft SQL Server:

■ Limiting T-SQL scripts to standard SQL elements found in the ANSI SQL-92 ISO standard will help increase portability of those scripts to other DBMS.

■ Using spaces in database object names is new to version 7.0.

■ The Query Analyzer will color code keywords for greater recognition.

■ Bitwise operators are still supported by T-SQL in SQL Server 7.0.

■ The precedence applied to logical operators may differ in T-SQL compared to other programming languages.

Other tips for using T-SQL include the use of a double-hyphen (--) as a comment separator rather than the /* ...*/ pair. This allows inline comments. Keep in mind that a double hyphen will include all text in the comment following the double hyphen, until the end of the line. T-SQL statements can also be constructed dynamically within an executing script. This involves using the EXECUTE command and parentheses to enclose the dynamically created string. Keep in mind that functions can not be used to create the strings, all items must consist of character data, and EXECUTE statements can be nested.

—Michael Lane Thomas,
MCSE+I, MCSD, MCP+SB, MSS, MCT, A+

■ **Stored Procedures**   Create "programs" for use in a query.

■ **Users and Roles**   Manage users and their access to the database tables.

- **Rules and Default values**   Set up constraints and initial values for columns.
- **User-defined data types**   Create your own data types.

To invoke the Enterprise Manager, follow these steps:

1. Click Start.

2. Select Programs.

3. Select Microsoft SQL Server 7.0.

4. Select Enterprise Manager, then open up your database.

5. Right-click one of the items such as Tables and click New Table, for example.

See Figure 2-1 for a graphical view of the Enterprise Manager.

FIGURE 2-1

Viewing the
Enterprise Manager

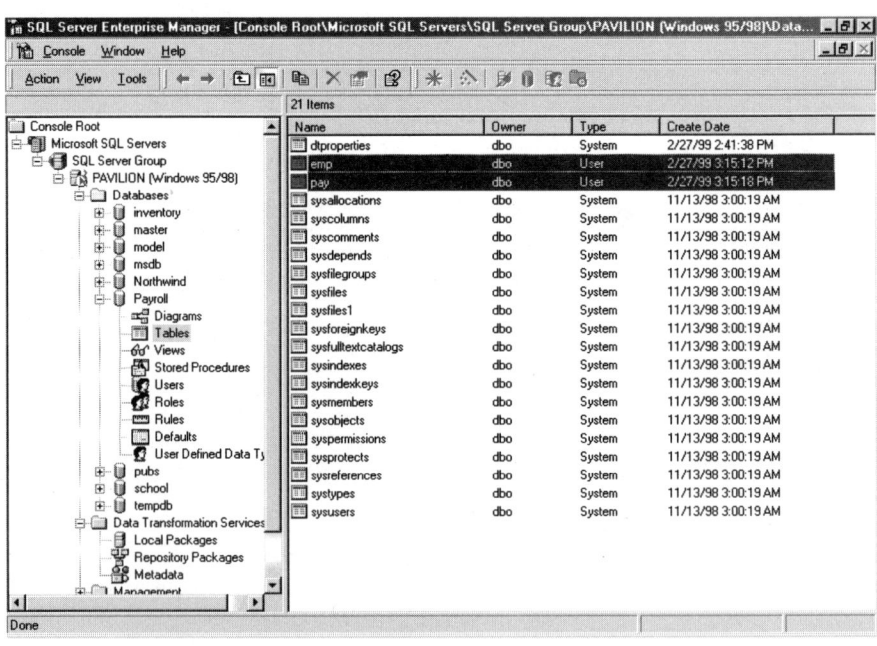

Query Analyzer

We will discuss the Query Analyzer in greater detail because it is the main tool used to generate Transact-SQL queries. It is invoked from the Microsoft SQL Server 7.0 icon, which is the same place that you find the Enterprise Manager.

How to Process Queries

One item to mention here is that queries are processed in two steps:

1. **Interpret**   Check for syntax.
2. **Execute**   Perform the processing.

How to Execute T-SQL Statements

In order to execute a query, you go into the Query Analyzer, type in your code, and click Execute, or press CTRL-E.

Bulk Copy Program

The bulk copy program utility, or bcp, allows you to take an already created data file and insert the data into a SQL Server 7.0 database. It is a command-line utility and executed as *bcp*. It requires a format file, but you can create the format file with bcp. Enter the following code, but note that the quotes are not required:

```
Bcp "payroll..emp" format d:\emp.dat /fd:\emp.fmt /U"sa" /P"" /Sserver_Name
```

This creates the format file *d:\emp.fmt* from the *payroll* database using the *emp* table. The format file specifies the layout of a column. The /U is for user, the /P is for password and the /S is for SQL Server name. A file similar to the following is created:

7.0						
3						
1	SQLSMALLINT	0	2	""	1	emp_id
2	SQLDECIMAL	1	19	""	2	hours
3	SQLDECIMAL	1	19	""	3	pay_rate

This file can then be used as a template to insert data into your database. A sample code listing to insert the data follows.

```
Bcp "payroll..pay" in d:\pay.dat /fd:\pay.fmt /U"sa" /P"" /Sserver_name
```

The *in* keyword sends the data to the payroll database into the *pay* table from d:\pay.dat and uses the format file d:\pay.fmt. To send the data out, change the keyword *in* to *out*. See the following example:

```
Bcp "payroll..pay" out d:\pay.dat /fd:\pay.fmt /U"sa" /P"" /Sserver_name
```

Data Transformation Services (DTS)

Data Transformation Services (DTS) is a powerful graphical tool used to copy data from database to database or even to a text file. To invoke DTS, open the Enterprise Manager and open your database. Once your database is open, right-click the table, click All Tasks, and then click Import or Export. This illustration shows the Export screen of DTS:

Generating a Script File

You can create a table within a database and use the Generate SQL Scripts command to create a query script file. You could then alter this as you see fit. In order to generate a script file, go into the Enterprise Manager and right-click your table. Next, select All Tasks and then Generate SQL Scripts. Here's the General tab of the Generate SQL Scripts screen:

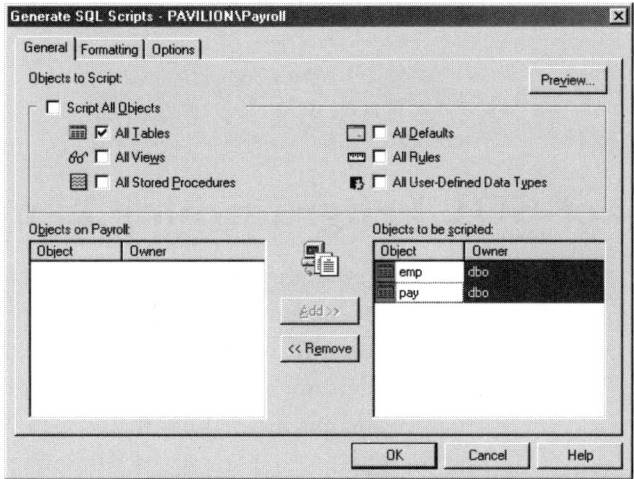

Shown next is the script file that was saved from the Generate SQL Script process. Be careful executing the script file after you have created a table with data. The first statement checks to see if the table exists and if it does, then the table will be dropped and your data will be deleted.

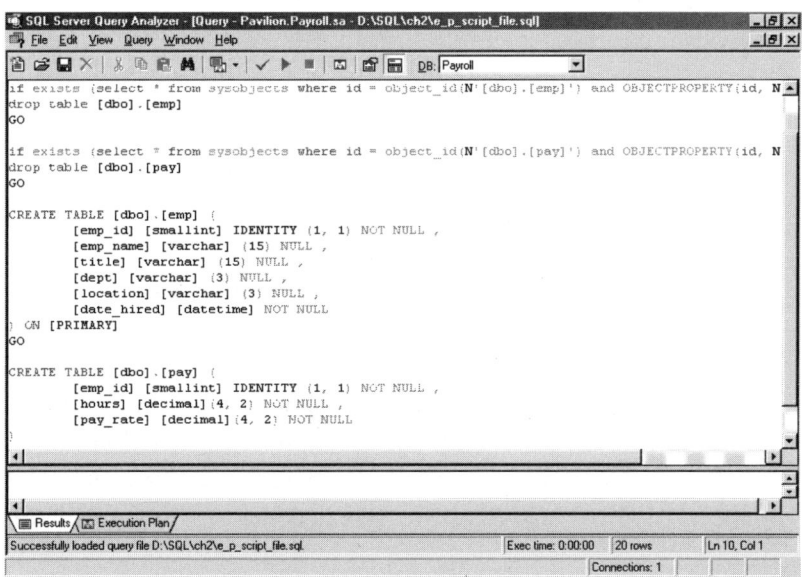

This section has focused on some of the SQL Server programming tools. Now, we will examine one of the most powerful tools—the Transact-SQL programming language.

CERTIFICATION OBJECTIVE 2.02

Transact-SQL Programming Language

This section defines the purpose of Transact-SQL. We will compare this programming environment to traditional programming environments. We will explore the modular divisions of Transact-SQL that set it apart from the cumbersome traditional programming arena. There are numerous figures and examples along the way, to help you understand.

Simply stated, Transact-SQL allows you to manage your database. It differs from more traditional programming language environments in which the data is defined in the same location as the actual programming logic, or code, statements.

Problems with Traditional Programming

One problem with languages such as COBOL, BASIC, and FORTRAN is that they define the size of the data field, and the type of data that the field can contain, within the actual program.

A second, related problem, is data placement. When data is defined with these languages, the data fields, or in SQL terms, columns, are located one after the other. We will explore these problems in the following section.

Data and Logic Coexistence

Because the data and programming logic are stored in the same location, or program file, problems arise when you add new data fields or change the size of existing data. For example, in a COBOL, program, a field such as CUST-NAME, could be defined as 25 characters; but it would be within the same file as the logic statements such as IF...THEN, ADD, MOVE, and COPY. If we were to add a new field, or increase the size of CUST-NAME to 30 characters, we would have to recompile our COBOL program. This could be a lengthy process and could require changing multiple programs that refer to CUST-NAME.

Data Placement and Dependence

Another problem is the fact that the data is strictly dependent upon its placement in the file. For example, assume in a data file that CUST-NAME is 30 characters, followed by CUST-ADDRESS, which is 35 characters. So, CUST-NAME starts in column one, whereas CUST-ADDRESS starts in column 31. In our program, we must define these the same way. We define CUST-NAME followed by CUST-ADDRESS. Then, we must compile the program to get the executable code:

```
|------------------CUST-NAME-|-CUST-ADDRESS-------------------|
123456789112345678921234567893123456789412345678951234567896123 45
        0         0         0         0         0         0
```

If we accidentally define CUST-NAME as 25 characters, instead of 30, then the program would think CUST-ADDRESS begins in column 26, instead of column 31. This would cause problems because our data would not match our definition. Because the definition and logic are housed in the same file, we could get compile errors and never get the executable code. Of course, even if the program compiled cleanly, the data would be incorrect. Part of CUST-ADDRESS would mistakenly have the data from CUST-NAME.

CERTIFICATION OBJECTIVE 2.03

Elements of Transact-SQL

Now, let's take a look at the elements that make up T-SQL. They are as follows:

- Data Definition Language (DDL)

- Data Manipulation Language (DML)
- Data Control Language (DCL)

Data Definition Language (DDL)

The Data Definition Language (DDL) is the subset of SQL statements used for modeling the structure (rather than the contents) of a database or cube. The DDL gives you the ability to create, modify, and remove databases and database objects.

The DDL allows you to create a database and the tables in the database. You create the columns and define column type and size. You can also set up a primary key in the DDL. A primary key allows the data to be accessed quickly in an index. Other DDL functions include setting up default values for a column, validating data to ensure that it is within a certain range of values, and altering a column's definition. Some of Transact-SQL's DDL statements are given here:

DDL Statement	Definition
CREATE DATABASE	Creates a database on disk for storing multiple tables. This defines a database name for SQL, the initial size, and growth factor. It can also specify log files that are used for transaction recovery.
CREATE TABLE	Allows you to define the data column characteristics based on predefined data types.
ALTER DATABASE	Allows you to modify the files associated with the database.
CREATE RULE	Enforces a range rule for a column of data.
CREATE DEFAULT	Sets the default or initial value for a column.

Creating a Database Using T-SQL

Now, let's take a look at a few of the DDL statements within Transact-SQL. There are two ways to create a database in SQL Server 7.0. You can use the Create Database Wizard or you can issue a Transact-SQL statement. We will explore how to create a database in Transact-SQL. See the steps in Exercise 2-1 for creating a database.

For this chapter, we will use a payroll database as our business model. We will build a database with several tables in it. One table will hold all employee information except pay and hours; the other will contain the pay and hours information.

In Exercise 2-1, the database is named *payroll* and the logical name is *payroll_dat*, which is associated with the actual file on disk. The initial file size is 5MB and the maximum size is 10MB. The file will grow by 5 percent when new space is needed by the database.

EXERCISE 2-1

Creating a Transact-SQL Database

1. Click Start | Programs | Microsoft SQL Server 7.0 | Query Analyzer. A screen such as this one appears:

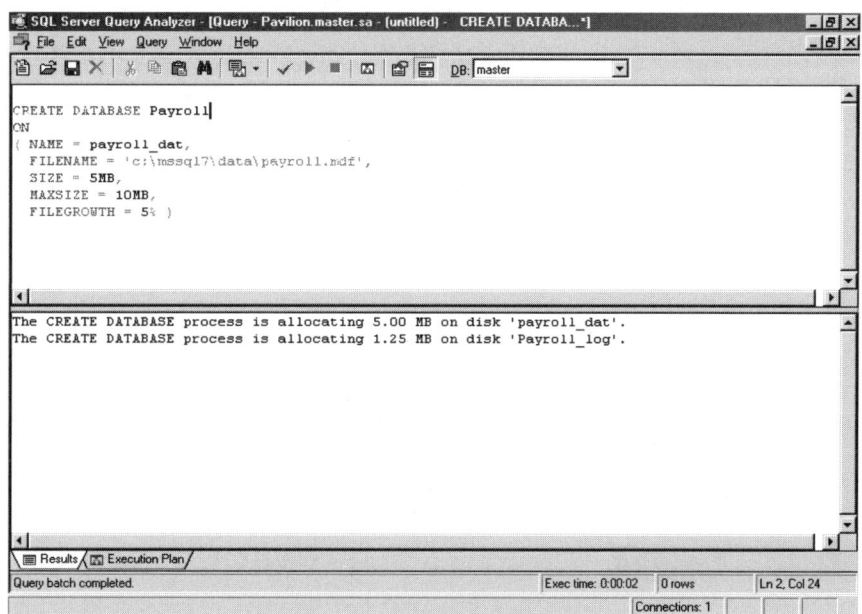

2. Enter the text shown in the top half of the screen.

3. Click Query | Execute. After the query is executed, the lower half of the screen shows you the results of the execution. If there are errors, then the appropriate error will appear. In the illustration, the execution is successful, as evidenced by the lower half of the screen.

Creating a Table Using T-SQL

Now we learn how to create a table. Remember from Chapter 1 that a table exists within the actual database. In Exercise 2-2, the table named *employees* is created within the payroll database. We will *parse* the query before executing it. Parsing merely checks the syntax of the query instead of executing it. A primary key will be defined along with other columns. We will also encounter other options with CREATE TABLE such as CHECK, and DEFAULT, which we will explore later in this chapter.

In Exercise 2-2, the columns are: emp_id, emp_name, title, dept, location, date_hired, and pay_rate. The primary key is emp_id on a nonclustered index. (See Chapter 1 for nonclustered and clustered indexes.) The IDENTITY (1,1) option indicates that SQL will automatically create this column and will increment it for each successive row. This will create a unique key field for us. The first number, 1, is the seed and the second is the increment number; so, it will increment each row by one, thus ensuring uniqueness.

The dept column has a CHECK constraint that lists the valid data such as ACT for Accounting, ENG for Engineering, and MIS for Management Information Systems. The location column has a DEFAULT of CAN, meaning if no data is entered in this column, then CAN, for Canada, will be supplied by Transact-SQL. The date_hired column uses the getdate() system function, which means it will use the current system date and time. We will discuss functions later in this chapter.

EXERCISE 2-2

Creating a Transact SQL Table

1. Click Start | Programs | Microsoft SQL Server 7.0 | Query Analyzer. A screen such as the following one appears.

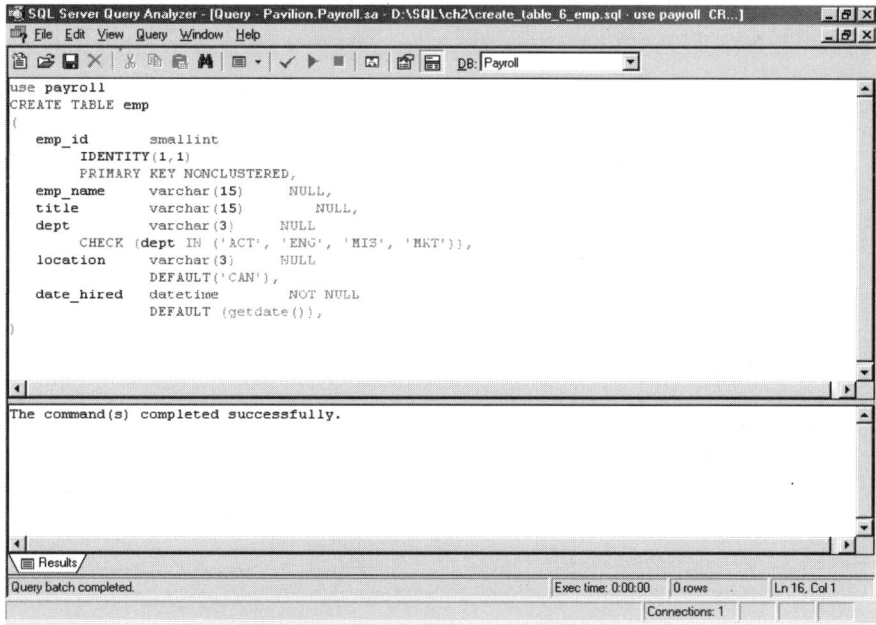

```
SQL Server Query Analyzer - [Query - Pavilion.Payroll.sa - D:\SQL\ch2\create_table_6_emp.sql - use payroll CR...]
File  Edit  View  Query  Window  Help
                                                        DB: Payroll
use payroll
CREATE TABLE emp
(
    emp_id          smallint
           IDENTITY(1,1)
           PRIMARY KEY NONCLUSTERED,
    emp_name        varchar(15)      NULL,
    title           varchar(15)          NULL,
    dept            varchar(3)       NULL
           CHECK (dept IN ('ACT', 'ENG', 'MIS', 'MKT')),
    location        varchar(3)       NULL
                    DEFAULT('CAN'),
    date_hired      datetime         NOT NULL
                    DEFAULT (getdate()),
)

The command(s) completed successfully.

Results
Query batch completed.                          Exec time: 0:00:00   0 rows        Ln 16, Col 1
                                                                     Connections: 1
```

2. Enter the text shown in the illustration. In this example, the database used is payroll. We created it in Exercise 2-1.

3. Click Query | Parse. This checks the query for valid syntax—it will not execute the query.

4. Click Query | Execute. As in Exercise 2-1, the query is executed successfully.

on the **job**

You can create a database or table within Transact-SQL. However, if you need to create a table quickly, then consider using the Create Table Wizard. Refer to the following illustration for a view of this wizard. To get to the wizard, click Start | Programs | Microsoft SQL Server 7.0 | Enterprise Manager. Then, click the icons on the left side of the screen, find your database and right-click on it.

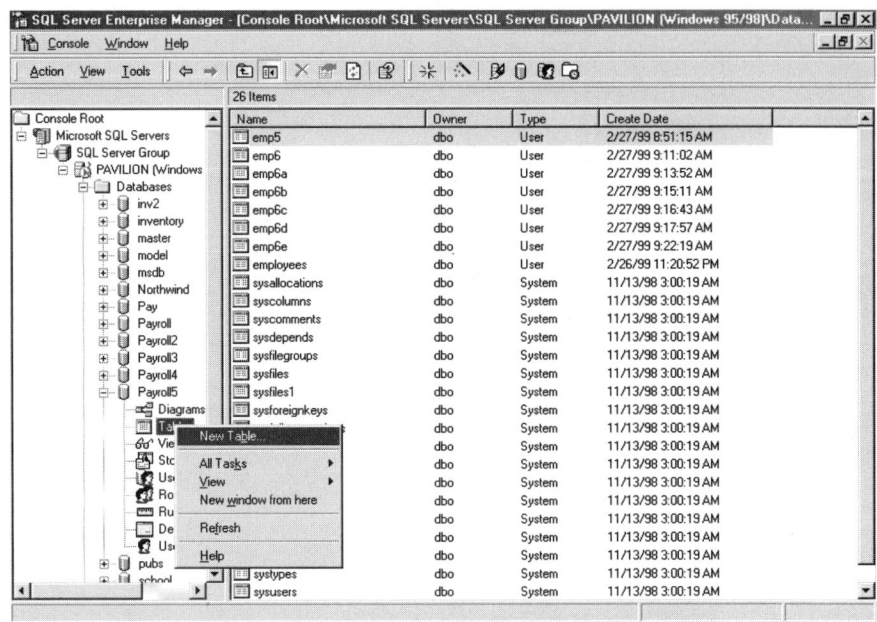

exam
⑩atch **Note the following rules for PRIMARY KEY constraints:**

- A table can contain only one PRIMARY KEY constraint.
- The PRIMARY KEY must be defined as NOT NULL.
- The primary key must be unique—there can be no duplicate primary key values in a table.
- Each primary key will generate an index.
- In order to modify a PRIMARY KEY constraint in T-SQL, you must first delete it and then re-create it.
- Multiple columns can be used as part of a primary key.

Now that we have discussed how to create a database and a table within the database, we will explore the Data Manipulation Language (DML).

Data Manipulation Language (DML)

The Data Manipulation Language (DML) is the subset of SQL statements used to retrieve and manipulate data. The DML lets you select rows in a view, or subset, of a database. It also allows you to insert, delete, and update rows and columns. This section has a number of sample figures that demonstrate some of the more important DML statements. The following table lists of a few of the Data Manipulation Language statements:

DML Statement	Definition
SELECT	The SELECT statement is used to extract data from a table.
INSERT	INSERT allows you to add a row to the table.
DELETE	With the DELETE statement, you can delete a row in a table.
UPDATE	UPDATE allows you to modify columns in a table.

Now, we will use the database and table created in Exercises 2-1 and 2-2 in combination with a few of the Transact-SQL DML statements. Expanding on our payroll database, we need to create another table. The following code listing is needed to add a new table called *pay* to our payroll database.

```
use payroll
CREATE TABLE pay
(
   emp_id smallint
      IDENTITY(1,1)
      PRIMARY KEY
        REFERENCES emp(emp_id),
   hours    decimal(4,2) NOT NULL
           CHECK (hours >= 0 and hours <= 50),
   pay_rate     decimal(4,2) NOT NULL
           CHECK (pay_rate >= 0.00 AND pay_rate <= 99.99)
    )
```

When executed, this query creates the following columns: emp_id, hours, and pay_rate. Notice there is a REFERENCES clause on the emp_id column. This refers to the emp_id primary key column in the emp table. This makes a foreign key assignment from the pay table to the emp table. A foreign key is a forced link between columns in different tables. This ensures data integrity. There is an emp_id column in both the pay and emp tables. This is the link between the two tables. We can later perform a query on multiple tables, or JOIN, them.

exam
ⓦatch

A foreign key is a column in one table that is linked to a column in another table. Here are some of the rules for FOREIGN KEY constraints:

- A FOREIGN KEY constraint can only reference a PRIMARY KEY constraint or a column with the UNIQUE constraint.

- There can be a maximum of 253 foreign keys in a table.

- A FOREIGN KEY constraint can reference a column in the same table; this is called a self-referencing key.

- A FOREIGN KEY constraint is commonly used to join multiple tables; the primary key and foreign key columns are linked.

- A FOREIGN KEY constraint ensures referential integrity by not allowing the PRIMARY KEY constraint it is linked with to be deleted. This ensures data integrity. You must first *delete the foreign key row in one table and then the primary key row in the other table.*

Relationships Between PRIMARY KEY Constraints and FOREIGN KEY Constraints

Let us now take a peek at what will occur if a PRIMARY KEY constraint in one table is deleted *before* the FOREIGN KEY constraint is deleted in another table. We will continue with our pay and emp tables. Remember, the pay table has the PRIMARY KEY constraint and the emp table has the FOREIGN KEY constraint. We want to delete the row with emp_id = 9. Take a look at the following sample code listing:

```
use payroll
delete from emp where emp_id = 9
delete from pay where emp_id  = 9
```

By attempting to delete the PRIMARY KEY constraint from within the emp table before deleting the FOREIGN KEY constraint in the pay table, this query would generate the following error:

```
Server: Msg 547, Level 16, State 1, Line 1
DELETE statement conflicted with COLUMN REFERENCE constraint
'FK__pay__emp_id__1AD3FDA4'.
The conflict occurred in database 'Payroll', table 'pay', column 'emp_id'.
The statement has been terminated.
```

However, if we used the following query to delete the foreign key row in the pay table prior to deleting the primary key in the emp table, the query will succeed.

```
use payroll
delete from pay where emp_id = 9
delete from emp where emp_id = 9
```

Now that we have proven that the FOREIGN KEY constraint maintains data integrity through the relationship with a key in another table, let's turn our focus to creating a table diagram.

Creating a Table Diagram

A diagram, or schema, is a very useful programming tool for showing the relationships between multiple tables. It is created using the Diagram Wizard in the Enterprise Manager. We will create a diagram to visualize the relationship.

Once you have created the code for the pay table and executed the query, you can go into Enterprise Manager and click the payroll database. Next, right click the Diagram icon and create a New Diagram. The New Diagram Wizard will take you through the set up. Remember to click the disk icon in the upper-left corner to save the diagram. See Figure 2-2 for a completed diagram of the visual relationship between the pay table and the emp table—both part of the payroll database.

Using the INSERT and SELECT DML Statements

Now that we have created two tables, it is time to put data in them. See Exercise 2-3 for the steps in inserting data using Transact-SQL.

FIGURE 2-2

Graphical diagram showing
the foreign key relationship
between the emp table and
the pay table

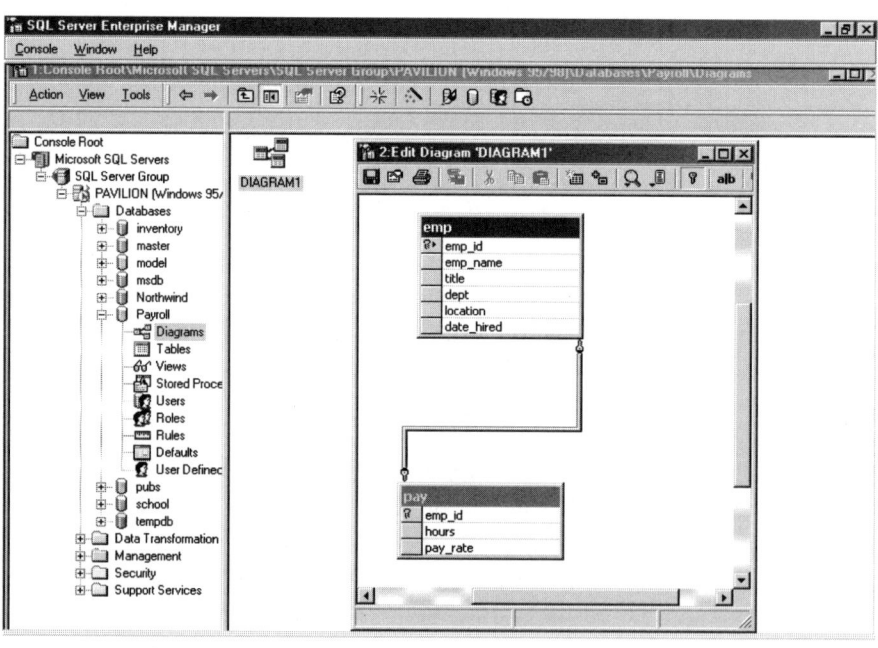

Inserting Data Using Transact-SQL

1. Click Start | Programs | Microsoft SQL Server 7.0 | Query Analyzer. A screen such as this one appears:

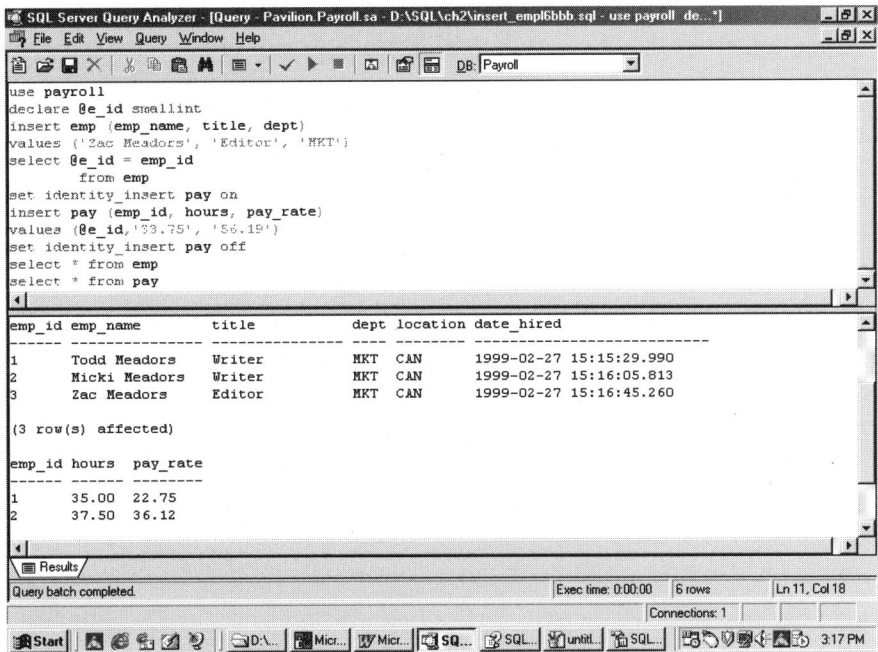

2. Enter the text that is in the top half of the screen.

3. Click Query | Execute. The query is executed successfully.

In the illustration, there are a few DML statements that need explaining. The following table contains descriptions of the DML statements:

DML Statement	Description
USE payroll	Identifies the database that the query will use.
DECLARE @e_id smallint	Declares an integer local variable, @e_id, which is available to the query.

DML Statement	Description
INSERT emp (emp_name, title, dept)	Inserts a new row in the emp table. The columns are: emp_name, title, and dept.
VALUES ('Zac Meadors', 'Editor', 'MKT')	Represents the data that will be inserted in the INSERT statement. The order of the data in the VALUES statement must match the order in the INSERT statement.
SELECT @e_id = emp_id from emp	Grabs the primary key, emp_id, from the emp table and places it into the local variable @emp_id. Remember the primary key was set with the IDENTITY statement. The system, in this case, will generate a unique key for us.
SET IDENTITY_INSERT pay ON	Allows us to modify a column set with the IDENTITY property. Normally, we could not set a value in an identity column because the system automatically generates this for us.
INSERT pay (emp_id, hours, pay_rate)	INSERTs a new row in the pay table. The columns are emp_id, hours, and pay_rate.
VALUES (@e_id, '33.75', '56.19')	Represents the data inserted in the table. Note the local variable @e_id is used for the data in the emp_id column in the pay table. It was previously set to the emp_id value from the pay table. This guarantees that the same primary key is used in both tables.
SET IDENTITY_INSERT pay OFF	Turns off the ability to insert a value in a identity column.
SELECT * FROM emp	Displays all the columns and their data from the emp table. The star (*) symbol implies all columns.
SELECT * FROM pay	Displays all the columns and their data from the pay table.

on the
job

Use the INDENTITY_INSERT tablename ON to put data in a column defined with the IDENTITY property. After you are through with the insert, make sure you turn it back off. This will prevent accidental changes.

Now that we have learned how to populate columns with data using the INSERT command, let's look at a few other ways to display the data with a SELECT statement. In Figure 2-3, a query is executed to display the name, title, and department of Canadian employees ORDERed (sorted) by department. Notice the comments, which are identified by /* at the beginning and a */ at the end of the comment. The top half is the query code, whereas the bottom half is the query execution results. More data has been added by using the INSERT and VALUES DML statements.

The next example shows how the UPDATE DML statement would give a 10 percent raise to the employee with emp_id = 5. Note the use of the SET statement, which computes the raise by SETting pay_rate = pay_rate * 1.10.

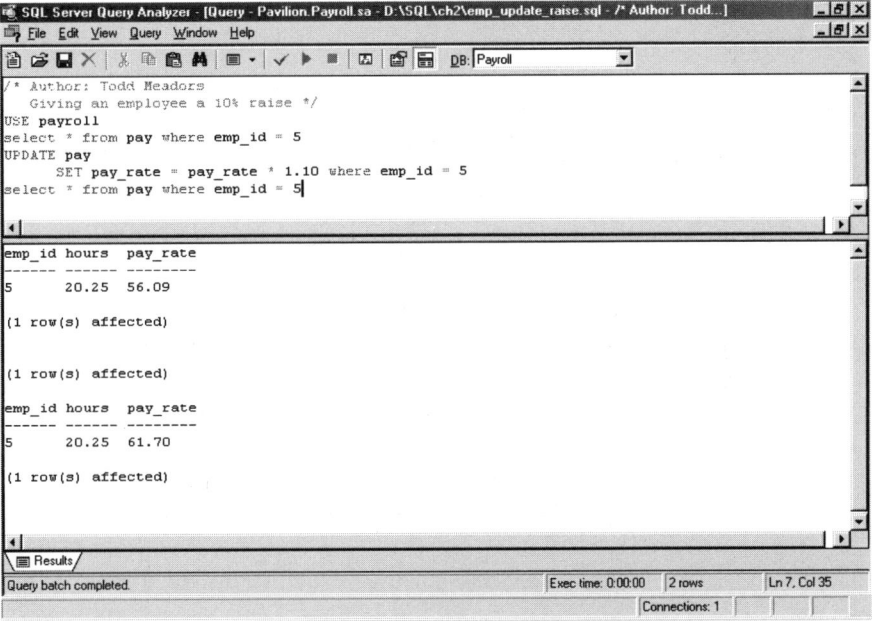

Up to this point, we have been looking at data from single tables. We have SELECTed, INSERTed, and UPDATEd columns from either the pay table or the emp table. It is possible to combine data from multiple tables. The data is separated into multiple tables because it is more efficient to process data that is in multiple tables. The primary key and foreign key

Selecting the name, title, and department of employees meeting a certain criterion

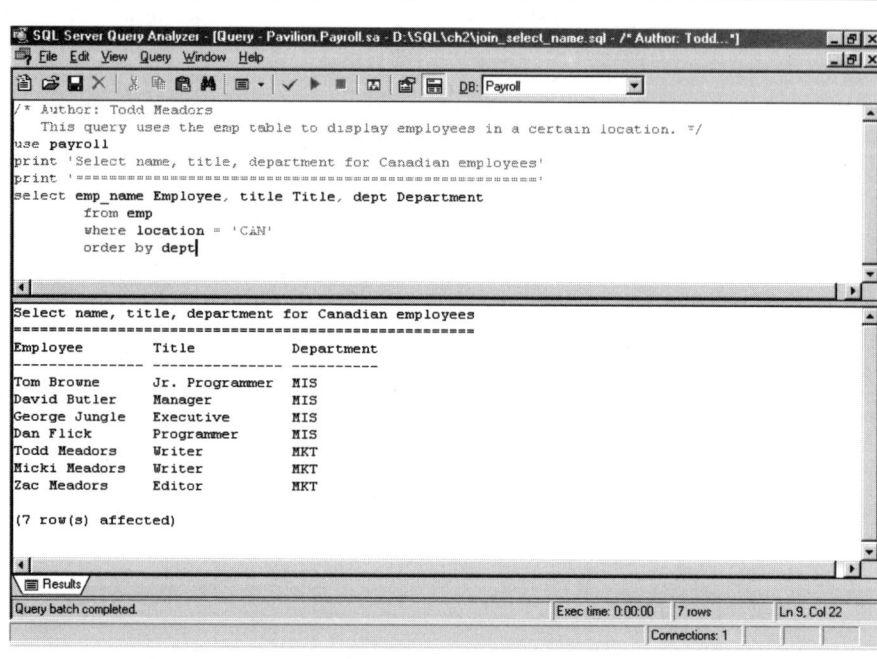

columns link the tables together. In our case, emp_id is a primary key in the emp table, and emp_id is a REFERENCEd foreign key in the pay table. Let's explore the technique of combining two tables.

Combining Data from Multiple Tables

There are two methods of combining multiple tables:

- Using the WHERE clause on the SELECT statement
- Utilizing the JOIN clause

Figure 2-4 demonstrates the use of the first method—combining multiple tables using the SELECT...WHERE statement. This is an older SQL construct. We can choose the columns we want by selecting columns based on the emp_id column being equal in both tables. In the SELECT

FIGURE 2-4

Combining data from
multiple tables using
SELECT…WHERE

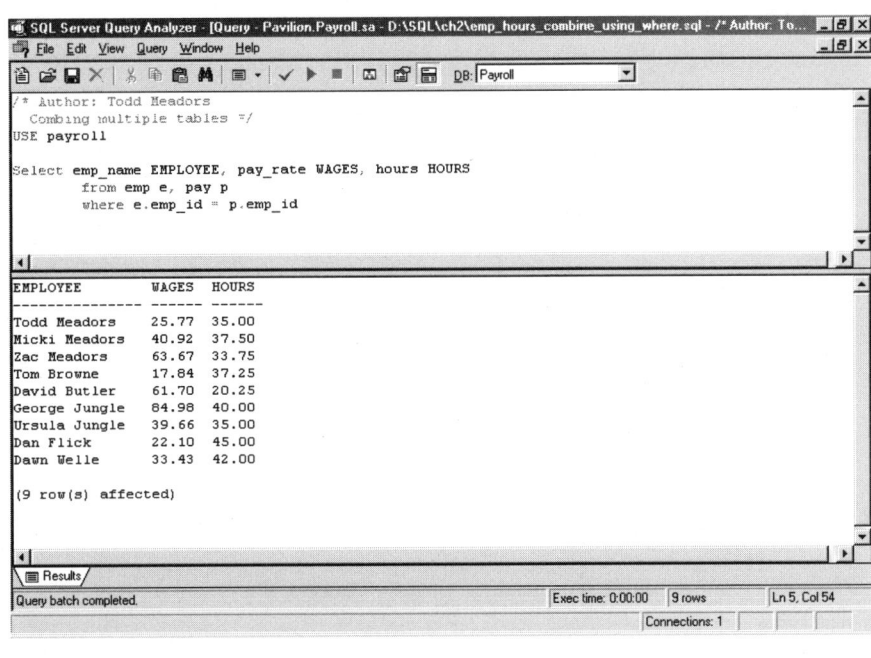

statement, an alias name is created for the emp table; it is called *e*. There is also an alias for the pay table; it is called *p*. You can refer to the columns in the table by either of the following two methods:

- *Table_name.column_name*
- *Table_alias_name.column_name*

Figure 2-5 demonstrates how to combine data from multiple tables using the INNER JOIN clause. An INNER JOIN is based on the equality of columns in a table. See the figure for the query and the resultant output. If you compare the output in Figure 2-4 and Figure 2-5, you see that they are equal; thus, proving that the statements perform the same logic.

Let's review JOINing tables. In Exercise 2-3, we use the JOIN command to combine table data.

FIGURE 2-5

Combining data from multiple tables using an INNER JOIN

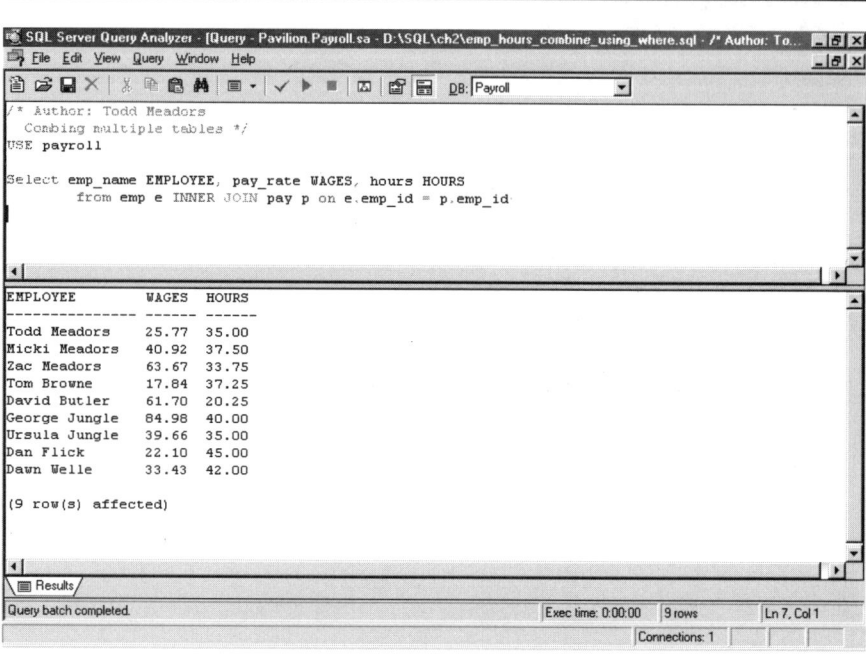

EXERCISE 2-4

Creating a JOIN Query

1. Click Start | Programs | Microsoft SQL Server 7.0 | Query Analyzer. A screen such as the one in Figure 2-5 appears.

2. Enter the text shown in the top half of the screen.

3. Click Query | Execute.

Data Control Language (DCL)

The Data Control Language (DCL) is the subset of SQL statements used to control permissions on database objects. Permissions are controlled using the GRANT and REVOKE statements. DCL statements control the data based on conditional processing. Examples include IF...ELSE, BEGIN...END, PRINT, WHILE, and CASE statements.

Control-of-Flow Methods

The following control methods exist:

- IF...ELSE
- BEGIN...END
- CASE
- WHILE
- GOTO

These conform to many of their traditional programming language counterparts. IF...ELSE tests a condition for true or false. If true, the statements immediately after the condition are executed; otherwise, if false, the statements after the false condition are executed.

An example of the IF...ELSE is as follows:

```
IF @status = 'A'
      SELECT 'Employee Active'
ELSE
      SELECT 'Employee not Active'
```

An example of a BEGIN...END block is as follows:

```
IF @status = 'A'
BEGIN
      SET @var = 1
PRINT 'ACTIVE'
END
```

BEGIN...END statements are necessary when you need to execute multiple statements in conjunction with a condition such as IF or WHILE.

A CASE statement is merely a different version of an IF...ELSE statement. A CASE sample is as follows:

```
CASE emp_status
WHEN 'A' THEN 'Active'
WHEN 'T' THEN 'Terminated'
WHEN 'D' THEN 'Disability Leave'
ELSE 'Invalid status'
END
```

CASE is appropriate to use when a variable has multiple conditions that we want to check. CASE could be used instead of a confusing IF statement. The WHILE statement is used for looping, as in this example:

```
WHILE @@fetch_status = 0
BEGIN
            Statement
            Statement
END
```

The GOTO statement is used to branch to a label. See the following example:

```
TOP:
      BEGIN
            Statement
            Statement
            Statement
      END
IF @var = 1
      GOTO TOP
```

In this example, the IF tests to see whether or not the local variable, @var, is set to 1. If set to 1, then the program will branch to the label TOP.

Local and Global Variables

There are two types of variables: local and global. A developer declares local variables using the query language. They are local to that specific procedure and cannot be seen outside of it. They are prefixed by a single @ sign. See the following example of how to declare a local variable:

```
DECLARE @status SMALLINT
```

Global variables are supplied by SQL Server and are not declared in the query language. So, what exactly makes a variable global? If the variable has two @ (ampersand) signs in front of it, then it is global. An example of a global variable is @@error. This stores the error number of the last SQL statement executed.

Variables are set using the SET command as follows:

```
SET @status = emp.emp_status
```

Functions

Functions are predefined SQL programs used by developers. They are usually given parameters. For example, UPPER(emp_name) will return the employee name in uppercase. There are numerous functions. Another is AVG(grade_score), which will compute the average of a student's score.

Error-Handling Methods

When an error condition occurs, you can use the RAISERROR statement to return information. We can trigger our own error message. First, we will add the error message via a system stored procedure. We will add the error code *50500*, with a severity code of *14* and a state code of *1*. This is done as follows:

```
exec sp_addmessage 50500, 14, 'Pay amount exceeded'
```

Then, if we set the pay amount too high, we can issue the following:

```
raiserror (50500,14,1)
```

The RAISERROR returns the following message:

```
Server: Msg 50500, Level 14, State 1, Line 1
Pay amount exceeded
```

Before moving onto another section, let's wrap up this section with a Q&A session.

QUESTIONS AND ANSWERS

How many primary keys can there be in a table?	There can be only one primary key; however, it can be made up of multiple columns.
Can I delete the primary key column in one table before I delete the foreign key in another table?	No! You must delete the foreign key first; then, delete the primary key.
My boss doesn't want to see all of the data in a table, how do I see only a few fields?	A field is a column. To display only a few columns, use the SELECT statement. For example, SELECT part_num, part_price FROM parts.
A consultant set up our database and we have few experienced SQL developers. They created multiple database tables, and I need data from both.	The primary and foreign keys link the databases. Use either a SELECT...WHERE or a SELECT...JOIN to match the primary and foreign keys.
My IT manager wants to see a graphical relationship of the tables in our database.	Use the Create Diagram Wizard to accomplish this.
I need to give an across-the-board raise to all of the employees in the current table.	Use the UPDATE DML statement to modify the pay column.
How can I put comments in my SQL query code?	Use the two symbols /* at beginning of the comment and then reverse them, */, at the end. For example: /* This statement is a comment. */. Note that the double hyphens, --, will also work in lieu of /* and */.
How do I put data into a table?	The INSERT and VALUE statements are used to insert a new row into a table.
An employee just gave her two-week notice, how can I remove her entry from the employee table?	In order to remove a row, use the DELETE statement.

Using Transact-SQL Cursors to Manipulate Data

Cursors are a method by which programmers store data into an area of memory, called the cursor. You can use the FETCH statement to fetch individual rows from the cursor. You can loop through the cursor in a query script, manipulating the data as needed.

Types of Cursors

There are two types of cursors: local and global. A global cursor is deallocated at the termination of the client/server connection. A local cursor is limited to a procedure and is terminated once the procedure exists. You must declare cursors as follows:

```
DECLARE emp_cursor CURSOR FOR
SELECT emp_id, emp_name FROM emp
```

You must open a cursor as follows:

```
OPEN EMP_cursor
```

The rows in the cursor can then be fetched. To fetch the next row, execute the DCL statement as follows:

```
FETCH NEXT FROM EMP_cursor
```

Once the processing of the rows in a cursor is finished, the cursor is closed and then deallocated as follows:

```
CLOSE EMP_cursor
DEALLOCATE EMP_cursor
```

Defining the Appropriate Level of Cursor Sensitivity

Cursors can be defined as either sensitive or insensitive. A cursor declared as INSENSITIVE will not reflect any updates or modifications to the data in the table. If the INSENSITIVE keyword is omitted, then the cursor is said to be sensitive to data changes or modifications in the table.

```
DECLARE emp_cursor INSENSITIVE CURSOR FOR
SELECT emp_id, emp_name
```

Choosing the Appropriate Navigation

The keyword SCROLL allows you to navigate through the rows in the cursor with the FETCH statement. If SCROLL is omitted, then you can only FETCH NEXT and not fetch backward in the cursor. So, FETCH

PRIOR would not work in this case. The following statement creates a scrollable cursor:

```
DECLARE emp_cursor SCROLL CURSOR FOR
SELECT emp_id, emp_name
```

You can FETCH NEXT, PRIOR, LAST, FIRST, ABSOLUTE *n*, and RELATIVE *n*. To fetch the first row in the cursor, use

```
FETCH FIRST FROM EMP_cursor
```

To fetch the previous row in a cursor, use

```
FETCH PRIOR FROM EMP_cursor
```

To fetch the fourth row from the top row in the cursor, use

```
FETCH ABSOLUTE 4 FROM EMP_cursor
```

To fetch a row three rows from the current row, use

```
FETCH RELATIVE 3 FROM EMP_cursor
```

To fetch the last row in the cursor, use

```
FETCH LAST FROM EMP_cursor
```

or

```
FETCH ABSOLUTE -1 FROM EMP_cursor
```

See Figure 2-6 for a query script using local and global variables, cursors, IF...ELSE, combining tables with INNER JOIN, and other techniques.

The @@FETCH_STATUS global variable will check the status of the fetch and will return a value of 0 if there are rows in the cursor and a value of –1 if no rows exist. Hence, the WHILE @@FETCH_STATUS = 0 test in Figure 2-6.

Now, let's wrap up this section with a comprehensive query script that incorporates cursors, variables, JOIN, BEGIN, WHILE, and IF statements. Exercise 2-5 incorporates all of these items.

Query using many tools
and techniques discussed
in this chapter

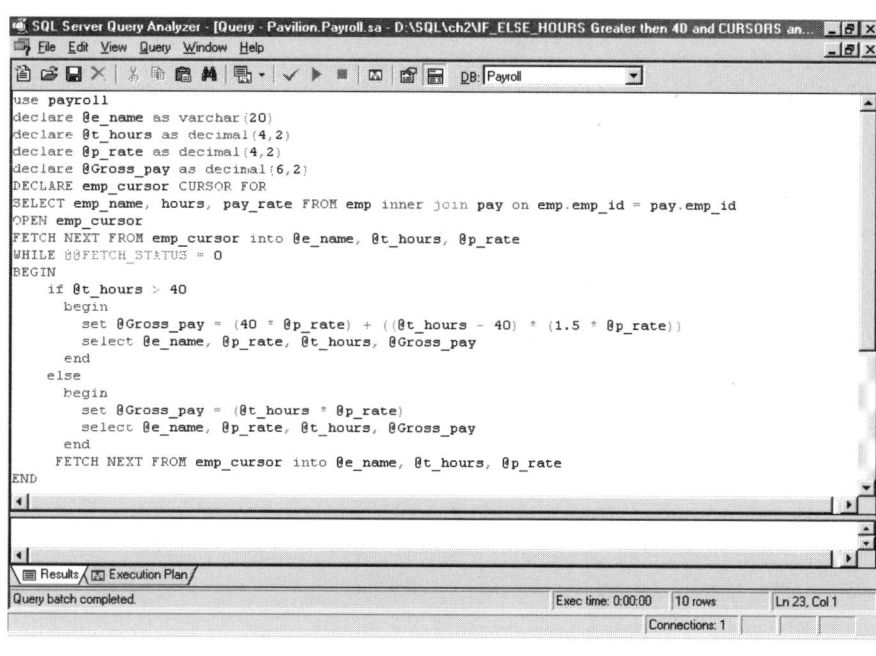

```
use payroll
declare @e_name as varchar(20)
declare @t_hours as decimal(4,2)
declare @p_rate as decimal(4,2)
declare @Gross_pay as decimal(6,2)
DECLARE emp_cursor CURSOR FOR
SELECT emp_name, hours, pay_rate FROM emp inner join pay on emp.emp_id = pay.emp_id
OPEN emp_cursor
FETCH NEXT FROM emp_cursor into @e_name, @t_hours, @p_rate
WHILE @@FETCH_STATUS = 0
BEGIN
    if @t_hours > 40
        begin
          set @Gross_pay = (40 * @p_rate) + ((@t_hours - 40) * (1.5 * @p_rate))
          select @e_name, @p_rate, @t_hours, @Gross_pay
        end
    else
        begin
          set @Gross_pay = (@t_hours * @p_rate)
          select @e_name, @p_rate, @t_hours, @Gross_pay
        end
    FETCH NEXT FROM emp_cursor into @e_name, @t_hours, @p_rate
END
```

Creating a Comprehensive Query

1. Click Start | Programs | Microsoft SQL Server 7.0 | Query Analyzer. A screen such as Figure 2-6 appears.

2. Enter the text located in the top half of the screen.

3. Click Query | Execute.

CERTIFICATION OBJECTIVE 2.04

Dynamic SQL Statements

A dynamic SQL statement uses a variable that can be built at run time. Take a look at the following code, which calculates retirement year based on the date hired. Retirement date is dynamically set when data is inserted in the table.

```
use payroll
CREATE TABLE emp3
(
   emp_id    smallint
      IDENTITY(1,1)
        PRIMARY KEY NONCLUSTERED,
   emp_name         varchar(15)     NULL,
   title    varchar(15)             NULL,
   dept             varchar(3)      NULL
      CHECK (dept IN ('ACT', 'ENG', 'MIS', 'MKT')),
   location         varchar(3)      NULL
           DEFAULT('CAN'),
   date_hired       datetime        NOT NULL
           DEFAULT (getdate()),
   retire_date      datetime
           default (dateadd(year, 30, getdate()))
))
)
```

Note in this example that the retirement date is 30 years from the hire date. It is dynamically set when the CREATE statement is executed. When an INSERT statement is executed, then the retire_date is *dynamically* built from the date_hired column. This yields the following sample output:

```
Emp_id  Emp_name       date_hired               retire_date
1       Dawn Wells     1999-03-06 16:38:52.723  2029-03-06 16:38:52.723
2       Michael Jones  1999-03-06 16:39:40.603  2029-03-06 16:39:40.603
```

CERTIFICATION SUMMARY

In this chapter we discussed the SQL Server programming tools. In the first section, we discussed the Enterprise Manager, bulk copy program, DTS, and generating scripts. Bulk copy program (bcp) and DTS are very powerful tools used to export and import data to and from tables.

In the next major section, we looked at Transact-SQL. We explored the divisions of Transact-SQL. The three divisions are DDL, DML, and DCL.

The DDL defines the data, the DML modifies the data, and the DCL controls how processing is accomplished.

We also investigated cursors. Cursors allow a programmer to fetch rows in a cursor. The cursor is a picture of a table. There are two types of cursors: insensitive and sensitive. Insensitive cursors don't change if the data in the table changes; sensitive cursors do change as table data changes.

We explored how to combine table data using the JOIN command. Tables can be JOINed based on the primary key and foreign key columns. This is a powerful tool. In the last section, Figure 2-6, demonstrates many, but not all, of the features outlined in earlier sections.

TWO-MINUTE DRILL

❑ T-SQL has been the variation of SQL utilized by Microsoft's flagship DBMS since its inception.

❑ Limiting T-SQL scripts to standard SQL elements found in the ANSI SQL-92 ISO standard will help increase portability of those scripts to other DBMS.

❑ Using spaces in database object names is new to version 7.0.

❑ The Query Analyzer will color code keywords for greater recognition.

❑ Bitwise operators are still supported by T-SQL in SQL Server 7.0.

❑ The precedence applied to logical operators may differ in T-SQL, compared to other programming languages.

❑ The Enterprise Manager allows you to create the following through a graphical interface: diagrams, tables, views, stored procedures, users and roles, rules and default values, and user-defined data types.

❑ The Query Analyzer is the main tool used to generate Transact-SQL queries. It is invoked from the Microsoft SQL Server 7.0 icon, which is the same place that you find the Enterprise Manager.

❑ The bulk copy program utility, or bcp, allows you to take an already created data file and insert the data into a SQL Server 7.0 database. It is a command-line utility and executed as *bcp*.

❑ Data Transformation Services (DTS) is a powerful graphical tool used to copy data from database to database or even to a text file.

❑ You can create a table within a database and use the Generate SQL Scripts command to create a query script file.

❑ Transact-SQL allows you to manage your database. It differs from more traditional programming language environments in which the data is defined in the same location as the actual programming logic, or code, statements.

❑ One problem with languages such as COBOL, BASIC, and FORTRAN, is that they define the size of the data field, and the type of data that the field can contain, within the actual program.

❑ A second, related problem, is data placement. When data is defined with these languages, the data fields, or in SQL terms, columns, are located one after the other.

❑ The elements that make up T-SQL are as follows: Data Definition Language (DDL), Data Manipulation Language (DML), and Data Control Language (DCL).

❑ The Data Definition Language (DDL) is the subset of SQL statements used for modeling the structure (rather than the contents) of a database or cube. The DDL gives you the ability to create, modify, and remove databases and database objects.

❑ You can create a database or table within Transact-SQL. However, if you need to create a table quickly, then consider using the Create Table Wizard.

❑ The Data Manipulation Language (DML) is the subset of SQL statements used to retrieve and manipulate data. The DML lets you select rows in a view, or subset, of a database.

❑ A foreign key is a column in one table that is linked to a column in another table.

❑ Use the INDENTITY_INSERT *tablename* ON to put data in a column defined with the IDENTITY property. After you are through with the insert, make sure you turn it back off. This will prevent accidental changes.

❑ The Data Control Language (DCL) is the subset of SQL statements used to control permissions on database objects. Permissions are controlled using the GRANT and REVOKE statements.

❑ Cursors are a method by which programmers store data into an area of memory, called the cursor. You can use the FETCH statement to fetch individual rows from the cursor. You can loop through the cursor in a query script, manipulating the data as needed.

❑ A dynamic SQL statement uses a variable that can be built at run time.

SELF TEST

The following questions will help you measure your understanding of the material presented in this chapter. Read all of the choices carefully, as there may be more than one correct answer. Choose all correct answers for each question.

1. What is the name of the column that uniquely identifies a row?

   A. Primary key

   B. Foreign key

   C. DUPLICATED KEY

   D. DEFAULT

2. What is used to make a cursor reflect modified table data?

   A. INSENSITIVE

   B. Omitting INSENSITIVE

   C. Global variable

   D. Local variable

3. What is used to make a variable local?

   A. @@

   B. @@@

   C. /*

   D. @

4. To display all the rows, what would you use?

   A. SELECT emp_name

   B. SELECT ONLY

   C. DELETE *

   D. SELECT *

5. What is used to test whether a condition is true or false?

   A. RAISERROR

   B. IF...ELSE

   C. SET

   D. DECLARE

6. What symbols identify a comment?

   A. ??

   B. @@

   C. @

   D. /* and */

7. Identify the two types of variables.

   A. Global and local

   B. Insensitive and sensitive

   C. IF and ELSE

   D. WHILE

8. What command removes a row?

   A. INSERT

   B. SELECT

   C. DELETE

   D. MOVE

9. What command will put data into a row?

   A. INSERT

   B. SELECT

   C. DELETE

   D. MOVE

10. What is used to assign a variable?

    A. MOVE

    B. INSERT

    C. DELETE

    D. SET

11. What is the looping construct?

    A. IF...ELSE

    B. WHILE

    C. CASE

    D. SELECT

12. What will allow you to export and import data? (Choose all that apply.)

    A. DTS

    B. Enterprise Manager

    C. Query Analyzer

    D. SELECT

13. What command line utility will copy data from and to a table?

    A. DTS

    B. bcp

    C. Query Analyzer

    D. INSERT

14. How can you get the next row in a cursor?

    A. FETCH NEXT

    B. FETCH LAST

    C. FETCH PREVIOUS

    D. FETCH ALL

15. How can you get the first row in a cursor?

    A. FETCH FIRST

    B. FETCH NEXT

    C. FETCH PRIOR

    D. FETCH LAST

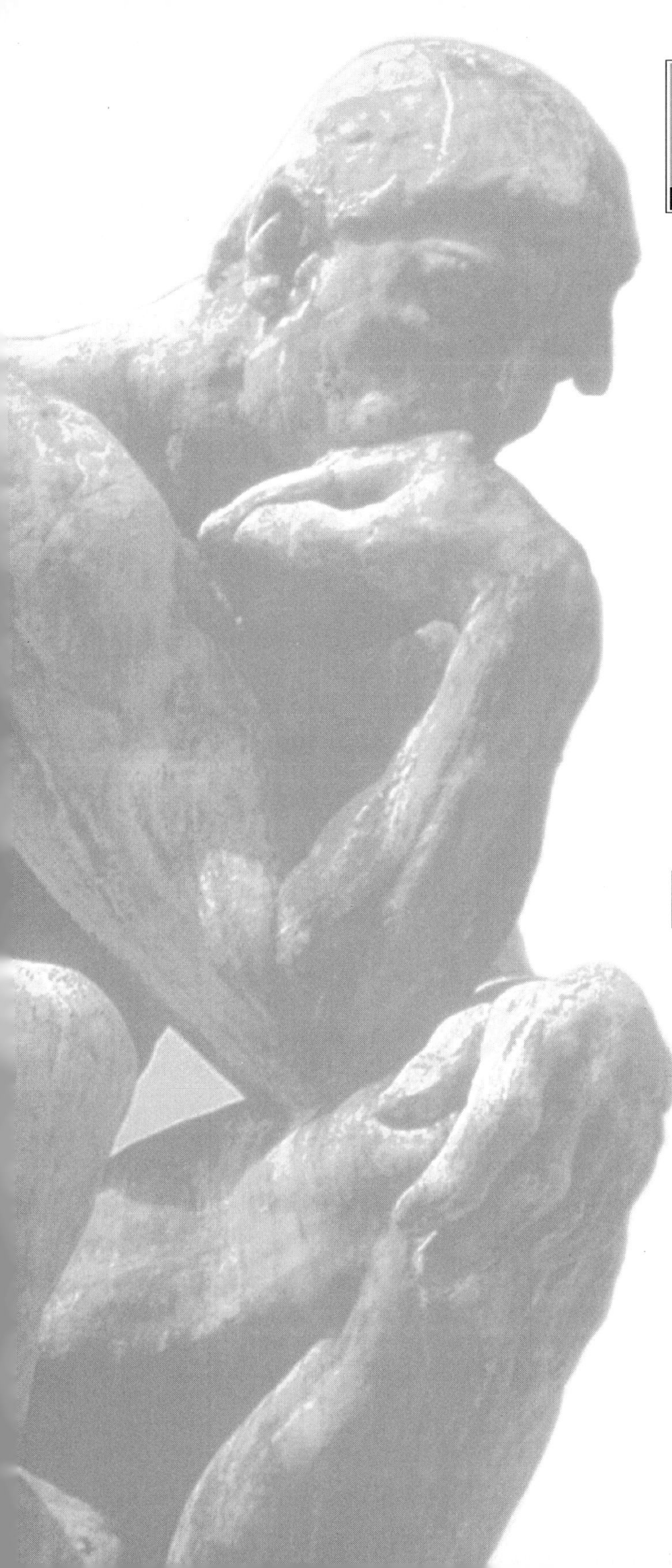

3

Creating and Managing Files and Databases

I n this chapter, we are going to take a closer look at the steps required to both create and modify a database. Although the graphical interface provided with SQL Server 7.0 makes this task very easy to perform, we need to look at the planning and maintenance necessary to obtain the best results in a stable production environment.

CERTIFICATION OBJECTIVE 3.01

Introduction to Databases

A database is loosely defined as a collection of data organized into files that make it easy to sort and retrieve this data. In this chapter, we will take a closer look at how the options that SQL Server provides to a database administrator (DBA) can be used to optimize the performance of your environment.

CERTIFICATION OBJECTIVE 3.02

Working with Databases

Microsoft SQL Server provides consistent interfaces for interacting with SQL Server. These interfaces are typically broken into two separate groups: data manipulation and database administration.

Microsoft provides multiple interfaces for manipulating data, including DB-Library, open database connectivity (ODBC), and Transact-SQL. The Transact-SQL interface is the sole proprietary interface to SQL Server. For SQL Server 7.0, Microsoft enhanced Transact-SQL to support Unicode data types, provided enhanced support for cursors, and increased capacities (such as column sizes) for compatibility with new limits supported by the database engine. Microsoft has also enhanced support for the standard ODBC and Object Link Embedding database (OLE DB) interfaces.

SQL Server 7.0 ships with an enhanced ODBC driver (version 3.7) that is compliant with the ODBC 3.51 specification. This driver provides full support for all SQL Server 6.0 and later databases. This driver is the recommended interface to use for Windows development outside of the Component Object Model (COM) environment. For developers working in a COM environment, Microsoft has provided an OLE-DB provider that is compliant with the OLE-DB 2.0 specification. This interface is used for OLE-DB and active data object (ADO) application development and includes support for functionality exclusive to SQL Server, such as bulk copy.

Microsoft provides SQL Distributive Management Objects (SQL-DMO) as an object-oriented interface that can be used to create administrative tools or integrate certain administrative functions into user applications. The primary administration tool, Enterprise Manager, which Microsoft ships with SQL Server 7.0, uses these standard components to perform its functions. The SQL-DMO interface is an evolution of earlier versions, yet it is recommended that you recompile applications using SQL-DMO interfaces to verify that functions continue to work properly and predictably.

CERTIFICATION OBJECTIVE 3.03

Configuring Session-Level Options

Although most configuration settings within SQL Server impact all users, Microsoft has also provided the option to set some configuration settings at a session level, which prevents them from impacting other users. The *SET* commands are used to modify the behavior of the database server. In the following example, you learn the syntax that you can use to modify the format used for handling dates in your application.

```
SET DATEFORMAT ydm
GO
DECLARE @thedate datetime
SET @thedate = '98/31/12'
SELECT @thedate
GO
```

FROM THE CLASSROOM

Database Management

Numerous tools and commands exist within Microsoft SQL Server to assist in working with databases. SQL Server provides a programming interface for use in manipulating database objects. This interface is known as SQL-DMO, or SQL Distributive Management Objects. SQL-DMO is a collection of OLE automation objects that expose all database objects and SQL Server functionality. SQL Server Enterprise Manager uses the SQL-DMO API to perform all of its functions. Therefore, through SQL-DMO, applications written in other languages can be used to administrator a SQL Server database. Since SQL-DMO provides the underlying automation and communication functionality of Enterprise Manager, replacement applications can be written using languages like Visual Basic or Visual C++. The administrative application is written as a custom Microsoft Management Console (MMC) plug-in, or as a stand-alone application, like previous versions of Enterprise Manager.

Certain aspects of database management, be it through Enterprise Manager or a custom application, are of critical importance in maintaining a well-implemented user database. Proper management of transaction logs is vital in ensuring that a database does not become inaccessible. If a transaction should happen to fill up, then changes cannot be made to the underlying database. The ability to make changes is impaired by the fact that the required record of the change cannot be made to a full transaction log, hence the change or modification is not allowed. Estimating the size of a transaction log involves three main issues: the time between transaction log backups, the rate of estimated activity, and the size of the entries in the transaction log. Getting a handle on estimating these factors will allow an accurate estimation of the optimal size of the transaction log.

—*Michael Lane Thomas, MCSE+I, MCSD, MCP+SB, MSS, MCT, A+*

This command is very powerful because it can alter the data that the server returns. Modifying this setting at a server level works well if all users can agree on a default format. For an international application for which users elect different formats, it is important to understand that SQL Server allows many options to be set at the session level. The duration of time that a SET option remains in effect is governed as follows:

■ SET options that are set by a script apply until reset by the user or the user's session with the SQL Server is terminated.

■ SET options that are set by a stored procedure (including triggers) apply until they are reset inside the stored procedure or until control returns to the code that called the stored procedure.

It is important to understand the full implications of these rules. Unless a configuration is explicitly reset, the configuration settings from all higher-level code apply within a stored procedure or trigger. Unless a configuration setting is reset, the SET options that have been set for a connection continue to apply after connecting to a different database under the same session.

Exercise 3-1 will demonstrate configuring session-level options.

| EXERCISE 3-1 | ## Configuring Session-Level Options |

1. Open the Query Optimizer.

2. Select the Pubs database.

3. Execute a query to determine how many rows are in the authors table. The syntax for this is shown next. Press CTRL-E to execute the command.

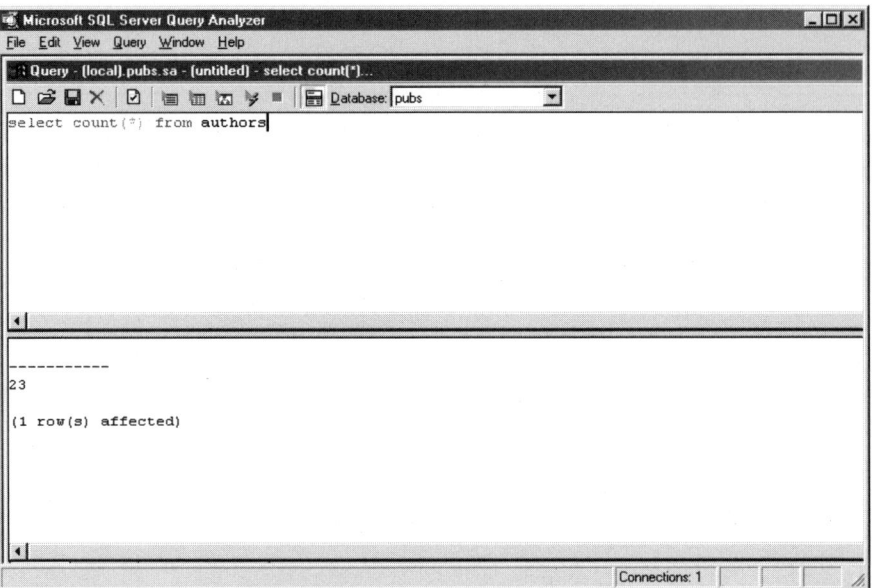

4. Now, let's add a SET command to set statistics input/output (I/O) on to the query and rerun it. The syntax is shown here:

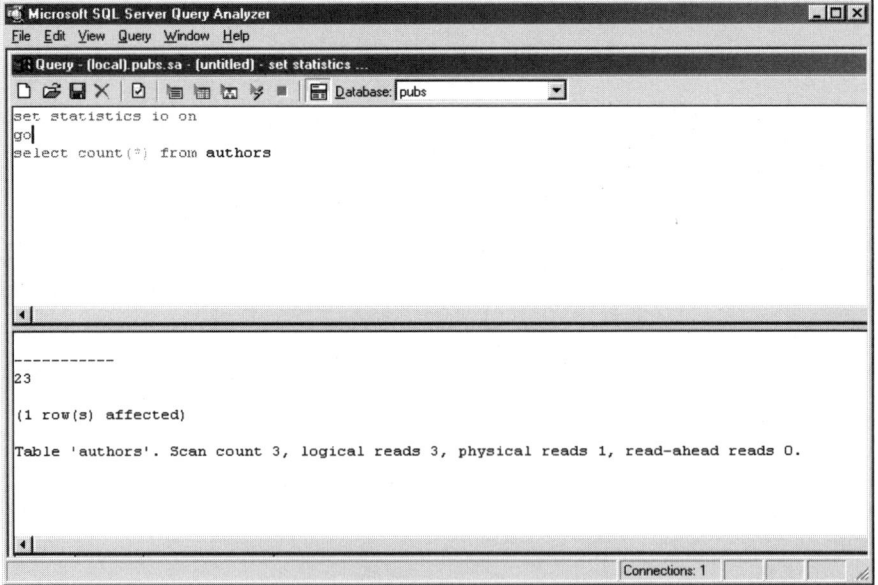

5. Without closing the Query Analyzer, remove all syntax other than the select statement and reexecute the query. Are the I/O statistics displayed? Why?

6. From the File menu, select Disconnect.

7. From the File menu, select Connect.

8. Run the original sample query again. Are the I/O statistics displayed? Why not?

CERTIFICATION OBJECTIVE 3.04

Modifying Databases

In a perfect world, we would all design our databases from the beginning to meet all current and future user requirements. Unfortunately, we are all stuck living in the real world where it is impossible to anticipate every user requirement, and attempting to do so would likely prove to be a terrible waste of time and money.

After accepting the fact that we cannot anticipate all changes to the requirements, it is easy to understand the need to modify the database after it is built. In earlier versions of SQL Server, the administrator could run commands to increase the size of a database. If the database became full, no further activity was possible until commands were run to increase the space allocated to the database. If the amount of space required to store data decreased (due to corporate restructuring, archiving of old information, or other changes in data requirements), earlier versions of SQL Server did not allow the administrator to shrink the database without rebuilding and repopulating it.

With version 7.0, Microsoft has significantly simplified the management of database size. At the time that databases are created, the *CREATE DATABASE* command allows the administrator to specify the initial size of a database, the maximum size the database is allowed to reach, and the size of the growth increments for the database when it is full. By using this technique, the database can grow automatically as necessary.

In addition, if your database is consuming more disk space than necessary, you can set the database to shrink automatically (by setting the autoshrink option to true) or manually using the DBCC SHRINKDATABASE command as follows:

```
DBCC SHRINKDATABASE (Northwind, 50)
GO
```

The DBCC SHRINKDATABASE command accepts two parameters. The first parameter is the name of the database being shrunk (Northwind) and the second parameter tells SQL Server what percentage of the database should remain empty (50 percent).

Creating and Managing Files, Filegroups, and Transaction Logs

Throughout most chapters of this book, you will find that we break the database server down into three primary groups of information that we must manage: data files, transaction logs, and backups. In this section we are going to take a closer look at the data files and transaction logs and the tools that SQL Server provides to a DBA for managing them.

Files

Microsoft SQL Server 7.0 has drastically simplified the management and placement of database files. In earlier versions of SQL Server, it was necessary to create disk devices that allocated file space for use by SQL Server. It was possible to place multiple databases on a single disk device or to span a single database across multiple devices. With version 7.0, Microsoft maps databases directly to a set of operating system files.

In earlier versions of SQL Server, it was necessary to separate data and transaction log information if you needed to back up the transaction log separately. With version 7.0, data and log information are separated by default, and individual files are used by only one database.

exam
ⓦatch

In earlier versions of SQL Server, it was critical to assign the transaction log to a separate disk device in order to back it up separately. SQL Server 7.0 forces the log on to a separate file by default.

SQL Server Files

In SQL Server 7.0, databases may be built on the following three types of files:

- The *primary data file* is the starting point of the database. This file contains pointers to all other files in the database. Every database has one primary data file. The recommended naming conventions for SQL Server give this file a file extension of *.MDF.*

- The *log files* hold all of the transaction log information that is used to recover the database. Every database must have at least one log file, but they can have more than one. The recommended file extension for all log files is *.LDF.*

- All data files other than the primary data file are called *secondary data files.* Some databases will not have any secondary data files, while others may have multiple secondary data files. Microsoft recommends a file extension of *.NDF.*

SQL Server Data Management

Unlike earlier versions, SQL Server 7.0 data and log files can grow automatically from their originally specified size. The growth increment is defined at the time the file is created. Each time the file fills, it increases its size by the growth increment. If there are multiple files in a filegroup, they do not grow automatically until all files have filled up. When all files are full, growth occurs in a round-robin algorithm.

Each file can also have a maximum size specified. If a maximum size is not specified, the file can continue to grow until it has used all available space on the disk. This feature is especially useful when SQL Server is used as the database in an application such as one for mobile users in which the user does not have access to administration tools. The user can let the files grow automatically as needed.

Microsoft made additional modifications to how SQL Server is stored on the disk. Let's take a closer look at those changes.

- All earlier versions of SQL Server were based upon 2KB pages. This structure limited rows of data to 1,962 bytes because rows cannot span multiple pages. As enterprise customers began to use SQL Server for larger applications, the limitations of 2KB pages became more apparent—and more limiting. SQL Server 7.0 is now based upon 8KB pages, which has extended the allowable size of columns and rows (8,060 bytes per page of usable space), providing far greater scalability.

- In earlier versions of SQL Server, database space was allocated to a particular table in *extents*, which consist of eight pages. With the growth in page size, this had the potential to increase wasted space. SQL Server 7.0 supports *mixed extents*. This means that extents allow multiple tables to share the space.

- By eliminating logical devices and allowing SQL Server to support native operating-system files, file management has become much simpler. It is easier to track files and manage the size of these databases.

These modifications to SQL Server file formats allow the server to scale from low-end to high-end systems, improving performance and manageability. The new page and row formats support row-level locking and improve performance when large blocks of data are accessed, because each I/O operation retrieves more data.

Exercise 3-2 will demonstrate creating files.

EXERCISE 3-2

Creating Files

1. Click Start | Programs | SQL Server 7.0 | Enterprise Manager and select your database server from the list.

2. Select the Northwind database.

3. Select Properties from the Context menu for this database.

4. Where is the primary data file located?

5. Where is the transaction log located?

In Figure 3-1, you see that the primary data file was placed on the D: drive, in the \MSSQL7\DATA\ folder using the default filename of NORTHWIND.MDF.

Filegroups

Depending upon your hardware configuration, your applications may benefit from spanning database objects across multiple physical drives. If your configuration does not include hardware or software Redundant Array of Inexpensive Disks (RAID) technology, it will be necessary to use filegroups. As

Identifying the primary data file location

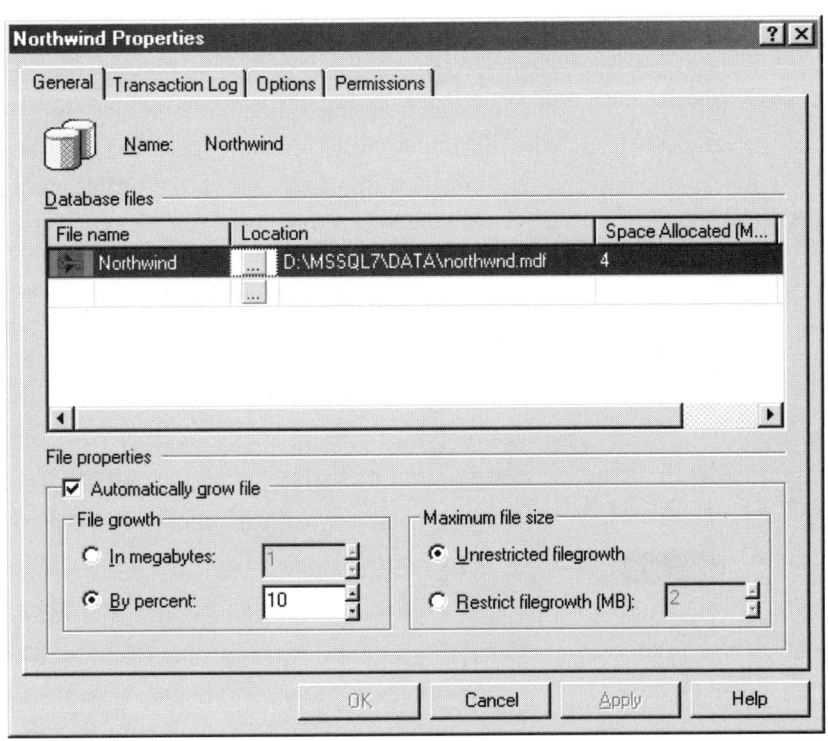

the name implies, filegroups consist of multiple data files. By creating a file on multiple disk drives, and combining them into a single filegroup, the administrator gets much of the benefit of RAID without the expense.

Planning the Use of Filegroups

We have already explained that a database consists of one or more data files and one or more log files. Microsoft has implemented filegroups to allow the data files to be grouped together. Tables and indexes can then be mapped to different filegroups to control data placement on physical disks.

Filegroups work well for advanced users who know where they want to place indexes and tables. If the administrator does not specify filegroups, all files are included in the default filegroup and SQL Server 7.0 allocates data within the database.

Using files and filegroups improves database performance by allowing a database to be created across multiple disks, multiple disk controllers, or RAID systems. For example, if your computer has four disks, you can create a database that comprises three data files and one log file, with one file on each disk. As data is accessed, four read/write heads can simultaneously access the data in parallel, which speeds up database operations. Files and filegroups can offer significant improvements in performance and recoverability of your SQL Server databases, but they must comply with the following rules:

- A file or filegroup cannot be used by more than one database. For example, files NORTHWINDS.MDF and NORTHWINDS.NDF, which contain data and objects from the Northwinds database, cannot be used by any other database.

- A file can be a member of only one filegroup. If the file named NORTHWINDS.NDF is a member of the NwindsRaid filegroup, you could not make it a member of the NwindsData filegroup.

- Log files are never part of any filegroups. Log files are always separate. We discuss the strategic placement of these files later in this chapter.

- Filegroups use a proportional fill strategy across all the files within each filegroup. As data is written to the filegroup, an amount proportional to the free space in the file is written to each file within the filegroup, rather than writing all the data to the first file until it is full, and then to the next file. For example, if file NW1 has 100MB free, and file NW2 has 200MB free, one extent is allocated from file NW1, and two extents from file NW2. This way both files become full at about the same time and simple striping is achieved.

Now that we have seen the rules that govern how files and filegroups can be implemented, let's take a look at the best practices for managing files and filegroups.

- Most small to mid-size databases work well with a single data file and a single log file. There is no reason to create complexity if there is not a measurable improvement in performance.

- If you plan to use multiple files, use the primary file only for system tables and objects, and create at least one secondary file to store user data and objects. This allows you to manage the user data separately from system files.

- To maximize performance, create files or filegroups on each different local physical disk that is available for your use and that does not have a physical or contention issue that restricts its performance. Creating filegroups on a physically slower drive may provide lower performance than having all files or filegroups on a single disk.

- Once you have created multiple files or filegroups, place objects that compete heavily for space in different filegroups. This reduces the likelihood of a drive filling up without warning.

- Place different tables that are commonly used in the same join queries in different filegroups. This will significantly improve the performance of these join queries due to parallel disk I/O searching for joined data.

- Place heavily accessed tables and their nonclustered indexes on different filegroups. This will improve performance due to parallel I/O if the files are located on different physical disks. It is important to remember that this cannot be done with clustered indexes, since they would move the data as the data makes up the leaf pages.

Placing Files and Filegroups for Optimal Performance

Now that we understand that files and filegroups provide the flexibility to place database objects, it is important that we understand how file placement impacts database performance. Let's take a look at the trends that will impact your decisions.

- Most database reads and writes occur randomly with respect to data and indexes. This is true for both online transaction processing and decision-support systems.

- Writes to the SQL Server transaction log are sequential and occur as large bursts of page-level I/O during the checkpoint process or update, insert, or delete operations.

- The fastest access to randomly accessed data and indexes is achieved by distributing the database over multiple physical disk units in a single striped volume. RAID 0 provides the optimal performance but lacks fault tolerance. RAID 5 provides slightly reduced performance while maximizing fault tolerance. Both approaches result in multiple heads being able to access the data and indexes.

- The most efficient access to sequential data is achieved by isolating it from the randomly accessed data and index volume(s). By placing sequentially accessed data on separate physical disk units, the read and write heads are in the desired location, minimizing overhead. Sequential access is faster via a single head, which is able to move in one direction. If it is necessary to have fault tolerance for these sequential accesses, disk mirroring or disk duplexing is the preferred solution. Disk mirroring and disk duplexing are implemented in RAID 1, and are discussed in Chapter 1.

Given these facts, it should make sense that optimal performance is obtained by placing the transaction log on an isolated drive and distributing the remaining data objects across multiple drives. For fault tolerance, transaction logs function best using disk mirroring, whereas RAID 5 is best for the remainder of the database.

Exercise 3-3 will take us through the steps in creating filegroups.

Creating Filegroups

1. Click Start | Programs | SQL Server 7.0 | Enterprise Manager, and select your server.
2. Select Action | New Database from the menu.
3. Enter a database name of **SampleDB**.
4. Select the second row and enter **SampleDB2** in the File name column.
5. Select the third row and enter **SampleDB3** in the File name column. At this point, you should see a screen similar to Figure 3-2.
6. Click OK.

At this stage, you have created the database SampleDB with a total size of 3MB spanning three separate data files. If these files are on separate physical disks, performance will be improved.

FIGURE 3-2

Creation of a filegroup

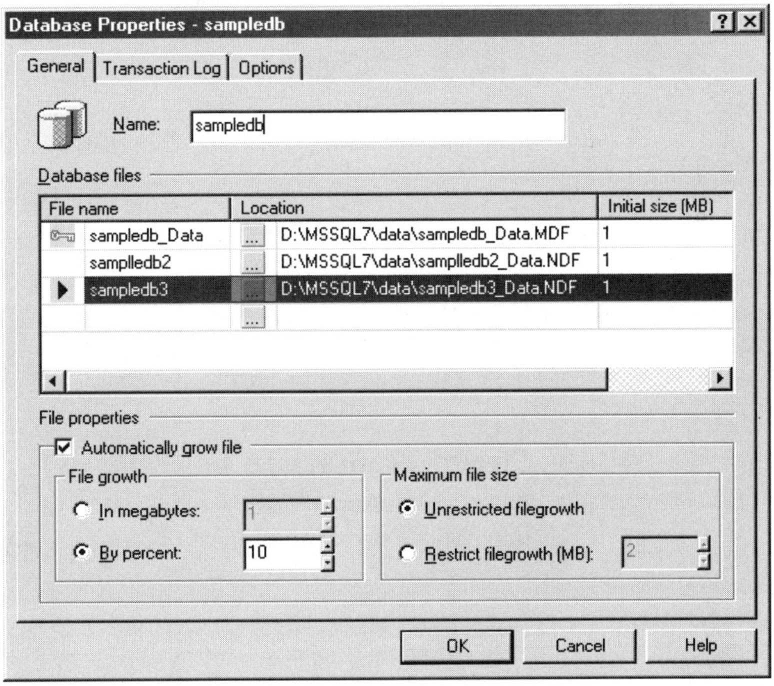

Transaction Logs

Transaction logs are a critical part of the successful implementation of a SQL Server user database. The transaction log is a serial record of all modifications that have occurred in the database. The log records the start of each transaction, the changes to the data, and enough information to undo the modifications. The transaction log contributes to the high performance and recoverability of these databases. A transaction log can only perform its function if adequate space is allocated. There aren't any hard-and-fast rules in determining the proper size for a transaction log. Determining the proper size depends on the following three main factors, and the size of the log is directly proportional to all three.

Time Between Transaction Log Dumps

As a serial record of all modifications that have occurred in the database, it is logical that the longer the transaction log is allowed to grow before it is dumped, the larger the log will get. To determine how often the transaction log should be dumped, you must determine how critical the data is to the business. If the data is critical to the operation of the business, the transaction log should be dumped more often. Typically, the transaction log for an online order-entry database will be dumped more often than a non-mission-critical database.

Rate of Transactions

The number of transactions that accumulate in the log is defined by the rate of activity, as well as the elapsed time between transaction log backups. In many instances, the transactional load is cyclical, which makes it critical for the database administrator to understand the business environment.

Size of Transaction Log Entries

Both the number of transactions to be stored and the size of the transactions drive the amount of space that must be allocated to the transaction log. For example, if an update transaction updates one row without changing the indexed columns and affects only the fixed-length columns, an in-place update takes place and the transaction log entries are minimal. On the other hand, if the update impacts multiple rows, variable-length columns, and an index, the number and total size of entries in the log would be much higher. If a row cannot be updated in place, it is deleted and inserted. If this happens, there will be two separate log entries corresponding to the delete and insert operations. If indexes are involved in the update, the changes to the index structures are recorded in the log as well. Microsoft has made efforts to minimize the impact of some maintenance commands on the log. For example, when a CREATE INDEX statement is issued, rather than recording the changes to each page of the index, SQL Server records only the fact that the operation took place.

The following exercise demonstrates creating a transaction log.

Creating a Transaction Log

1. Click Start | Programs | SQL Server 7.0 | Enterprise Manager, and select your server.

2. Select Action | New Database from the menu.

3. Enter a database name of **TransDB**.

4. Select the Transaction Log tab.

5. Change the folder location from the default of \MSSQL7\data\ to **\MSSQL7\log**. You should now see a window similar to Figure 3-3 (your drive letter may be different if SQL Server is installed on a different drive).

6. Click OK.

exam

ⓦatch

SQL Server will return an error (#5123) and fail to create the database if the directory that you attempt to place a file into does not already exist.

FIGURE 3-3

Specifying the location for
the transaction log

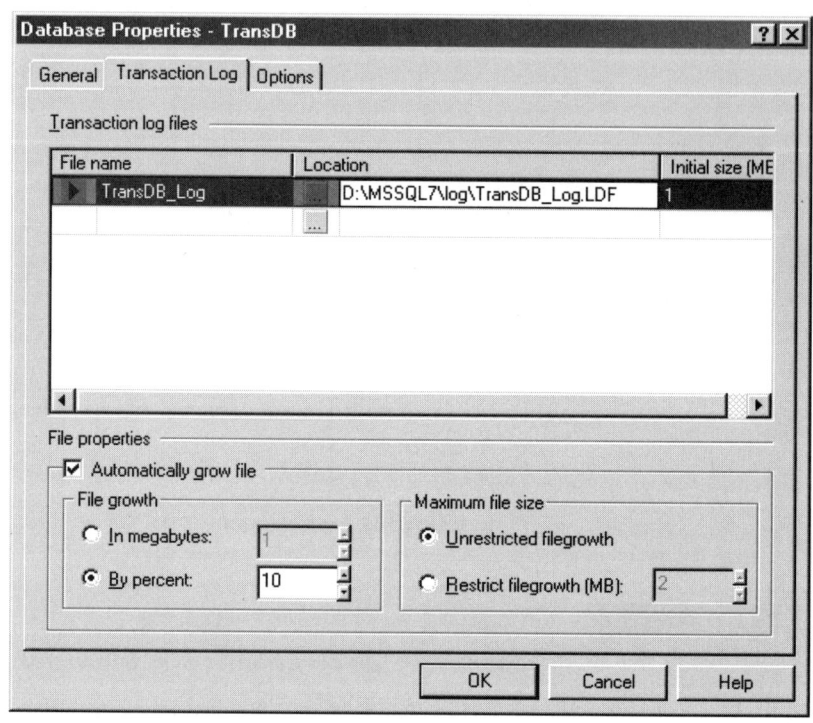

CERTIFICATION OBJECTIVE 3.06

Using Data Types

One of the important facts to keep in mind when working with SQL Server
is that every column, local variable, expression, and parameter has a data
type. There are two groups of data types used in SQL Server, system
supplied and user defined.

System-Supplied Data Types

The set of system-supplied SQL Server data types is shown in Table 3-1. These data types provide a number of services including the formatting and filtering of data, as well as space allocation.

The specification of data type defines the number of bytes allocated for storage of data and what data can be stored in a column. The filtering of data is performed as the data types limit what data can be placed in a field and what functions can be performed against them (without conversion). You cannot store the text *TWO* in a field that is defined as int. On the other hand, you could place the number *2* into a field with either a character or int data type. If the data was stored with a character data type, you would not be able to perform math functions against it.

The data types also perform the function of space allocation. For numeric data, this determines the range of data that can be stored in a field, as well as the amount of space that is allocated for this column in each row. For character data, you must choose between a variable-length field, which may save space but adds overhead, and a fixed-length field, which allocates the specified length for each row but performs some functions more efficiently.

TABLE 3-1		
Usage and Bytes for Each Data Type		

Data Type	Data Usage	Space Required
binary	Fixed-length binary data with a maximum length of 8,000 bytes.	As defined (0 to 8,000 bytes).
bit	Integer data with either a 1 or 0 value.	1 byte.
char	Fixed-length, non-Unicode character data with a maximum length of 8,000 characters.	As defined (0 to 8,000 bytes).
datetime	Date and time data from January 1, 1753, to December 31, 9999, with an accuracy of three-hundredths of a second, or 3.33 milliseconds.	8 bytes.
decimal	Fixed-precision and -scale numeric data from $-10^{38}-1$ through $10^{38}-1$.	2–17 bytes.

TABLE 3-1

Usage and Bytes for Each
Data Type *(continued)*

Data Type	Data Usage	Space Required
float	Floating precision number data from −1.79E + 308 through 1.79E + 308.	8 bytes.
image	Variable-length binary data with a maximum length of $2^{31} - 1$ (2,147,483,647) bytes.	16-byte pointer plus a minimum of 2,000 bytes for each initialized (non-null) column.
int	Integer (whole number) data from -2^{31} (−2,147,483,648) through $2^{31} - 1$ (2,147,483,647).	4 bytes.
money	Monetary data values from -2^{63} (−922,337,203,685,477.5808) through $2^{63} - 1$ (+922,337,203,685,477.5807), with accuracy to a ten-thousandth of a monetary unit.	8 bytes.
numeric	A synonym for decimal.	2–17 bytes.
real	Floating precision number data from −3.40E + 38 through 3.40E + 38.	4 bytes.
smalldate-time	Date and time data from January 1, 1900, through June 6, 2079, with an accuracy of one minute.	4 bytes.
smallint	Integer data from 2^{15} (−32,768) through $2^{15} - 1$ (32,767).	2 bytes.
smallmoney	Monetary data values from −214,748.3648 through +214,748.3647, with accuracy to a ten-thousandth of a monetary unit.	4 bytes.
text	Variable-length, non-Unicode data with a maximum length of $2^{31} - 1$ (2,147,483,647) characters.	16-byte pointer plus a minimum of 2,000 bytes for each initialized (non-null) column.
timestamp	A database-wide unique number.	8 bytes.

Data Type	Data Usage	Space Required
tinyint	Integer data from 0 through 255.	I byte.
varchar	Variable-length, non-Unicode data with a maximum of 8,000 characters.	Storage size is the actual length of the data entered.
varbinary	Variable-length binary data with a maximum length of 8,000 bytes.	Length of data entered plus 4 bytes.
nchar	Fixed-length Unicode data with a maximum length of 4,000 characters.	As defined (0 to 4,000 bytes).
nvarchar	Variable-length Unicode data with a maximum length of 4,000 characters.	Storage size is the actual length of the data entered.
ntext	Variable-length Unicode data with a maximum length of $2^{30} - 1$ (1,073,741,823) characters.	16-byte pointer plus a minimum of 2,000 bytes for each initialized (non-null) column.
unique-identifier	Stores 16-byte binary values that operate as a globally unique identifier (GUID). A GUID is a binary number that is guaranteed to be unique.	16 bytes.

When attempting to select the proper data type, it is important to keep the following guidelines in mind:

■ char and varchar columns can both be used to store letters, symbols, and numeric characters up to 8,000 bytes in length. Use char when every entry for a column will have virtually the same fixed length. Use varchar when a column's entries vary greatly in the number of characters that they contain, such as a comments field that may be 3,000 bytes long but is typically empty.

■ Money and smallmoney data types are limited to four decimal points. Use the decimal data type if more decimal points are required. Use the smallmoney data type to store values in the range of −214,748.3648 through 214,748.3647. Use the money data type to store values in the range of −922,337,203,685,477.5808 through +922,337,203,685,477.5807.

■ Use numeric data types for all fields that will have mathematical calculations performed against them. For all other columns, use character data types.

Microsoft SQL Server 7.0 complies with the entry level of the SQL-92 standard. This includes support for the basic set of data types specified. In Table 3-2, you see how the SQL Server data types map against the SQL-92 standard, even though the names are not the same due to backward-compatibility issues.

Exercise 3-5 demonstrates choosing the appropriate data types.

EXERCISE 3-5

Choosing the Appropriate Data Types

You are creating a customer database for Sutton Tool Company and determine that you need to create a table that consists of the following fields: last name, first name, phone number, customer date, and total orders. What data types would you assign to each?

1. We look at the last name field and know that we want a character field and that most names will be roughly the same length. We select a fixed-length character field with a length of 20 bytes—char(20).

2. We look at the first name field and know that we want a character field. We won't do as much searching on this column, but determine that the amount of space that could be saved doesn't justify the overhead of a variable-length column. We select a fixed-length character field with a length of 15 bytes—char(15).

3. Our phone number column could be stored as either a numeric or character column. We will not be performing any mathematical computations with the phone number, so we will choose the efficiency and flexibility of a character field—char(10).

4. The customer date is used to determine how long customers have been buying from Sutton Tool Company and to calculate the average monthly purchases since they became customers. We select a datetime data type.

5. After asking the users, we learn that the total orders column will track the total amount of money that this customer has spent with our company. After learning that purchases are tracked to the penny, we choose to use a money field to track this, because some customers have purchased more than $215,000 in tools.

TABLE 3-2 Mapping SQL-92 Data Types to SQL Server 7.0 Data Types	Synonym	Mapped to System Data Type
	binary varying	varbinary
	char varying	varchar
	Character	char
	Character	char(1)
	character(n)	char(n)
	character varying(n)	varchar(n)
	Dec	decimal
	double precision	float
	float[(n)] for n = 1–7	real
	float[(n)] for n = 8–15	float
	integer	int
	national character(n)	nchar(n)
	national char(n)	nchar(n)
	national character varying(n)	nvarchar(n)
	national char varying(n)	nvarchar(n)
	national text	ntext
	numeric	decimal

User-Defined Data Types

For a variety of reasons, companies find the need or desire for additional data types. SQL Server meets this need by providing functionality that allows administrators to create their own user-defined data types. User-defined data types are aliases for system-supplied data types that are more defined.

User-defined data types allow you to extend a SQL Server base data type (such as char) with a descriptive name and format tailored to a specific use.

```
sp_addtype
@typename =] type,
[@phystype =] system_data_type
[, [@nulltype =] 'null_type']
[@typename =] type
```

The parameters for this command are as follows:

- **@phystype** = *system_data_type*   The system-supplied data type (such as decimal and int) on which the user-defined data type is based. Quotation marks are required around all parameters that have embedded blank spaces or punctuation marks.

- **[@nulltype =]** '*null_type*'   Defines how the user-defined data type will handle null values. *null_type* defaults to NULL, and must be enclosed in single quotation marks ('NULL', 'NOT NULL', or 'NONULL'). If *null_type* is not explicitly defined by sp_addtype, it is set to the current default nullability. Note that the null_type parameter defines the default nullability for this data type; but, if nullability is explicitly defined when the user-defined data type is used during table creation, the table definition takes precedence over data type–defined nullability. However, the length specification cannot be changed; you cannot specify a length for a user-defined data type in a CREATE TABLE statement.

Now we look at an example of when you might use user-defined data types. In the United States, Social Security numbers have a format of *nnn-nn-nnnn*.

Although Social Security numbers contain numbers, these numbers are not subjected to mathematical operations. It is therefore common practice to create a user-defined Social Security number data type as char and create a CHECK constraint to enforce the format of the Social Security numbers stored in the table.

The syntax to support this is

```
EXEC sp_addtype SSN, 'CHAR(11)', 'NOT NULL'
GO
CREATE TABLE SSNTable
(EmployeeID INT PRIMARY KEY,
EmployeeSSN SSN,
CONSTRAINT CheckSSN CHECK ( EmployeeSSN LIKE
'[0-9][0-9][0-9]-[0-9][0-9]-[0-9][0-9][0-9][0-9]' ) )
GO
```

Exercise 3-6 gives a further example of the preceding concepts.

EXERCISE 3-6

Creating User-Defined Data Types

The database that we created for Sutton Tool Company in our earlier exercise is now being used by multiple applications. As users are entering data into our database using the different applications, some are complaining that the data in the phone number column has become unreliable because users are using different formats. We decide to solve this problem by re-creating the table and providing a user-defined data type of phonenumber that will be used in all SQL Server tables that require this information. The steps are as follows:

1. We need to add the data type with the following syntax:

   EXEC sp_addtype phonenumber, 'CHAR(13)', 'NOT NULL'
   GO

2. We will create the table giving the phone column a data type of phonenumber and a constraint that specifies a format of (*nnn*)*nnn-nnnn*. (This will be covered in greater detail in Chapter 4.)

Creating Tables

So far in this chapter, we have discussed the different data types and how they impact your ability to create tables. Many capacities have been increased with the release of SQL Server 7.0. We'll take a look here at the ones that impact the creation of tables.

It is now possible to have as many as two billion tables per database and 1,024 columns per table. The total size of the table is limited only by the amount of storage that is available. The maximum number of bytes per row is 8,060. Trying to insert more than 8,060 bytes into such a row or to update a row so that its total row size exceeds 8,060 produces an error message and the statement fails.

As we discuss tables, traditional permanent tables typically come to mind for most people. SQL Server also provides the ability to create local and global temporary tables. *Local temporary tables* are only visible to the current session, whereas *global temporary tables* are visible to all sessions. A local temporary table is created and referenced by prefixing the *table_name* with a single number sign (#*table_name*). Global temporary tables are designated using names with a double number sign (##*table_name*).

For local temporary tables that are created using stored procedures or other applications that can be executed at the same time by multiple users, it is critical that SQL Server be able to distinguish which tables were created by each user. SQL Server does this by internally appending a numeric suffix to each local temporary table name. To allow for the suffix, the *table_name* value specified for a local temporary name cannot exceed 116 characters.

Temporary tables are automatically dropped when they go out of scope, unless they have already been explicitly dropped using DROP TABLE. The specific guidelines are listed as follows:

- A local temporary table created in a stored procedure is automatically dropped when the stored procedure completes. These temporary tables can be accessed by any nested stored procedures executed by the stored procedure that created the table. The temporary tables cannot be accessed by the process that called the stored procedure that created the table.

■ All other local temporary tables are automatically dropped when the session is closed.

■ Global temporary tables are automatically dropped when the session that created the table ends and all other tasks have stopped referencing them.

Now we examine the process and syntax necessary to create both permanent and temporary tables.

```
CREATE TABLE table_name
( { <column_definition>
| column_name AS computed_column_expression
)
[ON {filegroup | DEFAULT} ]
[TEXTIMAGE_ON {filegroup | DEFAULT} ]
<column_definition> ::= { column_name data_type }
[ NULL | NOT NULL ]
[ IDENTITY [(seed, increment )
[NOT FOR REPLICATION] ] ]
[ ROWGUIDCOL ]
[ <column_constraint> ::=
[CONSTRAINT constraint_name]
{ { PRIMARY KEY | UNIQUE }
[CLUSTERED | NONCLUSTERED]
[WITH [FILLFACTOR = fillfactor]
]
[ON {filegroup | DEFAULT} ]
| [FOREIGN KEY]
REFERENCES ref_table
[ ( ref_column ) ]
[NOT FOR REPLICATION]
| DEFAULT constant_expression
| CHECK [NOT FOR REPLICATION]
(logical_expression)
}
] [ ...n]
<table_constraint> ::= [CONSTRAINT constraint_name]
{ [ { PRIMARY KEY | UNIQUE }
```

```
[ CLUSTERED | NONCLUSTERED]
{ ( column[,...n] ) }
[ WITH [FILLFACTOR = fillfactor]
]
[ON {filegroup | DEFAULT} ]
]
| FOREIGN KEY
[(column[,...n])]
REFERENCES ref_table [(ref_column[,...n])]
[NOT FOR REPLICATION]
| CHECK [NOT FOR REPLICATION]
(search_conditions)
}
```

The following list describes the parameters that are used in this syntax:

- *table_name*   This parameter specifies the name of the new table. Table names must conform to the rules for identifiers and the *owner.table_name* must be unique within the database. For all permanent tables, the length of the name cannot exceed 128 characters. The names of local temporary tables (tables prefixed with a single # symbol) cannot exceed 116 characters.

- *column_name*   This parameter specifies the name of a column in the table and is repeated for each column in the table. Column names must conform to the rules for identifiers and must be unique within the table. The *column_name* may be omitted for columns created using the timestamp data type. If this is done, the column is named *timestamp*. For all other columns, the *column_name* is required.

- *computed_column_expression*   This parameter is an expression that defines the value of a *computed column*. A computed column is a virtual column that is not physically stored in the table. It is computed using an expression that uses other columns in the same table. For example, a computed column could have the definition: salary AS wage * hours. Computed columns can be used in SELECT statements, WHERE clauses, ORDER BY clauses, or any other locations in which regular expressions can be used, with the following exceptions:

- A computed column cannot be used as a key column in an index or as part of any PRIMARY KEY, UNIQUE, FOREIGN KEY, or DEFAULT constraint definition.

- A computed column cannot be the target of an INSERT or UPDATE statement.

- **ON** {*filegroup* | **DEFAULT**} This optional parameter is used to specify the filegroup on which the table is stored. The filegroup must exist within the database. If you specify DEFAULT, or the clause is omitted, the table is stored on the default filegroup.

- **TEXTIMAGE_ON** This parameter specifies the filegroup on which the text, ntext, and image columns are stored. This parameter is not allowed if there are no text, ntext, or image columns in the table. If this parameter is not specified, the text, ntext, and image columns are stored in the same filegroup as the table.

- *data_type* This parameter specifies the data type of noncomputed columns. System- or user-defined data types are acceptable.

- **NULL** | **NOT NULL** These parameters/keywords determine the nullability of a column. Put another way, they determine whether or not that column can allow a null value (NULL) as the data in that column. A NULL is not 0 or blank. It means no entry has been made or an explicit NULL was supplied. It is recommended that you always explicitly define a column as NULL or NOT NULL. When not explicitly specified, column nullability follows these rules:

  - If the column is defined with a user-defined data type, SQL Server uses the nullability specified when the data type was created.

  - If the column is defined with a system-supplied data type, then one of the following rules apply:

    - If the system-supplied data type has only one option, it takes precedence. For example, timestamp data types must be NOT NULL.

- If any session settings are ON (turned on with the SET statement), then

  - If ANSI_NULL_DFLT_ON is ON, NULL is assigned.

  - If ANSI_NULL_DFLT_OFF is ON, NOT NULL is assigned.

- If any database settings are configured (changed with sp_dboption), then

  - If 'ANSI null default' is TRUE, NULL is assigned.

  - If 'ANSI null default' is FALSE, NOT NULL is assigned.

- When not explicitly defined (neither of the ANSI_NULL_DFLT options are set) for the session and the database is set to the default ('ANSI null default' is FALSE), then the SQL Server default of NOT NULL is assigned. Exercise 3-7 demonstrates defining columns as NULL or NOT NULL.

- **IDENTITY**   This parameter is a keyword that is associated with a single column and creates the new column as an identity column. When a new row is added to the table, SQL Server provides a unique, incremental value for that column. Identity columns are often used with the PRIMARY KEY constraints to serve as the unique row identifier for the table. The IDENTITY property can be assigned to a column with a tinyint, smallint, int, decimal, or numeric data type. An identity column accepts the following additional parameters:

- *seed*   The seed value is the value that is given to the column for the very first row.

- *increment*   The increment is the value that is added to the value that is in the last row loaded to create the value for the next row. You must specify both the seed and increment, or nothing at all. If neither is specified, the default is (1,1). There is a maximum of one identity column per table.

- **NOT FOR REPLICATION**   This property indicates that the IDENTITY property should not be enforced when a replication login, such as sqlrepl, inserts data into the table. This keeps the replicated record identical to that on the publisher.

- **ROWGUIDCOL**   This parameter designates a column as a row global unique identifier column. Only one uniqueidentifier column per table can be designated as the ROWGUIDCOL column. The ROWGUIDCOL property can only be assigned to a uniqueidentifier column. The ROWGUIDCOL property does not enforce uniqueness in the column, nor does it automatically generate values for new rows inserted into the table.

- **CONSTRAINT**   This property indicates the beginning of a constraint definition. Constraints are properties that enforce data integrity and create special indexes for the table and its columns. We will discuss Primary Key, Foreign Key, Check, and Unique constraints in greater detail in Chapter 4. We will discuss the indexes they create in Chapter 5.

- *constraint_name*   This property represents the name of the constraint being defined. The name must be unique within the database.

- **PRIMARY KEY**   This property is a constraint that enforces entity integrity for a given column or columns through a unique index. Only one PRIMARY KEY constraint can be created per table.

- **DEFAULT**   This property specifies the value placed in a column during an insert, when a value is not explicitly supplied for the column. The DEFAULT definitions can be applied to columns that have not been assigned the IDENTITY property and use any data type other than timestamp. This is particularly useful for columns with a uniqueidentifier data type. A GUID can be created without modifying the application by using the *newid()* function.

- *constant_expression*   This property represents a literal value, a NULL, or a system function used as the default value for a given column.

Defining Columns as NULL or NOT NULL

We modified the Customers table that we built for Sutton Tool Company in our earlier exercise by creating a user-defined data type. Now, many users are choosing to not place any data in the column rather than risk getting error messages from formatting it incorrectly. We have been asked to prevent this from happening, so we will rebuild the table to only allow NULLs in the CustDate and TotalOrders columns. Here is the syntax for creating our table.

```
CREATE TABLE Customers
(
LastName     char(20)     NOT NULL,
FirstName    char(15)     NOT NULL,
Phone        phonenumber  NOT NULL,
CustDate     datetime     NULL,
TotalOrders  money        NULL)
```

Exercise 3-8 demonstrates defining columns to generate values by using the IDENTITY property, the uniqueidentifier data type, and the newid() function.

Defining Columns to Generate Values by Using the IDENTITY Property, the uniqueidentifier Data Type, and the newid() Function

The Sutton Tool Company is growing quickly. As they have expanded their customer base, they are encountering problems with duplicate rows being added to their customer database. They recognize the need to create a unique ID. They have a second concern that because their sales staff will be traveling with the application, they want to prevent the staff from creating duplicate IDs.

How do we meet their needs? We are going to re-create the table and add a new column that creates a globally unique identifier (GUID) for each customer. What is the proper syntax for handling this?

```
CREATE TABLE Customers
(
CustID       uniqueidentifier NOT NULL DEFAULT newid(),
LastName     char(20)     NOT NULL,
FirstName    char(15)     NOT NULL,
```

```
Phone       phonenumber NOT NULL,
CustDate    datetime    NULL,
TotalOrders money       NULL)
```

The DEFAULT command is used in the new table to place a value in the CustID column without modifying the application. The newid() function generates a GUID that is used as the default.

CERTIFICATION OBJECTIVE 3.08

Generating Scripts

When Microsoft first added the Enterprise Manager to SQL Server, many DBAs were reluctant to use it due to the fact that configuration changes made using the Graphical User Interface (GUI) could not be duplicated on other servers, or during a disaster recovery.

This need was addressed by the addition of a script generating tool within the Enterprise Manager. From the Context menu of any database, select Generate SQL Server Script from the All Tools menu. If you perform this function on the Northwind database, you will see a window similar to Figure 3-4.

The main menu allows you to select the database objects for which you wish to create a script. Additional options are available from the Formatting tab. Among the available choices, you are given the option to generate scripts for dependent objects. Notice in Figure 3-5 that when prompted to generate scripts for dependent objects, the sp_addtype is added to the script to generate the user-defined data type SampleUDT.

The final page of configuration settings is available under the Options tab, shown in Figure 3-6. On this page you must decide if you want to create scripts to manage your security and indexes. You also determine how the file output will be formatted. Your scripts can be standard text or Unicode, and the information can be stored in a single file or multiple files.

FIGURE 3-4

The General tab of the
SQL Script Generator

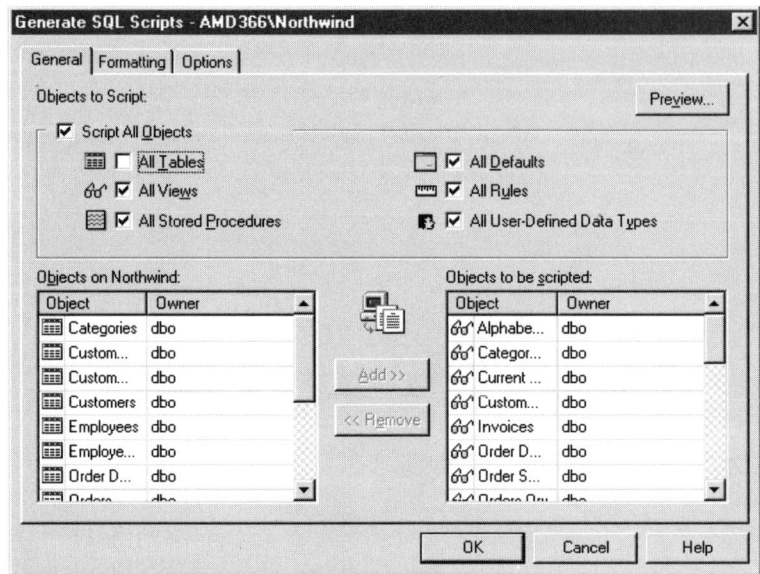

FIGURE 3-5

Generating scripts for
dependent objects

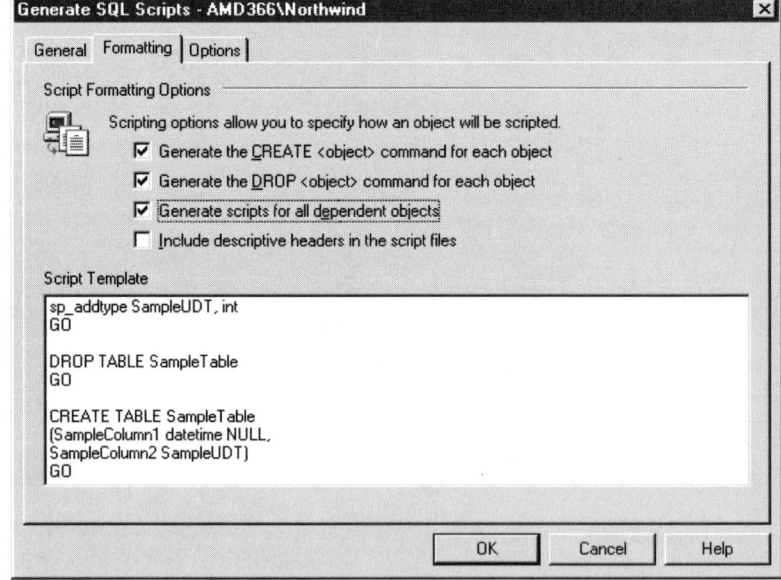

FIGURE 3-6

Setting script options

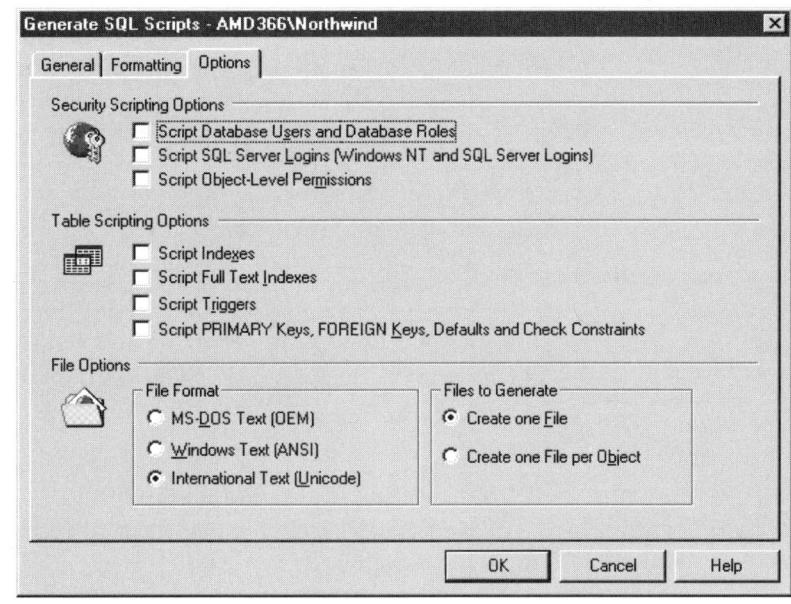

CERTIFICATION OBJECTIVE 3.09

Maintaining Databases

To this point in the chapter, our focus has been how to create your database. As any database administrator would tell you, this is only half the battle. Once you have created the database and placed it into production, it is time to perform maintenance. This encompasses tuning, optimization, and troubleshooting. Let's look closer at the tools SQL Server provides for these functions.

Tools for Evaluating and Optimizing Performance

As we look at the function of evaluating and optimizing the performance of your database, we are going to focus on two families of tools—the

SHOWPLAN functions and the database consistency checker (DBCC). The DBCC commands can be used for tuning and optimization as well as for finding and repairing some corrupted data.

SHOWPLAN_TEXT

The SHOWPLAN_TEXT option of SQL Server is turned on and off at run time. When SHOWPLAN_TEXT is turned on, the SQL Server database engine returns the detailed plan of how the command would be executed rather than processing the actual query.

Look at the example in Figure 3-7 and you see that rather than returning all rows from the authors table, SHOWPLAN_TEXT tells us that the query would be processed using a specific clustered index. If we ran this query and found that SQL Server was performing a table scan (sequential read), we would know the cause of our performance concerns when we run the command.

You notice in Figure 3-7 that the SET SHOWPLAN_TEXT command is followed by the GO statement. This is required, as the SET SHOWPLAN_TEXT command must be the only statement in a batch. The command cannot be executed as a part of a stored procedure. After

FIGURE 3-7

Demonstration of the SHOWPLAN_TEXT command

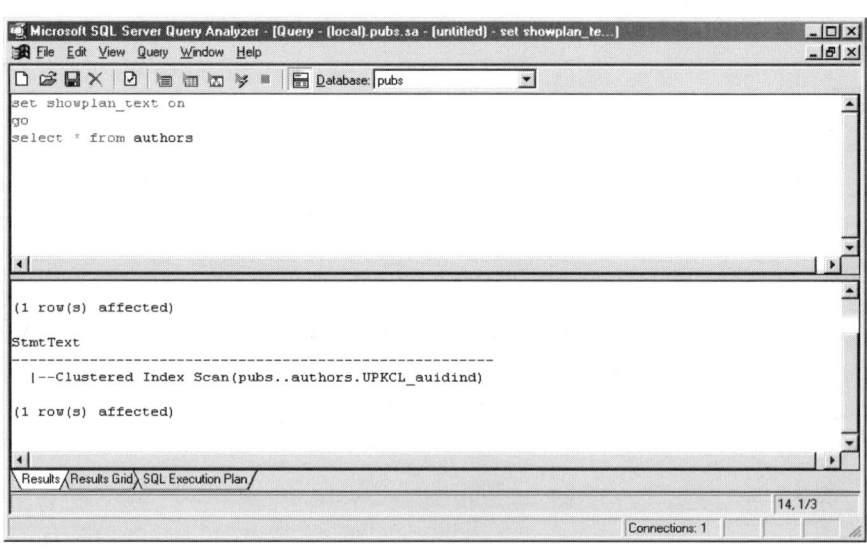

this option is turned on, all subsequent Transact-SQL statements return this information until the option is set to OFF. The parameter is set for the duration of the session, or until explicitly turned off. By default, all users have permission to run the SET SHOWPLAN_TEXT command.

SHOWPLAN_ALL

The SET SHOWPLAN_ALL command is similar to the SET SHOWPLAN_TEXT command as it returns execution information rather than data. The SET SHOWPLAN_ALL command returns information as a set of rows that represent the steps taken by the SQL Server query processor as it executes each statement. Each statement reflected in the output contains a single row with the text of the statement, followed by several rows with the details of the execution steps. This command is intended to be used by applications that are written to handle its output rather than by simple command-line tools. When you look at Figure 3-8, you see that this command returns more information than we received with the SET SHOWPLAN_TEXT statement. Not only do we see the index that will be used, we see resource costing estimates along with column details.

FIGURE 3-8

Demonstration of the
SET SHOWPLAN_ALL
command

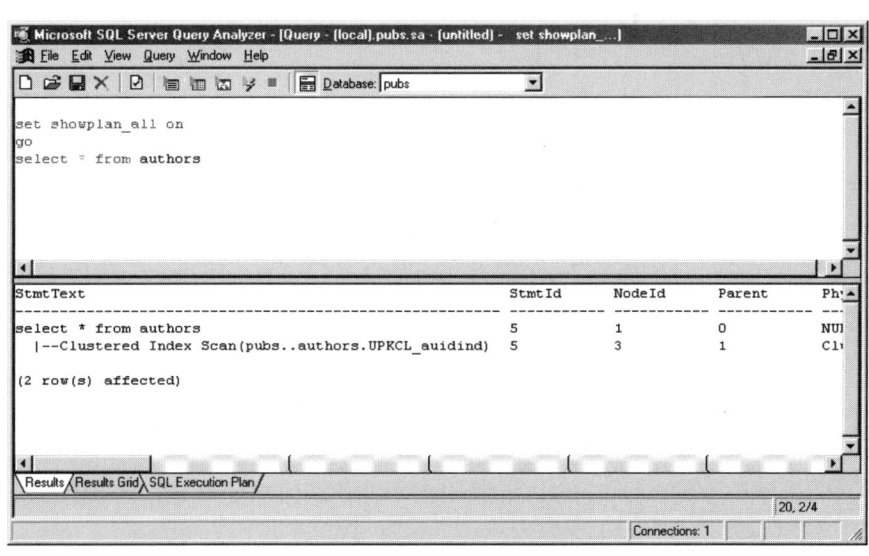

Graphical SHOWPLAN

The SQL Server Query Analyzer provides an additional method for reviewing how the SQL Server database engine executes a command. The graphical SHOWPLAN provides a method to analyze graphically the plan of a query, execute multiple queries simultaneously, view data, and choose indexes. The graphical SHOWPLAN reports data retrieval methods chosen by the SQL Server Query Optimizer and recommends optimal indexes to improve performance. After running a query in the Query Analyzer, select Display SQL Execution Plan from the Query menu. In Figure 3-9, you see how the results are laid out for you.

The icons displayed by the graphical SHOWPLAN represent the logical and physical operators used by SQL Server to execute statements. The SHOWPLAN output is read from left to right and from top to bottom. When the cursor is placed over each icon, additional details are provided.

FIGURE 3-9

Graphical SHOWPLAN output

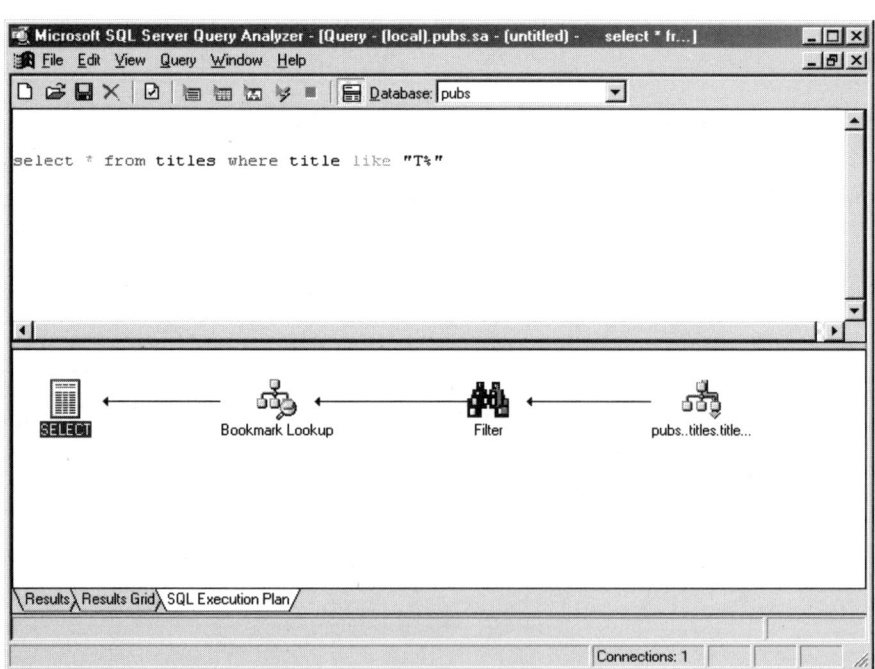

In Figure 3-9, the SELECT statement results in a bookmark lookup of the titles table. The WHERE clause results in the filter being applied to the query and limiting what is retrieved from *pubs.titles* using the *titleind* index.

DBCC SHOWCONTIG

If you run SHOWPLAN and determine that SQL Server is using the proper indexes but performance is still suffering, your performance problem may be caused by fragmentation. To analyze this, SQL Server provides the DBCC SHOWCONTIG utility. The syntax and parameters for this are as follows:

```
DBCC SHOWCONTIG [( table_id [, index_id])]
```

■ *table_id*   This parameter represents the table identification number (ID) for which to check fragmentation information. If not specified, all tables in the current database are checked. The table ID can be obtained using the OBJECT_ID function shown in Figure 3-10. It can also be obtained by querying the system tables directly: select * *from sysobjects where xtype = "U".*

■ *index_id*   This parameter represents the index identification number (ID) for which to check fragmentation information. If not specified, the statement processes all indexes for the specified table. To obtain the index ID, you can query the system table named sysindexes. For example, to get the ID of the *titleind* index in the Pubs database, you would run the following query: select *id from sysindexes where name = "titleind".*

In Figure 3-10, you see how the OBJECT_ID function is used to retrieve the table ID and input into the DBCC SHOWCONTIG command. The returned information, shown in the figure, is explained in this table:

Statistic	Description
Pages Scanned	Number of pages in the table or index.
Extents Scanned	Number of extents that contain pages that were scanned.

Statistic	Description
Extent Switches	Number of times the DBCC statement left an extent while it traversed the pages of the extent.
Avg. Pages per Extent	Number of pages per extent in the page chain.
Scan Density [Best Count: Actual Count]	The number in scan density is 100 if everything is contiguous; if it is below 100, some fragmentation exists. Scan density is reported as a percentage. The best count is the ideal number of extent changes that would be necessary if everything were contiguously linked. The actual count is the actual number of extent changes.
Logical Scan Fragmentation	The percentage of out-of-order pages returned from scanning the leaf pages of an index. An out-of-order page is one for which the next page indicated in an IAM is a different page than the page pointed to by the next page pointer in the leaf page.
Extent Scan Fragmentation	Percentage of out-of-order pages in scanning the leaf pages of an index. An out-of-order page is one where the next page indicated in an IAM is a different page than the page pointed to by the next page pointer in the leaf page.
Avg. Bytes free per page	Average number of free bytes on the pages scanned. The higher the number, the less full the pages are; and, therefore, lower numbers are better. This number is also affected by row size; a large row size can result in a higher number.
Avg. Page density (full)	Average page density (as a percentage). This value takes into account row size, so it is a more accurate indication of how full your pages are. The higher the percentage, the better.

There are many more DBCC commands available for use by the administrator. I recommend that you review the Books Online or other SQL Server documentation to understand other options.

Update Statistics

If you run the SHOWPLAN tools and find that the SQL Server Query Optimizer is not using the indexes appropriately, it is most likely because the

FIGURE 3-10

Results of OBJECT_ID and
DBCC SHOWCONTIG

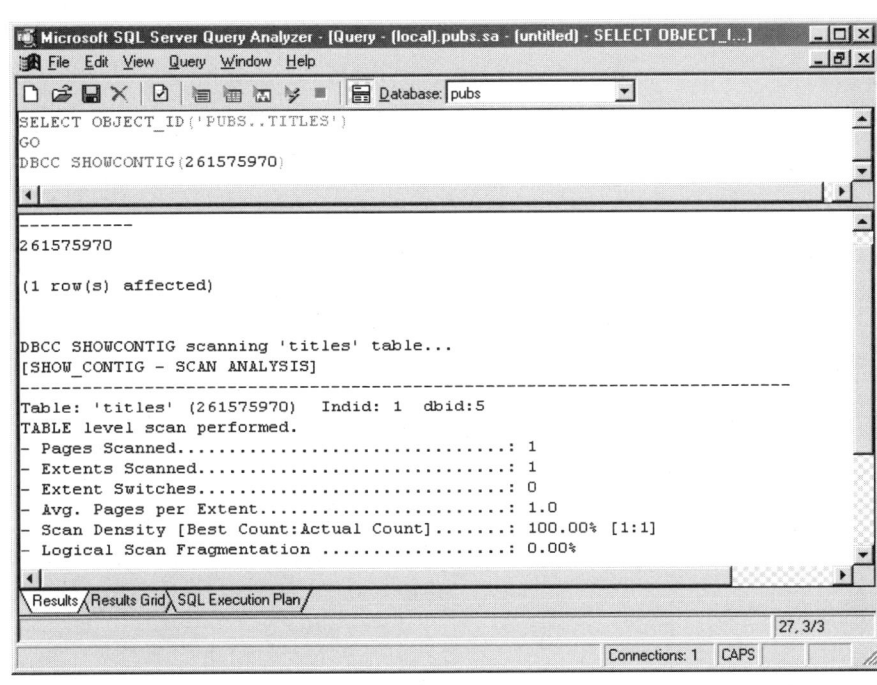

statistics pages are out of date. SQL Server keeps statistics about the distribution
of the key values in each index and uses these statistics to determine which
index to use in query processing. The *UPDATE STATISTICS* command
updates information about the distribution of key values for one or more
indexes in the specified table. UPDATE STATISTICS is run automatically
when an index is created on a table that already contains data. The syntax and
a definition of the parameters for this command are as follows:

```
UPDATE STATISTICS {table} [index | (index_or_column[, ...n])]
[WITH
[
[FULLSCAN]
| SAMPLE number {PERCENT | ROWS}]]
[[,] [ALL | COLUMNS | INDEX]
[[,] NORECOMPUTE]]
```

- *table*   This parameter represents the table for which statistics are being updated. Because index names are unique to tables rather than databases, the *table* must be specified. Specifying the database or table owner is optional.

- *index*   This parameter represents the index for which statistics are being updated. If no *index* is specified, the command will update the distribution statistics for all indexes in the specified table.

- *index_or_column*   This parameter is the name of the column(s) or index(es) for which statistics are being updated. *index_or_column* is required only when the INDEX or COLUMN options are specified.

- **FULLSCAN**   If this parameter is specified, SQL Server performs a full scan of the index or table when gathering statistics. In situations in which the developer feels a random sampling might return skewed results, it is advisable to perform a full scan. This situation might occur if 15 percent of records contain identical or closely grouped keys while remaining keys are evenly distributed.

- **SAMPLE** *number* {**PERCENT | ROWS**}   This parameter specifies the percentage of the table or the number of rows that are being sampled when collecting statistics for larger tables. If the PERCENT, ROWS, or *number* option results in too few rows being sampled, SQL Server automatically corrects the sampling based on the number of existing rows in the table.

- **ALL | COLUMNS | INDEX**   These parameters specify whether the UPDATE STATISTICS statement affects column statistics, index statistics, or all existing statistics. If no option is specified, the UPDATE STATISTICS statement affects existing indexes only. When COLUMN is specified, statistics are created or updated for columns that do not have preexisting statistics.

- **NORECOMPUTE**   This parameter specifies that statistics that become out of date are not automatically recomputed. Statistics become out of date over time as INSERT, UPDATE, and DELETE operations are performed on indexed columns. If the UPDATE STATISTICS command is run without the NORECOMPUTE option, automatic recompilation is restarted.

To determine the last time statistics were updated for an index, you can run the STATS_DATE function. By default, the table owner has UPDATE STATISTICS permissions and cannot transfer these permissions to anyone else.

Exercise 3-9 will demonstrate the preceding tools for evaluating and optimizing the performance of an execution plan.

EXERCISE 3-9

Evaluating and Optimizing the Performance of an Execution Plan by Using DBCC SHOWCONTIG, SHOWPLAN_TEXT, SHOWPLAN_ALL, and UPDATE STATISTICS

The users at Sutton Tool Company are complaining that during your recent three-week vacation to Europe, the CEO's nephew was maintaining the database server and the performance of their queries has degraded significantly. The interim administrator tells you that he didn't change anything. What are the steps you would go through to troubleshoot the problem?

1. We start out looking at the problem and decide that if nothing changed, our indexes should be maintained, which leaves us suspecting excessive fragmentation of our data. What command are we going to use to check this? DBCC SHOWCONTIG.

2. After running our test, we learn that there is very little fragmentation, so that cannot be the problem. We decide to run the application and determine whether or not the appropriate indexes are being run. What command are we going to run from the command-line utility (OSQL) to determine if the index is being used? SHOWPLAN_TEXT.

3. The results of our test come back and tell us that the index is not being used. We decide to take a closer look at the execution plan from the Query Analyzer. What tool can we use to get additional information about the execution plans for your application queries? SHOWPLAN_ALL.

4. These tests confirm that the indexes are not being used properly. We suspect that our statistics pages are out of date, but don't know how this is possible since SQL Server automatically maintains them. What command can we run to determine if the statistics pages have been updating? STATS_DATE(*table_id*).

5. We learn that the indexes have not been updating. What did our interim administrator run that caused SQL Server to not update these pages? UPDATE STATISTICS NORECOMPUTE.

6. How do we correct this? Rerun UPDATE STATISTICS without the NORECOMPUTE.

SQL Server Profiler

The SQL Server Profiler provides the ability to monitor server and database activity such as the number of deadlocks or login activity. As you see in Figure 3-11, the profiler tracks activity. The information you see includes SQL Server replication services in action as well as the execution and closing of the query shown in Figure 3-10. The profiler provides you with the option to capture data to a SQL Server table or to a file for later analysis. The profiler also provides the option of replaying the events captured on SQL Server to allow the administrator or developer to see exactly what happened. This functionality can also be very helpful to administrators for regression testing when changes are made to a production environment. SQL Server Profiler tracks engine process events, such as the start of a

---

FIGURE 3-11

SQL Server Profiler tracing a DBCC SHOWCONTIG command

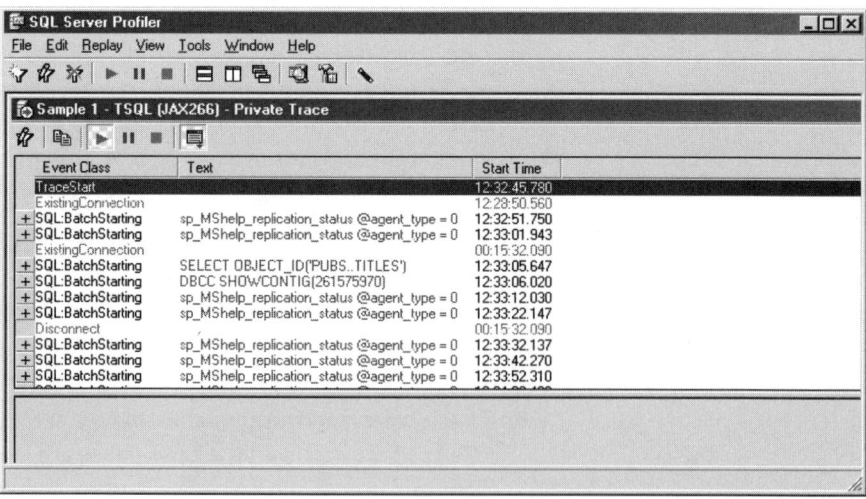

batch, or a transaction. Exercise 3-10 will demonstrate using SQL Server Profiler to identify SQL Server events and performance problems.

EXERCISE 3-10

Identify SQL Server Events and Performance Problems by Using SQL Server Profiler

The users at Sutton Tool Company are now experiencing good performance from their application. Their only complaint is that sometimes they enter records in the system but then cannot retrieve them. You ask them for examples but they can't come up with specific users. They tell you that they enter the customer again and have no problems the second time. How can we track the functions performed by the users to find a solution?

By running the SQL Server Profiler for an entire day, we can see exactly what the user is entering and retrieve inserts and updates that the users performed that are later not found. By doing this, we find that the users are placing a space in front of the username and the stored procedure used for inserts is erring out without returning an error message to the application. We must update the application to provide correct data validation.

CERTIFICATION SUMMARY

In this chapter, we looked at the commands that are needed to create and maintain a SQL Server user database. We reviewed how data files and transaction log files are used and the impact they can have on your system's performance. We discussed how to configure session-level options using the SET commands. We reviewed the Create Database syntax and laid the groundwork for a closer look at constraints and indexes in the upcoming chapters. You should now understand the system-defined data types that SQL Server provides and how you may extend these using user-defined data types.

After your database was created, we showed you how to use the script generator to create a SQL script that can be used to create a duplicate configuration or a subset of it. You also learned how to effectively monitor the behavior of your database using tools such as SHOWPLAN and DBCC SHOWCONTIG. You also saw how to monitor server and database activity using the SQL Server Profiler.

TWO-MINUTE DRILL

❑ A database is loosely defined as a collection of data organized into files that make it easy to sort and retrieve this data.

❑ Microsoft SQL Server provides consistent interfaces for interacting with SQL Server. These interfaces are typically broken into two separate groups: data manipulation and database administration.

❑ The Transact-SQL interface is the sole proprietary interface to SQL Server. For SQL Server 7.0, Microsoft enhanced Transact-SQL to support Unicode data types, provided enhanced support for cursors, and increased capacities (such as column sizes) for compatibility with new limits supported by the database engine.

❑ Unless a configuration setting is reset, the SET options that have been set for a connection continue to apply after connecting to a different database under the same session.

❑ With version 7.0, Microsoft has significantly simplified the management of database size. At the time that databases are created, the CREATE DATABASE command allows the administrator to specify the initial size of a database, the maximum size the database is allowed to reach, and the size of the growth increments for the database when it is full.

❑ The database server is broken down into three primary groups of information that must be managed: data files, transaction logs, and backups.

❑ In earlier versions of SQL Server, it was critical to assign the transaction log to a separate disk device in order to back it up separately. SQL Server 7.0 forces the log onto a separate file by default.

❑ As the name implies, filegroups consist of multiple data files. By creating a file on multiple disk drives, and combining them into a single filegroup, the administrator gets much of the benefit of RAID without the expense.

❑ Filegroups work well for advanced users who know where they want to place indexes and tables. If the administrator does not specify filegroups, all files are included in the default filegroup and SQL Server 7.0 allocates data within the database.

❑ Using files and filegroups improves database performance by allowing a database to be created across multiple disks, multiple disk controllers, or RAID systems.

❑ The transaction log is a serial record of all modifications that have occurred in the database. The log records the start of each transaction, the changes to the data, and enough information to undo the modifications.

❑ SQL Server will return an error (#5123) and fail to create the database if the directory that you attempt to place a file into does not already exist.

❑ One of the important facts to keep in mind when working with SQL Server is that every column, local variable, expression, and parameter has a data type.

❑ There are two groups of data types used in SQL Server, system supplied and user defined.

❑ The specification of data type defines the number of bytes allocated for storage of data and what data can be stored in a column. The filtering of data is performed as the data types limit what data can be placed in a field and what functions can be performed against them (without conversion).

❑ The data types also perform the function of space allocation. For numeric data, this determines the range of data that can be stored in a field, as well as the amount of space that is allocated for this column in each row.

❑ Microsoft SQL Server 7.0 complies with the entry level of the SQL-92 standard. This includes support for the basic set of data types specified.

❑ User-defined data types are aliases for system-supplied data types that are more defined.

❑ User-defined data types allow you to extend a SQL Server base data type (such as char) with a descriptive name and format tailored to a specific use.

❑ It is now possible to have as many as two billion tables per database and 1,024 columns per table. The total size of the table is limited only by the amount of storage that is available. The maximum number of bytes per row is 8,060.

❑ Once you have created the database and placed it into production, it is time to perform maintenance. This encompasses tuning, optimization, and troubleshooting.

❑ The SHOWPLAN_TEXT option of SQL Server is turned on and off at run time. When SHOWPLAN_TEXT is turned on, the SQL Server database engine returns the detailed plan of how the command would be executed rather than processing the actual query.

❑ The SET SHOWPLAN_ALL command is similar to the SET SHOWPLAN_TEXT command because returns execution information rather than data.

❑ The graphical SHOWPLAN provides a method to analyze graphically the plan of a query, execute multiple queries simultaneously, view data, and choose indexes.

❑ If you run SHOWPLAN and determine that SQL Server is using the proper indexes but performance is still suffering, your performance problem may be caused by fragmentation. To analyze this, SQL Server provides the DBCC SHOWCONTIG utility.

❑ The DBCC commands can be used for tuning and optimization, as well as for finding and repairing some corrupted data.

❑ The SQL Server Profiler provides the ability to monitor server and database activity such as the number of deadlocks or login activity.

SELF TEST

The following questions will help you measure your understanding of the material presented in this chapter. Read all of the choices carefully, as there may be more than one correct answer. Choose all correct answers for each question.

1. What syntax can you use to change the format in which SQL Server presents dates to your session without impacting other users?

    A. SET DATEFORMAT

    B. CHANGE DATETIME

    C. DBCC FORMATDATE

    D. UPDATE DATESTAT

2. What command would you execute if you wanted to determine how many logical and physical reads SQL Server is performing to resolve your query?

    A. SET SHOWPLAN ON

    B. SET SHOWTEXT ON

    C. SET STATISTICS_IO ON

    D. SET DATA ON

3. Which of the following is not a valid SQL Server file type?

    A. Primary data file

    B. Secondary data file

    C. Primary log file

    D. Log file

4. How large are the data pages in SQL Server 7.0?

    A. 2KB

    B. 4KB

    C. 6KB

    D. 8KB

5. Which of the following were added to SQL Server in version 7.0?

    A. 8KB pages

    B. Mixed Extents

    C. Native Operating System File Support

    D. All of the above

6. Which of the following is the correct term for groups of data files that can be used to strategically locate database objects?

    A. Filegroups

    B. Datagroups

    C. Clusters

    D. SMP support

7. Which of the following is *not* a performance trend within SQL Server 7.0?

    A. Transaction log writes are sequential and thus benefit from being on an isolated device to minimize physical movement of read and write heads.

    B. Data files benefit from being spread across multiple physical disks.

    C. RAID 5 provides the most efficient fault tolerance for transaction logs.

    D. RAID 5 provides the most efficient fault tolerance for data files.

8. How many fixed-length fields are in the following table?

```
CREATE TABLE testtable
(
lname          varchar(25),
fname          char(15) NULL,
ssnum          char(15) NOT NULL,
score int
)
```

   A. 1
   B. 2
   C. 3
   D. 4

9. Which of the following is the correct syntax for creating a user-defined data type?

   A. Create Type
   B. Create Data type
   C. sp_addtype
   D. sp_addatatype

10. Which of the following is the correct syntax for creating a new table?

    A. CREATE TABLE
    B. Disk Init
    C. sp_createtable
    D. sp_addtable

11. What command would you execute to determine if the SQL Server database engine is using the index that you created?

    A. SET SHOWPLAN_TEXT ON
    B. SET SHOWINDEX ON
    C. SET SHOWPLAN_TEXT OFF
    D. SET INDEXUSAGE

12. What tool would you use if you want to see a graphical representation of what indexes SQL Server would use to resolve a query?

    A. SQL Server Profiler
    B. SQL Server Query Analyzer
    C. Enterprise Manager
    D. Client Network Utility

13. What command would you execute to determine if your database is suffering from excessive disk fragmentation?

    A. SET SHOWPLAN_TEXT ON
    B. SET SHOWFRAGMENTATION ON
    C. DBCC SHOWCONTIG
    D. DBCC SHOWFRAGMENTS

14. What command can you issue to update information about the distribution of key values for one or more indexes in the specified table?

    A. DBCC SHOWINDEX
    B. DBCC REINDEX
    C. UPDATE INDEX
    D. UPDATE STATISTICS

15. What tool would you use to trap the activity between clients and a SQL Server database to flat files?

    A. SQL Server Profiler
    B. SQL Server Query Analyzer
    C. Enterprise Manager
    D. Client Network Utility

MICROSOFT CERTIFIED DATABASE ADMINISTRATOR

4

Developing a Logical Data Model

A s you begin to investigate the keys to developing good database applications, you are likely to run into many sources that tell you the key to good, reliable application performance lies in good database design. Unfortunately, there are far fewer sources that are willing to share with you the keys to good database design. In the next few chapters, we are going to take a closer look at the guidelines for good database design and help you to understand the whys as well as the whats. With a focus on integrity, constraints, defaults, and rules, let's get started learning about database design.

Grouping Data into Entities Using Normalization Rules

The first step in creating a successful relational database implementation comes from the creation of a good logical design for the database. This includes designing the tables and defining the relationships between them. Designing SQL Server databases effectively begins with a normalized database design. A well thought-out, logical database design provides the foundation for optimal database and application performance. A poor logical database design can provide a very negative impact on the performance of the entire system. *Normalization* is the process of removing redundancies from the data. There are five commonly accepted rules of normal forms that dictate the creation of a relational database. The first three forms carry a higher importance and broader acceptance than the last two. All five rules are identified as follows:

1. The first normal form dictates that tables must be flat. This means that each row of the table can contain only one set of data values. Each data value must be stored in its own column, rather than an item in the database containing a list of values for a specific piece of information. For example, a book in the pubs database could be coauthored. If there is a column in the *titles* table for the name of the author, this would present a problem. One solution is to store the

name of both authors in the column, but this makes it difficult to show a list of the individual authors. A second solution is to change the structure of the table to add another column for the name of the second author, but this solution does nothing to accommodate more than two authors. For each additional author, another column must be added. If your design requirements dictate that you need to store a list of values, the first normal form states that you should place the duplicated data in another table with a link back to the primary table. In the example of the pubs database, there is one table for book information, one table for author information, and a third that stores the ID values for the books and the IDs of the books' authors. This design allows any number of authors for a book without modifying the table definition, and does not allocate any unnecessary storage space for books with a single author.

2. The second normal form requires that all nonkey fields in a table must be related to all key fields. The table cannot contain information that is not related to the key fields. This means that even when payments are recorded, the customer's address should not be stored in the payment table because the address describes the customer rather than the payments.

3. The third normal form dictates that any column that is not a key column cannot be dependent upon another nonkey column. For example, if your table includes columns for the area code and city entry and neither are key columns, it would not be appropriate to have the area code column filled based upon the value placed in the city column.

4. The fourth normal form (Boyce Codd Normal Form) requires that only related data entities be included in a single table. A table should store only data for a single type of entity. In the example of the pubs database, the titles and publishers information is stored in two separate tables. Although it is possible to have columns for both the book's information and its publisher's information in the same table, this design generates several undesirable results. The publisher information is added and stored redundantly because it must be

added for every book that is published by the publisher. This consumes additional storage space in the database. In addition, if the address for the publisher changes, the change must be made for each book. Finally, if the last book for a publisher is removed from the table, the publisher's information is lost. A better solution is implemented in the pubs database. The information for books and publishers is stored in the titles and publishers tables, respectively. The publisher information is entered once and linked to each book. When the publisher information is changed, it is changed in one place. In addition, the publisher information is stored in the publisher table, even if the publisher has no books in the database.

5. The fifth normal form requires that a table that has been divided into multiple tables must be capable of being reconstructed to its exact original structure by one or more joins. In some situations, the logical database design is fixed and total redesign is not feasible. Even then, however, it might be possible to normalize a large table by dividing it into several smaller tables. If the insurance company divides information about an individual customer into multiple tables (such as policyholder information, billing information, phone information, and underwriting information), they must be able to reconstruct the information by performing a query that retrieves all related data.

Prior to normalization, database designs often consist of a few wide tables. The process of normalizing a database consists of breaking the tables down to represent the smallest data entities possible. This process usually results in the creation of a greater number of tables, with each table decreasing in width (that is, reducing the number of columns). Some of the benefits of narrow tables include

- Faster performance when retrieving data from the tables due to the decreased amount of data contained in the narrower tables. This benefit also applies to table-level administrative tasks such as database consistency checks (DBCC) and index maintenance (particularly clustered indexes).

■ Improved performance when retrieving data in ranges. As we will discuss in Chapter 5, we are limited to a single clustered index in each table because clustered indexes physically sort the data. By breaking the data into more tables, we are able to maintain data elements in the order they are most likely to be retrieved.

■ A reduced number of indexes. Narrow tables contain fewer fields that benefit from being indexed for query purposes. Since indexes typically benefit SELECT statements but reduce the performance of INSERT, UPDATE, and DELETE statements, narrower tables provide a better compromise for systems used for dual purposes.

In addition to the five normal forms, there are a number of rules that identify attributes that must be either present or absent in a well-designed database. There are additional considerations that you must take into account when working with a SQL Server database.

SQL Server allows columns to be defined to allow null values. A null value indicates that a field has no value. Although it can be useful to allow null values in isolated cases, it is best to use them sparingly because null values require special handling that increases the complexity of data operations. If your logical database design requires a table with several nullable columns, it may be more efficient to consider placing these columns in another table linked to the primary table. Storing the data in two separate tables will allow the primary table to be simple in design while still accommodating the need for storing null information. Exercise 4-1 demonstrates how to group data using normalization rules.

EXERCISE 4-1

Grouping Data into Entities Using Normalization Rules

You have been hired by a country club to create the database that they will be using to track their membership. In your first meeting with the club, you ask them what they intend to do with the information. They have provided the list that follows.

■ Track all members (including all people in a household)

■ Monthly billing

■ Generating golf handicaps

- Managing reservations for golf, tennis, and the restaurant
- Staff scheduling
- Locker assignments
- Pro shop inventory
- Calendar of events

Let's look at the information that our user gave us and determine what entities we need to track this information. (Note: I have provided one set of solutions. There is more than one right answer. If your answers are different, then make sure you can justify the differences.)

1. What entities do we need to track all members? _____

   There are two entities—*the membership* and *the members.*

2. What entities do we need to track monthly billing? _____

   Typically two entities—*invoices* and *payments.*

3. What entities are needed to generate golf handicaps? _____

   This is a single entity—*handicaps.*

4. What entities are needed for managing reservations for golf, tennis, and the restaurant? _____

   This is most likely to be three separate entities—*golf tee times, tennis court time,* and *restaurant reservations.*

5. What entities are needed to manage staff scheduling?_____

   There are two entities involved—*employees* and *scheduling.*

6. What entities do we need to manage locker assignments? _____

   Most likely one entity—*the lockers.*

7. What entities are needed to manage the pro shop inventory?

   _____

   Most likely two entities (but one was already created)—*inventory* and *invoices.*

8. What entities do we need to create a calendar of events? _____

   A single entity of events.

FROM THE CLASSROOM

Normalization Normalities

The process of normalization cannot be understated when designing the tables in a database. Removing redundancies from a database design is critical in avoiding what could easily become a highly inefficient database. Without the process of normalization, queries might have drastically increased execution times. Although normalization consists of five rules, called forms, only the first three Normal Forms are generally a concern for producing a normalized database. The First Normal Form simply states that no multivalue columns may exist within a table. The Second Normal Form states that nonkey columns must be related to all columns that comprise the primary key. The Third Normal Form states that any nonkey column cannot depend on another nonkey column.

If these normalization rules are implemented when designing a database, then queries will be significantly more efficient. It is important to note that normalization for the sake of normalization does not guarantee that a database will be efficient and optimized. Careful denormalization activities are recommended to selectively denormalize tables for increasing the efficiency of selective queries that are performed often, but cannot be conveniently performed with a fully normalized design.

—Michael Lane Thomas,
MCSE+I, MCSD, MCP+SB, MSS, MCT, A+

When to Use Denormalization

When you design a database, you have to ensure that the database performs all the important functions correctly and quickly. If a database has a solid database design, other performance issues can be resolved after the database is in production. If the database schema is designed poorly, the related performance issues can only be addressed by changing the design of the database. Normalization often leads down the path of efficient database design, but there are tradeoffs to normalization. A database that is used primarily for decision support (as opposed to update-intensive transaction processing) may not have redundant updates and may be more understandable and efficient for queries if the design is not fully normalized.

As with most database configurations, normalization provides benefits; however, if it is taken to the extreme, it may restrict performance. As normalization increases, so does the number and complexity of joins required to retrieve data. If your database requires too many complex relational joins between too many tables, you can hinder performance. A generally accepted rule of thumb for reasonable normalization allows the inclusion of few regularly executed queries that use joins involving more than four tables. After creating your fully normalized database design, it may become necessary to make changes that intentionally violate the normalization rules. Typically, these changes are made to eliminate joins or arithmetic calculations that are necessary to resolve frequently run or very complicated queries. This process includes identifying the largest tables in the database and any complex processes that the database will perform (especially those that will be performed frequently). These portions of your database must be given special performance consideration when designing the tables.

For example, you determine that many of the queries run against your pubs database are queries against the titles table, and require a join with the publishers table to retrieve the publisher's name. You may decide that adding the publisher's name to the titles table will improve performance (despite the fact that it violates the second normal form).

On the other hand, if you work for ACME Insurance Company and your database is being built to track catastrophe claims as a result of major disasters, you may have other needs. The management in the claim offices will run daily reports to determine the funds available for each claim by comparing policy limits to the amount already paid. Using your fully normalized database schema, this would require that a one-to-many relationship be established between the claim table and the payment table for each claim. You determine that it is more efficient to add a column to the claim table that stores the total payments for each claim. Exercise 4-2 demonstrates the process for choosing when to use denormalization.

How to Decide If Denormalization Is Appropriate

In Exercise 4-1, we determined what entities we needed to create for the database that will support our customer. We decided on a group similar to the following list:

- Membership
- Members
- Invoices
- Payments
- Handicaps
- Golf tee times
- Tennis court time
- Restaurant reservations
- Employees
- Scheduling
- Lockers
- Inventory
- Events

In the first meeting with the club, they stated that they would be performing the following functions:

- Tracking all members (including all people in the household)
- Monthly billing
- Generating golf handicaps (based on last 20 scores)
- Managing reservations for golf, tennis, and the restaurant
- Staff scheduling
- Locker assignments
- Pro shop inventory
- Calendar of events

Note that I have provided answers based upon one interpretation of the described environment. These answers are not all inclusive; your correct answers may differ from those provided here. It is more important that you be able to defend your answer than have it match these answers.

1. If each entity represents a table in your database, select an example of an entity that might be modified to violate the first normal form (flat rows) to improve performance.

   ■ Golf handicaps may be modified to store 20 scores rather than one per row.

   ■ The membership table may include the head male and head female on the membership.

   ■ The golf tee times or tennis court times may list four participants because that is the set limit for participation.

2. If each entity represents a table in your database, select an example of an entity that might be modified to violate the second normal form (nonkey fields relate to the key) to improve performance.

   ■ The scheduling table may include employee names as well as their IDs.

   ■ In the golf tee times table, we store member names as well as the member numbers. The name refers to the member rather than the tee time.

3. If each entity represents a table in your database, select an example of an entity that might be modified to violate the third normal form (nonkey field dependency) to improve performance.

   ■ The membership table may contain an area code that is dependent upon the city column when membership ID is the key field.

   ■ The inventory field may have a flag to indicate whether an item is taxable, based upon the item type rather than the item ID, which is the key field.

4. If each entity represents a table in your database, select an example of an entity that might be modified to violate the fourth normal form (only related entities in a single table) to improve performance.

   ■ The invoices table may contain information about the member making the purchase.

■ The payments table may contain information about the member making the payment.

You notice in performing this exercise that changes to the database that improve performance of your application will often break more than one normal form.

Types of Data Integrity

It is difficult to discuss database design without the conversation quickly turning to data integrity. When we look at this term from a high level, we define it simply as the quality of the data. It is very important that a database maintain the quality of the data stored in it. We are going to take a closer look at the different types of data integrity that define the quality of the data. In this chapter, we discuss the following forms of data integrity:

■ **Entity integrity**   Entity integrity defines a row as a unique entity within a particular table. Entity integrity enforces the integrity of the identifier columns (also called the primary key) and, therefore, the rows of the table itself. When you place the data in the table, it is important that it be uniquely identifiable so that it can be retrieved for update or delete.

■ **Domain integrity**   Domain integrity specifies the validity of a specific data entry within a given column. The term *domain* is used to represent the group of allowable values for a column. When you store data in a column, it is important that it be stored in a manner that allows it to be retrieved and compared to other values in the same table. This may be as simple as verifying character or numeric data, or as complicated as specifying a format for storing phone number information.

- **Referential integrity**   Referential integrity is used to preserve a defined relationship between two tables when records are added or deleted. Referential integrity is often used to enforce business rules. In SQL Server, referential integrity is based on relationships between foreign keys and primary keys or between foreign keys and unique keys. Referential integrity ensures that key values are consistent across tables. When you enforce referential integrity, SQL Server prevents users from

  - Adding records to a related table if there is not an associated record in the primary table. For example, a store would not allow someone to purchase an item (invoices table) on credit if no credit line had been previously established (customer table) for the individual.

  - Changing values in a primary table that results in orphaned records in one or more related tables. For example, if you have purchased a new suit and charged it to your account number 12345, we cannot update your information to change your account number without updating it for the debt that you have accumulated.

  - Deleting records from a primary table if there are related records. For example, a relationship exists between the accounts receivable table and the customer table. I can't delete my record from the customers table as this action would orphan the record in the accounts receivable and leave the store unable to track who purchased the suit.

- **User-defined integrity**   User-defined integrity allows the administrator to define additional business rules that do not fall into any of the other integrity categories. User-defined integrity can be established through the use of constraints, stored procedures, or triggers. User-defined integrity may be as simple as limiting the subset of area codes based upon the state code entered with a record (custom domain integrity), or as complicated as an insurance company enforcing completely different sets of policy number constraints depending upon the policy type (auto, fire, health, or life).

Enforcing Data Integrity

A well-designed and -written application protects data integrity through the necessary edits to data. Although this form of data protection will function in simple environments, it is inconsistent with the goals of multitier development because it is placing responsibility for the server data integrity on the client. If we used this design, we would need to build these edits into every client application that modified the data. This strategy is inefficient at best and very difficult in others (such as users that use Excel in addition to a custom application to access data). For this reason, Microsoft has provided the tools in SQL Server to maintain data integrity on the server side.

Let's take a closer look at the options that an administrator uses to provide each type of data integrity.

Entity Integrity

Microsoft has provided three separate mechanisms that are used to guarantee entity integrity. The following list describes each approach.

PRIMARY KEY CONSTRAINT   A table typically has a column or combination of columns whose values can be used to uniquely identify each row in the table. This column (or columns) is called the primary key of the table. In early versions of SQL Server, the primary key was used to diagram relationships with other tables but did not provide any enforcement of integrity. In SQL Server 7.0, we can define a PRIMARY KEY constraint when we create (or alter) the table. If we do this, SQL Server creates an index (default is a clustered index) and enforces the entity integrity. Let's look at the syntax to add a column with a PRIMARY KEY constraint to a table.

```
ALTER TABLE EXAMPLE ADD
Primary_column INT
CONSTRAINT newcolumn_pk PRIMARY KEY,
```

There are a few limitations to the use of the PRIMARY KEY constraint. Tables are limited to only one PRIMARY KEY constraint, but the constraint can span multiple columns (indexes on multiple columns are referred to as a composite index). In addition, no column that participates in the PRIMARY KEY constraint can be configured to accept null values. By default, when a PRIMARY KEY constraint is established, SQL Server creates a clustered index on the primary key columns.

UNIQUE CONSTRAINT   The UNIQUE constraint is used to enforce uniqueness on non-primary key columns. The UNIQUE constraint has a function that is similar to that of the PRIMARY KEY constraint, but it can allow null values. The syntax is very similar to the syntax we saw for the PRIMARY KEY constraint.

```
ALTER TABLE EXAMPLE ADD
Unique_column varchar(30) NULL
UNIQUE NONCLUSTERED
```

An administrator can specify multiple UNIQUE constraints within a table. Although it is possible to use unique indexes to enforce entity integrity, you should specify a unique index only when uniqueness is a characteristic of the data itself. If uniqueness must be enforced to ensure data integrity, create a UNIQUE constraint on the column rather than a unique index. By default, when the UNIQUE constraint is placed on a column (or group of columns), a nonclustered index is created.

IDENTITY PROPERTY   A third method of enforcing entity integrity is provided through the IDENTITY property. The IDENTITY property can be applied to a column with a decimal, int, smallint, tinyint, or numeric data type. The IDENTITY property generates a value that is unique within the table. In the following syntax, we see that two parameters can be passed to the ALTER TABLE command. The IDENTITY property allows the database owner to specify both a starting number (IdentitySeed property) and the increment (IdentityIncrement property) to be added to the seed to set successive identity numbers.

```
ALTER TABLE EXAMPLE ADD
Identity_column INT IDENTITY(1,1)
```

When data is inserted into a table with an identifier column, SQL Server automatically generates the next identity value by adding the increment to the seed. There are a few limitations to the use of the IDENTITY property. A table can have only one column defined with the IDENTITY property. The identifier column cannot allow null values.

The column that has the IDENTITY property can be referenced in a select list by using the IDENTITYCOL keyword. The OBJECTPROPERTY function can be used to determine if a table has an identity column.

Domain Integrity

Microsoft has provided four separate mechanisms that are used to guarantee domain integrity. The following list describes each approach.

DEFAULT DEFINITION   Within SQL Server, every column in each record must contain a value, even if that value is NULL. If the column allows null values, you can load the row with one or more null values. In many situations, nullable columns are not desirable or do not fit the format that is needed in a column. In situations where nulls do not meet the requirements, and the desired data is not available, a better solution is to define a DEFAULT definition for the column. This configuration inserts a predefined value into the column if a value is not given. For example, it is common to specify zero as the default for numeric columns, or n/a as the default for string columns when no value is specified. Only one default can be defined for a table. That default can contain a literal, a function, or a SQL-92 *niladic* function (see Table 4-1). If it is desirable to place one of several results depending upon other data provided, a stored procedure is a better solution. As you see with the following syntax, the default is established when the table is created or altered.

```
ALTER TABLE SampleTable
ADD SampleDate smalldatetime NULL
CONSTRAINT AddDateDflt
DEFAULT getdate() WITH VALUES
```

When you load a row into a table with a DEFAULT definition for one or more columns, SQL Server loads the default value into all columns that do not have a value specified.

exam
Watch

You cannot place a default on a column with a timestamp data type or on a column with the IDENTITY property specified. In either situation, the system is attempting to provide the value by default.

FOREIGN KEY CONSTRAINT   A FOREIGN KEY constraint consists of a column or combination of columns used to enforce a link between data in two tables. The link is created between the tables by tying the column or columns that contain one table's primary key values to another table's column(s). This column becomes a foreign key in the second table. As you see in the following syntax, the FOREIGN KEY constraint is defined by establishing a FOREIGN KEY constraint when you create or alter a table.

```
ALTER TABLE SampleTable
column_c INT NULL
CONSTRAINT column_c_fk
REFERENCES doc_exe(column_a),
```

The FOREIGN KEY constraint can be linked to a UNIQUE constraint as well as the more common PRIMARY KEY constraint. A FOREIGN KEY constraint can contain null values; however, if any column of a composite FOREIGN KEY constraint contains null values, verification of the FOREIGN KEY constraint will be skipped. When a new row is added

TABLE 4-1	SQL-92 niladic Function	Value Returned
	CURRENT_TIMESTAMP	Current date and time
SQL-92 Niladic Function Descriptions	CURRENT_USER	Name of user performing insert
	SESSION_USER	Name of user performing insert
	SYSTEM_USER	Name of user performing insert
	USER	Name of user performing insert

to a table or the data in an existing row is changed, values in the foreign key columns must either exist in the primary key columns of the other table or be NULL.

CHECK CONSTRAINT   A CHECK constraint is used to enforce domain integrity by limiting the acceptable values for a column. The CHECK constraint is similar to a FOREIGN KEY constraint in that they both control the valid data values that are allowed in a column. It is different in how they determine which values are valid. The FOREIGN KEY constraint retrieves a list of valid values from another table, while the CHECK constraint determines the valid values from a logical expression that is not based on data in another column. As you look at the syntax, keep in mind that the CHECK constraint can be configured with any logical (Boolean) expression that returns a true or false value based on the logical operators.

```
ALTER TABLE SampleTable
Emp_id char(9) NULL
CONSTRAINT CK_emp_id CHECK (emp_id LIKE
'[A-Z][A-B][M-Z][1-2][0-9][0-9][0-9][0-9][AM]' OR
emp_id LIKE '[A-Z]-[R-Z][1-2][0-5][0-9][0-9][0-9][DC]')
```

The CHECK constraint provides two acceptable patterns for the value that can be placed in each digit of the 9-byte character field. A valid value being placed into this column must match one of the two patterns. Multiple CHECK constraints can be placed on a single column. The constraints are evaluated in the order in which they were created, so it is logical that you would place the most limiting constraint first. It is also acceptable to apply a single CHECK constraint to multiple columns by creating it at the table level. For example, a multiple-column CHECK constraint can be used to verify that if a row contains a value of *US* in the country column, a valid state is entered in the state column.

Because our database environments and user requirements are constantly evolving, it is important that we are able to modify the CHECK constraints that we have created. To modify a CHECK constraint through command-line syntax, you must first delete the existing constraint (using the drop constraints command or Enterprise Manager) and then re-create it with the new definition.

When you add a check constraint to an existing table, you must choose whether the CHECK constraint should apply to existing data, or only to new data being added to the table. By default, the CHECK constraint will apply to all existing data as well as new data being put into the table. The ability to add a CHECK constraint and have it only apply to new data can be very useful for situations in which business rules have recently changed. In this situation, creating the check for all new data allows us to put the new rule into effect and prevent creating more data that will require modification.

NOT NULL CONSTRAINT   The most fundamental option for enforcing domain integrity comes from specifying the NOT NULL constraint on a column. By not allowing null values a valid entry must be made in the column. The NOT NULL constraint can be used in combination with the FOREIGN KEY constraint to eliminate alternatives to meeting the foreign key constraints.

Referential Integrity

Microsoft has provided a mechanism with the PRIMARY KEY and FOREIGN KEY constraints to enforce referential integrity.

PRIMARY KEY / FOREIGN KEY CONSTRAINTS   The PRIMARY KEY and FOREIGN KEY constraints that we detailed earlier can be used together to enforce referential integrity as well as entity and domain integrity. To provide referential integrity, this implementation of a foreign key must be linked to a primary key in another table. In the following syntax, we create the publishers table and the titles table. Notice that we created a PRIMARY KEY constraint in the publishers table and a FOREIGN KEY constraint that references the publishers table.

```
CREATE TABLE publishers
(
pub_id char(4) NOT NULL
CONSTRAINT UPKCL_pubind PRIMARY KEY CLUSTERED,
pub_name varchar(40) NULL,
city varchar(20) NULL,
state char(2) NULL
```

```
)
GO
CREATE TABLE titles
(title_id char(5) NOT NULL ,
 title varchar (80) NOT NULL ,
 pub_id char (4) NULL
      CONSTRAINT pubid_fk
      REFERENCES publishers(pub_id) ,
 price money NULL ,
 pubdate datetime NOT NULL
)
GO
```

In the example just shown, the publishers table is created with the UPKCL_PUBIND constraint, which defines the pub_id column as the primary key and creates a clustered index. When the titles table is created, a foreign key relationship is established between the pub_id column in titles and the pub_id column in publishers. With this relationship established, records cannot be added to the titles table if they include a pub_id that is not in the publishers table. In addition, rows cannot be deleted from the publishers table if there are rows in the titles using the pub_id that is being deleted.

User-Defined Integrity

User-defined integrity allows you to define specific business rules that do not fall into one of the other integrity categories. The primary tools that Microsoft provides for enforcing business rules are triggers. Because CHECK constraints can reference only the columns on which they have been defined, any cross-table constraints (such as business rules) must be defined as triggers.

A *trigger* is a special type of stored procedure that is automatically invoked whenever the data in the table is modified. Although stored procedures can perform similar functions, they are bypassed if the data is accessed directly. Triggers can be invoked in response to INSERT, UPDATE, or DELETE statements. These triggers possess all functionality allowed other stored procedures, as well as having access to all rows being deleted and inserted. The trigger becomes a part of the transaction that fires it and thus can be used to roll back the transaction if appropriate. If a severe error is detected, the entire transaction automatically rolls back.

Triggers are typically used in one or more of the following ways:

- Triggers can cascade changes through related tables in the database to assist in keeping all parent-child relationships intact and prevent the orphaning of any rows. For example, a DELETE trigger on a column in the titles table may cause a corresponding deletion of matching rows in other tables, such as sales or titleauthor.

- Triggers can roll back inappropriate changes that would otherwise violate referential integrity. For example, if you attempted to delete a customer record, the trigger would check for an outstanding balance. If a nonzero balance is found, the trigger does not allow the customer to be deleted.

- Triggers can enforce restrictions other than those that can be defined in a CHECK constraint. Triggers have the added ability to reference other tables and act accordingly. For example, a trigger can use a SELECT statement from another table to roll back updates that attempt to increase a salesperson's income by more than 1 percent of their annual sales for the past year.

- The ability to act upon all rows being inserted and deleted allows triggers to determine the difference between the state of a table before and after a data modification and take action based on that difference.

An example of how triggers are used to enforce business rules is found in the following syntax.

```
USE pubs
CREATE TRIGGER empl_salarycheck
ON employee
FOR INSERT, UPDATE
AS
DECLARE          @maximum tinyint,
@salary tinyint,
@job_id smallint
/* We are selecting the id and salary just inserted as well as the maximum
salary allowed for this job ID. */
```

```
SELECT          @maximum = max,
@salary = i.salary,
@job_id = i.job_id
/* We are joining the employee table, the row we inserted and the jobs table.
The jobs table tracks the maximum salary for a job class. */
FROM employee INNER JOIN inserted ON employee.emp_id = inserted.emp_id
JOIN jobs ON jobs.job_id = inserted.job_id
/* The salary being paid is compared to the highest salary level allowed for a
given job ID. If the salary is higher than allowed, the transaction an error is
returned and the transaction is rolled back. */
IF NOT (@salary < @max_lvl)
  BEGIN
   RAISERROR ('The salary for job_id:%d should be less than %d. ',
             16, 1, @job_id, @max_lvl)
  ROLLBACK TRANSACTION
END
```

In the trigger that is created in our example, when an employee job level is inserted or updated, the trigger verifies that the specified job level is within the range defined for the job. To get the appropriate range, the jobs table must be referenced.

CERTIFICATION OBJECTIVE 4.04

Using Constraints

As we have discussed, constraints provide a method for SQL Server to enforce automatically the integrity of data within a database. The constraints define the values allowed in columns and provide the preferred method for enforcing data integrity. Constraints are typically more efficient than triggers, rules, and defaults. The query optimizer uses constraints to improve performance in selectivity estimation, cost calculations, and query rewriting.

We have discussed the following five classes of constraints:

- **NOT NULL**   Specifies that the column does not accept NULL values.

- **CHECK constraints**   Enforce domain integrity by limiting the values that can be placed in a column.

- **UNIQUE constraints**   Enforce the uniqueness of the values in a column or set of columns. This action enforces entity integrity.
- **PRIMARY KEY constraints**   Identify the column or set of columns whose values uniquely identify a row in a table.
- **FOREIGN KEY constraints**   Identify the relationships between tables. A foreign key in one table points to a primary key in another table.

exam
ⓦatch

A table may have more than one combination of columns that could uniquely identify the rows in a table; each combination is a candidate key. The database administrator picks one of the candidate keys to be the primary key.

There are two primary levels of constraints: column constraints and table constraints. Earlier in this chapter, we focused on column-level constraints. A column constraint is specified as part of a column definition and applies only to that column. Table constraints are different because they are declared independently from a column definition and can apply to more than one column in a table. Table constraints must be used when more than one column is included in a constraint. Either type can be used when only one column is included in a constraint.

There are many practical situations that require the use of table constraints. For example, many tables use two or more columns to define the primary key. In this situation, you must use a table constraint to specify multiple columns as the primary key. As a result of this constraint, a composite index is created.

If you are building a claim database for an insurance company, they may wish to use the policy number or date and time as the primary key for their claim database. When we look closer at the database we realize that an insured may have the misfortune of having multiple claims over time so that a single field cannot be used as the primary key. In addition, the company has the potential to enter multiple claims at the same date and time so this field cannot be used as the primary key by itself. We inform the company that they must use a combination of these two fields as the primary key. Let's take a closer look at the syntax to create this table and constraint.

```
CREATE TABLE claims
(policy_no char(10),
 date_reported datetime,
 description char(200),
 amount_paid money,
CONSTRAINT claim_key PRIMARY KEY (policy_no, date_reported))
```

As you probably noticed, the syntax for table constraints is very similar to the syntax we used for column constraints.

CERTIFICATION OBJECTIVE 4.05

Using Defaults and Rules

Defaults and rules are both database objects available in SQL Server 7.0 to help with the enforcement of data integrity. Both defaults and rules are created as objects within the database and are then bound to specific data columns or user-defined data types. Let's take a closer look at the functionality they provide and how they are used.

Defaults

In earlier sections of this chapter, we discussed the DEFAULT definition that can be applied to a given column of a table during the CREATE DATABASE or ALTER DATABASE commands. Microsoft continues to provide *Default objects*, which provide similar functionality. Defaults are created and bound to either columns or user-defined data types. The defaults specify what value is inserted into the column or user-defined data type the object is bound to when no value is supplied during an insert. Default object is a backward-compatibility feature that overlaps the functionality provided by DEFAULT definitions. DEFAULT definitions are the preferred method to restrict column data because the definition is stored with the table and automatically dropped when the table is dropped. A Default object can still be beneficial, however, when the default is being used multiple times for multiple columns. Let's take a closer look at the syntax used to create a default and bind it to the phone column of the authors table in pubs.

```
USE golfhandicap
GO
CREATE DEFAULT default_par AS 72
GO
sp_bindefault default_par, 'scores.par'
```

Rules

In earlier sections of this chapter, we discussed CHECK constraints and the functionality they provide. SQL Server provides database objects called *rules* that can be used to provide similar functionality. Rule objects are similar to defaults in how they are implemented. Rules are created and then bound to columns or user-defined data types. Like a CHECK constraint, a rule specifies the acceptable values that can be inserted into a column. Rule objects are primarily provided with SQL Server 7.0 for backward compatibility and are more limited than the CHECK constraints that provide the same functionality. A column or user-defined data type can have only one rule bound to it, whereas multiple CHECK constraints can be attached to a column. However, a column can have both a rule and one or more CHECK constraints associated with it. When this is true, all restrictions are evaluated. The syntax used to create a rule and bind it to a user-defined data type (named *wage*) is as follows:

```
CREATE RULE salary_range
@salary >= $2000 AND AS @salary < $20000
USE master
EXEC sp_bindrule 'salary_range', 'wage'
```

Identify the Business Rules That Relate to Data Integrity

As you work with your tables and identify the relationships that exist between them, it is important to understand the business rules that govern these relationships. It is best to break this down into the following two phases:

■ Determine the impact that inserts and deletes to each table will have on all related tables. Determine the impact that updates to each column will have on related tables. If you identify conditions under which these inserts or deletes should not be allowed to continue or additional changes are necessary, you must create a trigger.

■ Evaluate every column in every table to determine if the business has requirements that impact the data type, properties, or CHECK constraints that must be applied to enforce the rules.

Exercise 4-3 will demonstrate how to incorporate business rules and constraints into the data model.

EXERCISE 4-3

Incorporate Business Rules and Constraints into the Data Model

Now that we have outlined the entities that we will be using to design the database for the Country Club that has hired us, we meet with them again to learn more about their business and how it is managed. From this meeting, we learn the facts in the following list. What changes need to be made to the database to support this information?

1. A member can get only one golf reservation during any four-hour period. _____

   A trigger must be added to check a range of four hours on each side of the desired time to verify no other reservations exist.

2. No more than four members can share a golf reservation together. _____

   If we denormalized the database and made four columns for members in the reservation table, no changes are necessary. If not, we must modify the business tier to count the number of golfers at that tee time.

3. When a child reaches the age of 21, he or she must obtain a membership or lose membership benefits. _____

   No changes are necessary. This will run as a scheduled batch process.

4. When a member resigns, he or she must pay the full balance of accounts receivable. _____

   A trigger must be built that doesn't allow us to delete from the members table if the balance between the invoices and payments table is not 0.

Deciding Which Enforcement Method to Use

In this chapter, we have outlined multiple methods of maintaining data integrity. Several of these techniques have provided overlapping functionality, which may leave you wondering which to implement. Use the following guidelines to help you with this decision:

- Constraints and properties are the preferred method for maintaining data integrity. They are stored with the tables.

- Null values hinder performance in SQL Server. When possible, specify NOT NULLS and provide a default definition.

- Avoid using Rule or Default objects. These items exist primarily for backward compatibility.

- Indexes should be used to optimize query performance—not to enforce data integrity.

- Don't rush the logical design phase of development—the performance of your application depends on it.

Assess the Potential Impact of the Logical Design on Performance, Maintainability, Extensibility, Scalability, Availability, and Security

The logical plan serves both as a guide to use when implementing the database and as a functional specification for the database after it has been implemented. The complexity and size of the database application and its user community dictate the complexity and detail of the database design. For a small, single-user database, the database design may be little more than a hand drawing on notepaper. For larger databases with more extensive uses, the design typically contains formal documents with many pages that contain very detailed information about the database design.

In planning the database, regardless of its size and complexity, you should go through these basic steps:

- Assess and define scope
- Identify the entities
- Identify the types of information for each entity
- Identify the relationships between entities
- Normalize and evaluate denormalization
- Apply business rules

Assess and Define Scope

Before creating a database, you must have a good understanding of how the database will be used. Examining the existing processes and interviewing users will provide most of the information that you need. It is important to pay particular attention to problems with the existing system to prevent these problems from being duplicated. It is often useful to collect copies of all forms (input and output) that are used in the current system. These forms will help you identify entities and their relationships as we move forward.

Identify the Entities

As you gather information about the database that you will be designing, most entities will become apparent. These entities may be physical objects, such as people, or intangible items, such as business transactions, golf tee times, or memberships. Typically, you will identify a few main objects very quickly. Each of these items will have its own table in your logical design.

Identify the Types of Information for Each Entity

After you have identified the primary entities in the database, it is time to identify what information will need to be tracked about each of them. Each item of information that needs to be tracked will be a column in the entity's table. For each entity, it is important to have a data column that can be used to uniquely identify the information. This may come naturally or be added in the form of an ID column. Other descriptive information will be more obvious to you.

Identify the Relationships Between Entities

Although some isolated information may be stored in your database, the majority of information is stored in the database because it relates to other entities you have selected. The next step in creating your database is to identify the natural relationships that exist between entities. It is not uncommon to identify a relationship between two entities, only to find out that you don't currently have the relational information in one or both tables. If this happens, go back to the previous step and add the appropriate columns to your tables.

Normalize and Evaluate Denormalization

By this point, we have a basic understanding of the columns that will make up each of the tables in our database. The next step is to evaluate our tables against the five normal forms to verify that we are in compliance with standard SQL relational theory. (There is a reason these standards exist—they lead to the best database design.) Once we have developed a fully normalized database, it is time to review the key tasks that we have been told will be performed on our database. If we find that a significant number of joins or very complex arithmetic calculations can be eliminated by denormalization, we should consider doing this.

Assess the Potential Impact of the Logical Design on Performance, Maintainability, Extensibility, Scalability, Availability, and Security, and Apply Business Rules

At this stage, we have a very good understanding of our database structure and the data that will be stored within it. It is now time to review our interview notes and business guidelines to determine what combination of constraints and triggers will need to be applied to verify that our data maintains its integrity in production. We will also consider indexes and other modifications to maximize the performance. Exercise 4-4 will help us get started.

EXERCISE 4-4

Assess the Potential Impact of the Logical Design on Performance, Maintainability, Extensibility, Scalability, Availability, and Security

In Exercise 4-2, we outlined the database schema that we would be using and made decisions about normalization. Let's review these decisions and determine how they impact our database. Do you recognize any issues with these decisions?

1. The golf tee times and tennis court tables were modified to list four participants because that is the set limit for participation. _____

   This improves the performance for retrieving reservations but may have a negative impact on maintainability and extensibility if the club decides to allow five golfers to play together.

2. The scheduling table may include employee names as well as their IDs. _____

   This improves performance by eliminating a join between the employee table and the schedule table. This also eliminates contention for the employee table if there are a large number of users. We may impact security because employee names are stored in multiple locations.

3. The invoices table may contain information about the member making the purchase. _____

   This improves performance by eliminating joins between the membership table and the invoices table, but may have a negative impact on security if a member's billing information, such as credit cards, are stored in multiple locations.

CERTIFICATION SUMMARY

In this chapter, we have examined the key concepts that govern the creation of a logical database design and the SQL Server functionality that can be used to implement them. You should now understand how to identify entities, make tables of them, and identify the relationships that exist between them. In your first pass at developing the database, you will create a fully normalized database that complies with the five normal forms that we discussed in detail. If this database were implemented, we would typically find reasonable performance. This is the science portion of creating a database. After the normalized database is designed, it is time to apply the art of database design.

Some databases will not provide adequate performance in a fully normalized state. In these situations, you will use denormalization strategies to reduce the number of joins required to complete frequent queries as well as maintain totals and subtotals, in an effort to reduce the number of intense arithmetic functions competing for system resources.

With the entities identified and defined, we outlined how to use complete logical design through constraints, properties, and triggers. We were able to establish entity integrity, domain integrity, referential integrity, and any necessary user-defined integrity. We also identified how defaults and rules continue to be supported in SQL Server 7.0 for the sake of backward compatibility, but are not the preferred mechanism for enforcing integrity. You now have the tools needed to build a logical database model.

 # TWO-MINUTE DRILL

❑ The first step in creating a successful relational database implementation comes from the creation of a good logical design for the database. This includes designing the tables and defining the relationships between them.

❑ Designing SQL Server databases effectively begins with a normalized database design. A well thought-out, logical database design provides the foundation for optimal database and application performance.

❑ *Normalization* is the process of removing redundancies from the data.

❑ Prior to normalization, database designs often consist of a few wide tables. The process of normalizing a database consists of breaking the tables down to represent the smallest data entities possible.

❑ SQL Server allows columns to be defined to allow null values. A null value indicates that a field has no value. Although it can be useful to allow null values in isolated cases, it is best to use them sparingly, because null values require special handling that increases the complexity of data operations.

❑ Although normalization consists of five rules, called *forms*, only the first three normal forms are generally a concern for producing a normalized database. The first normal form simply states that no multivalue columns may exist within a table. The second normal form states that nonkey columns must be related to all columns that comprise the primary key. The third normal form states that any nonkey column cannot depend on another nonkey column.

❑ If a database has a solid database design, other performance issues can be resolved after the database is in production. If the database schema is designed poorly, the related performance issues can only be addressed by changing the design of the database.

❑ Normalization often leads down the path of efficient database design, but there are tradeoffs to normalization. A database that is used primarily for decision support (as opposed to update-intensive transaction processing) may not have redundant updates and may be more understandable and efficient for queries if the design is not fully normalized.

❑ A generally accepted rule of thumb for reasonable normalization allows the inclusion of few regularly executed queries that use joins involving more than four tables.

❑ Entity integrity defines a row as a unique entity within a particular table.

❑ Domain integrity specifies the validity of a specific data entry within a given column.

❑ Referential integrity is used to preserve a defined relationship between two tables when records are added or deleted.

❑ User-defined integrity allows the administrator to define additional business rules that do not fall into any of the other integrity categories.

❑ A table typically has a column or combination of columns whose values can be used to uniquely identify each row in the table. This column (or columns) is called the primary key of the table.

❑ The UNIQUE constraint is used to enforce uniqueness on nonprimary key columns. The UNIQUE constraint has a function that is similar to that of the PRIMARY KEY constraint, but it can allow null values.

❑ An administrator can specify multiple UNIQUE constraints within a table.

❑ The IDENTITY property can be applied to a column with a decimal, int, smallint, tinyint, or numeric data type. The IDENTITY property generates a value that is unique within the table.

❑ The column that has the IDENTITY property can be referenced in a select list by using the IDENTITYCOL keyword. The OBJECTPROPERTY function can be used to determine if a table has an identity column.

❑ A DEFAULT definition for the column inserts a predefined value into the column if a value is not given.

❑ You cannot place a default on a column with a timestamp data type or on a column with the IDENTITY property specified. In either situation, the system is attempting to provide the value by default.

❑ A FOREIGN KEY constraint consists of a column or combination of columns used to enforce a link between data in two tables.

❑ The FOREIGN KEY constraint can be linked to a UNIQUE constraint, as well as the more common PRIMARY KEY constraint.

❑ A CHECK constraint is used to enforce domain integrity by limiting the acceptable values for a column.

❑ The NOT NULL constraint can be used in combination with the FOREIGN KEY constraint to eliminate alternatives to meeting the FOREIGN KEY constraints.

❑ The PRIMARY KEY and FOREIGN KEY constraints can be used together to enforce referential integrity, as well as entity and domain integrity. To provide referential integrity, this implementation of a foreign key must be linked to a primary key in another table.

❑ User-defined integrity allows you to define specific business rules that do not fall into one of the other integrity categories. The primary tools that Microsoft provides for enforcing business rules are triggers.

❑ A *trigger* is a special type of stored procedure that is automatically invoked whenever the data in the table is modified. Although stored procedures can perform similar functions, they are bypassed if the data is accessed directly.

❑ Triggers can be invoked in response to INSERT, UPDATE, or DELETE statements.

❑ Constraints are typically more efficient than triggers, rules, and defaults. The query optimizer uses constraints to improve performance in selectivity estimation, cost calculations, and query rewriting.

❑ A table may have more than one combination of columns that could uniquely identify the rows in a table; each combination is a candidate key. The database administrator picks one of the candidate keys to be the primary key.

❑ Both defaults and rules are created as objects within the database and are then bound to specific data columns or user-defined data types.

❑ Default object is a backward-compatibility feature that overlaps the functionality provided by DEFAULT definitions. DEFAULT definitions are the preferred method to restrict column data because the definition is stored with the table and automatically dropped when the table is dropped.

❑ Rule objects are similar to defaults in how they are implemented. Rules are created and then bound to columns or user-defined data types.

❑ Rule objects are primarily provided with SQL Server 7.0 for backward compatibility and are more limited than the CHECK constraints that provide the same functionality.

❑ Constraints and properties are the preferred method for maintaining data integrity. They are stored with the tables.

❑ Null values hinder performance in SQL Server. When possible, specify NOT NULLS and provide a default definition.

❑ Avoid using Rule or Default objects. These items exist primarily for backward compatibility.

❑ Indexes should be used to optimize query performance—not to enforce data integrity.

❑ The logical plan serves both as a guide to use when implementing the database and as a functional specification for the database after it has been implemented.

SELF TEST

The following questions will help you measure your understanding of the material presented in this chapter. Read all of the choices carefully, as there may be more than one correct answer. Choose all correct answers for each question.

1. Which normal form requires that a query be able to reassemble a table that was divided into multiple tables for normalization purposes?

    A. First normal form

    B. Second normal form

    C. Third normal form

    D. Fourth normal form

    E. Fifth normal form

2. Which normal form specifies that nonkey fields in a table must relate to the key field(s) in the table?

    A. First normal form

    B. Second normal form

    C. Third normal form

    D. Fourth normal form

    E. Fifth normal form

3. Which normal form specifies that tables must be flat and that each row must contain only one set of values?

    A. First normal form

    B. Second normal form

    C. Third normal form

    D. Fourth normal form

    E. Fifth normal form

4. Which normal form requires related data entities to be included in one table?

    A. First normal form

    B. Second normal form

    C. Third normal form

    D. Fourth normal form

    E. Fifth normal form

5. Which form dictates that no column in a normalized table can be dependent upon a nonkey column in the table?

    A. First normal form

    B. Second normal form

    C. Third normal form

    D. Fourth normal form

    E. Fifth normal form

6. Which of the following is not a benefit of narrow normalized tables?

    A. Reduce the amount of data returned for simple queries.

    B. Improve performance of range searches due to clustered indexes.

    C. Improve performance from multitable joins.

    D. Lower overhead by reducing the number of indexes in each table.

7. Which of the following is not a good reason to denormalize your database schema?

   A. To reduce the number of joins required to satisfy frequent queries

   B. To benefit a decision-support database with standard queries

   C. To store the results of frequently performed arithmetic calculations

   D. To reduce overhead by decreasing the number of tables

8. When designing your table, you specify a PRIMARY KEY constraint on the empl_id column. Which of the following is this an example of?

   A. Entity integrity

   B. Domain integrity

   C. Referential integrity

   D. User-defined integrity

9. When designing the schedule table, you specify the empl_id column as a foreign key related to the employee table. What type of integrity are you building into your database?

   A. Entity integrity

   B. Domain integrity

   C. Referential integrity

   D. User-defined integrity

10. When designing our database, we set a trigger to make sure that if the country code is set to US, the Zip1 column contains five numeric characters. What type of integrity have you created?

    A. Entity integrity

    B. Domain integrity

    C. Referential integrity

    D. User-defined integrity

11. When designing a table, you add a check constraint to verify that the employee ID contains nine characters and has valid characters in each position. What type of integrity are you enforcing?

    A. Entity integrity

    B. Domain integrity

    C. Referential integrity

    D. User-defined integrity

12. What is the best method to enforce uniqueness for values being placed into a nonkey column?

    A. Create a Unique Index on the field.

    B. Set a UNIQUE constraint.

    C. Set a PRIMARY KEY constraint.

    D. Set a FOREIGN KEY constraint.

13. You are migrating your application from Microsoft Access to SQL Server 7.0. The Access database has a column with a *counter* data type that automatically assigns a member number (by adding one to the member number of the last row added) when records are added to the

member table. What data type and property can accomplish the same function in SQL Server?

A. Varchar(10) with the count property

B. Varchar(10) with the IDENTITY property

C. Int with the count property

D. Int with the IDENTITY property

14. You are creating a database to support a Human Resources application. Your users explain that when the support staff first enters records, they do not have a way to enter the starting salary. You know that you don't want NULLs in this field and decide that because it is a money data type, you will enter 0 if a value is not specified. What is the recommended method to implement this solution?

A. Modify the application to enter a 0 if the user doesn't set a value.

B. Create a Default object and bind it to the money data type.

C. Set a DEFAULT definition of 0 for the column.

D. Do nothing; the money data type defaults to 0.

15. Which of the following is not a good use of a trigger?

A. Verify that the data in the state column matches the data in the area code column.

B. Verify that the data entered for starting salary falls within the range stored in another table for this job class.

C. Roll back the deletion of a customer record if a search of the orders table shows they have placed an order in the past 90 days.

D. Roll back an update to the salary field if it is increasing by more than 20 percent.

MCDBA

MICROSOFT CERTIFIED DATABASE ADMINISTRATOR

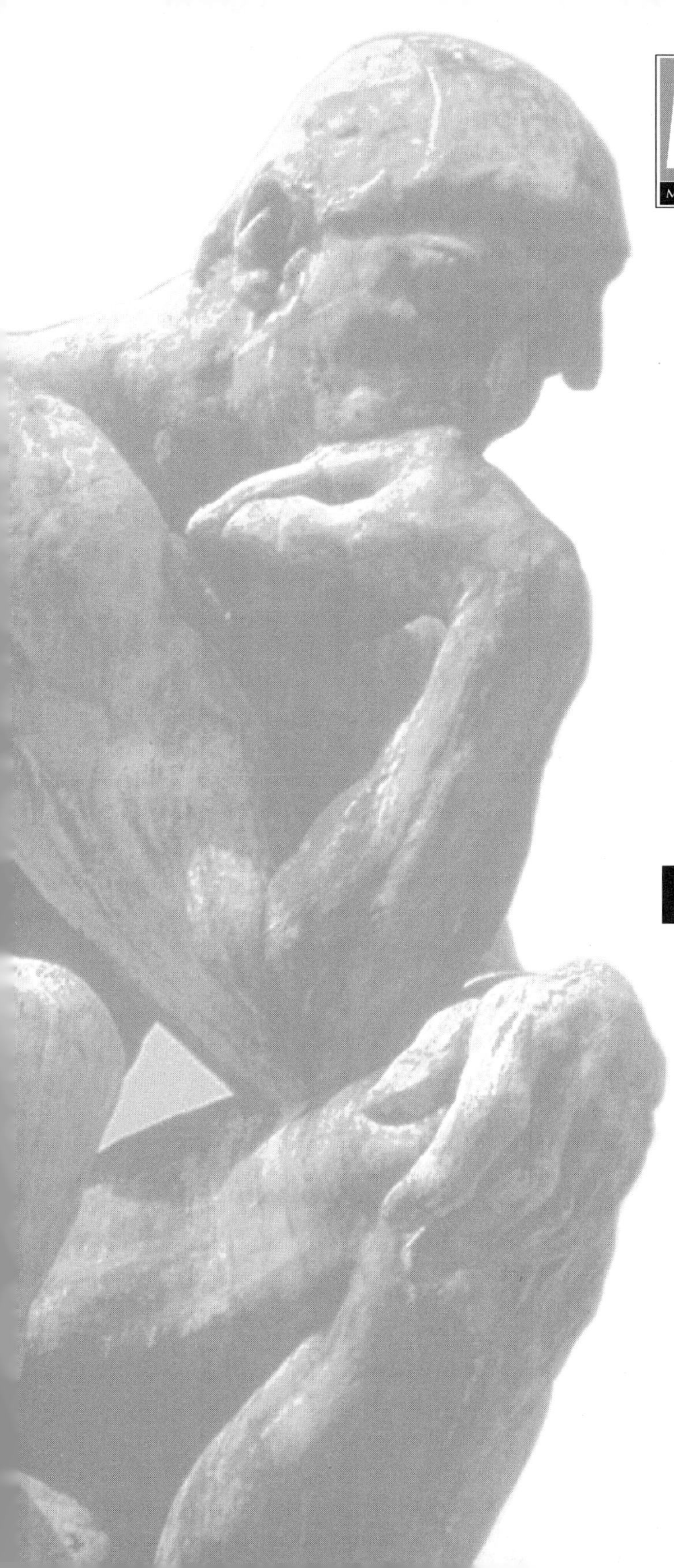

5

Planning and Creating Indexes

CERTIFICATION OBJECTIVES

5.01	Introduction to Indexes
5.02	Creating Indexes
5.03	Index Architecture
5.04	CREATE INDEX Syntax

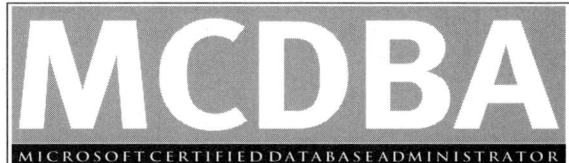

W hen working to improve the performance of Microsoft SQL Server (all versions), it is important to understand that the performance gains come from reducing the amount of physical disk activity. There are a number of hardware changes that can be made to assist in these efforts, including the addition of more physical memory to increase the percentage of queries resolved from the data cache rather than requiring a read from the physical disk. There are also a number of SQL Server configuration and database design changes that will reduce the amount of disk input/output (I/O), if configured properly.

In this chapter we are going to focus on the use of indexes to improve performance by reducing the amount of data that must be read from the disk to retrieve the desired information. We will also discuss the total impact of indexes and provide you with the framework to understand why it is not efficient to create indexes on all fields within your database. Let's get started.

Introduction to Indexes

If you have ever picked up a book to search for a small piece of information that you know is contained inside, did you read from the beginning of the book until you find the information you were looking for? Although this approach would have worked, most likely you counted on either the table of contents or an index in the book to assist you in finding the desired information. Indexes within a book are very similar to the database indexes that we are going to teach you how (and when) to create and use within your database. The book index helped you to find the desired information quickly without reading from the beginning of the book. A database index allows you to retrieve information from your database without reading from the beginning of the table. The book's index contains a list of words (the keys) and a page number where that topic is discussed (the pointer). Our database indexes contain a list of values from one or more columns of the table (the keys) and the address of the data page in which the data is contained (the pointer).

Although many books that you come across will contain a single index grouping all keywords in alphabetical order for your reference, some will contain multiple indexes. For example, I recently picked up a book of Bruce Springsteen's lyrics. This book provides two separate indexes. The first index sorts the title of each song in alphabetical order and provides the page on which it is located. The second index sorts the first line of each song into alphabetical order and provides the page number where the song is located. By having two indexes, I only need to know one of the two pieces of information to find the complete song and related information. This same concept applies to database tables. You may elect to create multiple indexes on a table so that the table may be accessed using indexes, if any indexed information is available.

In the Northwind database, many of the tables have more than one index. In Figure 5-1, we see that the Customers table for example, contains five separate indexes to accelerate searches by name, city, postal code, region, or customer ID. With these indexes in place, if the user queries the table looking for a company by name, SQL Server looks for this name in the appropriate index (CompanyName) and finds the address of the data page where the record is stored. Once it has that address, SQL Server goes directly to that 8KB data page and retrieves the record. If this index did not exist, SQL Server would go to the beginning of the table and read every 8KB page used by the table—we call this process a table scan. Tables that are created without a clustered index are referred to as *heaps*.

CERTIFICATION OBJECTIVE 5.02

Creating Indexes

There are two primary methods for an administrator to create an index: using a graphical tool such as the Enterprise Manager or through an SQL

Indexes on the Customers
table in Northwind

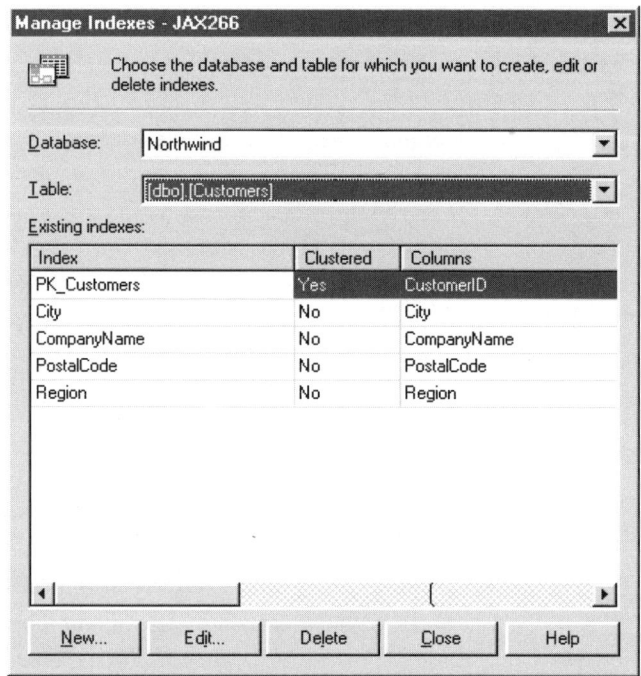

query. We will take a look at both of these approaches in this chapter, but let's begin with the Enterprise Manager.

Creating Indexes Using the Enterprise Manager

With the ease of administration provided by the Enterprise Manager, many administrators will prefer to create and administer indexes on their tables. For example, as the administrator of the Northwind database, your users are complaining that when they access information about employees, the system is too slow in providing information. Within the Enterprise Manager, you choose the Manage Indexes option on the Employees table and see the screen shown in Figure 5-2.

You now have the information you need to meet with the users. At the meeting, they explain that the CEO often asks them for a list of employees who

FIGURE 5-2

Indexes on the Northwind
Employees table

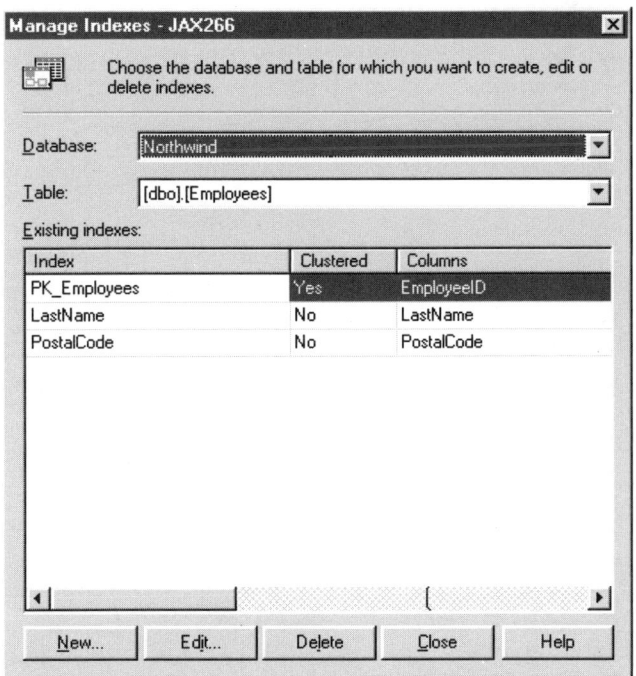

are working in a particular city. These queries often take 30 seconds or more to return the information. Although this doesn't sound like a lot, other queries are returning in less than five seconds and the CEO does not like waiting for this information. As a database administrator with career aspirations, you decide to add an index on the city field to help the performance. As you can see in Figure 5-3, you selected the New button and specified the name and fields to include in the index.

With the new index created, you ask your users to test performance before meeting with you later in the day. You enter the meeting expecting to hear that you have saved the day, but instead, the users tell you there was no improvement. You ask them further information about their application and learn that when querying for employees in a city, they provide region and city information. Further investigation tells you that the query is on region, then city. You now must modify the index that you have created. In

FIGURE 5-3

Creating a new index in
Enterprise Manager

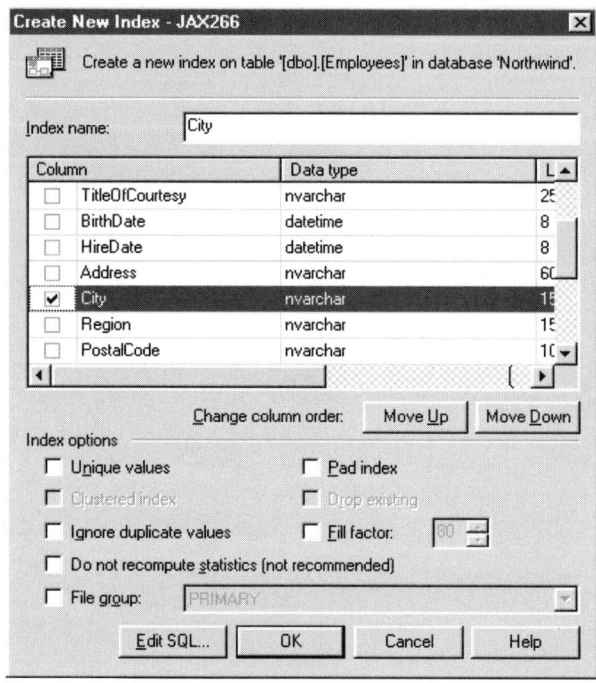

Figure 5-4, you see how you are rebuilding the index to include the region and city fields.

You will notice that we used the Move Up button to move the region field to the top, making it the left column in our index. If we had not done this on our query which matched on Region, then City would not have used our index. We have one more meeting with our users, and they tell us they are now experiencing performance in less than five seconds.

In this section, we learned about the process of creating and administering indexes, as well as a little about how indexes impact performance. Exercise 5-1 puts this knowledge into practice.

EXERCISE 5-1

Creating and Maintaining Indexes

Our users are very happy with the responsiveness for their searches for employees based on the city in which they work. They have since

FIGURE 5-4

Modifying the City index

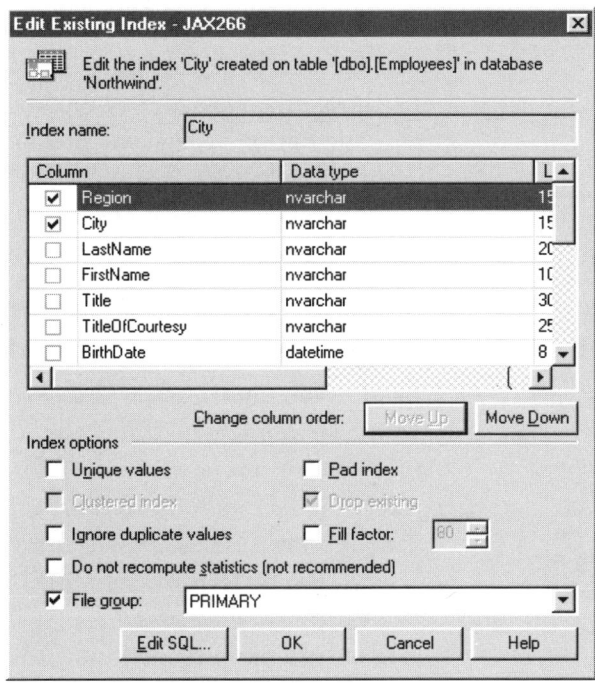

discovered that when they attempt to perform a similar search for
suppliers, they continue to have a 30-second response time. They would
like us to help them improve the performance if possible.

1. Is there currently an index on the region and city within the
   suppliers table? _____ Where did you go in the Enterprise
   Manager to determine this? _____

   There is not an index by default. We can determine this by opening
   the Manage Indexes window of SQL Server (under All Tasks on the
   right-click shortcut menu) and selecting the Northwind database and
   Suppliers table.

2. What columns currently have indexes on them?

   _____

   SupplierID, CompanyName, and PostalCode

3. Create the necessary index with a name of SupplierLocation. What steps did you go through?

Press the New button, enter the name, **SupplierLocation**, select the Region column and press the Move Up button until it is the top field, select the City column and press the Move Up button until it is right below the Region column, and press OK.

Check the index list to verify that you have added the desired index.

Choosing an Indexing Strategy to Optimize Performance

Now that you understand that indexes speed the retrieval of information, your intuition might be telling you to create indexes on every column. Avoid this urge for now, and we'll discuss why this is unlikely to create an optimal configuration. Indexes are similar to other database design decisions—their use can provide benefits to some transactions while inhibiting the performance of other transactions.

Indexes provide a performance trade-off, so let's take a closer look at which indexes optimize performance and which have a negative impact. The overall performance of each database depends on interaction between the indexes and the mix of queries performed against the database. Many applications have a complex mixture of queries with directly opposing performance demands. In these situations, interviewing users provides details about what is important to them but may not provide the details needed to understand the priority and frequency of use. In these situations, it is necessary to make your best estimate of indexes, place the database into production, and monitor performance; making adjustments as appropriate. When developing your index strategy, it is important to plan for indexes that are created as a result of other design activities. SQL Server 7.0 automatically creates indexes when PRIMARY KEY and UNIQUE constraints are created.

Database work can be broken into two primary categories: data manipulation and data retrieval. An index on the fields that you are using to retrieve your data typically improves the performance of the SQL Server database. On the other hand, the process of inserting new data is slowed down by the existence of indexes because SQL Server must write the new row in the table and insert new rows into each index on the table. For updates, the performance implications are mixed. Indexes can speed the process of retrieving the record but may slow the writing of changes.

The performance benefits of indexes, however, do come with a cost. Tables with indexes require more storage space in the database. Also, commands that insert, update, or delete data can take longer and require more processing time to maintain the indexes. When you design and create indexes, you should ensure that the performance benefits outweigh the extra cost in storage space and processing resources.

Microsoft has supplied administrators with a tool to provide assistance in creating indexes in SQL Server version 7.0. The Index Tuning Wizard is provided to help administrators create the proper indexes in a database. When the Index Tuning Wizard is launched, you are presented with the screen in Figure 5-5. This screen prompts you to provide the server and database name on which you wish to establish indexes. In addition, it allows

FIGURE 5-5

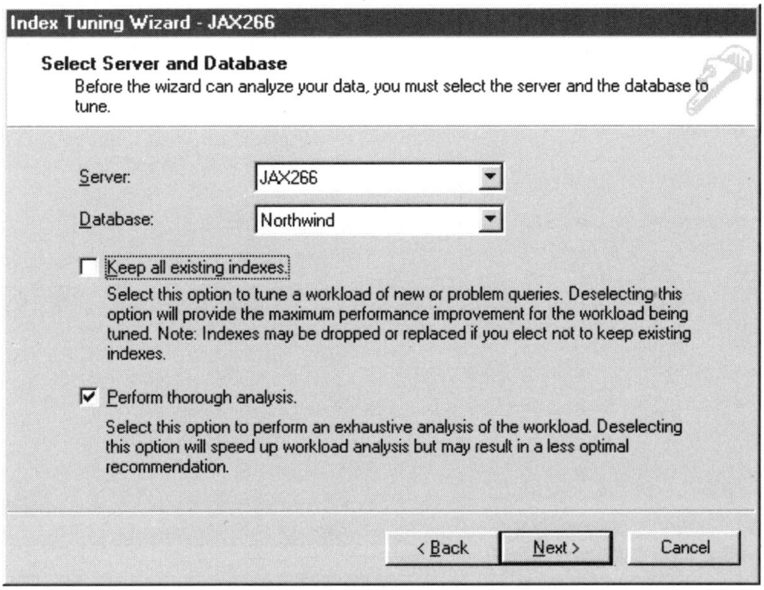

Use the Index Tuning Wizard to help create the proper indexes in a database

the administrator to determine if he or she wants to keep the existing indexes or begin with a clean slate.

If the administrator has a solid understanding of the user's requirements and usage of the database, it is recommended that a thorough analysis be performed. If not, it is more efficient to perform a high-level analysis to get the server into production, and perform a detailed analysis after the database is in production and more detailed information is available. When performing a thorough analysis, the Index Tuning Wizard presents the screen in Figure 5-6. The wizard needs to know if the administrator has saved a SQL Server Profiler trace to provide a sample of the production workload that the database will experience. If the database is new, it's not possible to have a production trace, so the designer must create a sample file by executing specific queries.

In either case, you need to have a SQL Server Profiler trace file in order to use the wizard to set indexes. SQL Server uses the screen in Figure 5-7 to prompt for the appropriate trace file to use.

FIGURE 5-6

Selecting a SQL Server Profiler trace for the Index Tuning Wizard

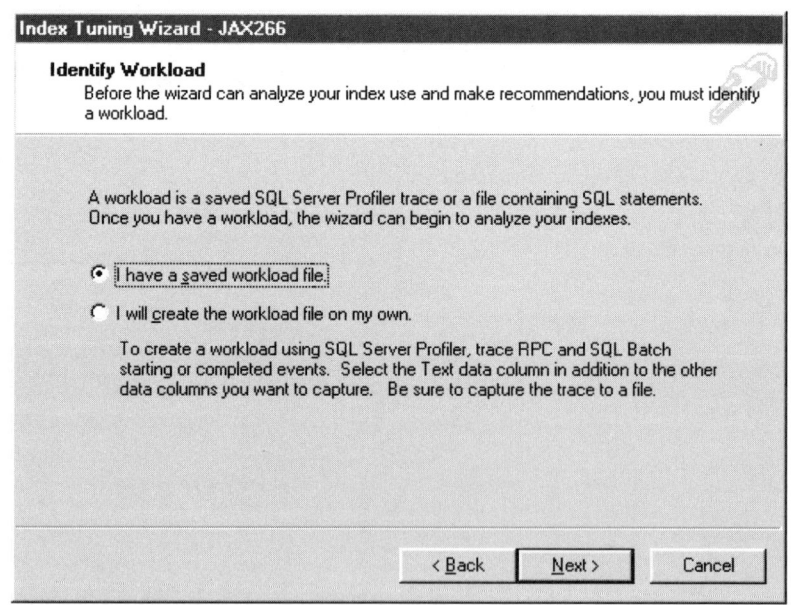

FIGURE 5-7

Specifying the trace file
for the Index Tuning
Wizard

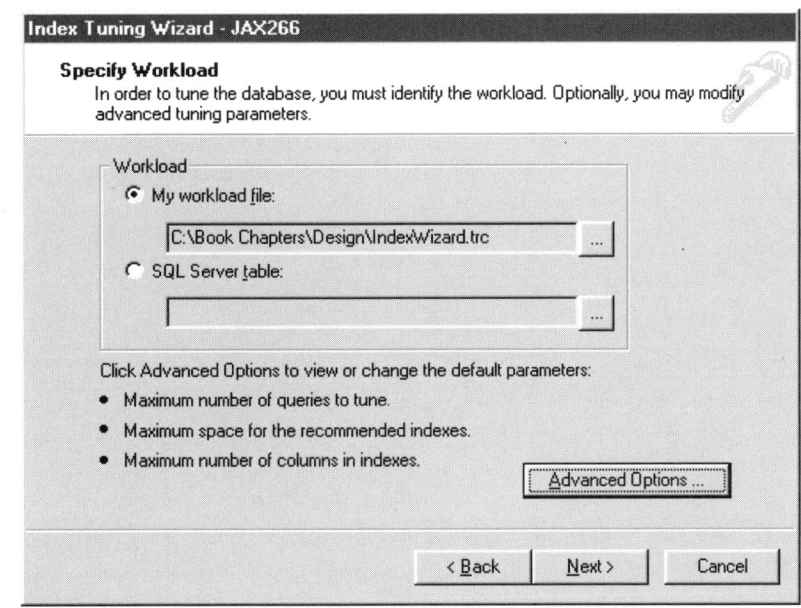

If desired, you may select Advanced Options and establish the specific details, as shown in Figure 5-8. The wizard calculates the space consumed by the existing database and indexes. The advanced features allow us to control how many columns can be used in a single index, how much total space can be dedicated to indexes, and how many queries from the trace file should be used to generate indexes.

After you have established what trace file to use and established any additional requirements, you will see the screen in Figure 5-9, and will need to identify the tables for which you wish to create or modify indexes. Best practices dictate that you select the entire database for initial setup, but you may perform updates and ongoing maintenance on one table at a time.

The Index Tuning Wizard now has all of the information that it needs to calculate what indexes will provide the greatest benefit based upon the queries contained in the trace file. The screen in Figure 5-10 shows sample results of the wizard. In this particular example, SQL Server is recommending indexes that already exist, so no performance gains are expected.

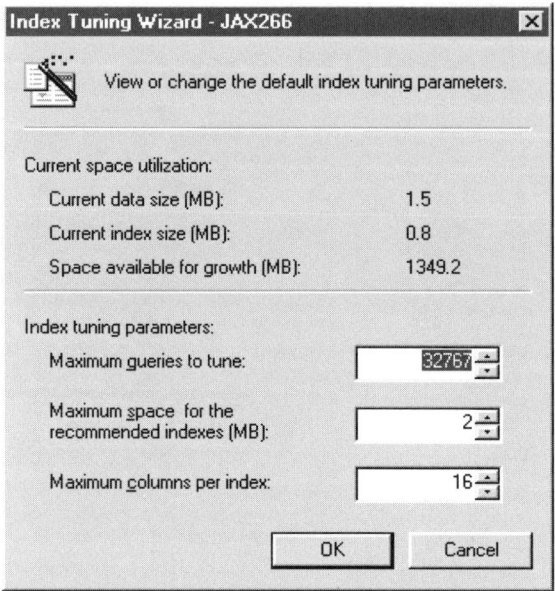

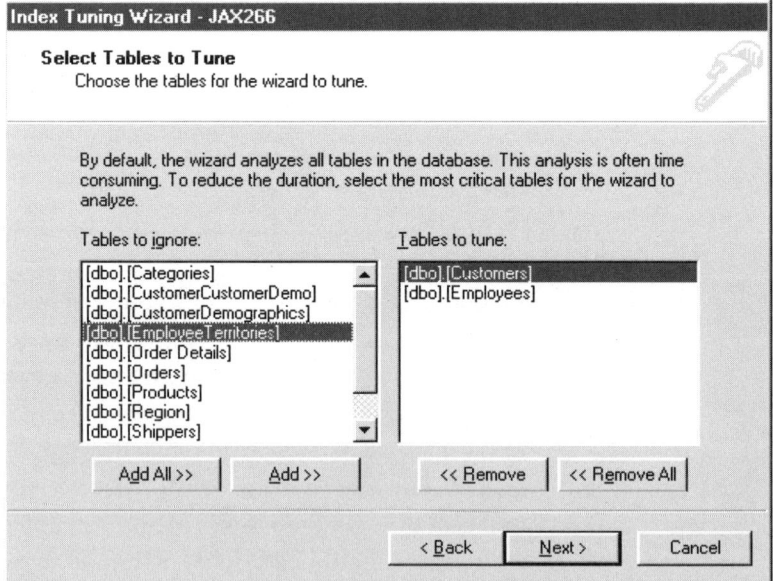

FIGURE 5-10

The Index Tuning Wizard
recommends indexes for
the selected tables

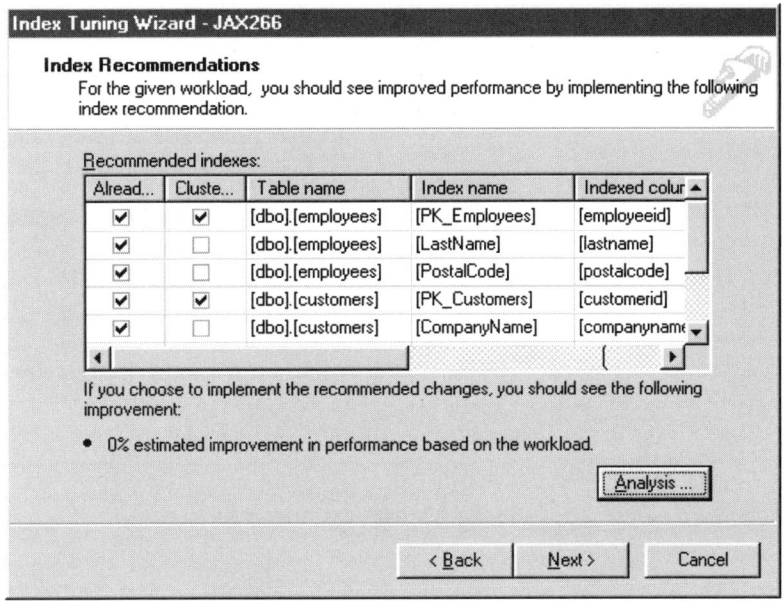

If desired, you can select the Analysis button and get greater detail
about the recommendations being made by SQL Server. In Figure 5-11,
the Index Tuning Wizard shows the cost-based performance improvements
related to each query. This report allows you to verify that accepting
changes will not have a significantly negative impact on critical queries.
Other analysis information is available, such as the Index Usage Report
which documents the percentage of queries (in the trace file) that will be
resolved using the recommended indexes.

After you have reviewed the information provided, the only step left to
perform is to decide whether the changes should be implemented. You see in
Figure 5-12 that the wizard provides you with the option of implementing
changes immediately, scheduling them for a point in the future, or merely
saving them as a script that can be implemented in the future if you so desire.

Exercise 5-2 will take us through the steps in developing an indexing
strategy.

Reviewing the analysis of the index recommendations

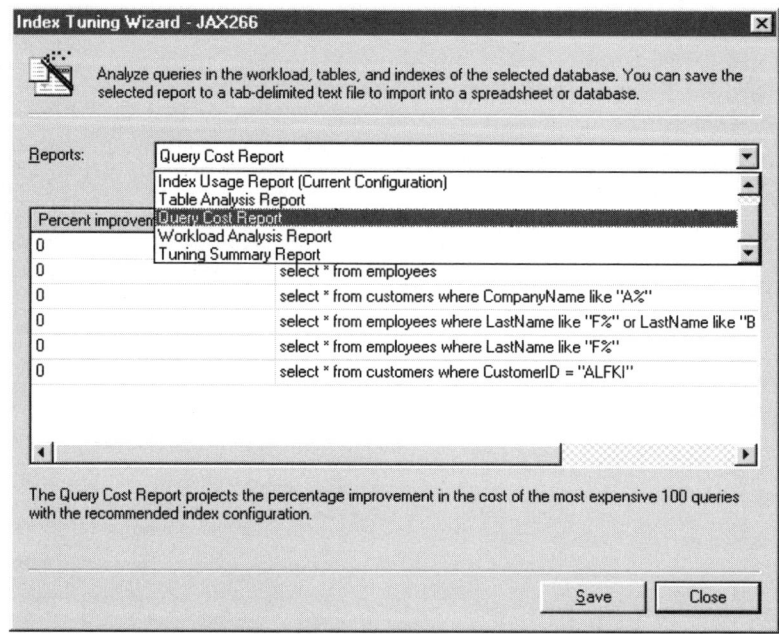

Choosing the Column or Columns to Index

In Chapter 4 we designed a database for a local country club. We now must review the tables and develop an indexing strategy. We are going to focus on the Members table and the Invoices table. The table designs are listed as follows:

Members	Invoices
Member_No—Primary Key	Invoice_No—Primary Key
Last_Name	Date
First_Name	Amount
Address	Member_No—Foreign Key
City	Taxable
State	Location

Members	Invoices
Zip	Description
Phone	
PIN	

We know that the business applications allow members to be looked up by their full member number or by any portion of their last name. Invoices are accessed by their invoice number or by date. The members also have the flexibility to check the balance on their account by calling the club from their home phone. The application uses TAPI to look up the member information, based upon the phone number they call from and the PIN number they enter.

Please note that there is not sufficient information to state that there is only one right answer for this indexing exercise. The most important factors in this exercise are to create your own answers and the reasons for

FIGURE 5-12

Accepting the Index Tuning Wizard recommendations

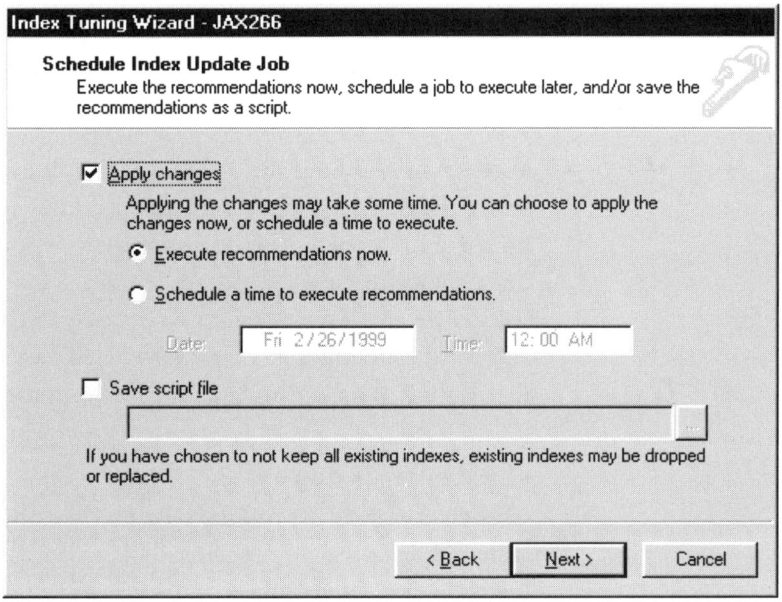

Index Tuning Wizard - JAX266

Schedule Index Update Job
Execute the recommendations now, schedule a job to execute later, and/or save the recommendations as a script.

☑ Apply changes
Applying the changes may take some time. You can choose to apply the changes now, or schedule a time to execute.

○ Execute recommendations now.

○ Schedule a time to execute recommendations.

Date: Fri 2/26/1999   Time: 12:00 AM

☐ Save script file

If you have chosen to not keep all existing indexes, existing indexes may be dropped or replaced.

< Back   Next >   Cancel

them, as well as to understand the answers that are provided. You will find this skill to be critical to your success with production SQL Server databases as well as a primary goal in preparing for your SQL Server exam.

1. On what fields in the Members table would you place an index? Why? _____

   We would place an index on the following fields:

   ■ **Member_No**   The application looks up member information and also is used in all joins of the Members table and the Invoices table.

   ■ **Last_Name**   The application looks up member information.

   ■ **Phone**   The application looks up user information and account balances based upon the phone number the user is calling from.

2. On what fields in the Invoices table would you place an index? Why? _____

   We would place an index on the following fields:

   ■ **Invoice_No**   The application looks up invoice information based upon this field.

   ■ **Date**   The application look up invoices based upon the date field.

Types of Indexes

You now understand the purpose that indexes serve and the right place to use them. We now need to take this knowledge a step further and understand the details of how indexes function. It is also important to understand the types of indexes and how their behaviors differ. In this section we are going to look more closely at clustered, nonclustered, unique, and composite indexes. It is this detailed level of understanding that allows the administrator to implement indexes in the optimal configuration.

Clustered Indexes

Clustered indexes are unique because they physically sort the data in the table to which they are applied. This means that in a clustered index, the lowest level of index nodes, known as leaf nodes, contain the actual data rows. The data pages and the rows in them are ordered on the value of the clustered index key. The only time the rows in a table are stored in a presorted order is when there is a clustered index on the table. As rows are inserted, they are placed at the location where the key value in the inserted row fits in the ordering sequence. Because a clustered index sorts the physical data, there can only be one clustered index on a table. The clustered index can be a composite index spanning multiple columns.

For a clustered index, the sysindexes.root points to the top of the clustered index. SQL Server navigates down the index (intermediate pages) to find the row corresponding to a clustered index key. To find a range of rows based on the clustered index keys, SQL Server navigates through the index to find the starting key value in the range, and then performs a table scan until it finds the first key value that no longer meets the query requirements. For example, an application executes a query to retrieve records within a range of dates. A clustered index will efficiently locate the first row that meets the search criteria and then retrieve all consecutive rows until the last row that meets the date criteria is reached. As a result of this search technique, clustered indexes are particularly efficient when used on columns that are often searched for ranges of values. SQL Server is greatly impacted by physical disk I/O. The ability to return a range of records while minimizing the movement of the read/write heads greatly improves the performance of this query, as well as the overall performance of SQL Server. The same technique can benefit queries that use columns to sort the data retrieved from a table. Clustered indexes on these columns can greatly improve the performance of these queries.

Microsoft has modified the relationship between clustered and nonclustered indexes with the release of SQL Server 7.0. In earlier versions of SQL Server, nonclustered indexes contained keys with a pointer to the location of the data. With the release of version 7.0, all nonclustered indexes that are defined on a table that has a clustered index contain their key and the clustering key. While this change can improve performance, it also increases the importance of limiting the number of columns included in the clustered index key. If a large key is defined in the clustered index, all nonclustered indexes on this table will also be larger.

When deciding which indexes should be clustered, it is important to understand your application, as well as the following guidelines that help you select the column(s) on which to place a clustered index.

- Columns that contain a limited number of distinct values (such as auto manufacturers when identifying a vehicle), often benefit from clustered indexes. Note that this guideline does not supercede the fact that columns with very few distinct values (such as sex—M/F) should not have any indexes.

- If your application submits queries that return a series of rows using operators such as *like, between,* >, >=, <, and <=, a clustered index may significantly improve performance. This is not true if these queries typically return more than 50 percent of the rows in the table. In these situations, the Query Analyzer typically performs a table scan rather than an indexed search.

- Any columns that are frequently used in the ORDER BY or GROUP BY clauses of queries benefit from clustered indexes. When a clustered index is placed on the column(s), SQL Server no longer needs to sort the data to resolve the query because the rows are already in the desired order.

- It is not a good idea to place a clustered index on a column that changes frequently, such as an account balance column. When this is done, every time the column is updated, the entire row has to be moved to a new location to keep the data sorted by the key value. This is an important consideration in high-volume transaction processing systems where data tends to be volatile.

The creation of a clustered index requires free space equal to approximately 120 percent of the data space currently used by the table. The table is duplicated during the process of creating the index.

Nonclustered Indexes

Unlike clustered indexes, nonclustered indexes build a structure that is completely separate from the data rows. The data is not sorted or otherwise moved when a nonclustered index is created or modified. Each index row of the leaf nodes of a nonclustered index contains the index key value and a pointer to the data row that contains the key value. This pointer to the data row is known as the row locator. The structure of the row locator varies, depending on whether there is a clustered index on the table. If no clustered index exists, the row locator is a pointer to the row. For a table that does have a clustered index, the row locator is the clustered index key.

exam
ⓦatch

While there is a limit of one clustered index per table due to the physical sorting of data, SQL Server allows as many as 249 nonclustered indexes per table.

Composite Indexes

Indexes that are created on more than one column are referred to as composite indexes. Composite indexes can contain up to 16 columns. It is important to understand that these indexes are used only when the left portion of the key is being compared. For example, if a composite index is created on the last name followed by the first name, a query matching against the last name or the last name and the first name will use this index. On the other hand, a query matching the first name or the first name and the last name would not use this index.

Exercise 5-3 demonstrates how to create a clustered index.

EXERCISE 5-3

Choosing the Appropriate Type of Index to Create in a Given Situation

In Exercise 5-2 we assigned indexes to the Members and Invoices tables of the CountryClub database. We now realize that our tables might benefit from a clustered index. Our plan is to place indexes on the boldfaced columns in the following table:

Members	Invoices
Member_No—Primary Key	**Invoice_No**—Primary Key
Last_Name	Date
First_Name	Amount
Address	Member_No—Foreign Key
City	Taxable

Members	Invoices
State	Location
Zip	Description
Phone	
PIN	

Let's review what we know about our application. The business application allows members to be looked up by their full member number or by any portion of their last name. Invoices are accessed by their invoice number or by date. The members also have the flexibility to check the balance on their account by calling the club from their home phone. The application uses TAPI to look up the member information based upon the phone number the member calls from and the PIN number they enter.

1. On which field in the Members table would you place the clustered index? _____ Why?

   _____

   We would place the clustered index on the Last_Name field because this is the field that the application uses to retrieve a range of records. For example, it returns all of the members with a last name of Smith.

2. On which field in the Invoices table would you place the clustered index? _____

   Why?

   _____

   We would place the clustered index on the Date field because this is the field that the application uses to retrieve a range of records from the Invoices table.

FROM THE CLASSROOM

Indexes—Supercharged Data Access

The use of indexes to speed up the retrieval of data from tables is an essential part of implementing a database design. Therefore, knowing the ins and outs of index design is a high priority for both efficient design, and for tackling Microsoft's certification exam. Familiarity with some of the following characteristics of indexes is highly recommended:

- Reversing the order of columns in a composite index affects the use of the index.

- Adding indexes to columns with only a very small number of unique values adds overhead to the data retrieval command without any significant benefit.

- Indexes should not be used when a large number of rows will be returned (over 50 percent).

- Increasing the size of a clustered index increases the size of nonclustered index leaf nodes.

In SQL Server 7.0, the architecture of nonclustered indexes created on tables using a clustered index differs from the architecture of these nonclustered indexes in earlier versions. The leaf nodes of the nonclustered indexes contain a row locator comprised of the clustered index key, as you can see in the illustration shown next. Failure to understand this architectural change could result in bloated and inefficient nonclustered indexes.

—*Michael Lane Thomas, MCSE+I, MCSD, MCP+SB, MSS, MCT, A+*

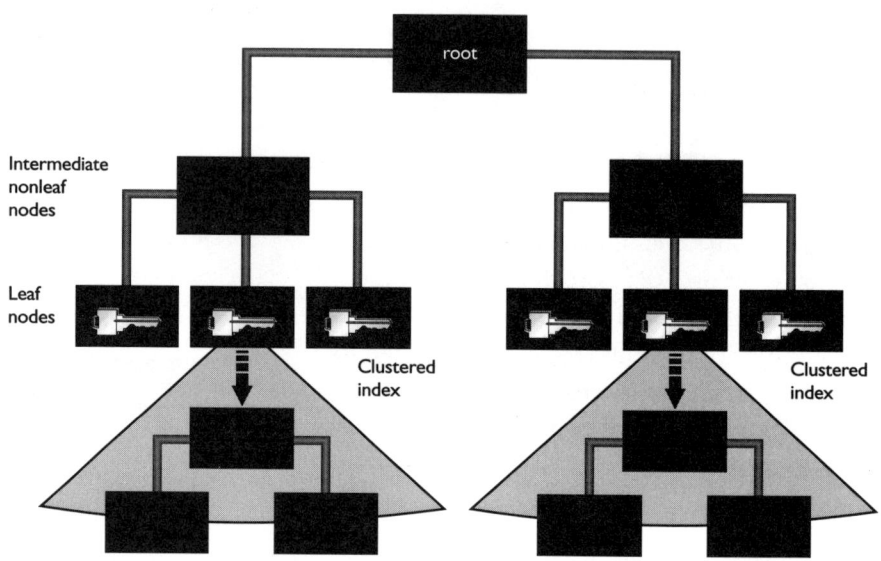

Index Architecture

SQL Server indexes are organized as B-trees. Each index page holds a page header, followed by index rows. Each page of the index is referred to as an index node. There are three levels of index nodes. The top node of the B-tree is called the root node, while the bottom layer of nodes is called the leaf nodes (or leaf pages). All index pages between the root and the leaves are known as intermediate pages.

As we discussed earlier, Microsoft has modified the structure of index pages in version 7.0. The leaf pages of a clustered index continue to contain the actual data rows. On the other hand, the leaf pages of the nonclustered index have been modified. The record contains the key and a pointer to the data row. This pointer, known as the row locator, has one of two structures.

For tables with a clustered index, the row locator is the clustered index key. For tables without a clustered index, the row locator contains a pointer to the data row. As you see in Figure 5-13, the SQL Server index pages also contain headers, which are used by to link the index pages.

The key of a SQL Server index does have a pair of capacity limitations. The key may have a maximum size of 900 bytes. This applies to individual fields being indexed and the total size of composite indexes. In addition, composite indexes may contain up to 16 columns. A 17th column cannot be added, even if the key would contain less than 900 bytes.

on the
job

The best practices for database administration include running the database consistency checker (DBCC) on a regular schedule. The DBCC CHECKTABLE command is used to check database linkages and sizes. This command can be run against specific indexes to verify the integrity of the headers.

In addition to the node pages mentioned above, SQL Server maintains statistics pages for indexes. These pages contain statistical information about the distribution of values in indexed column. The query optimizer uses this statistical information to determine the most cost-effective manner to resolve a query. Although SQL Server used statistics pages in the past, Microsoft modified version 7.0 to provide automated updates of the statistical information. This modification allows the optimizer to have current information on which to base its decisions.

FIGURE 5-13   SQL Server index page structure

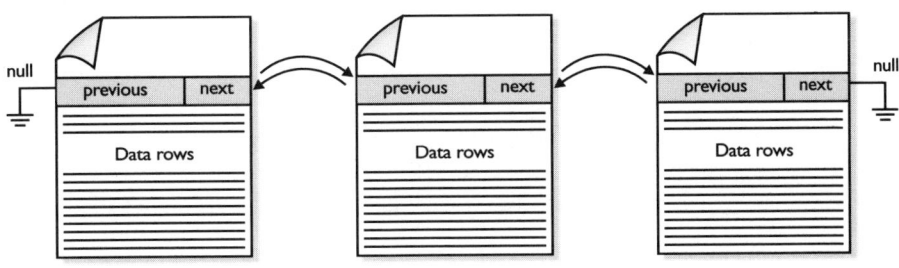

CERTIFICATION OBJECTIVE 5.04

CREATE INDEX Syntax

There are two types of commands that SQL Server supports for the creation of indexes. The first type includes the CREATE DATABASE and ALTER DATABASE commands, and can be used to create indexes if the creator specifies a PRIMARY KEY, FOREIGN KEY, or UNIQUE constraint. The PRIMARY KEY constraint creates a clustered index by default (provided a clustered index doesn't already exist on the table), whereas FOREIGN KEY and UNIQUE constraints create nonclustered indexes by default.

The second type of command that can be used for the creation of indexes is the CREATE INDEX command. This command is used to create indexes that are not used as a part of constraints. Let's take a closer look at this syntax and the options that it provides.

```
CREATE [UNIQUE] [CLUSTERED | NONCLUSTERED]
INDEX index_name ON table (column [,...n])
[WITH
[PAD_INDEX]
[[,] FILLFACTOR = fillfactor]
[[,] IGNORE_DUP_KEY]
[[,] DROP_EXISTING]
[[,] STATISTICS_NORECOMPUTE]
]
[ON filegroup]
```

Although you likely recognize some of the parameters from earlier information, some are new, so we will take a more detailed look at all of the parameters:

■ The UNIQUE parameter can be used to create an index that does not allow more than one row to contain the exact same information in its key field(s). If duplicate keys exist at the time that the CREATE INDEX command is issued, the index creation terminates and returns an error including key information for the first duplicate row. This includes tables that contain more than one row with keys that are completely NULL. Once a unique index has been created, any inserts or updates that result in duplicate keys are rolled back. If this option is not specified, a nonunique index is created.

■ The CLUSTERED and NONCLUSTERED parameters are used to determine what type of index should be created. If the CLUSTERED parameter is specified, SQL Server checks to determine if a clustered index already exists on the table. If there is another clustered index, the command will error out, and the index is not created. If no other clustered index exists, the table is sorted based on the specified key. If neither the CLUSTERED or NONCLUSTERED parameter is provided, SQL Server creates a nonclustered index.

■ The *index_name* parameter allows the creator to specify the name for the index. It is recommended that you create a standard which allows someone looking at the index name to determine whether it is unique, clustered, or nonclustered and what fields are included in the key. For example, if someone looked at an index on the pubs employees table, the name CL_UN_LNAME_FNAME could tell them a clustered, unique, composite index was created on the lname and fname columns. The index name must be unique within a table but does not need to be unique within the database.

■ The FILLFACTOR parameter allows an administrator to specify what percentage of each leaf level of the index pages should be filled with data. This parameter only impacts the index pages at a single point in time. After the index has been created, SQL Server adds information to these pages as rows are inserted and updated. Tables that receive a large volume of changes, such as those in online transaction processing systems (OLTP), can benefit from a low FILLFACTOR value, as this reduces the overhead of splitting pages. On the other hand, tables used in Decision Support Systems benefit from a high FILLFACTOR, as the data will fit in a smaller number of data pages, which reduces the number of reads required to resolve queries. It is important to remember that setting a FILLFACTOR of 50 requires close to double the number of leaf pages for the index. If the index is a clustered index, this doubles the space used by the data. If no FILLFACTOR is specified, SQL Server fills each page to a point that allows at least one additional row to be added to each page.

■ The PAD_INDEX parameter specifies that the intermediate pages of an index should accept the FILLFACTOR value, providing the same level of free space.

■ The IGNORE_DUP_KEY parameter is the most commonly misunderstood parameter in the CREATE INDEX command. This command does not allow a duplicate key to be placed into a unique index. This command determines how SQL Server reacts when a transaction attempts to insert a duplicate row. If the IGNORE_DUP_KEY parameter is set, SQL Server rejects the insert, returns an error message, and allows the remainder of the transaction to continue. If the IGNORE_DUP_KEY parameter is not specified, SQL Server rejects the insert, returns an error message, and rolls back the transaction.(17)

■ The DROP_EXISTING parameter removes an existing index by the same name as the index that is being created. There are two benefits in using this parameter rather than issuing a DROP INDEX statement before the CREATE INDEX command. First, we have discussed how the existence of a clustered index alters the pointers of all nonclustered indexes. If the delete and create are run as two separate commands against a clustered index, the pointers for every nonclustered index are rebuilt twice (once after the delete, and again after the create). When the DROP_EXISTING parameter is used to rebuild a clustered index, the pointers in nonclustered indexes are rebuilt once. The second benefit comes from the fact that if the index keys do not change, SQL Server will create the new index without resorting the data. This is particularly useful when the indexes are being compacted.

■ The STATISTICS_NORECOMPUTE command instructs SQL Server not to automatically recalculate the statistics page for this index. In version 7.0, Microsoft has added the feature of automatically updating these pages. Automated recompute can be enabled by running the UPDATE STATISTICS command without the NORECOMPUTE parameter.

■ The ON *filegroup* parameter allows you to specify where the index should be placed when it is created. It is important to keep in mind that when a clustered index is being created, specifying the location will move the actual data to the specified location.

Exercise 5-4 demonstrates how to modify a clustered index.

Choosing the Appropriate Index Characteristics: FILLFACTOR, DROP_EXISTING, and PAD_INDEX

The users of the Northwind database have informed us that the Orders table will only be used for Decision Support, and they would like us to modify the indexes as necessary to best support this. We determine that the clustered index could be improved.

1. What is the name of the clustered index?

   _____

   PK_orders is the clustered index.

2. What is the desired FILLFACTOR for this clustered index?

   _____

   We would recommend a FILLFACTOR of 100 to limit the number of reads necessary to resolve queries.

3. Should we include the PAD_INDEX option? _____ Why?

   _____

   Yes we should include this option. This will compress all intermediate pages to limit further the number of pages that must be read to resolve a query.

4. What is the full syntax to rebuild this index?

   ```
   Create Clustered Index PK_Orders
   on Orders(OrderID)
   with PAD_INDEX , FILLFACTOR = 100,DROP_EXISTING
   ```

5. Run the above syntax. Does it succeed? _____ Why?

   _____

The command will not execute because this index was created with a PRIMARY KEY constraint, so first, you have to drop the constraint.

CERTIFICATION SUMMARY

In this chapter we have outlined the use and structure of indexes. The two primary types of indexes are clustered and nonclustered. You can create a maximum of one clustered index per table because these indexes physically sort the data in the table. Nonclustered indexes don't sort the data but do provide sorted pointers to the data pages. There is a maximum of 249 nonclustered indexes per page.

We outlined how indexes can benefit query performance but can have a negative impact on the performance of online transaction processing systems. You have to combine this trade-off in performance with the fact that clustered indexes sort the data (and the fact that there is only one allowed per table), in order to prepare a proper indexing strategy. The clustered index is best used for queries that return multiple rows with a serial range of values.

You can create these indexes using graphical tools such as Microsoft Enterprise Manager or via Transact-SQL syntax. When you create the index, you can specify the name of the index, what fields are included in the key, where the index should be created, and how full each index should be. SQL Server uses files and filegroups to specify location. The FILLFACTOR is used to determine what percentage of each leaf page should be filled, but we know that this FILLFACTOR only applies when the index is created—SQL Server does not keep the leaf pages at this fill level.

 # TWO-MINUTE DRILL

❑ When working to improve the performance of Microsoft SQL Server (all versions) it is important to understand that the performance gains come from reducing the amount of physical disk activity.

❑ A database index allows you to retrieve information from your database without reading from the beginning of the table.

❑ Database indexes contain a list of values from one or more columns of the table (the keys) and the address of the data page where the data is contained (the pointer).

❑ There are two primary methods for an administrator to create an index: using a graphical tool such as the Enterprise Manager or through an SQL query.

❑ With the ease of administration provided by the Enterprise Manager, many administrators will prefer to create and administer indexes on their tables.

❑ Indexes are similar to other database design decisions—their use can provide benefits to some transactions while inhibiting the performance of other transactions.

❑ The overall performance of each database depends on interaction between the indexes and the mix of queries performed against the database. Many applications have a complex mixture of queries with directly opposing performance demands.

❑ When developing your index strategy, it is important to plan for indexes that are created as a result of other design activities.

❑ SQL Server 7.0 automatically creates indexes when PRIMARY KEY and UNIQUE constraints are created.

❑ Database work can be broken into two primary categories: data manipulation and data retrieval. An index on the fields that you are using to retrieve your data typically improves the performance of the SQL Server database.

❑ The Index Tuning Wizard is provided to help administrators create the proper indexes in a database.

❑ Clustered indexes are unique because they physically sort the data in the table to which they are applied. This means that in a clustered index, the lowest level of index nodes, known as leaf nodes, contain the actual data rows.

❑ With the release of SQL Server 7.0, all nonclustered indexes that are defined on a table that has a clustered index contain their key and the clustering key. While this change can improve performance, it also increases the importance of limiting the number of columns included in the clustered index key.

❑ Unlike clustered indexes, nonclustered indexes build a structure that is completely separate from the data rows. The data is not sorted or otherwise moved when a nonclustered index is created or modified.

❑ While there is a limit of one clustered index per table due to the physical sorting of data, SQL Server allows as many as 249 nonclustered indexes per table.

❑ Indexes that are created on more than one column are referred to as composite indexes. Composite indexes can contain up to 16 columns.

❑ Reversing the order of columns in a composite index affects the use of the index.

❑ Adding indexes to columns with only a very small number of unique values adds overhead to the data retrieval command without any significant benefit.

❑ Indexes should not be used when a large number of rows will be returned (over 50 percent).

❑ Increasing the size of a clustered index increases the size of nonclustered index leaf nodes.

❑ SQL Server indexes are organized as B-trees. Each index page holds a page header, followed by index rows. Each page of the index is referred to as an index node.

❑ There are three levels of index nodes. The top node of the B-tree is called the root node, while the bottom nodes are called the leaf nodes (or leaf pages). All index pages between the root and the leaves are known as intermediate pages.

❑ The best practices for database administration include running the database consistency checker (DBCC) on a regular schedule.

❑ There are two types of commands that SQL Server supports for the creation of indexes. The first type includes the CREATE DATABASE and ALTER DATABASE commands, and can be used to create indexes if the creator specifies a PRIMARY KEY, FOREIGN KEY, or UNIQUE constraint.

❑ The second type of command that can be used for the creation of indexes is the CREATE INDEX command. This command is used to create indexes that are not used as a part of constraints.

❑ The UNIQUE parameter can be used to create an index that does not allow more than one row to contain the exact same information in its key field(s).

❑ The CLUSTERED and NONCLUSTERED parameters are used to determine what type of index should be created.

❑ The *index_name* parameter allows the creator to specify the name for the index. It is recommended that you create a standard that allows someone looking at the index name to determine whether it is unique, clustered, or nonclustered and what fields are included in the key.

❑ The FILLFACTOR parameter allows an administrator to specify what percentage of each leaf level of the index pages should be filled with data.

❑ The PAD_INDEX parameter specifies that the intermediate pages of an index should accept the FILLFACTOR value, providing the same level of free space.

❑ The IGNORE_DUP_KEY parameter is the most commonly misunderstood parameter in the CREATE INDEX command. This command does not allow a duplicate key to be placed into a unique index. This command determines how SQL Server reacts when a transaction attempts to insert a duplicate row.

❑ The DROP_EXISTING parameter removes an existing index by the same name as the index that is being created.

❑ The STATISTICS_NORECOMPUTE command instructs SQL Server not to recalculate automatically the statistics page for this index.

❑ The ON *filegroup* parameter allows you to specify where the index should be placed when it is created.

SELF TEST

The following questions will help you measure your understanding of the material presented in this chapter. Read all of the choices carefully, as there may be more than one correct answer. Choose all correct answers for each question.

1. What is the term for SQL Server accessing data if it does not use an index?

   A. Direct read

   B. Page scan

   C. Table scan

   D. Page read

2. What option under All Tasks on the shortcut menu in the Enterprise Manager can you use to determine what indexes exist on a table?

   A. View Indexes

   B. Manage Indexes

   C. Table Properties

   D. Index Properties

3. Which of the following wizards does SQL Server 7.0 offer to help you identify changes to your indexes that might help performance?

   A. Create Index Wizard

   B. Delete Index Wizard

   C. Database Maintenance Plan Wizard

   D. Index Tuning Wizard

4. Which of the following SQL Server 7.0 tools provides an input file to the SQL Server Index Tuning Wizard?

   A. SQL Query Analyzer

   B. Enterprise Manager

   C. SQL Server Profiler

   D. SQL Server Service Manager

5. Which of the following types of indexes always sort the data rows?

   A. Clustered indexes

   B. Nonclustered indexes

   C. Composite indexes

   D. Unique indexes

6. Which of the following are included in the leaf pages of a clustered index?

   A. Pointers to disk location

   B. Pointers to the clustered key

   C. Data rows

   D. All of the above

7. How many clustered indexes are allowed on a table?

   A. One

   B. 249

   C. 250

   D. There is no limit.

8. Which of the following columns is a good candidate for a clustered index?

A. A column that must contain 1 of 50 valid values

B. A column that is frequently queried for a serial range of values

C. A column that is frequently used in the order by portion of a query

D. All of the above

9. How much additional space is needed to create a clustered index on a table?

   A. None, the clustered index merely rearranges data

   B. 10 percent more space than the current space consumed by the data

   C. 50 percent more space than the current space consumed by the data

   D. 120 percent more space than the current space consumed by the data

10. Which of the following is found in the row locator of a nonclustered index if the table has a clustered index?

    A. The data row

    B. A pointer to the data row

    C. The clustered index key

    D. None of the above

11. Which of the following is found in the row locator of a nonclustered index if the table does not have a clustered index?

    A. The data row

    B. A pointer to the data row

    C. The clustered index key

    D. None of the above

12. What is the maximum number of columns that can be included in a composite index?

    A. 2

    B. 4

    C. 8

    D. 16

13. Which of the following is not one of the types of nodes in a SQL Server index?

    A. Home node

    B. Root node

    C. Intermediate node

    D. Leaf node

14. What is the maximum size allowed for the key in a SQL Server index?

    A. 100 bytes

    B. 300 bytes

    C. 900 bytes

    D. None of the above

15. If you execute the CREATE INDEX command with the UNIQUE parameter, what happens if rows with duplicate keys exist?

    A. The command terminates.

    B. Nothing, if the IGNORE_DUP_KEY parameter is included.

    C. The command executes and returns a list of duplicate rows.

    D. The command executes.

16. Which of the following is not true if the create index command is run with a FILLFACTOR of 100 percent?

    A. Inserts and updates are slowed down.

    B. The index consumes less space.

    C. Database queries run faster.

    D. None of the above

17. Which of the following is true when the IGNORE_DUP_KEY parameter is applied to an index ?

    A. If duplicate rows exist when the index is created, they are ignored.

    B. If a transaction inserts rows that would duplicate an existing key, the rows are inserted.

    C. If a transaction inserts rows that would duplicate an existing key, those rows are rejected but the transaction completes.

    D. None of the above

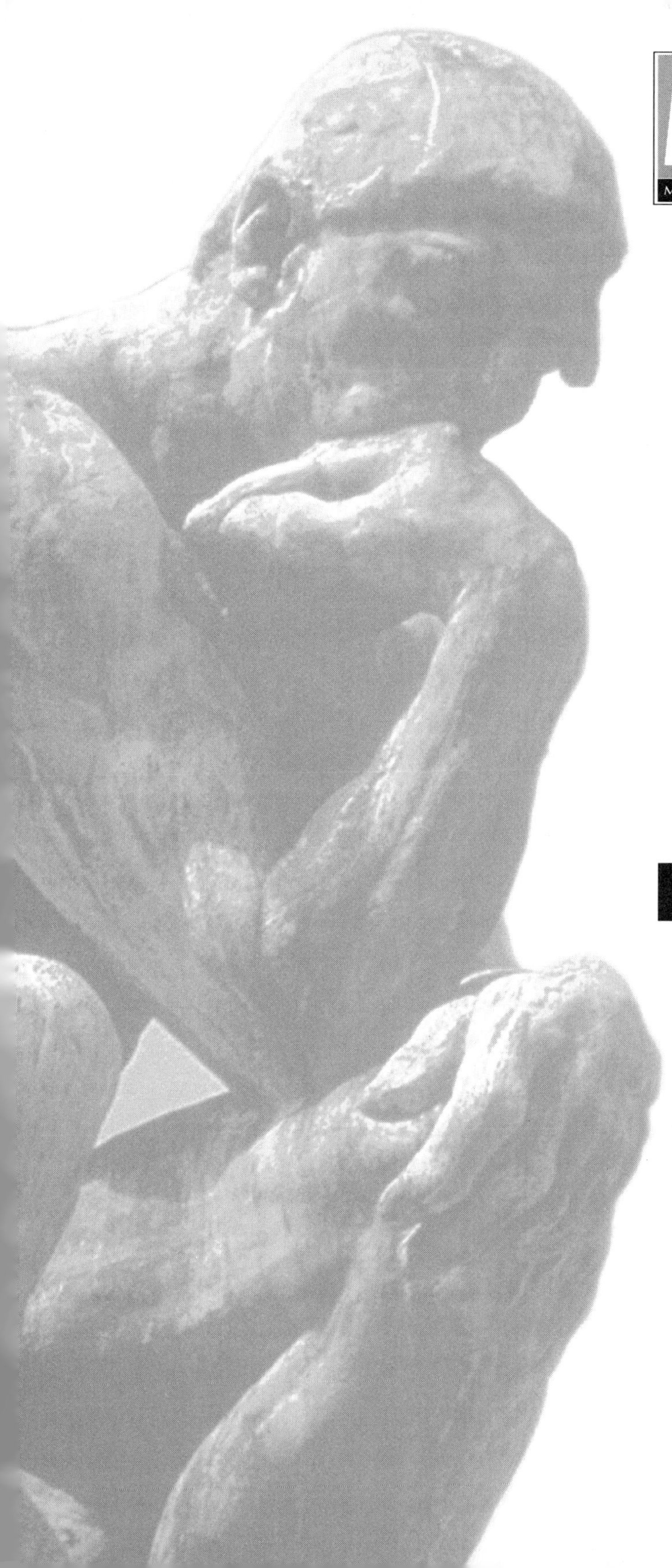

MCDBA

MICROSOFT CERTIFIED DATABASE ADMINISTRATOR

6

Queries

CERTIFICATION OBJECTIVES

6.01	Developing Query Execution Plans
6.02	Combining Data from Multiple Tables
6.03	Combining Multiple Result Sets
6.04	Creating a Table from a Result Set
6.05	Introduction to Subqueries
6.06	Nested Subqueries
6.07	Correlated Subqueries
6.08	Using the EXISTS and NOT EXISTS Keywords
6.09	Modifying Data
6.10	Full-Text Searches

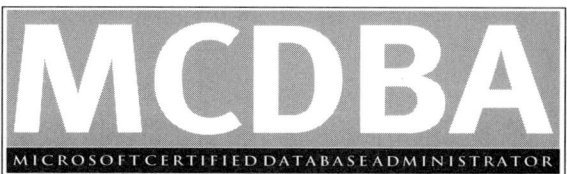

I n Chapter 2 we observed that table normalization can make your database more efficient, but this requires you to create queries to reconstruct the needed data sets. These queries can retrieve data in many different ways. They can compare data from multiple sources, they can use data from one table to provide a filter for another table, and they can be encapsulated within other queries. In addition to retrieving information from tables, queries can also be used to modify content in tables, or even to create brand new tables. This chapter discusses the creation of queries, their construction, and their use.

CERTIFICATION OBJECTIVE 6.01

Developing Query Execution Plans

In this chapter, we will focus on the creation of queries, and the use of Transact-SQL to define what data we want retrieved from the available tables. However, we will not be specifying how this data should be retrieved. Although our requirements are defined in the queries, the actual plan to retrieve this data is created by SQL Server. The database uses what it knows about the tables to estimate the most efficient program for retrieving the data. This algorithm is known as a *query execution plan.*

Several different factors influence SQL Server when it develops a query execution plan. Even if SQL Server has had excellent performance when executing a query in the past, it may choose a new execution plan if the size of the table changes, if indexes are changed, or if the percentage of unique values in an indexed column changes.

Although it is not possible to define the plan for SQL Server, you can view the plan that SQL Server has created. After observing the choices made, you can then adjust other design elements accordingly.

There are a few different techniques for observing these choices. If you execute the command, SET SHOWPLAN_ALL ON, a textual representation of this plan is returned when a query is submitted. There is also a new tool in SQL Server 7.0, the Query Analyzer, which presents these plans visually. These tools make it much easier to understand how these queries are being executed, and how to address any bottlenecks.

For example, you can use the Query Analyzer to connect to the pubs database, and execute the query, **SELECT * FROM employee WHERE emp_id = 'ard36773F'**. If you select Show Execution Plan from the Query menu, you will see a plan that looks like the following one, presented first as text, then graphically in Figure 6-1:

```
|--Bookmark Lookup(BOOKMARK:([Bmk1000]), OBJECT:([pubs].[dbo].[employee]))
       |--Index Seek(OBJECT:([pubs].[dbo].[employee].[PK_emp_id]),
SEEK:([employee].[emp_id]=[@1]) ORDERED)
```

However, if you analyzed **SELECT * FROM employee WHERE hire_date = "1993-01-27"** you would get the same content in the Results Grid, but you would generate a different execution plan, again presented first as text, then graphically in Figure 6-2:

```
|--Clustered Index Scan(OBJECT:([pubs].[dbo].[employee].[employee_ind]),
WHERE:([employee].[hire_date]=Convert([@1])))
```

FIGURE 6-1

Use the Query Analyzer to graphically display the execution plan for SELECT * FROM employee WHERE emp_id = 'ard36773F'

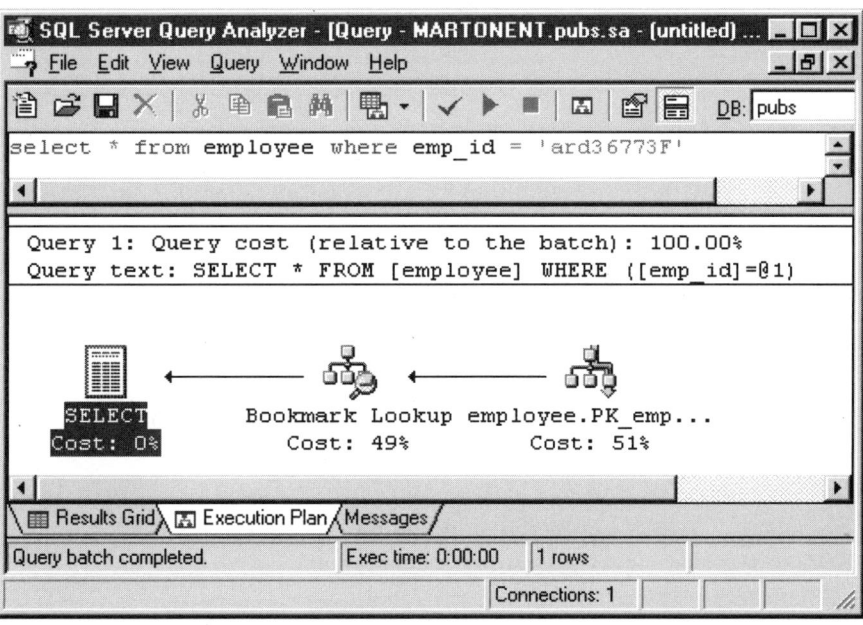

FIGURE 6-2

SELECT * FROM employee
WHERE hire_date =
"1993-01-27"

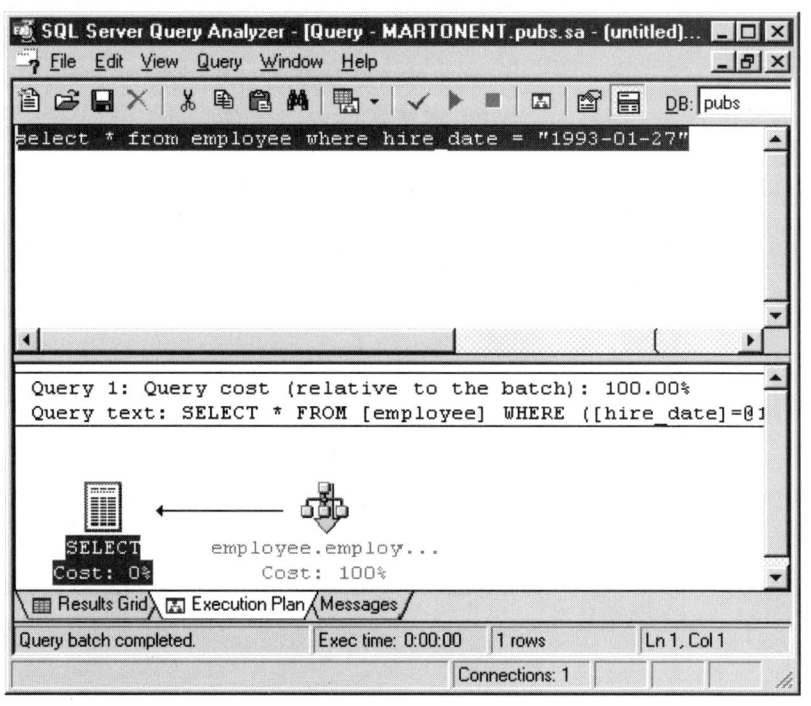

Although the two queries are quite similar, the first one searched a field
with an index, whereas the second one searched a field with no index.
Although it looks like the second query requires fewer steps (two instead
of three), the first query actually executes more efficiently.

When working with data sets this small, poor programming isn't
punished. However, as you start to work with larger tables, understanding
execution plans can be critical for achieving improved performance of the
queries you build.

There are three primary ways to improve the performance of your
queries: adding indexes, updating statistics, and changing the query
definition.

FROM THE CLASSROOM

Joins, Queries, and Such—Pulling It All Together

Pulling data together from multiple sources is the forte of high-end database servers such as Microsoft SQL Server. The query processors that are part of the server product are designed to be highly efficient in retrieving the data from the proprietary data structures. The inclusion of structures such as indexes increase the options, and therefore the complexity, of the data retrieval methods. With index varieties including clustered, nonclustered, and composite, a query processor has a great deal of choices to make to produce the most efficient algorithm for data retrieval. This algorithm, known as the execution plan, is the optimized series of instructions that the database engine uses when actually retrieving the data from the database. A poorly chosen or poorly developed execution plan can result in significantly increased data retrieval times.

Fortunately, the SQL Server 7.0 Query Analyzer provides a graphical display of the estimated and actual execution plans. By becoming familiar with the execution plans that result from the variety of queries that are performed, a better understanding of the underlying decision-making process can be established, thereby improving the design of the queries. Unfortunately though, a graphical representation requires numerous icons to represent the various decisions made in the resulting decision tree. It is therefore recommended that you look up and study the list of possible icons in the SQL Server Books Online. This will increase the recognition rate of the individual analyzing the execution plan, as well as aid anyone planning on taking the certification exam.

—*Michael Lane Thomas, MCSE+I, MCSD, MCP+SB, MSS, MCT*

Improving Performance by Adding Indexes

As illustrated in Chapter 5, you can create multiple indexes on the same tables. As you observed in the sample execution plans, SQL Server usually uses an index when one is available. However, sometimes adding an index to improve query performance can do more harm than good.

Keep the following issues in mind when deciding whether to add indexes:

- What kind of operations does the table support? If you use many INSERT, UPDATE, or DELETE statements, then the indexes must be updated whenever the data changes. This slows down the process of updating the data.

- How many records are in the table? If there is no index, the query must loop through every record to find the matching records. However, if the table is very small, it may actually be faster to perform this looping than to look up the matching values in an index.

- How many discrete values are in the column? A clustered index can offer faster performance than a nonclustered index, but if you have many different values, then the server may have to spend significant time resorting your data on the hard drive.

- Do you have control over what queries are executed? If the needed queries are known, it may be wise to create a few multicolumn, nonclustered indexes that are optimized for these queries. On the other hand, if the needed queries are unknown, then you may want to implement a larger number of single-column indexes. This way, no matter what criteria are selected for the query, SQL Server has a better chance of finding an appropriate index.

These principles are not absolute, and they should be weighed against each other, as well as against other database priorities. However, in determining these priorities, you are not limited to empirical observation. Microsoft also provides an Index Tuning Wizard to help make recommendations. This wizard usually recommends no action while working on the pubs or Northwest databases due to their small size, but when working on real-world data, it can help analyze several factors at once.

Improving Performance by Updating Statistics

SQL Server estimates the performance costs of a query and selects the most efficient possibility before executing it. When SQL Server is trying to decide what index (if any) to use to find the requested data, it refers to internal statistics that it has generated on that column. Because of this, it is useful to have up-to-date statistics generated on a table; if you don't, SQL Server may not choose the most efficient plan.

For example, imagine that you created a Patient table for a hospital, with indexes on social_security and on last_name. As you start with a small number of records, both of these indexes will probably be highly unique, and they should offer roughly comparable search performances. However, as the database grows, you will start to get significant duplication in the last_name field. This results in the key on this field becoming less useful than the key on the social_security field (which should remain unique).

If the server has up-to-date statistics on both of these keys, it will "know" that the social_security key is more unique, and will probably use it when possible. However, if the statistics have not been updated, it might still consider both keys to be equally useful, and it may waste time performing inefficient queries.

Table 6-1 lists the commands and stored procedures provided by SQL Server to support the maintenance of these statistics.

Keep the following in mind when working with statistics:

- If a database is smaller than 8MB, SQL Server will scan the entire table; otherwise, only a sample of the data will be analyzed to generate the statistics.

- In previous versions of SQL Server, you could specify *hints* in a query to override the judgement of SQL Server and manually define which index should be used. Though these hints are still supported in SQL Server 7.0, Microsoft now discourages their use. This is because Microsoft believes that the *judgement* of SQL Server is better than it was in the past, and in most cases developers should not override it.

- Even though statistics are not necessarily updated when new content is added, the index itself is still automatically updated.

Improving Performance by Changing the Query Definition

Much of the effort required to process a query involves the joins between tables. There are three main join techniques that Microsoft uses: nested loops, merge joins, and hash joins.

TABLE 6-1	Commands for Administrating Statistics	
Command or Stored Procedure	**Name**	**Description**
Command	CREATE INDEX	Creates statistics on a column when the index is generated. (If you include the STATISTICS_NORECOMPUTE option, statistics will not be automatically updated.)
Command	CREATE STATISTICS	Creates the initial statistics on the specified column or columns
Command	UPDATE STATISTICS	Refreshes existing statistics. (If you select the NORECOMPUTE option, then the statistics will not be automatically updated.)
Command	DROP STATISTICS	Removes all statistics in an entire table. (If you select the NORECOMPUTE option, then the statistics will not be automatically updated.)
Command	DBCC SHOW_STATISTICS	Displays the density of an existing statistics set.
Command	STATS_DATE	Displays when the statistics were last updated.
Stored Procedure	sp_autostats	Determines whether a particular statistic will be automatically updated.
Stored Procedure	sp_createstats	Creates statistics on every column supporting statistics in the current database.

When SQL Server develops a plan for a query, it analyzes the indexes and statistics of the query to estimate which join type will have the best performance. Although you cannot directly define the execution plan, if you have an awareness of these join types, you can design your queries with a better understanding of how they will execute.

The type of query chosen depends upon the size of the tables. For example, suppose that you created a query drawing fields from two tables: a publishers table containing 100 records, and an authors table containing 10,000 records. Both tables have a Publisher_ID field, and the authors table uses this field as a foreign key into the publishers table. The two tables can be joined together in the following ways:

- **Nested loop join**   Loops through all 100 publishers. For each publisher, it loops through all 10,000 authors to find matches.

- **Hash join**   Reads all 100 publishers into memory. It then loops through all 10,000 authors and compares them to the publishers in memory. (The record set stored in memory is known as the *build input*. If there are too many records to store in memory, some records may be swapped onto the hard drive temporarily.)

- **Merge join**   Sorts on Publisher_ID in both tables and then loops through both tables at the same time. Where Publisher_ID matches in both tables, merge join returns the row; otherwise, it moves to the next record in the table with the lower current Publisher_ID. If both join fields have indexes and both tables are large, merge joins can provide better performance than the other options.

Understanding these joins can help you create efficient queries, especially when you must join more than two tables in a single query. For example, suppose you have a query that runs very slowly. You might consider adding another index, but because the table is updated frequently, you don't want to do this unless you are confident that there will be a payoff in performance.

If your join involves a very large table and a very small table, then SQL Server may be using a hash join or a nested loop join. In this situation, adding an index may not significantly improve performance. However, if you are joining two medium-sized tables, it may be more likely that you are using a merge join. In this situation, adding an index on the join field could greatly accelerate performance.

In Exercise 6-1, we will look closely at the two queries presented earlier in this chapter, compare their efficiency, and show how performance could be improved.

Evaluating and Optimizing the Performance of Query Execution Plans

1. Load the Query Analyzer, and connect to the pubs database.

2. Enter the following SQL statement in the top pane:
   SELECT * FROM employee WHERE emp_id = 'ard36773F'.
   Execute the query.

3. Confirm that one record (Anabela Domingues) was returned by the query.

4. From the Query menu, select Show Execution Plan. Execute the query again. You should now see a new tab, *Execution Plan*, in the bottom pane.

5. Click the Execution Plan tab. You should see three icons representing the steps required to execute this query. (Each of these three icons will have a percentage label underneath it. When working with more complicated queries, you can use these estimates to find bottlenecks.)

6. Because the flow of operation is from right to left, move your mouse over the rightmost icon. You should see a yellow rectangle, *Index Seek*. Because this query searches on the emp_id field, which has an index, the first step in the execution plan is to search through this index. Observe that the estimated row size is 47 bytes.

7. Right-click this third icon. From the shortcut menu, select Manage Indexes. Observe that the nonclustered index is PK_emp_id, and that the index is on the emp_id field only. After selecting this key, click Edit. Note that the checkbox "Do not recompute statistics" is not selected, and therefore you would not need to manually update statistics on this field. Click Cancel, then Close to return to the main screen.

8. Right-click the icon again, and select Manage Statistics. Note that there is a set of statistics for each of the two keys. Click the Update button. You should see a screen similar to Figure 6-3. If you had configured the statistics not to update automatically, you could use this screen to update them manually. Click Cancel and then Close.

9. Hover your mouse over the arrow connecting the second and third icons. Notice that the estimated row size is 47—the same as you observed with the third icon.

FIGURE 6-3

Recomputing statistics on
a field

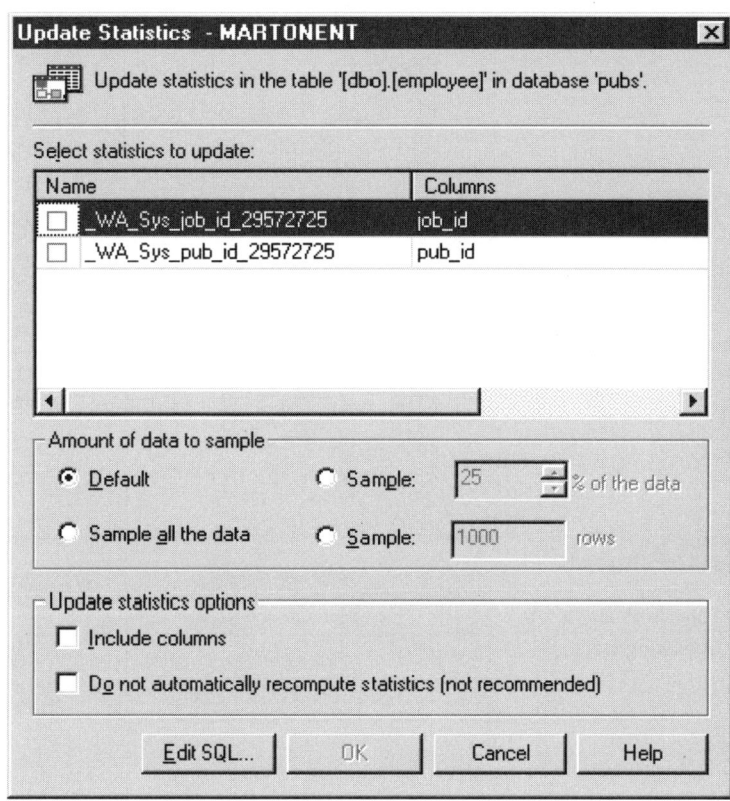

10. Hover your mouse over the arrow connecting the first and second
    icons. Notice that the estimated row size is now 63 bytes. Whereas
    the third icon represented the search for records in the index, the
    second icon represents the use of this index to find the records in the
    actual table. Because the table has few columns, the estimated size
    of the row is only slightly larger than the estimated size of the index.

11. Replace the existing query in the top pane with the following:
    **SELECT * FROM employee WHERE hire_date =
    "1993-01-27"**
    Execute the query and confirm that the result set has not changed.

12. In the execution plan, observe that there are now only two icons. This is because there is no index on the hire_date column, so SQL Server has to search directly through the table itself.

13. Note that the second icon is red. Hover your mouse over the icon and you should see a warning that statistics are missing for this table. This is illustrated in Figure 6-4. By making the icon red, Query Analyzer is encouraging the developer to generate statistics for the table.

14. Right-click this icon. You should see an option that you didn't have before: Create Missing Statistics. Select this option.

15. You should see a screen similar to the one used to update statistics. Observing the available defaults, click Edit SQL to observe the syntax used to create new statistics for a column. Click Cancel, then Cancel again. Exit the Query Analyzer.

FIGURE 6-4

Query Analyzer issuing a
warning of missing statistics

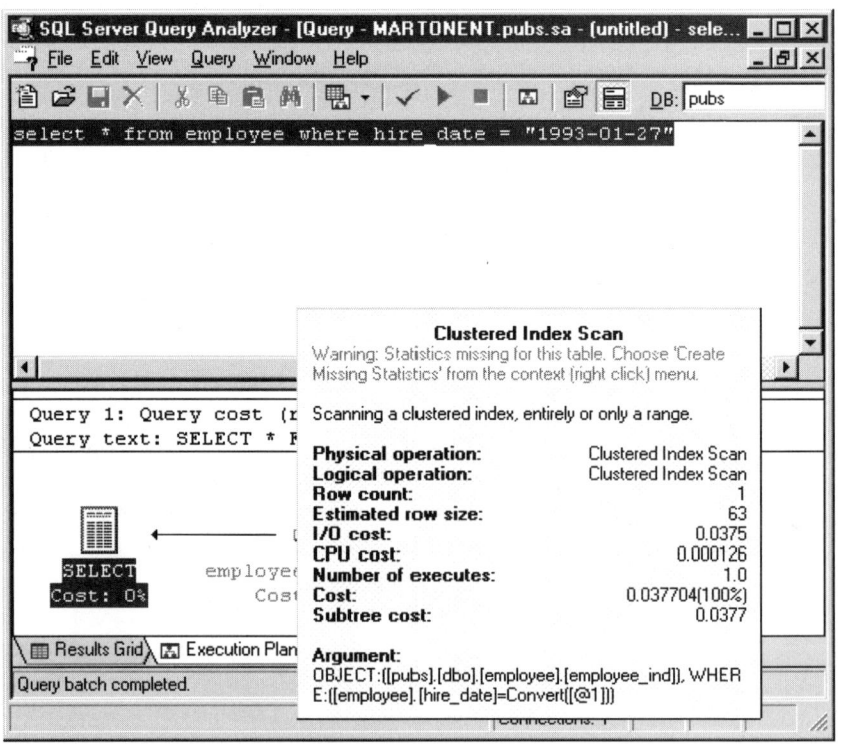

We did not add the statistic because we didn't want to change the database. However, if you did add the statistic, then the next time you executed the query, the second icon would change from red to black.

Querying Multiple Tables

In Chapter 2, you observed an overview of the techniques for combining the content in multiple tables. In this chapter we examine these techniques in more detail.

There are three primary ways to combine data from multiple sources:

- **Joins** Combine columns from multiple data sources.
- **Unions** Combine rows from multiple data sources.
- **Subqueries** Encapsulate one query inside another query.

CERTIFICATION OBJECTIVE 6.02

Combining Data from Multiple Tables

As you observed in Exercise 6-1, joins match up data in two or more tables and combine the resulting data by columns. For example, if you had one table that listed a city for each employee, and another table that listed a state for each city, you could create a join that provided the state for each employee.

A good way to understand joins is to start with a terrible example. Recall that there is a foreign key in the titles table relating to the publishers table. Suppose you want to retrieve the publisher name for each of the 18 books in the titles table. You might try the following query:

```
SELECT * FROM Titles, Publishers
```

This would return 144 records, which is not what we wanted. Every possible combination of title and publisher is returned. However, we could limit the record set to return only the combinations where the pub_id field in both tables was the same:

```
SELECT * FROM Titles, Publishers WHERE Titles.pub_id = Publishers.pub_id
```

Because this join is presented in the WHERE clause, it is possible to think of a join as a specialized filter. When you create a join, however, SQL Server derives it very differently than it does a filter. In fact, Microsoft recommends that you use a newer syntax to express the same functionality:

```
SELECT * FROM Titles INNER JOIN Publishers ON Titles.pub_id = Publishers.pub_id
```

This returns exactly the same content as the previous query using the old syntax, and you will want to use the new syntax whenever possible, for several reasons.

Although the data returned by both queries are identical, you want to use INNER JOIN where possible. First, it can be more legible because it is easier to understand the distinction between the WHERE conditions used for filtering, and those used for joins. Second, the new syntax is less ambiguous in more complicated queries. Third, FULL OUTER JOIN, described below, is not supported with the old syntax. Finally, the new syntax is closer to the industry standard, and the old syntax is likely to be phased out by Microsoft in the future.

There are five kinds of joins: inner join, left outer join, right outer join, full outer join, and cross join. These joins are summarized in Table 6-2.

Note the following about Joins:

- If you don't specify any join, the cross join is the default. Unfortunately, it is easy to make large errors using the cross join. If you have 30 rows in the left table and 50 rows in the right table, you will get 1500 rows in the result set. If you have 10,000 rows in the left table and 120,000 rows in the right table, you get angry phone calls from your DBA. Most of the time that cross joins are created, the developer really meant to use another kind of join. However, an example of a case where a cross join is useful is described in the section entitled Advanced Query Techniques.

- Although the = (equal) operator is usually used in joins, it is possible to use inequality operators as well. For an example of when this would be useful, see "Self Joins" in Advanced Query Techniques.

TABLE 6-2   Comparing Types of Joins

New Syntax	Old Syntax	Description
INNER JOIN	Where...=	Returns all rows that have the same value on the left side and the right side of the join.
LEFT OUTER JOIN	Where...*=	Returns all rows from the table on the left side, and only those rows from the table on the right where there is a match. If a match doesn't exist, a null value is placed in the missing fields.
RIGHT OUTER JOIN	Where...=*	Returns all rows from the table on the right side, and only those rows from the table on the left where there is a match. If a match doesn't exist, a null value is placed in the missing fields.
FULL OUTER JOIN	N/A	Returns all rows on both sides. Where there is a match, it reports both sides, otherwise it fills in nulls as appropriate.
CROSS JOIN	WHERE clause omitted	Returns all combinations of all rows from the left and right side. (Also known as *Cartesian Product*)

■ Normally, you will want to join fields of the same data type. However, if the field types can be implicitly converted, then the join will succeed even if the field types are different.

■ Joins are almost always expressed in the FROM clause. However, to maintain compatibility with the SQL-92 standard, inner joins can also be expressed in the WHERE clause. (This is not an option with outer joins.)

■ Even if there is a matching NULL on both sides of the join, they will not be considered a match by SQL Server. Because of this, you will not see a null value in a join column when using an inner join. Null values in a join column in an outer join signify that no match could be found, not that there was a matching NULL.

Using Joins or Subqueries to Combine Data from Multiple Tables

Exercise 6-2 demonstrates how joins can be used to combine content from multiple tables.

Writing a Transact-SQL Statement That Uses Joins or Subqueries to Combine Data from Multiple Tables

1. Load the Query Analyzer, and connect to the pubs database.

2. Execute **SELECT * FROM Titles**. Observe that 18 rows are returned.

3. Execute **SELECT * FROM Publishers**. Observe that eight rows are returned.

4. Execute **SELECT * FROM Titles, Publishers**. Observe that 144 rows (18 * 8) rows are returned. Because no join was specified, a cross join was inferred, and all title records were erroneously joined to all publisher records, whether or not they were related.

5. Execute **SELECT * FROM Titles INNER JOIN Publishers ON Titles.pub_id = Publishers.pub_id**. Observe that only 18 rows were returned. This filtered the content from the previous query so that each title only contains publisher information for the correct publisher.

6. Observe the execution plan for the query. It should look similar to Figure 6-5. Note that the Nested Loop physical operator was chosen to join these two tables. Although this can be an inefficient join when used with larger data sets, with such small tables SQL Server often predicts that it will have the best performance.

   Scroll through the Results Grid. Observe that every column from both tables was returned. This is because the * operator was used.

8. Execute the query **SELECT title, pub_name FROM Titles INNER JOIN Publishers ON Titles.pub_id = Publishers.pub_id**. You should still see 18 records, but now only

FIGURE 6-5

Execution plan for a
simple join

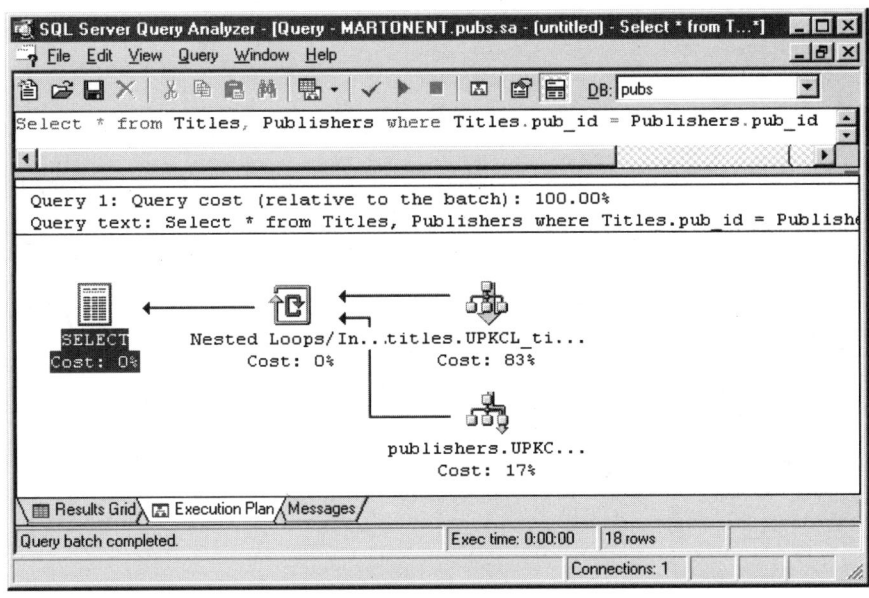

two columns are returned. Note that because the fields, title and
pub_name, exist in only one of the tables, it is not necessary to
specify their source.

9. Attempt to execute the query **SELECT title, pub_name, pub_id
   FROM Titles INNER JOIN Publishers ON Titles.pub_id =
   Publishers.pub_id.** You should get an error stating "Ambiguous
   column name 'pub_id'." Because the pub_id column is in both tables,
   you can not retrieve the field without qualifying it.

10. Execute the query **SELECT title, pub_name, Titles.pub_id
    FROM Titles INNER JOIN Publishers ON Titles.pub_id =
    Publishers.pub_id**. Because you have specified that you want to
    draw pub_id from the titles table, the query can now execute.

CERTIFICATION OBJECTIVE 6.03

Combining Multiple Result Sets

Joins are very useful when you want to combine the content from multiple tables into the same row. However, there are times when you want to view the data from multiple tables in the same column. This can be best accomplished using the UNION operator.

For example, in the pubs database, there is one table for Employees, and a separate table for authors. Suppose that you needed to populate the content in these two tables into three fields: LastName, FirstName, and Position. SQL Server allows you to do this with the UNION operator, as follows:

```
SELECT lname as LastName, fname as FirstName, 'employee' AS Position FROM employee
UNION
SELECT  au_lname, au_fname, 'author' AS Position FROM authors
ORDER by lname
```

The results of this query should appear similar to Figure 6-6.

This operation "stacks" the results from the two queries "on top of each other." Keep the following in mind when using UNION queries:

- The resulting field names are adopted from the field names as defined in the first SELECT statement, and all of the other field names are ignored.

- You must have the same number of fields in every SELECT statement.

- All of the fields sharing a column have compatible data types. If the fields are not of the same type, there must be an implicit conversion available among the types.

- You can use HAVING and GROUP BY only on the individual queries, and not on the data set as a whole. By contrast, you can use COMPUTE and ORDER BY only on the whole data set, and not on the individual queries.

FIGURE 6-6

Using a UNION query

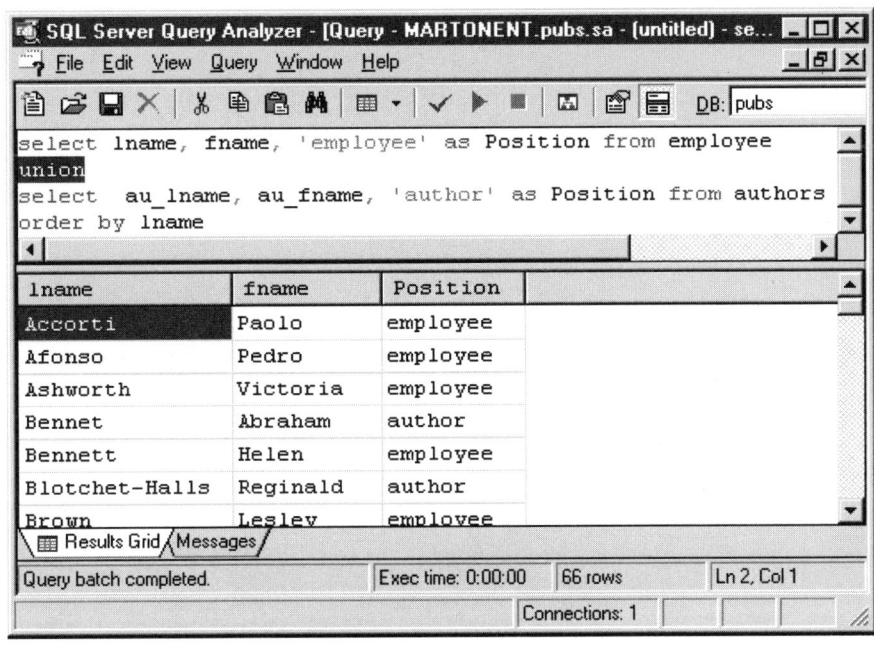

CERTIFICATION OBJECTIVE 6.04

Creating a Table from a Result Set

So far, we have taken our returned data sets, which we created with queries, and returned them directly to the user. It is also possible to take this data and place it into entirely new tables. This is done using the SELECT INTO statement.

The syntax of this statement is as follows:

```
SELECT * INTO #JustPsychBooks FROM titles WHERE type = 'psychology'
```

Note the single number sign (#) preceding the name of the table. In SQL Server, this indicates that a table is a local temporary table. If it were preceded with two number signs (# #), it would be a global temporary table. When the *select into/bulkcopy* option is set, you can also use SELECT INTO to create permanent tables by omitting the number sign, but you should use temporary tables when experimenting with this feature.

To create a permanent table you must have the CREATE TABLE permission in the database. If you do not have this permission, you still can create a local or global temporary table.

Each field in the new table will have the field name of the source query. Therefore, if your query draws from more than one table and two fields have the same name, you must use an alias for one of them.

After the table has been created, it can be used just like any other table. For example, after running the SELECT INTO statement, you could select from it, as follows:

```
SELECT * FROM #JustPsychBooks
```

This command would return the same five records that were selected by the SELECT INTO statement.

Although SELECT INTO can provide flexibility, there are disadvantages associated with the frequent creation of new tables, including the following:

- More server resources can be consumed
- Precise table definition can be degraded
- Centralized table control can be lost

If you find yourself using SELECT INTO too frequently, you may wish to investigate alternatives. For example, you could use INSERT INTO (discussed later in this chapter) to add new rows to existing tables, or use views (discussed in Chapter 9) to simulate new tables without actually creating them.

Advanced Query Techniques

The following are some advanced techniques that you can use with joins, SELECT INTO statements, and UNION operators:

Self-Joins

Most joins involve connecting two distinct tables. However, there are times that you will want to join a table to itself. For example, if you have a manager ID field in an employee table, you may want to link the employee table to itself in order to report the name of a particular employee next to the name of its manager. SQL Server supports linking a table to itself, and this is known as a *self-join*.

There are two things to keep in mind when using a self-join. First, because the same table is referenced in two different places, you need to distinguish between the two instances. You can do this by providing different names, or aliases, for at least one of the tables. You would then refer to these aliases in the query, instead of referring to the table itself.

Second, depending upon how your query is constructed, you may want to use inequality operators for your joins. Usually, in joins you would use an = operator. However, if you use an = operator in a self-join, you often would get twice as many records as you want: instances where the records matched each other going from left to right, and the same record, going right to left. Because the tables are symmetrical, the data returned is redundant. By using the < (less than) operator, the record is only be returned for one of these two matches.

Cross Joins

Imagine that you have a table of regions, a table of products, and a table of sales. The user wants a report of all of the sales, grouped by region and then by product. The user also wants the products with no sales to be included in the query. If you create a cross join of the products and regions, you can return a table including every product and every region, but without sales. You can then UNION this with the sales table, and then group the results to provide the desired results.

UNION

One of the nicest features of using the UNION operator is that it allows you to pseudonormalize your data through a query. For example, you could have a single row of data that recorded employee data, including four consecutive years of performance evaluations. Using a UNION query, you could "stack" the data using four queries, repeating all fields but changing the performance evaluation, and simulating a normalized data source. You might ask "But why would you have a denormalized table in the first place?" One example involves HTML development. When you submit a Web page, the values you entered on that page are provided through HTTP as a one-dimensional array of values, even if some of the data was presented to the user as an array. By using a UNION query on this data in conjunction with a SELECT INTO, you can quickly migrate a full set of these data rows into a normalized data table with much less effort than would be required to do it programmatically.

CERTIFICATION OBJECTIVE 6.05

Introduction to Subqueries

We have learned how joins can be used to combine tables. However, there is another technique that you can use to combine tables in a similar manner. You can use one SQL statement to return records or criteria used by another SQL statement. The encapsulating query is called a *parent query*, and the inner query is a *subquery*.

For example, assume that you had a theory that people bought more books from stores that had the word "book" in them than from stores that didn't. You could create the following query to find all of these stores:

```
SELECT stor_id FROM stores WHERE stor_name LIKE "%book%"
```

You could then encapsulate this query in parentheses, and use it inside of another query, as follows:

```
SELECT sales.*, stor_id AS Store FROM sales WHERE (stor_id IN
    (SELECT stor_id FROM stores WHERE stor_name LIKE '%book%'))
```

In the preceding query, the IN command is used with subqueries to see if a value is present in the records returned by a subquery. This query returns all of the sales figures from all of the stores with the word "book" in their name. The following issues should be remembered when using subqueries:

■ You can use a subquery as a replacement for a value in the SELECT clause, as part of the WHERE clause, or as part of the HAVING clause.

■ When you introduce a subquery with an operator, there are restrictions on the columns and rows that can be returned by that subquery. These restrictions are summarized in the following table.

	One Column	Many Columns
One Row	Use =, >, <, and the other comparison operators	Use EXISTS
Many Rows	Use ANY, ALL, IN, and EXISTS	Use EXISTS

■ If you are using the comparison operator with a subquery, or if you are using the subquery without an operator in the SELECT clause, you will receive an error if the subquery returns more than one row.

■ Because a subquery used with a comparison operator requires that only one row be returned, it is often used with a subquery containing an aggregation function, such as MAX or MIN.

■ Many subqueries can be rewritten as joins. For example, the subquery regarding books could also have been written using a join, as follows:

```
SELECT sales.*, sales.stor_id AS Store, stores.stor_name AS Name
FROM sales INNER JOIN stores ON sales.stor_id = stores.stor_id
WHERE (stores.stor_name LIKE '%book%')
```

When you have multiple ways of returning the same record set, you can use the Query Analyzer to help define the most efficient technique for retrieving the needed data.

Nested Subqueries

It is possible to extend the technique learned earlier, and have your subqueries call subqueries of their own. When this is done, it is called *nested subqueries*. (Do not confuse this with *nested queries*, which is a term sometimes used to describe simple subqueries.)

According to the specification, it is possible for queries to be nested 32 levels deep, but it is unlikely that performance of such a query would be satisfactory.

Correlated Subqueries

In many queries containing subqueries, the subquery needs to be evaluated only once to provide the values needed by the parent query. This is because in most queries, the subquery makes no reference to the parent query, so the values in the subquery remain constant.

However, if the subquery refers to the parent query, the subquery needs to be reevaluated for every iteration in the parent query. This is because the search criteria in the subquery is dependent upon the value of a particular record in the parent query. When a subquery retrieves parameters from its parent query, it is known as a *correlated subquery*.

For example, the following query lists all stores that do not have any sales with payment terms categorized as *on invoice*:

```
SELECT stor_id FROM stores WHERE 'ON invoice' NOT IN
    (SELECT payterms FROM sales WHERE sales.stor_ID = stores.stor_id)
```

Because the subquery refers to a field (stores.stor_id) from the parent query, this is a correlated subquery.

As you may have predicted, a correlated subquery is more demanding of server resources than most other subqueries, so care should be taken with their use.

CERTIFICATION OBJECTIVE 6.08

Using the EXISTS and NOT EXISTS Keywords

Most subqueries return a single field, and the values in this field are returned to the parent query. By contrast, the EXISTS statement is permitted to select multiple fields. This is because the actual values in these fields are not passed to the parent query—only the presence or absence of the rows is reported.

For example, you could use the following query to return the stores having sales with payment terms equal to *On Invoice*:

```
SELECT stor_name, state FROM stores
WHERE EXISTS
(SELECT * FROM sales WHERE sales.stor_id = stores.stor_id AND
 payterms = 'On Invoice')
```

Although you should be familiar with EXISTS for the certification exam, be aware that most queries using EXISTS could be rewritten using the ANY or IN functions instead, or by using joins.

With all of these options to combine tables, it can be difficult choosing which approaches to use. The following scenarios provide some common issues and recommended resolutions.

QUESTIONS AND ANSWERS

I am building a query that combines an employees table and a sales table. Because the sales data is periodically imported from a remote source, I'm not using foreign keys. Now, when I create an inner join, I am not reporting sales for employees that are not present in the employees table.	When your business processes impede your implementation of referential integrity, you will sometimes get orphan records. However, by using outer joins instead of inner joins, at least you can include these orphan records in your report.
I have two different tables on two different servers in two different cities. The structure of the tables is the same. The reason they are separated is to provide improved performance for views in the cities. I need to generate monthly reports that combine this data. How should I do this?	By using the UNION statement, you can combine these tables in the same columns and present them as a single data source.
I took your advice and used a UNION query, and it worked well for the monthly reports. But now the users want to view these reports in real time. The performance accessing the remote server using UNION queries was unacceptable.	You could select a process to run overnight, using SELECT INTO to create a table based upon the content from both cities. Although updates made during the day would not be immediately available in other cities, the performance of queries accessing this data would be greatly improved.
The queries I am building are nested several levels deep, and they are becoming difficult to understand.	You may want to encapsulate some of the complexity of the query in a view. Views are discussed in Chapter 9.

CERTIFICATION OBJECTIVE 6.09

Modifying Data

Of course, all of these methods of retrieving data from a database are of no use if the tables are empty. This section focuses upon the three main statements used in Transact-SQL to modify the content in tables: INSERT, DELETE, and UPDATE.

Adding Records with **INSERT**

New records are inserted into a table using the INSERT statement. The most commonly used syntax is shown in Table 6-3.

You can use the INSERT command to create a single record of data, or to insert an entire record set. Examples of both of these approaches are provided in the following sections.

Inserting a Single Row

You can add a new job category into the Jobs table using the following line of code:

```
INSERT INTO JOBS (job_desc, min_lvl, max_lvl) VALUES('Co-op', 15, 25)
```

The keyword, DEFAULT, may be used in place of a value. You can also replace the entire list of values by using the DEFAULT VALUES command. (When you do this, SQL Server will insert a NULL into every field where there is no default value defined. Therefore, it is not possible to

TABLE 6-3	Syntax	Description
Syntax of INSERT Statement	INSERT [INTO] {	Specifies command. (The *INTO* is optional.)
	table_name }	Defines the table or view that will be receiving the new record.
	{ [(column_list)]	Specifies which fields should receive the new content, and in which order. (When omitted, all legal fields are populated.)
	{ VALUES ({	Provides the list of parameters to insert into the record.
	expression | NULL | DEFAULT }	Defines whether the new value for the field should be provided by the query, should be NULL, or should be the default from the table definition.
	[,...n]) }}	Completes the list of fields to insert.
	| DEFAULT VALUES	Populates the entire row with the defined default values.

use DEFAULT VALUES on a table where there are NON NULL fields that have no defaults defined.)

Not only are the values optional, so are the fields themselves. If you omit the field list, the columns will be populated in the order in which they were originally created. For example, the following line of code performs the same action as the previous example, because the three non-identity columns in the Jobs table are job_desc, min_lvl, and max_lvl, in that order.

```
INSERT INTO JOBS VALUES('Co-op', 15, 25)
```

In general this approach is not recommended, for the following reasons:

- The INSERT statement stops working if more columns are added or deleted to the table.

- It is more difficult for other developers to understand the query.

- If the query is executed on a copy of the table where the columns were created in a different order, the results could range from an improperly populated table to an error being generated.

Inserting Multiple Rows

Instead of adding a single record at a time, it is possible to insert the entire result set of a SELECT query. For example, suppose that you want to automatically create new job categories that describe the location of the employees at the stores. The following query automatically computes and adds six records:

```
INSERT INTO JOBS (job_desc, min_lvl, max_lvl) select city +
    ' employee' as Type, 15, 35 from stores
```

Special Fields

Normally, you cannot use the INSERT statement to populate an identity field, because SQL Server maintains this field internally. However, if you must insert content into an identity column, the SET IDENTITY_INSERT statement can be used to enable this behavior temporarily. However, you normally would only want to use this for data maintenance, and this option should be left off for normal operations.

e x a m
ⓦa t c h *In contrast to an identity field, SQL Server does not automatically maintain the contents of a uniqueidentifier field. (A uniqueidentifier is a globally unique record identifier, and it is useful when merging record sets originally generated at different sources.) If you are using a uniqueidentifier as a primary key, you will need to initialize its value by using the NEWID() function.*

Removing Records with **DELETE**

The DELETE command is used to delete entire rows of data from a table. The most commonly used syntax of the DELETE statement is shown in this table:

Syntax	Description
DELETE [FROM] {	Specifies the command. (The FROM keyword is optional.)
table_name	Defines the table or view from which you will be deleting.
[WHERE { <search_condition>]	Defines the search criteria. (If this clause is omitted, then all records are deleted.)

For example, you could delete all of the psychology books with the following query:

```
DELETE FROM titles WHERE type = 'psychology'
```

In some other database systems (Microsoft Access, for example) the preferred syntax is *DELETE * FROM Table* instead of *DELETE FROM Table*. However, this syntax is not supported in SQL Server 7.0.

Although the WHERE clause is optional when using the DELETE statement, omitting it is usually a poor choice. When you omit the WHERE clause, all the records in the table are deleted.

If you truly intend to delete all of the records from a table, you may want to consider using the TRUNCATE TABLE statement instead. This statement also deletes all the rows in a table, but because each row deletion is not logged, the deletion is much faster. However, it is not possible to use the TRUNCATE TABLE statement on a table that is referenced by foreign keys. Also, because the records removed using TRUNCATE TABLE are not logged, the action can not be rolled back.

In the previous example, the WHERE clause referred to the same table as the DELETE clause, but it is also possible to draw the criteria from another table. For example, you could use the following query to terminate every employee working for a publisher in cities with names that start with a *B*:

```
DELETE FROM employee WHERE employee.pub_id IN
    (SELECT pub_id FROM publishers WHERE city LIKE 'b%')
```

The DELETE operation does not override any constraints defined in the table. If a DELETE operation on a table would remove rows that are referenced by foreign keys, then the entire operation is cancelled. (This is why TRUNCATE TABLE cannot be used on a table referenced by foreign keys, because each record has to be individually validated.) For example, when we deleted the computer books in the first DELETE query, this would only execute successfully if other tables did not have foreign keys that referenced these records.

Modifying Records with UPDATE

The UPDATE statement allows you to make modifications to specific columns of an existing row or rows. The most common syntax for the UPDATE statement is listed in Table 6-4.

The UPDATE statement modifies all records that meet the criteria specified in the WHERE clause. For example, you could recategorize all of the cookbooks with the following command:

```
UPDATE titles SET type = "cooking" WHERE type = "mod_cook"
```

The values used to update the fields can be constants, values from another table, values from another field in the same table, or even values from the same field in the same table. If you assign a field to a modified version of itself, it will calculate correctly.

The UPDATE statement modifies all records that meet the specified criteria. This can lead to unfortunate errors if you make an error in your WHERE criteria. An alternative version of the statement is available to allay these worries. If you are using a cursor to scroll through the records, you

	Syntax	Description
TABLE 6-4		
Syntax of the UPDATE Statement	UPDATE {	Specifies the command.
	table_name	Defines the table or view to update.
	SET {column_name =	Defines which fields to update.
	expression | NULL | DEFAULT }	Defines whether the new value for the field should be provided by the query, should be NULL, or should be the default from the table definition.
	[,...n]	Completes the list of fields to update.
	{{[FROM {<table_source>} [,...n]]	Defines the table or tables from which the content should be drawn.
	[WHERE <search_condition>] }}	Filters the records to update. (If this is omitted, then all records will be modified.)

can use WHERE CURRENT OF to modify the existing record. By doing this, you can be sure that you are only modifying a single row.

Exercise 6-3 demonstrates the uses of the INSERT, DELETE, and UPDATE statements, and illustrates some of the conditions required for successful execution of these statements.

EXERCISE 6-3

Writing INSERT, DELETE, UPDATE, and SELECT Statements That Retrieve and Modify Data

1. Enter the Query Analyzer tool, and connect to the pubs database.

2. Execute **SELECT COUNT(*) FROM titles**, and confirm that there are 18 entries in this table. (If there is a different number, just remember this number as your starting point instead of 18.)

3. Execute **BEGIN TRANSACTION**. We will be making changes to the content in the tables in this exercise, and this will make it easier for these changes to be rolled back.

4. Execute **INSERT INTO titles (title_id, title, type) VALUES (20001, 'My New Book', 'business')**.

5. Execute **SELECT COUNT(*) FROM titles** again. Observe that you now have 19 records.

6. Execute **SELECT * FROM titles**. Observe your new title in the Results Grid.

7. Attempt to execute **INSERT INTO titles (title_id, title, type) VALUES (20001, 'My Other New Book', 'business')** again. It should fail, warning you that you "Cannot insert duplicate key in object 'titles'." The title_id column is the primary key in the titles table, so we cannot enter two books with the same key of 20001.

8. Execute **INSERT INTO titles (title_id, title, type) VALUES (20002, 'My Other New Book', 'business')** By using a new key value, this should now be successful.

9. Execute **SELECT COUNT(*) FROM titles** again. Observe that you now should have 20 records.

10. Execute **DELETE FROM titles WHERE title_ID = 20002**. This will remove the book you just added.

11. Attempt to execute **DELETE FROM titles WHERE title_ID = 'BU1032'**. You should receive a message that it fails, because your request conflicted with a column reference constraint.

12. Display the estimated execution plan for this DELETE query. (This is available under the Query menu.) Observe that in order to execute this query, SQL Server must perform an Index Seek on the titleauthor, sales, and roysched tables. When performing a DELETE query, all tables with a foreign key into the table where the record is being deleted must be checked to confirm that no violations will be created by this deletion.

13. Execute **SELECT * FROM titles** again, and observe that in the record for *My Other New Book* that you created, most of the fields are NULL, including the pub_id field.

14. Execute **UPDATE titles SET pub_id = '0736' WHERE title_ID = '20002'**. Then execute **SELECT * FROM titles** and observe that My Other New Book now has a publisher listed.

15. Try to execute **UPDATE titles SET pub_id = '0737' WHERE title_ID = '20002'**. This will fail because there is a foreign key reference to the publishers table, and there is no publisher with an ID of 0737.

16. Enter **ROLLBACK TRANSACTION**. This should return your data to its original state.

Full-Text Searches

If you have already used wildcard searches, then you are familiar with how useful they can be in finding records when the exact content is not known. In SQL Server 7.0, Microsoft introduces full-text search functionality, Microsoft Search Service. This complements the existing functionality set and provides more features, but requires additional configuration and data maintenance.

A comparison of these two approaches is provided in Table 6-5.

on the **Job**

For simple situations, you can also use the SOUNDEX and DIFFERENCE functions to provide some of the functionality of a full-text search without requiring all of the configuration.

Setting Up Microsoft Search Service

Full-text indexes are necessary in order to perform a full-text search. Although the use of full-text searches is fairly simple, the initial configuration required to support them can be quite involved.

TABLE 6-5 Comparing Examples of Wildcard and Full-Text Searches

Search Condition	Wildcard Search	Full-Text Search
	LIKE	CONTAINS, FREETEXT
Can determine if a string appears in a field?	Yes	Yes
Can search for word variants (inflectional forms of words)?	No	Yes
Can rank and sort quality of matches from high to low?	No	Yes
Can search for "noise" words, such as *a*, *an*, or *the*?	Yes	No
Supports a phrase search?	Yes	Yes
Supports a proximity search?	No	Yes

Even before performing this configuration, the Microsoft Search service must be installed and started. (The Microsoft Search service is not a part of the Desktop installation of SQL Server 7.0, and therefore is not available if you're using Windows 95, Windows 98, or Windows NT Workstation.) If you are having trouble using full-text searches, confirm that the service is started, as shown here:

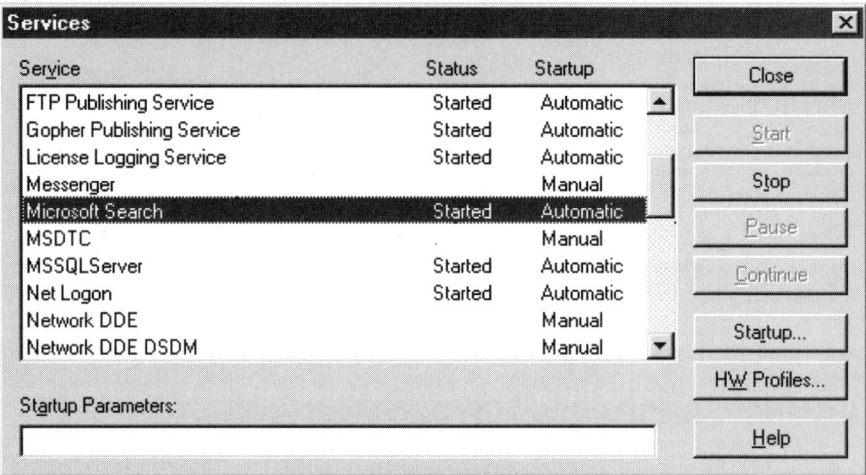

There are several stored procedures that are required to configure full-text indexing. These are summarized in the following table:

Stored Procedure	Action
sp_fulltext_database	Enables full-text indexing in the current database
sp_fulltext_catalog	Generates a blank full-text catalog, and performs the initial population of the catalog
sp_fulltext_table	Registers a table within your new catalog, and activates full-text indexing on the table
sp_fulltext_column	Identifies a column for full-text indexing

Although you should be familiar with all of these stored procedures for the exam, the fastest way to initialize full-text indexing is to run the Full-Text Indexing Wizard. The use of this wizard is illustrated in Exercise 6-4.

Unlike traditional indexes, full-text indexes are not automatically recalculated when data is inserted or modified. Therefore, it is necessary to define a strategy for recalculating these indexes. Usually you will want to recalculate them during periods of low utilization, but occasionally you may want to manually initialize this recalculation immediately preceding a query. You can rebuild all indexes by scheduling the sp_fulltext_catalog stored procedure.

If the index is out of date, the search will not provide satisfactory results. A query using a full-text index can only match data compared to the most recent population; thus, if the index has never been populated, it will return no matches.

Implementing a Full-Text Search

Once you have configured your full-text indexes as specified in the previous section, full-text searches may be performed. There are two main functions used for full-text searching, and two ways in which each of these functions can be used, as shown in this table:

Condition	Predicates	Rowsets
Match on spelling	CONTAINS	CONTAINSTABLE
Match on meaning	FREETEXT	FREETEXTTABLE

The CONTAINS and FREETEXT functions are quite similar. They both allow you to define a word or phrase and find it in the source content. However, the details of their use differ.

CONTAINS

The CONTAINS operator is invoked as follows:

```
SELECT title, notes FROM titles WHERE CONTAINS (notes, 'computer')".
```

When used in this format, the CONTAINS operator seems very similar to the LIKE operator. However, there are additional features of this command that provide more flexibility:

■ You can use the ISABOUT...WEIGHT syntax to determine which terms should have more influence in calculating which records were the best matches.

■ You can use the FORMSOF...INFLECTIONAL syntax to search for forms of words that are related, even when they are spelled differently. For example, you could search on *bring* and still return instances of the word *brought*.

■ You can use the NEAR operator to search not just on all the matching terms, but also on how closely the matching terms appear to each other.

FREETEXT

The FREETEXT operator is invoked as follows:

```
SELECT title, notes FROM titles WHERE FREETEXT (notes, 'What
are easy meals for the computer user in the modern world?')
```

Although FREETEXT doesn't offer as many options as CONTAINS, it can be more useful when the search details are being defined not by a developer but by an end user. You can pass an entire phrase to the FREETEXT function, and SQL Server automatically breaks the phrase into words and smaller phrases, and search for them in the table. Because of this, as a developer you can prompt a user for an entire string to search, and pass it directly to SQL Server using FREETEXT.

Both of these commands can be used either as a *predicate*, to filter on a field, or as a *rowset*, to return an entire table. When you use these operators as a rowset, you append TABLE to the end of the operator. An example of the FREETEXTTABLE operator follows:

```
SELECT  au_id, SEARCH_TABLE.RANK FROM titleauthor INNER JOIN
FREETEXTTABLE(titles, notes,  'What are easy meals for the
computer user in the modern world?') AS SEARCH_TABLE  ON
titleauthor.title_id = SEARCH_TABLE.[KEY]
```

Rowsets

There are two primary advantages of using the rowset variants of these commands. First, it is easier to construct subqueries that reference this functionality. Second, when you use these rowset variants, you are provided with two additional columns—*KEY* and *RANK*. KEY is only used to help construct the join and doesn't provide new uses of its own, whereas RANK provides a numerical rating of how well the record matched the search criteria. This field can be sorted or filtered just like any other field, and it provides the developer more flexibility in presenting the data returned.

The uses of CONTAINS and FREETEXT are illustrated in Exercise 6-4.

Performing a Full-Text Search

The following steps demonstrate how to use full-text searching on your server. To perform these steps you must create the index on your server, so if you do not have permissions to do this (or if you just don't want to modify your server), you may choose to just read along.

1. From the Tools menu, select Full-Text Indexing. This should bring you to the first page of the Full-Text Indexing Wizard. Click Next.

2. From the second screen (Select a Table), select the pubs database. Click Next.

3. From the third screen (Select an Index), select the unique index, UPKCL_titleidind. (It is necessary for the full-text search to be able to uniquely identify a record to perform any needed joins.) Click Next.

4. From the fourth screen (Select Table Columns), add the fields **title**, **type**, and **notes**. The screen should look like the one shown next. Click Next.

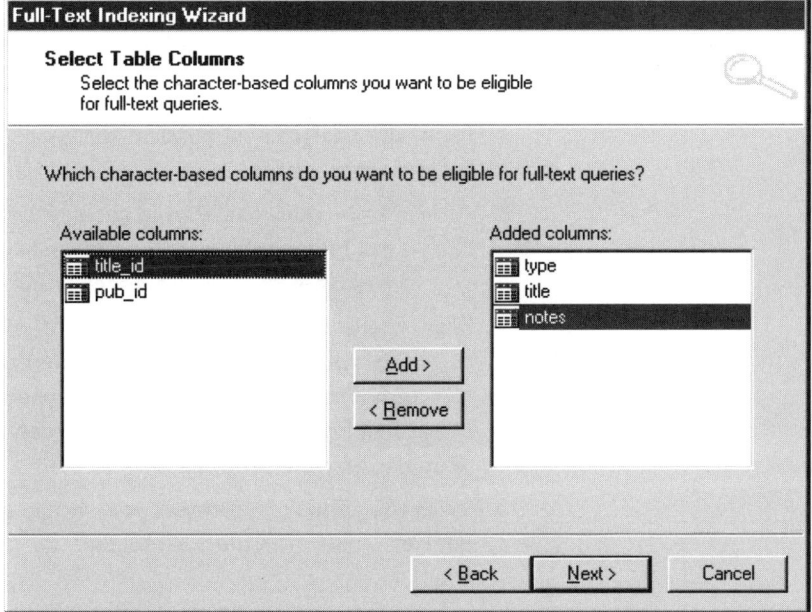

5. From the fifth screen (Select a Catalog), enter a name of **TitleCatalog**. Keep the other defaults. (If you have not used created a catalog before, you will be required to create a new catalog.) Click Next.

6. From the sixth screen (Select or Create Population Schedules), click New Schedule. On the screen that appears, enter a Schedule Name of **IndexTitles**. (This should be the same as the one shown next.) Accept the other defaults. Click OK; then click Next.

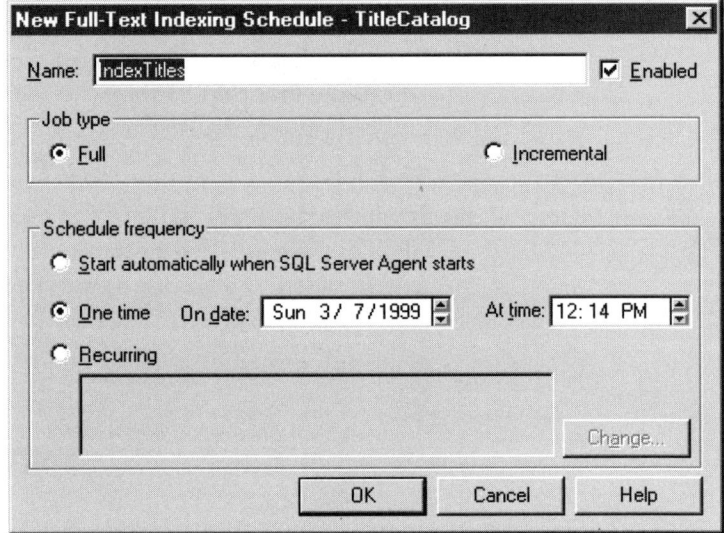

7. From the final screen, confirm that your selections are summarized as you entered them, and click Finish.

8. After a brief wait, you should receive a message stating that the "Full-Text Indexing Wizard completed successfully" and instructing you to populate the full-text index. Click OK.

9. From the Enterprise Manager, in Full Text Catalogs in the pubs database, you should now see a single item: TitleCatalog. Right-click this item. From the shortcut menu, select Start Population, and then select Full Population. You should receive a message that the "Population of full-text catalog started successfully."

10. With the catalog populated, you should be able to build full-text queries. Load the Query Analyzer.

11. Execute the following query: **SELECT title, notes FROM titles WHERE CONTAINS (notes, 'computer')**. Note that three records are returned, each containing the word *computer* in the Notes field.

12. Execute the following query: **SELECT title, notes FROM titles WHERE CONTAINS (notes, 'FORMSOF(INFLECTIONAL, "cook")')** You should return two different records, containing two different verb tenses of the word *cook*.

13. Execute the following query: **SELECT title, notes FROM titles WHERE FREETEXT (notes, 'What are easy meals for the computer user in the modern world?')** This should return nine records containing the various words and phrases in the text submitted, excluding words such as *the* and *in*.

14. Execute the following query: **SELECT au_id, SEARCH_TABLE.RANK FROM titleauthor INNER JOIN FREETEXTTABLE(titles, notes, 'What are easy meals for the computer user in the modern world?') AS SEARCH_TABLE ON titleauthor.title_id = SEARCH_TABLE.[KEY]**. This should return 12 records showing which authors wrote the kinds of books matched in the previous query. (There are more authors than books, because some books had multiple authors.)

CERTIFICATION SUMMARY

Developers create queries to select content from a table or from a combination of tables. The developers can define the content they want retrieved, but the actual algorithm to retrieve the data is called a query execution plan, and it is generated by SQL Server. However, by observing this query execution plan, the developer can better understand the query and avoid production bottlenecks.

Tables can be combined in a variety of ways. Columns can be combined using joins, rows can be combined using UNIONs, and subqueries can encapsulate queries inside of other queries.

Most data modification is done with the INSERT, DELETE, and UPDATE statements. If the use of one of these commands violates a table constraint, the command will not execute.

There are two kinds of searches that can be performed: wildcard searches, and full-text searches. Full-text searches provide more flexibility, but they require more effort for initial configuration and for index maintenance.

✓ TWO-MINUTE DRILL

❑ In addition to retrieving information from tables, queries can also be used to modify content in tables, or even to create brand-new tables.

❑ The database uses what it knows about the tables to estimate the most efficient program for retrieving the data. This algorithm is known as a *query execution plan*.

❑ Even if SQL Server has had excellent performance when executing a query in the past, it may choose a new execution plan if the size of the table changes, if indexes are changed, or if the percentage of unique values in an indexed column changes.

❑ There are three primary ways to improve the performance of your queries: adding indexes, updating statistics, and changing the query definition.

❑ You can create multiple indexes on the same tables. As you observed in the sample execution plans, SQL Server usually uses an index when one is available. However, sometimes adding an index to improve query performance can do more harm than good.

❑ SQL Server estimates the performance costs of a query and selects the most efficient possibility before executing it. When SQL Server is trying to decide what index (if any) to use to find the requested data, it refers to internal statistics that it has generated on that column.

❑ If a database is smaller than 8MB, SQL Server will scan the entire table; otherwise, only a sample of the data will be analyzed to generate the statistics.

❑ Even though statistics are not necessarily updated when new content is added, the index itself is still automatically updated.

❑ Much of the effort required to process a query involves the joins between tables. There are three main join techniques that Microsoft uses: nested loops, merge joins, and hash joins.

❑ There are three primary ways to combine data from multiple sources: joins, unions, and subqueries. Encapsulate one query inside another query.

❑ Joins match up data in two or more tables and combine the resulting data by columns.

❑ There are five kinds of joins: inner join, left outer join, right outer join, full outer join, and cross join.

❑ If you don't specify any join, the cross join is the default.

❑ Although the = (equal) operator is usually used in joins, it is possible to use inequality operators as well.

❑ Normally, you will want to join fields of the same data type. However, if the field types can be implicitly converted, then the join will succeed even if the field types are different.

❑ Joins are very useful when you want to combine the content from multiple tables into the same row. However, there are times when you want to view the data from multiple tables in the same column. This can be best accomplished using the UNION operator.

❑ So far, we have taken our returned data sets, which we created with queries, and returned them directly to the user. It is also possible to take this data and place it into entirely new tables. This is done using the SELECT INTO statement.

❑ The following are some advanced techniques that you can use with joins, SELECT INTO statements, and UNION operators: self-joins, cross joins, and UNION.

❑ You can use one SQL statement to return records or criteria used by another SQL statement. The encapsulating query is called a *parent query*, and the inner query is a *subquery*.

❑ You can use a subquery as a replacement for a value in the SELECT clause, as part of the WHERE clause, or as part of the HAVING clause.

❑ When you introduce a subquery with an operator, there are restrictions on the columns and rows that can be returned by that subquery.

❑ It is possible to have your subqueries call subqueries of their own. When this is done, it is called *nested subqueries*. (Do not confuse this with *nested queries*, which is a term sometimes used to describe simple subqueries.)

❑ When a subquery retrieves parameters from its parent query, it is known as a *correlated subquery*.

❑ A correlated subquery is more demanding of server resources than most other subqueries, so care should be taken with their use.

❑ Most subqueries return a single field, and the values in this field are returned to the parent query. By contrast, the EXISTS statement is permitted to select multiple fields.

❑ Although you should be familiar with EXISTS for the certification exam, be aware that most queries using EXISTS could be rewritten using the ANY or IN functions instead, or by using joins.

❑ The three main statements used in Transact-SQL to modify the content in tables are INSERT, DELETE, and UPDATE.

❑ You can use the INSERT command to create a single record of data, or to insert an entire record set.

❑ The DELETE command is used to delete entire rows of data from a table.

❑ The UPDATE statement allows you to make modifications to specific columns of an existing row or rows.

❑ In SQL Server 7.0, Microsoft introduces full-text search functionality. This complements the existing functionality set and provides more features, but requires additional configuration and data maintenance.

❑ For simple situations, you can also use the SOUNDEX and DIFFERENCE functions to provide some of the functionalityof a full-text search without requiring all of the configuration.

❑ Although the use of full-text searches is fairly simple, the initial configuration required to support them can be quite involved.

❑ Even before performing this configuration, the Microsoft Search service must be installed and started. (The Microsoft Search service is not a part of the Desktop installation of SQL Server 7.0, and therefore is not available if you're using Windows 95, Windows 98, or Windows NT Workstation.)

❑ There are two main functions used for full-text searching: CONTAINS and FREETEXT.

SELF TEST

The following questions will help you measure your understanding of the material presented in this chapter. Read all of the choices carefully, as there may be more than one correct answer. Choose all correct answers for each question.

1. Which of the following could have an impact upon the query execution plan determined by SQL Server? (Choose all that apply.)

   A. Removing a clustered index

   B. Querying the table from an administrative account

   C. Adding 10,000 records to a 100 record table

   D. Reducing the number of unique values in a column while keeping the number of rows constant

2. When using the Query Analyzer, you get a warning that the statistics are out of date. Which of the following could fix this? (Choose all that apply.)

   A. DBCC SHOW_STATISTICS

   B. DROP STATISTICS on the table; then CREATE STATISTICS

   C. Drop the index; then create the index

   D. UPDATE STATISTICS

3. You execute the following query: *SELECT table1.name, table2.number FROM table1 INNER JOIN table2 ON table1.keyfield = table2.keyfield ORDER BY name.* Which of the following joins would SQL Server most likely use if both tables had

5,000,000 rows, and *keyfield* was indexed in both tables?

   A. Nested loop

   B. Hash

   C. Build input

   D. Merge

4. What is an advantage of using JOIN (the new syntax) instead of WHERE (the old syntax) to define your joins? (Choose all that apply.)

   A. The WHERE syntax may not be supported in future versions of SQL Server.

   B. More database vendors support the JOIN syntax.

   C. It is not possible to represent a right outer join using the WHERE syntax.

   D. It is easier to distinguish between joins and filter criteria.

5. Using the pubs database, you want to view all the authors and titles. You use the following query:
   SELECT authors.au_lname, authors.au_fname, titleauthor.title_id FROM authors, titleauthor
   You receive far too many rows.
   What went wrong?

   A. No join was specified, so a cross join was implied.

   B. You didn't include the primary keys in the SELECT clause.

C. A foreign key needs to be created for the titleauthor table.

D. There is nothing wrong with the query.

6. Can two fields with different data types be joined?

   A. They cannot be joined with any join.

   B. They can only be joined with a cross join.

   C. If the field can be implicitly converted, they can be joined.

   D. The fields will not be implicitly converted, but if the developer CASTs or CONVERTs one of the fields, they can be joined.

7. What would be the caption of the second field in the following UNION query: *SELECT CompanyName, ShipperID, Phone FROM Shippers UNION SELECT CompanyName, SupplierID AS ID, Phone.*

   A. Suppliers

   B. ShipperID

   C. SupplierID

   D. ID

8. How do you define local and global temporary tables when using SELECT INTO?

   A. One dollar sign for a local temporary table, two number signs for a dollar temporary table

   B. One dollar sign for a global temporary table, two number signs for a dollar temporary table

   C. One number sign for a local temporary table, two number signs for a global temporary table

   D. One number sign for a global temporary table, two number signs for a local temporary table

9. Assuming that the select into/bulkcopy option is set, which of the following must also be true for a SELECT INTO statement to successfully create a new permanent table? (Choose all that apply.)

   A. The source and destination tables must have the same number of fields.

   B. In the database, the user must have the permission CREATE TABLE.

   C. There can be no computed fields in the SELECT list.

   D. All fields in the SELECT list must be unique.

10. If you look at a query and see a < as the join operator, which of the following is most likely?

    A. The developer was using a right outer join.

    B. The developer was using a self-join.

    C. The developer was using a cross join.

    D. The developer was using a full outer join.

11. Which clauses can have a subquery? (Choose all that apply.)

    A. HAVING

    B. GROUP BY

    C. SUMMARIZE

    D. WHERE

12. How many rows can be returned by a subquery without generating an error?

    A. Only one

    B. Only one, unless preceded by the ANY, ALL, EXISTS, or IN operators

    C. Unlimited

    D. Unlimited, unless preceded by the ANY, ALL, EXISTS, or IN operators

13. How many levels deep can subqueries be nested?

    A. Up to 32, memory permitting

    B. Up to 16, memory permitting

    C. Up to 8, memory permitting

    D. Up to 4, memory permitting

    E. Up to 2, memory permitting

14. Which of the following is true for a correlated subquery? (Choose all that apply.)

    A. The subquery is evaluated once.

    B. The subquery is evaluated multiple times.

    C. The subquery can refer to a field in the parent query.

    D. The subquery cannot refer to a field in the parent query.

15. How many fields can be returned by a subquery?

    A. One, always

    B. One, unless preceded by the EXISTS clause

    C. The same number of fields as the outer query, always

    D. The same number of fields as the outer query, unless preceded by the EXISTS clause

16. Which of the following can be successfully excluded from an INSERT statement? (Choose all that apply.)

    A. An identity column that is a primary key

    B. A uniqueidentifier column that is a primary key

    C. A NOT NULL field with no default

    D. A NOT NULL field with a default

17. If you run the query, DELETE FROM Director, when the Name field of the Director table is used as a foreign key constraint by the Films table, what would happen?

    A. All rows would be deleted from Director, and no rows would be deleted from Films.

    B. All rows would be deleted from Director, and all referenced rows would be deleted from Films.

    C. No rows would be deleted from Director or from Films.

    D. The rows in Director that were not referenced by Films would be deleted.

18. Which of the following is guaranteed to modify, at most, one record?

    A. UPDATE...WHERE

    B. UPDATE...WHERE CURRENT OF

    C. UPDATE FIRST...WHERE

    D. UPDATE...WHERE ROWCOUNT=1

19. You have confirmed that the Microsoft Search service is running, and you have used the Full-Text Indexing Wizard to create a full-text index. However, you have not yet scheduled the population of this full-text index. What will you get when you run a query using CONTAINS?

   A. You will receive the following warning: "Cannot use a CONTAINS or FREETEXT predicate on table 'Categories' because it is not full-text indexed."

   B. The query will execute, automatically creating the indexes on an as-needed basis.

   C. The CONTAINS operator will automatically be converted to a LIKE command.

   D. The query will execute, but return no data.

20. What is an advantage of FREETEXTTABLE over CONTAINSTABLE?

   A. FREETEXTTABLE can be used to rank the results by how well they match.

   B. FREETEXTTABLE can automatically parse the search parameter into words and phrases to be found in the destination table.

   C. FREETEXTTABLE doesn't require Microsoft Search service to be running.

   D. FREETEXTTABLE allows you to search for tense variants of nouns and verbs.

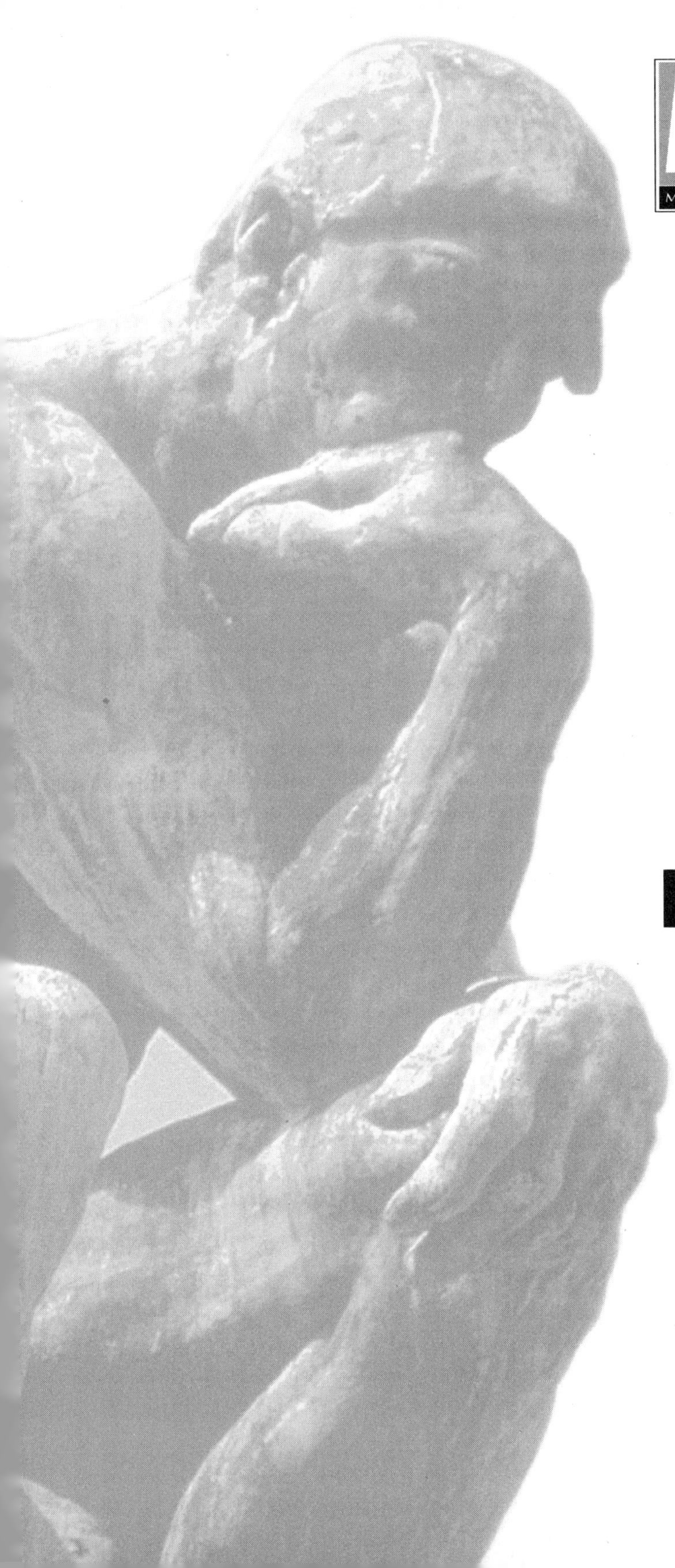

7

Summarizing Data

CERTIFICATION OBJECTIVES

U sing Transact-SQL, you can retrieve data from a database, create databases and database objects, add data, modify existing data, and perform complex operations. In addition, Transact-SQL also supports the ability to summarize data. To accomplish this task using Transact-SQL, you employ the use of aggregate functions.

Aggregate functions return summary values, such as averages and sums, from values in a particular column. The returned values represent a single value for each set of rows to which an aggregate function was applied.

Transact-SQL commands can be executed within the utilities provided by SQL Server 7.0, as well as in third-party applications that support embedded Transact-SQL. The primary tool used to create and test Transact-SQL in SQL Server 7.0 is the Query Analyzer.

The Query Analyzer is a graphical tool used to build and test your Transact-SQL statements; therefore, it is the tool that we will use during the hands-on exercises for this chapter. The Query Analyzer can be launched from within the SQL Server 7.0 program group, or from within the Enterprise Manager by selecting Query Analyzer from the Tools menu.

In this chapter, we will learn how to use the aggregate functions to return summary information from SQL Server database tables.

CERTIFICATION OBJECTIVE 7.01

Using Aggregate Functions

Aggregate functions can be used to return values for each row returned by an SQL statement, or to produce a single value for each group of rows. The new values that are generated appear as new columns. It is important to remember that when using aggregate functions, each column specified in the SELECT clause must use an aggregate function or your statement will return an error. This requirement results in an inability to see the row details. Furthermore, aggregate functions cannot be used in a WHERE clause. If a SELECT statement uses a WHERE clause but not a GROUP BY clause, an aggregate function will produce a single value for the subset of rows specified by the

FROM THE CLASSROOM

Summarizing Summarizing Data

Microsoft SQL Server 7.0 provides numerous Transact-SQL commands for use in summarizing, aggregating, or combining data automatically into cumulative values. If used properly, these commands can provide a convenient method for generating summary data as a part of a single command. Being more complex in nature, aggregate functions are naturally prone to producing more usage errors than normal. Errors can often occur when using aggregate functions together with NULL values. Unexpected, or inaccurate results may occur, due to the nature of aggregate function functionality when encountering NULL values. Additionally, aggregate commands often involve higher than normal amounts of guidelines for proper usage. It's important to keep track of the requirements for using commands such as GROUP BY, ORDER BY, COMPUTE (BY),

or any of the assorted aggregate functions supported by SQL Server 7.0.

One of the most complex pairs of operators, keywords, or functions used to generate summary information includes the CUBE and ROLLUP operators. The results produced by these commands are often misunderstood, especially when dealing with more than two or three columns at a time. ROLLUP is preferred over COMPUTE (BY), which is maintained for backward compatibility. ROLLUP has the advantage of producing relational data result sets, instead of the row aggregate information returned by COMPUTE (BY). COMPUTE (BY) is considered useful for testing purposes, but not recommended for use in application development.

—Michael Lane Thomas, MCSE+I, MCSD, MCP+SB, MSS, MCT, A+

WHERE clause. When aggregates produce a single value per column, whether or not the SELECT statement included a WHERE clause, the function is called a *scalar* aggregate. When a SELECT statement includes a GROUP BY clause, each subset produces a value per function. When used in this way, the aggregate function is called a *vector* aggregate.

When row details are needed, we can use *row aggregates* to summarize data and maintain the ability to view the row details. Row aggregate functions generate summary values that appear as additional rows in the results set. This is accomplished by using the COMPUTE clause, which will be covered later in this chapter.

Aggregate Functions and Syntax

Let's begin by examining the aggregate functions supported by SQL Server. We will discuss their syntax and usage.

AVG

AVG returns the average of all the values in an expression. AVG can be used with numeric columns only and will automatically ignore null values. Valid numeric columns refer to *decimal, float, int, money, numeric, real, smallint, smallmoney,* and *tinyint.*

Syntax:

AVG(*expression*)

Scenario:

Tiffany is in the process of hiring a new sales person for her department. She knows that each sales person's salary has been stored in the Employees table. In order to determine an appropriate salary range for the new employee, she would like to find out the average salary of all the sales personnel. This type of scenario is an example of the need to create a SQL statement that uses the AVG function. In order to accomplish this task, Tiffany might enter the statement below:

Example:

```
SELECT AVG(Salary) FROM Employees WHERE Title='Sales'
```

Returned value:

```
--------------------
28866.68
(1 row(s) affected)
```

Use the AS clause as an option to provide a column head for the resulting column values, so that the information being viewed in the results set can be more easily identified.

Example:

```
SELECT AVG(salary) as AvgSalary FROM Employees WHERE Title='Sales'
```

Returned value:

```
AvgSalary
--------------------
28866.68
(1 row(s) affected)
```

COUNT

COUNT returns the number of non-null values in the expression provided. If used in conjunction with DISTINCT, COUNT finds the number of unique non-null values. COUNT supports the use of both numeric and character columns. All null values will be ignored, therefore it is important to use COUNT against a column for which you are sure that each row you want included in your count will have a value. Columns that should be safe to use as your COUNT expression will be your *primary key* and *foreign key* columns. As explained in Chapter 5, a primary key is a column or a group of columns that is used to uniquely identify each row within a table. A foreign key is a value that already exists in another table as a primary key, and is being used in the current table to create a relationship between rows that exist in different tables.

As another alternative you can use the asterisk (*) as the COUNT expression. Using the asterisk eliminates specifying a particular column and will count all rows, therefore null values in a column will not be a factor.

Syntax:

COUNT(*expression*) or
COUNT(*)

Scenario:

Sean has been put in charge of sending out invitations to his company's annual staff meeting. Before he can call the printer with the number of invitations to be printed, he needs to have a head count. In order to accomplish this task, Sean might use the following SQL statement:

Example:

```
SELECT COUNT(*) FROM Employees
```

Returned value:

```
-----------
9
(1 row(s) affected)
```

MAX

MAX returns the maximum value in an expression. MAX can be used with numeric, character, and date/time columns, but not with *bit* columns. When using MAX with character columns, MAX returns the highest value in the collating order. MAX ignores null values. DISTINCT is available for ANSI compatibility, but is not used by MAX. Therefore, the use of DISTINCT in conjunction with MAX does not generate an error. However, because MAX is designed to return only one value; that being the maximum value, uniqueness is not an issue.

Syntax:

MAX(*expression*)

Scenario:

Jennifer is conducting research on the types of products that her company sells. She would like to know what is the highest-priced beverage that her company offers. Each product that is sold is categorized based on a column named CategoryID; in the case of beverages, the CategoryID = 1. The price for each product is in a column named UnitPrice. Using these two columns, Jennifer might devise the following statement:

Example:

```
SELECT MAX(UnitPrice) FROM Products WHERE CategoryID=1
```

Returned value:

```
--------------------
263.5000
(1 row(s) affected)
```

MIN

MIN returns the minimum value in an expression. MIN can be used with numeric, character, and date/time columns, but not with *bit* columns. When using MIN with character columns, MIN returns the lowest value in the collating order. MIN ignores null values. DISTINCT is available for ANSI compatibility but is not used by MIN.

Syntax:

MIN(*expression*)

Scenario:

Tiffany is coordinating a recruiting project for her employer. As part of her research, she would like to know the age range of the personnel currently employed. To find out the oldest person employed by her company, she needs to know the earliest birth date that exits in the Employees table. To do this Tiffany might use the following statement:

Example:

```
SELECT MIN(BirthDate) FROM Employees
```

Returned value:

```
--------------------------
1937-09-19 00:00:00.000
(1 row(s) affected)
```

SUM

SUM returns the sum of all values in an expression. SUM supports the use of DISTINCT to summarize only unique values in the expression. Null values are ignored and SUM can only be used against numeric columns.

Syntax:

SUM(*expression*)

Scenario:

Sean is working on a proposal to request more personnel for the U.S. Territory sales staff. As supportive information, he needs to know the total revenue generated by customers in the United States. Unfortunately the information that he needs spans three different tables.

Sean can readily compute total sales because the Order Details table contains the UnitPrice per product and the Quantity that was ordered. However, Sean also needs to know the country of each customer who placed an order. That information is located in the Customers table in a column named Country. Because there is not a direct link or relationship between the Customers table and the Order Details table, Sean has to find a *junction table*. That is to say, a table that has a relationship to both the Customers table and the Order Details table.

The junction table needed in this example is the Orders table. The Orders table contains as foreign key, CustomerID, which is the primary key for the Customers table. The Order Details table contains as a foreign key, OrderID, which is the primary key for the Orders table. Having this knowledge about the tables involved, Sean could execute the following statement:

Example:

```
SELECT SUM([UnitPrice]*[quantity]) AS ExtPrice
FROM (Customers INNER JOIN Orders ON Customers.CustomerID = Orders.CustomerID)
INNER JOIN [Order Details] ON Orders.OrderID = [Order Details].OrderID
WHERE (((Customers.Country)='USA'))
```

Returned value:

```
ExtPrice
--------------------
263566.9800
(1 row(s) affected)
```

DISTINCT

You can use DISTINCT to eliminate duplicate values before an aggregate function is applied. DISTINCT can be used with AVG, COUNT, and SUM. DISTINCT cannot be used with COUNT(*) and will be ignored when used in conjunction with MIN and MAX.

Syntax:

DISTINCT (*expression*)

Scenario:

Michael is coordinating a marketing campaign for his employer. He needs to determine in which markets to run the new advertising campaign. To do this he needs to know in what cities the company's current clients are located. He knows that the Customers table contains address information, and that a customer's city is held in a column named City. He knows that many customers come from the same city, but he only needs a unique listing of all the cities that appear in the Customers table. With this information, Michael might use the following statement:

Example:

```
SELECT DISTINCT City FROM Customers
```

Returned value:

```
City
---------------
Aachen
Albuquerque
Anchorage
list continued ...
(69 row(s) affected)
```

exam

ⓦatch

Before testing, be sure to know the syntax, exceptions, and rules involved in using the aggregate functions. Know the data types of the column values that are allowed for each of the function aggregates. For example, AVG and SUM can only be used against numeric values, whereas COUNT, MAX, and MIN support text values.

Using the Northwind Traders Sample Database

During Exercises 7-1 and 7-2, and all future exercises for this chapter, we use one of the sample databases that ship with SQL Server 7.0, Northwind. The Northwind database contains the sales data for a fictitious company called Northwind Traders, which imports and exports specialty foods from around the world.

If you are not familiar with the tables that comprise Northwind, you should spend a few moments looking at the tables, fields, and relationships.

EXERCISE 7-1

Examining Northwind Using the Enterprise Manager

Follow these steps to use the Enterprise Manager to view the contents of Northwind.

1. From the SQL Server 7.0 Program Group, start the Enterprise Manager.

2. Expand the SQL Server Group by clicking the plus sign (+) associated with it.

3. Expand the server on which you installed the SQL Server sample databases.

4. Locate the Databases folder and expand its contents by selecting the associated plus sign (+).

5. Locate the Diagrams folder contained in the Databases folder.

6. Click the Diagrams folder to view its contents.

7. With your cursor still on the Diagrams folder, you should see an icon named Relationships in the Items pane on the right.

8. Double-click the Relationships icon to see the Northwind tables and relationships.

9. Spend a few minutes familiarizing yourself with the tables and relationships.

10. Choose File | Exit to exit the Query Analyzer.

It's time to put to work some of the aggregate functions we've discussed. In Exercise 7-2, we use one of the tables from Northwind to practice the concepts learned thus far.

EXERCISE 7-2

Using Aggregate Functions

1. From the SQL Server 7.0 Program Group, start the Query Analyzer. Log on to your server if prompted. Alternatively, if you are inside the Enterprise Manager, you can start the Query Analyzer by selecting it from the Tools menu.

2. Located on the Query Analyzer toolbar is a drop-down list for a database selection. Drop down the list of available databases and choose Northwind.

3. Below the Query Analyzer toolbar is the Transact-SQL area. Enter the following statement into the Transact-SQL area:

```
SELECT COUNT (*) AS NumberOfCustomers
FROM Customers
```

4. Use the Execute Query icon on the toolbar to execute your SQL statement. If you prefer, you can use the keyboard combination CTRL-E to execute your query.

5. The results of your query are displayed in the Results pane.

6. Select File | Exit to close the Query Analyzer.

CERTIFICATION OBJECTIVE 7.02

GROUP BY Fundamentals

The GROUP BY clause allows you to partition a table into one or more subsets that have a value or expression in common. If aggregate functions are used in the SELECT clause, the GROUP BY clause produces a single value per aggregate. The GROUP BY subsets are produced by collecting rows with the same values, in the columns specified in the GROUP BY list.

You can refer to new summary information that is produced by the GROUP BY clause by using the HAVING clause. When selecting your columns for the GROUP BY clause, you cannot include columns with the following data types: text, image, and bit. When building your SELECT field list, each column specified in the SELECT list must also appear in the GROUP BY clause unless the column is being used in an aggregate function.

You cannot GROUP BY an alias, which means that all the fields in the GROUP BY field list must be columns physically located in the table(s) specified in the FROM clause.

You can use a WHERE clause in your statement, and rows that don't meet your criteria will be eliminated before any grouping occurs. If an ORDER BY clause is not specified, groups returned using the GROUP BY clause will not be in any particular order. It is recommended that you use the ORDER BY clause to specify the ordering desired.

A maximum of 10 grouping expressions are allowed in a GROUP BY clause when using CUBE or ROLLUP. Both CUBE and ROLLUP are discussed later in the section. If neither CUBE or ROLLUP is present, GROUP BY is limited not by the number of groupings, but by the size of the columns referenced in the GROUP BY, the aggregate functions, and the aggregate values involved in the query. The size of the resulting query is limited, like all query results, to 8060 bytes.

Syntax:

GROUP BY [ALL] *field1,field2...*

ALL

ALL is meaningful only when the SELECT statement also includes a WHERE clause. If you use ALL, the query results include all groups produced by the GROUP BY clause, even if some of the groups have no rows that meet the search conditions. Without ALL, a SELECT statement that includes GROUP BY does not show groups for which no rows qualify.

Let's examine two different scenarios that give examples of using the GROUP BY clause. Using the GROUP BY clause is the first step in providing summarized data. This information can be used to assist you in making informed business decisions based on data that has accumulated in your database tables. However, in order to make good use of the information that is being stored, you have to have a good understanding of the database's tables, fields, and relationships.

Scenario 1:

The warehouse manager is working on his staff schedule for next week. He called Cameron, one of Northwind's DBAs, for his assistance. In order to know how many employees will be needed in the warehouse, the warehouse manager needs to know the number of items that will have to be pulled from the shelves and packaged for each open order. Cameron knows that the Order Details table contains the OrderID for each order and the number of items purchased per product in a Quantity column. However, in order to know which orders are still outstanding, Cameron will have to pull information from the Orders table. The Orders table contains a column named ShippedDate that is used to store the date that an order was shipped from the warehouse to a customer. If the ShippedDate column is empty, an order has yet to be shipped. Knowing this information, Cameron could use the following statement to produce the results for the warehouse manager.

Example:

```
SELECT [Order Details].OrderID, Sum([Order Details].Quantity) AS NumberOfItems
FROM Orders INNER JOIN [Order Details] ON Orders.OrderID = [Order Details].OrderID
WHERE (((Orders.ShippedDate) Is Null))
GROUP BY [Order Details].OrderID
ORDER BY [Order Details].OrderID
```

Returned value:

```
OrderID      NumberOfItems
----------   -------------
11008        181
11019        5
11039        132
list continued …
(21 row(s) affected)
```

Scenario 2:

To provide the warehouse manager with some additional information, Cameron decides to produce a report that shows sales trends. He wants to produce a report that shows how many orders are being placed per month, for each country. To assist in determining the warehouse staff that's necessary to process these orders, Cameron also includes the average number of items for the orders. Most of the columns that Cameron needs are found in the Orders table. But, in order to find out the number of items contained in each order so that they can be averaged, Cameron has to pull that information from the Order Details table. In order to produce this report, Cameron could use the following statement:

Example:

```
SELECT MONTH(OrderDate) AS SaleMonth, Orders.ShipCountry, COUNT(Orders.OrderID) AS
CountOfOrderID, AVG([Order Details].Quantity) AS AvgNumberOfItems
FROM Orders INNER JOIN [Order Details] ON Orders.OrderID = [Order Details].OrderID
GROUP BY MONTH(OrderDate), Orders.ShipCountry
ORDER BY SaleMonth,ShipCountry
```

Returned value:

```
SaleMonth   ShipCountry       CountOfOrderID
AvgNumberOfItems
----------  ---------------   --------------
----------------
1           Argentina         1                1
1           Austria           22               42
1           Belgium           4                21
```

```
list continued …
(211 row(s) affected)
```

Using the *Month* function is necessary to group the order dates based on the month rather than the exact date the order was placed. The Month function returns values 1 through 12, representing the twelve months of the year. The syntax for Month is: *Month(date)*.

Cameron could have grouped the order dates based on the week of the year, or possibly the quarter. In order to accomplish either of those, Cameron could use the *DatePart* function. DatePart returns a numeric value based on the date interval provided. For example, had he asked to return quarters, DatePart returns 1 through 4 representing the four quarters of the year. On the other hand, had he requested weeks, DatePart would return 1 to 52, representative of the 52 weeks in a year. The syntax for DatePart is *DatePart(dateinterval,date)*. The date interval argument for DatePart is an abbreviation for the interval desired. For instance, DatePart(qq,GetDate()), would return 1 to 4, indicating in what quarter today's date occurs. The GetDate function returns today's date.

on the job

Have you noticed all of the additional typing that is required any time we have to reference the Order Details table from Northwind? We continually have to enclose the name of the table inside of square brackets ([ ]) because the table name contains a space. The same holds true for column names that contain spaces. Although SQL Server supports the use of spaces when naming database objects, I suggest you use either upper- and lowercasing or the underscore instead. This will give you the readability you need without requiring the extra syntax.

HAVING

The HAVING clause sets conditions for the GROUP BY clause in the way that the WHERE clause sets conditions for the SELECT clause. Because HAVING is used to restrict the rows being returned by GROUP BY, the use of HAVING without GROUP BY is meaningless and would ultimately function as a WHERE clause.

The HAVING search conditions are similar to WHERE, except that HAVING supports the use of aggregates and HAVING can reference the values being returned by the GROUP BY clause. When multiple conditions are specified, they are combined with AND, OR, or NOT. The HAVING clause supports the use of up to 128 conditions. HAVING can also reference any of the items that appear in the select list.

Syntax:

HAVING *search condition(s)*

Scenario:

Robert is assisting in compiling information on Northwind sales trends. He would like to see how many orders are being shipped to each country per year. He is most interested in shipments that are occurring with frequency; therefore, he would like to eliminate data on countries that receive only a couple of shipments each year. All of the information that Robert needs can be found in the Orders table. He will have to employ the use of the *Year* function to assist in grouping his data. The Year function accepts a date as its required argument, and returns the date's year. To accomplish this task Robert could use the following statement:

Example:

```
SELECT YEAR(Orders.OrderDate) as YearOrdered,
Orders.ShipCountry,COUNT(Orders.OrderID) as NumOfOrders
FROM Orders
GROUP BY YEAR(Orders.OrderDate), Orders.ShipCountry
HAVING COUNT(*) > 2
ORDER BY YEAR(Orders.OrderDate)
```

Returned value:

```
YearOrdered ShipCountry      NumOfOrders
------------ ---------------- -----------
1994         Austria          5
1994         Belgium          3
1994         Brazil           10
list continued …
(60 row(s) affected)
```

CUBE

CUBE is an aggregate operator that can be used to produce result sets that are typically used in reports. CUBE produces a *super-aggregate* row, which is a summary of the row information generated by the GROUP BY clause. The super-aggregate rows are generated by creating all possible combinations of groupings from the list of columns in the GROUP BY clause. Distinct aggregates such as COUNT(DISTINCT column) are not supported when using CUBE. If used, the SQL Server returns an error, and stops processing your query.

You use CUBE to cross-reference information without having to create additional procedures. CUBE expands the information being returned by adding an additional accumulative value, represented by *(null)* for each column used in the GROUP BY clause. Therefore, the number of columns in the GROUP BY clause causes the resulting super-aggregate rows to shrink and grow accordingly. A maximum number of 10 columns or expressions can be used in a GROUP BY clause when using CUBE. GROUP BY ALL is not supported.

Syntax:

WITH CUBE

Let's compare the differences in results being returned by a GROUP BY with and without the use of the CUBE operator. We use four slightly different SQL statements to compare our results.

Scenario:

Robert wants to know how many products Northwind offers in each of its product categories. To accomplish this, Robert can use columns from the Products table. To begin, Robert decides to group and count the products. He can use the following statement to produce the results he needs. Notice that the *rows affected* returns the number of groupings found. In other words, it returns the number of rows that are returned by the SQL SELECT statement.

Example:

```
SELECT Products.CategoryID,COUNT(Products.ProductID) as NumOfProds
FROM Products
GROUP BY Products.CategoryID
```

Returned value:

```
CategoryID  NumOfProds
----------- -----------
1               12
2               12
3               13
4               10
5               7
6               6
7               5
8               12
(8 row(s) affected)
```

In this next statement, Robert decides to use the CUBE operator to provide summary information on the result sets produced by the GROUP BY clause. Notice that when the CUBE operator is used, a new row is added to the results set. *Null* is added as though it is a row value. It behaves like a stop gap or subdivision. Null represents all values in the CategoryID column. The value placed in the NumOfProds column uses the same aggregate function, but the function is applied against *all* of the subgroup rows. Hence, it counts all the ProductIDs (NumOfProds).

Example:

```
SELECT Products.CategoryID,COUNT(Products.ProductID) as NumOfProds
FROM Products
GROUP BY Products.CategoryID
WITH CUBE
```

Returned value:

```
CategoryID  NumOfProds
----------- -----------
1               12
2               12
```

```
3              13
4              10
5              7
6              6
7              5
8              12
NULL           77
(9 row(s) affected)
```

In this example we are going to include the HAVING clause. Notice that the value returned by CUBE is not affected by the HAVING clause.

Example:

```
SELECT Products.CategoryID,COUNT(Products.ProductID) as NumOfProds
FROM Products
GROUP BY Products.CategoryID
WITH CUBE
HAVING COUNT(*)>10
```

Returned value:

```
CategoryID  NumOfProds
----------- -----------
1           12
2           12
3           13
8           12
NULL        77
(5 row(s) affected)
```

Finally, Robert decides to add an additional column reference to both his SELECT clause and the GROUP BY clause. Robert adds the SupplierID column from the Products table. With more than one column in the GROUP BY clause, you can really see the effect of the CUBE operator. CUBE produces super-aggregate rows for all possible combinations for both columns that have been placed in the GROUP BY.

First you see a super-aggregate row added that counts all products by category, followed by a count of all products in all categories. Finally, CUBE produces super-aggregate rows, counting all products by each SupplierID.

Example:

```
SELECT Products.CategoryID,Products.SupplierID,COUNT(Products.ProductID) as
NumOfProds
FROM Products
GROUP BY Products.CategoryID,Products.SupplierID
WITH CUBE
```

Returned value:

```
CategoryID   SupplierID   NumOfProds
-----------  -----------  -----------
1            1            2
1            7            1
1            10           1
1            12           1
1            16           3
1            18           2
1            20           1
1            23           1
1            NULL         12
list continued ...
2            1            1
2            2            4
2            3            2
2            6            1
2            7            1
2            12           1
2            20           1
2            29           1
2            NULL         12
list continued ...
NULL         NULL         77
list continued ...
NULL         1            3
NULL         2            4
NULL         3            3
list continued ...
(87 row(s) affected)
```

ROLLUP

Like CUBE, the ROLLUP operator creates aggregates and super-aggregates for elements within a GROUP BY clause. ROLLUP supports cumulative aggregates such as running sums and averages. ROLLUP reflects the positions of the columns and expressions used in the GROUP BY clause. Aggregate groupings are made up of columns to the right of the current column.

The ROLLUP operator creates groups in only one direction, from right to left, along the list of columns in the GROUP BY clause. It then applies the relative aggregate function to these groupings.

The ROLLUP operator can be used to create reports by extracting statistics and summary information from the results sets. This information can then be applied to reports, charts, and graphs.

Syntax:

WITH ROLLUP

Scenario:

Jeffrey is compiling information on how many sales orders are being processed by each Northwind employee. Within each employee grouping, Jeffrey would like the orders to be grouped based on the CustomerID column. This would be simple enough to accomplish with nothing more than a GROUP BY clause that uses both the EmployeeID column and the CustomerID column from the Orders table. However, Jeffery wants to see subtotals for each employee and a cumulative total that represents information for all employees. In order to return the subtotals, Jeffrey needs to use the ROLLUP operator.

Example:

```
SELECT Orders.EmployeeID, Orders.CustomerID, COUNT(Orders.OrderID) as
NumberOfOrders, SUM( [Order Details].UnitPrice * [Order Details].Quantity) as
GrossSalesBeforeDisc
FROM Orders
INNER JOIN [Order Details] ON Orders.OrderID=[Order Details].OrderID
GROUP BY Orders.EmployeeID, Orders.CustomerID
WITH ROLLUP
```

Returned value:

```
EmployeeID  CustomerID NumberOfOrders
GrossSalesBeforeDisc
----------- ---------- --------------
--------------------
1           ALFKI      4              1342.2000
1           ANTON      2              956.9000
1           AROUT      8              2931.9000
list continued ...
1           NULL       345            202143.7100
2           BERGS      3              613.2000
2           BLONP      2              1176.0000
list continued ...
2           NULL       241            177749.2600
3           ALFKI      2              960.0000
3           ANATR      4              799.7500
list continued ...
3           NULL       321            213051.3000
list continued ...
9           AROUT      4              5166.5000
9           BERGS      6              5464.5000
9           BLAUS      5              1632.0000
9           NULL       107            82964.0000
NULL        NULL       2155           1354458.5900
(474 row(s) affected)
```

EXERCISE 7-3

Using the GROUP BY Clause

It's time to use the Query Analyzer to practice the concepts we've learned about using the GROUP BY clause.

1. From the SQL Server 7.0 Program Group, start the Query Analyzer.

2. Connect to your server if prompted.

3. In the Database selection drop-down list, select Northwind.

4. Enter the following statement into the Query Analyzer:

```
SELECT Orders.EmployeeID, COUNT(Orders.OrderID) as NumberOfOrders, SUM( [Order
Details].UnitPrice * [Order Details].Quantity) as GrossSalesBeforeDisc
FROM Orders
INNER JOIN [Order Details] ON Orders.OrderID=[Order Details].OrderID
GROUP BY Orders.EmployeeID
```

5. Use the Execute Query icon on the toolbar to execute your SQL statement. If you prefer, you can press CTRL-E to execute the query.

6. The Results tab will display the results of your SQL statement. They should be similar the to results in Figure 7-1.

7. Choose File | Exit to close the Query Analyzer. Do not save your query.

CERTIFICATION OBJECTIVE 7.03

Using the **COMPUTE** and **COMPUTE BY** Clauses

COMPUTE generates summary values that appear as additional rows within a results set for row aggregate functions. You can use the COMPUTE BY clause to generate values based on subgroups, or generate values for more than one

---

FIGURE 7-1

Using the Query Analyzer on the GROUP BY clause

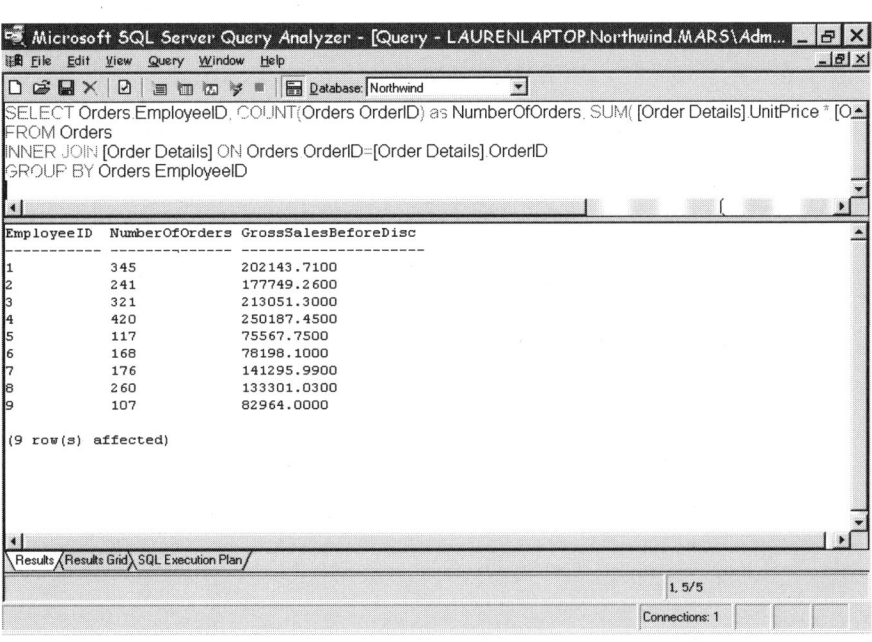

column by employing an aggregate against it. COMPUTE supports the use of summary aggregates AVG, COUNT, MIN, MAX, and SUM. Although SQL Server 7.0 supports COMPUTE, it is available mainly for backward compatibility—it is suggested that you use ROLLUP instead.

The summary values that are generated appear as additional rows. This allows you to see the detail rows and the summary rows within the same results set. The COMPUTE clause cannot be used with INTO because COMPUTE creates summary information, and not new values that would be placed into a table. COMPUTE does not support the use of DISTINCT and must be applied against columns that actually exist in the tables referenced. Therefore, aliases are not supported unless they are aliases that were established in the select list.

If you use COMPUTE BY, you must also include an ORDER BY clause. The columns appearing in a COMPUTE BY must be identical to or a subset of the columns listed in the select list, and they must be in the same left-to-right order. You must start with the same expression as was used in the select list, and you cannot skip over any expressions.

Keep in mind that an ORDER BY is optional if you only use COMPUTE. When you are working with integer data, whether using AVG or SUM, SQL Server returns your values as int.

Syntax:

COMPUTE expression1, expression2, ... [BY] expression1, expression2, ...

Scenario:

Sean wants to produce a report of all products being sold by Northwind, but he still wants the ability to see row details. He knows that he could produce a total by using GROUP BY with an aggregate in the SELECT list to produce the totals per grouping. However, using a GROUP BY does show the rows that are attributed to creating the values for each group.

Example:

```
SELECT ProductID,SUM(Quantity)
FROM   [Order Details]
```

```
GROUP BY ProductID
ORDER BY ProductID
```

Returned value:

```
ProductID
----------- -----------
1              828
2              1057
3              328
list continued …
(77 row(s) affected)
```

Scenario:

Because Sean wants to see the rows that make up each grouping, he decides to change the GROUP BY clause into a COMPUTE clause. Sean quickly sees that using COMPUTE allows him to see the rows per grouping, but only returns a grand total when he needs to see a total per grouping.

Example:

```
SELECT ProductID,Quantity
FROM   [Order Details]
ORDER BY ProductID
COMPUTE  SUM(Quantity)
```

Returned value:

```
ProductID   Quantity
----------- --------
1              2
1              3
1              4
list continued …
2              3
2              5
2              5
list continued …
77             2
```

```
77              2
77              2
(2155 row(s) affected)
sum
-----------
51317
(1 row(s) affected)
```

Scenario:

Finally, Sean decides to use a COMPUTE BY clause so that he can have his row details and his subtotals.

Example:

```
SELECT ProductID,Quantity
FROM  [Order Details]
ORDER BY ProductID
COMPUTE  SUM( Quantity) BY ProductID
```

Returned value:

```
ProductID   Quantity
----------- --------
1           45
1           18
1           20
list continued ...
(38 row(s) affected)
sum
-----------
828
list continued for each product number until the last product ...
ProductID   Quantity
----------- --------
77          12
77          15
77          10
list continued ...
(38 row(s) affected)
```

```
sum
-----------
791
```

Listing the Top *n* Values

TOP *n* specifies that only a certain number of rows will be returned by your results set, where *n* is an integer indicating the number of rows to return. The ORDER BY clause determines which rows are returned. It specifies that the first *n* rows will be returned. If you do not use an ORDER BY clause, then the rows returned are arbitrary. Therefore, most TOP *n* statements use an ORDER BY clause that uses the DESC operator to position the rows into descending order.

Optionally, TOP supports the use of the PERCENT operator. PERCENT specifies that only the first *n* percent of rows are returned. If the percentage returns a fractional number, TOP rounds to the next integer value.

Syntax:

TOP *n* [PERCENT]

Scenario:

Jennifer is working to produce a report that reflects the top selling products for Northwind. At first, Jennifer simply wants to know the top five best-selling products. To accomplish this, Jennifer uses the following statement:

Example:

```
SELECT TOP 5 ProductID,SUM(Quantity) as NumSold
FROM  [Order Details]
```

```
GROUP BY PRODUCTID
ORDER BY SUM(Quantity) DESC
```

Returned value:

```
ProductID    NumSold
----------   -----------
60           1577
59           1496
31           1397
56           1263
16           1158
(5 row(s) affected)
```

Scenario:

After seeing the first set of results, Jennifer decides she wants to know the top 5 percent of the products being sold. She uses the following statement:

Example:

```
SELECT TOP 5 PERCENT ProductID,SUM(Quantity) as NumSold
FROM   [Order Details]
GROUP BY PRODUCTID
ORDER BY SUM(Quantity) DESC
```

Returned value:

```
ProductID    NumSold
----------   -----------
60           1577
59           1496
31           1397
56           1263
(4 row(s) affected)
```

As a refresher for some of the aggregate functions we have discussed, let's take a look at some common questions that might arise.

QUESTIONS AND ANSWERS

You want to know the total number of rows from a table and aren't very familiar with the columns or column values in the table. What would be the safest way to proceed?	Use COUNT(*). Using COUNT and supplying an explicit column name leaves you open to the possibility that the column you selected contains null values. COUNT ignores null values, and therefore will not return the true row count that you are seeking.
Can I use MIN to return the lowest value, when the values are text?	Yes, MIN returns the lowest value in the collating order.
I am returning values from a column that has duplicates. How do I return just one occurrence of each value?	Use DISTINCT to eliminate your duplicate values.
I am trying to return the top five values from a column. I am not getting any syntax errors, but the values returned are not the highest.	Remember that TOP returns the top number of values or the top percentage of values, based on the current collating order. Make sure that your ORDER BY clause is using DESC to place your records in descending order.

CERTIFICATION SUMMARY

In this chapter, we have focused on the functions and clauses available in Transact-SQL that make summarizing data possible. While working with scalar functions such as AVG, COUNT, MAX, MIN, and SUM, we have seen how to create SQL statements that return one value per column. We have seen that the syntax required for each of these functions is to simply supply the name of a column or expression to which the function should be applied. Of the functions that we covered, AVG and SUM had the distinction of supporting only numeric data type expressions. All of these aggregate functions support the ability to ignore duplicates by using DISTINCT. Although DISTINCT is supported, it plays no role when used in conjunction with MIN or MAX.

Scalar aggregates are useful when you only need to see one value per column; however, there are times when we need to partition the information being returned into subgroups by including a GROUP BY clause. The GROUP BY clause divides your data based on common values found in the specified columns. The columns specified in the GROUP BY must be a subset of the columns or expressions used in your select list.

Often times, your GROUP BY produces new values because of aggregate functions that are employed. If this is the case, and you would like to filter your results set based on the values being produced in the GROUP BY, you can use the HAVING clause. Remember that if you are not actually referring to new values being generated by aggregates in the GROUP BY, you are better off using a WHERE clause instead of the HAVING clause. The added performance is due to the fact that the WHERE clause is used to filter the rows that are being delivered to the GROUP BY clause. By filtering the rows before they get to the GROUP BY clause, we limit the rows that the GROUP BY clause needs to calculate.

Whether you are using scalar or vector aggregates, the summarizing of your data prevents your ability to see the details of the rows that produced the results. When it is necessary to view the actual rows that produced the summarized data, we can use CUBE and ROLLUP. CUBE produces super-aggregate rows that are combinations of all the possible groupings based on the columns or expressions used in the GROUP BY clause. On the other hand, ROLLUP supports cumulative values such as running sums and averages. Both of these functions assist in providing the detailed and summarized data that can be found in reports, charts, and graphs.

Finally, we used TOP in order to control the number or percentage of rows returned by a results set. Make sure that you feel comfortable with employing all of these functions and operators before taking your test. Be sure of the exceptions and exclusions when using the operators such as CUBE and ROLLUP.

The syntax for using all of these items is as follows:

```
SELECT [ALL | DISTINCT]
  [TOP n [PERCENT] <select list>
[FROM <table(s)>]
[WHERE <search conditions>]
  [GROUP BY [ALL] <group expression>]
    [HAVING <search conditions>]
    [WITH {CUBE | ROLLUP}]
[ORDER BY <column list> [ASC | DESC]]
[COMPUTE {AVG | COUNT | MAX | MAX | SUM} (expression)}, …]
```

TWO-MINUTE DRILL

❑ Using Transact-SQL, you can retrieve data from a database, create databases and database objects, add data, modify existing data, and perform complex operations.

❑ Aggregate functions return summary values, such as averages and sums, from values in a particular column. The returned values represent a single value for each set of rows to which an aggregate function was applied.

❑ Microsoft SQL Server 7.0 provides numerous Transact-SQL commands for use in summarizing, aggregating, or combining data automatically into cumulative values. If used properly, these commands can provide a convenient method for generating summary data as a part of a single command.

❑ Errors can often occur when using aggregate functions together with NULL values. Unexpected or inaccurate results may occur, due to the nature of aggregate function functionality when encountering NULL values.

❑ It's important to keep track of the requirements for using commands such as GROUP BY, ORDER BY, COMPUTE (BY), or any of the assorted aggregate functions supported by SQL Server 7.0.

❑ Aggregate functions can be used to return values for each row returned by an SQL statement, or to produce a single value for each group of rows. The new values that are generated appear as new columns.

❑ It is important to remember that when using aggregate functions, each column specified in the SELECT clause must use an aggregate function or your statement will return an error.

❑ AVG returns the average of all the values in an expression. AVG can be used with numeric columns only and will automatically ignore null values.

❑ COUNT returns the number of non-null values in the expression provided. If used in conjunction with DISTINCT, COUNT finds the number of unique non-null values.

❑ MAX returns the maximum value in an expression. MAX can be used with numeric, character, and date/time columns, but not with *bit* columns.

❑ MIN returns the minimum value in an expression. MIN can be used with numeric, character, and date/time columns, but not with *bit* columns.

❑ SUM returns the sum of all values in an expression. SUM supports the use of DISTINCT to summarize only unique values in the expression.

❑ You can use DISTINCT to eliminate duplicate values before an aggregate function is applied.

❑ The GROUP BY clause allows you to partition a table into one or more subsets that have a value or expression in common.

❑ ALL is meaningful only when the SELECT statement also includes a WHERE clause. If you use ALL, the query results include all groups produced by the GROUP BY clause, even if some of the groups have no rows that meet the search conditions.

❑ The HAVING clause sets conditions for the GROUP BY clause in the way that the WHERE clause sets conditions for the SELECT clause.

❑ CUBE is an aggregate operator that can be used to produce result sets that are typically used in reports. CUBE produces a *super-aggregate* row, which is a summary of the row information generated by the GROUP BY clause.

❑ Like CUBE, the ROLLUP operator creates aggregates and super-aggregates for elements within a GROUP BY clause. ROLLUP supports cumulative aggregates such as running sums and averages.

❑ COMPUTE generates summary values that appear as additional rows within a results set for row aggregate functions. You can use the COMPUTE BY clause to generate values based on subgroups, or generate values for more than one column by employing an aggregate against it.

❑ TOP *n* specifies that only a certain number of rows will be returned by your results set, where *n* is an integer indicating the number of rows to return. The ORDER BY clause determines which rows are returned. It specifies that the first *n* rows will be returned.

SELF TEST

The following questions will help you measure your understanding of the material presented in this chapter. Read all of the choices carefully, as there may be more than one correct answer. Choose all correct answers for each question.

1. What type of aggregate function produces a single value for each column found in the select list?

   A. Scalar

   B. Vector

   C. Singular

   D. Modular

2. Which data type is not valid for SUM and AVG?

   A. Int

   B. Smallint

   C. Text

   D. Tinyint

3. What is the safest and easiest way to return a full row count from a table without having to worry about null values?

   A. COUNT ALL

   B. COUNT(*)

   C. COUNT (NOT NULL)

   D. COUNT(ALL)

4. What operator can be used with a column in order to eliminate duplicate values?

   A. UNIQUE

   B. NOMATCH

   C. ALL UNIQUE

   D. DISTINCT

5. Which clause can you use to refer to the rows that are being returned by the GROUP BY clause?

   A. WHERE

   B. GROUP WHERE

   C. HAVING

   D. You can't refer to the GROUP BY rows.

6. How many columns or expressions can be used in the GROUP BY clause if you plan to use CUBE or ROLLUP?

   A. 10

   B. 20

   C. 15

   D. No limit

7. What is the purpose of the ALL statement that contains a GROUP BY clause?

   A. ALL nullifies the use of a WHERE clause.

   B. ALL bypasses the HAVING statement.

   C. ALL returns the number of rows in a table.

   D. ALL returns all rows produced by the GROUP BY, ignoring the WHERE clause.

8. Jennifer is trying to group date values by the month; however, the value she has to work with is a whole date value. What

function can Jennifer use to pull out the month?

A. DateMonth( )

B. Month( )

C. ReturnMonth( )

D. GetMonth( )

9. How many conditions does HAVING support?

A. 256

B. 10

C. 128

D. 15

10. Which aggregate can be used to produce super-aggregate rows that summarize the data being returned by the GROUP BY clause?

A. CUBED

B. ROLLED

C. SUMMARIZE

D. CUBE

11. Which aggregate functions are supported by COMPUTE BY?

A. AVG, MIN, MAX, and SUM

B. COUNT, MIN, MAX, and SUM

C. AVG, COUNT, MIN, MAX

D. AVG, COUNT, MIN, MAX, and SUM

12. Which statement best explains the rules about the field list in the COMPUTE BY clause?

A. You must start with the same expression as the SELECT clause.

B. You must start with the same expression as the SELECT clause; the remaining columns maybe in any order you desire.

C. You must start with the same expression as the SELECT clause, and the remaining columns must be identical to or a subset of the columns found in the SELECT list.

D. You must start with the same expression as the SELECT clause, and you must include all columns found in the SELECT list.

13. When you add or average integer data in SQL Server, what type of value is returned?

A. Int

B. Tinyint

C. LargeInt

D. Smallint

14. Which clause can be used to limit the number of rows being returned in a results set?

A. TOP n

B. COUNT n

C. RETURN n

D. SELECT n

15. Tiffany has written the following SQL statement:
SELECT Customers.CustomerID, Customers.Country, Customers.Region FROM Customers

GROUP BY Customers.Region,
Customers.Country
ORDER BY Region, Country
Why will this statement return an error?

A. The ORDER BY clause doesn't
    specify the table names for the Region
    and Country columns.

B. Her use of the CustomerID column
    will generate an error. CustomerID
    must either have an aggregate function
    applied to it in the SELECT clause, or
    the CustomerID must be part of the
    column list in the GROUP BY clause.

C. The GROUP BY clause will generate
    an error because you cannot group by
    more than one column.

D. The GROUP BY clause will generate
    an error because the order of fields or
    expressions in the GROUP BY must
    match the order used in the SELECT
    clause.

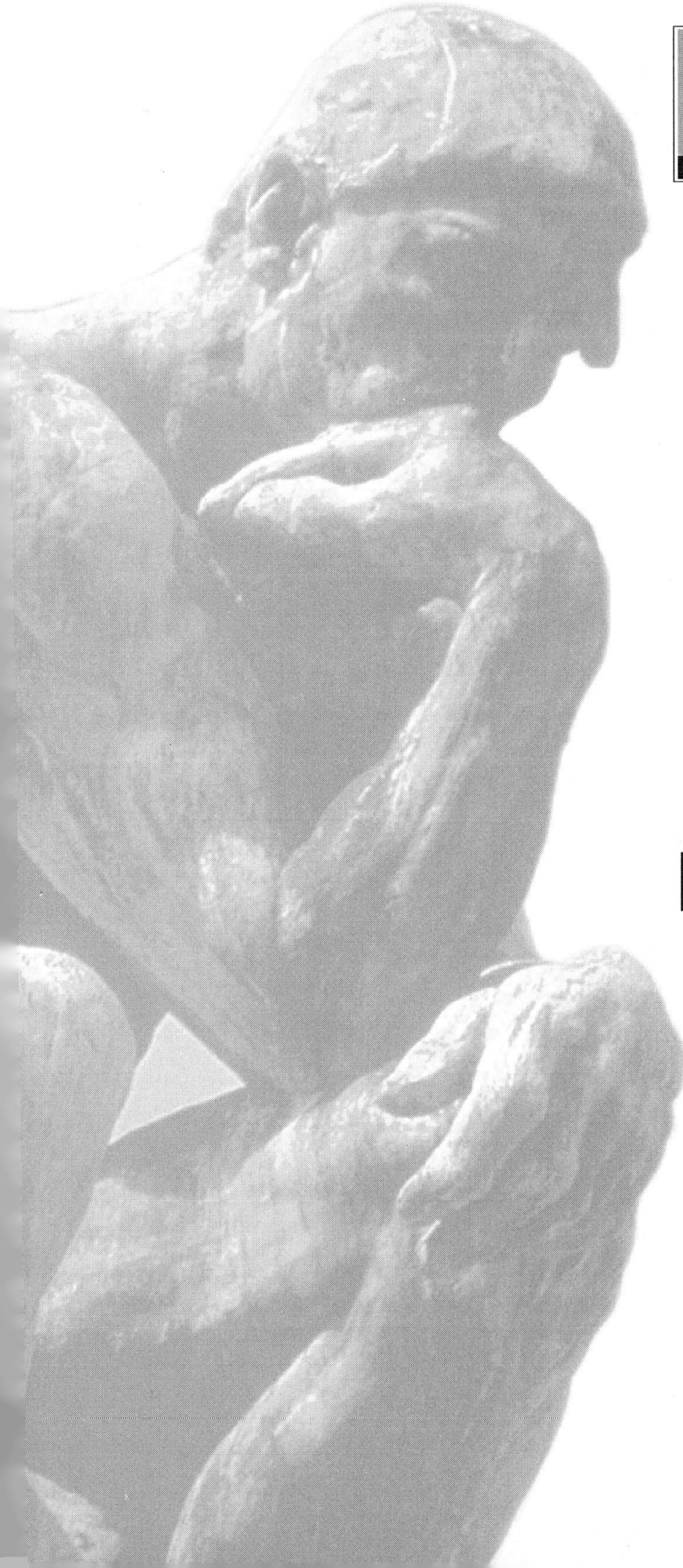

MCDBA

MICROSOFT CERTIFIED DATABASE ADMINISTRATOR

8

Managing Transactions and Locks

CERTIFICATION OBJECTIVES

- 8.01 Introduction to Transactions and Locks
- 8.02 Managing Transactions
- 8.03 Distributed Transactions
- 8.04 Microsoft SQL Server Locking
- 8.05 Managing Locks

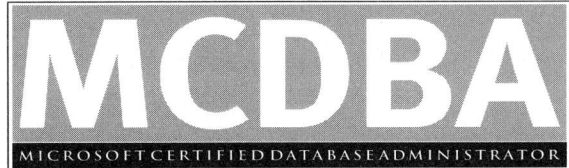

The most basic unit of work in Microsoft SQL Server 7.0 is a transaction. SQL Server developers are responsible for setting up transactions so that the data is logically consistent. Therefore, it is imperative that you know how to properly set up transactions so they preserve data integrity. This chapter will discuss the importance of transactions and locks in SQL Server, which will assist you in properly optimizing the design of your database.

Introduction to Transactions and Locks

SQL Server developers are responsible for the database design. One of the most important parts of a database's design is to ensure that the data on the SQL Server is logically consistent. Consistent data is necessary to ensure that all applications and queries accessing the data will return accurate and timely data. With *transactions* playing the biggest part of designing and implementing the database design, transactions must be tuned and set up properly.

A transaction is the smallest logical unit of work for the database. All actions that occur on the database break down to one or more transactions. Transactions consist of four properties, called the *ACID* properties. Each level of work must contain all of these properties before they are considered transactions. The four ACID properties are

■ **Atomicity**   A transaction must completely succeed or fail. If any statement in the transaction fails, the entire transaction completely fails. All previous successful statements in the transaction are rolled back or reverted to their previous states.

■ **Consistency**   Data consistency is enforced for all successful or failed transactions. All rules must be enforced on the transactions in order to maintain data integrity. All parts of the database, including indexes and lists, must support the state that the data is currently in.

■ **Isolation**   All transactions that modify data are isolated from each other, meaning they do not access the same data at the same time. A modifying transaction can access the data only before or after another transaction has completed. These types of transactions do not affect the state of other transactions.

■ **Durability**   Transaction durability implies that the transaction modifications are permanent and persistent. Even during a reboot or a computer crash, the data is guaranteed to be complete when the computer restarts. This is possible with the use of SQL Server log records, which are explained later in this chapter.

Since client applications often access data at the same time, it is crucial that transactions either completely succeed or completely fail. Transactions that are partially complete can upset the consistency of the data. The use of *locks* guarantees that a transaction must be complete in order for the transaction to be successful. During a transaction, locks can put holds on your data so that no other transaction can access the database. This is done to minimize the possibility that the data will be corrupt. Since managing transactions plays a large role in the SQL Server database administrator's job, you must be aware of what happens during a SQL Server transaction.

1. A transaction starts with the BEGIN TRAN or BEGIN TRANSACTION statement. When that command is sensed, the SQL Server parser begins the transaction. Since no work has started yet, SQL Server won't allocate any memory for the log records.

2. When the INSERT, SELECT, UPDATE, DELETE statement is detected, SQL Server allocates a new transaction ID and creates a log record in memory. If any records are altered, a new record is created and recorded in memory. The data page will be modified in memory and recorded in the transaction log.

3. The next statements run similarly to step 2 above. All altered rows are recorded in the logs and then the data page is actually changed in memory.

FROM THE CLASSROOM

ACID, the Foundation of Transactions!

The concept of a transaction plays the most fundamental of roles in the sweeping wave of E-commerce, data processing, and information management needs. Maintaining the integrity of information modifications, be they updates, additions, or deletions, is the primary footing in the ascension of the mountain of information and feedback generated in today's business world. The concept of a single unit of work, known as a transaction, serves as the fundamental building block in daily business activity. Now that the value of information storage and data mining has been brought to the forefront of company activities, high volumes of information retrieval and storage demand certain guarantees with the data events. These guarantees surface in the form of a comical acronym ACID. The acronym stands for Atomicity, Consistency, Isolation, and Durability. These attributes are inherently required of transactions to ensure reliable movement and transformation of data within the

system. All DBMSs should support the concept of transactions to be a serious contender for anything but the smallest of data storage needs.

From these simple attributes, most of the hardcore functionality of a DBMS is affected. ACID contributes directly to the concepts of locking, scalability, logging, concurrency, pages, and recoverability. Aggressively designing data modifications, retrievals, or updates with the mindset of transactions can provide numerous benefits in a scaled-up environment down the road. Being thrifty with locking needs and the batching up of data commands can yield increasingly large dividends as usage increases.

Fully understanding these concepts can support the full understanding of deeper or more complex concepts used within Microsoft SQL Server 7.0.

—Michael Lane Thomas, MCSE+I, MCSD,
MCP+SB, MSS, MCT, A+

4. After all SQL Server statements have finished running and SQL Server receives the COMMIT TRAN or COMMIT TRANSACTION statement, the log records are written to the transaction log for the database. This ensures that all transactions can be recovered, even in the

event of a power outage or crash. The log records are separate temporary files that cannot be accessed with any Transact-SQL statements. Only SQL server internal processes can access them. This ensures that no human error can corrupt or change the logs before the change is applied to the SQL Server database.

5. Once the transaction logs are written, the changes are automatically applied to the database.

To enforce isolation and durability in the transactions, Microsoft SQL Server utilizes locks to prevent concurrent users from modifying data that has been changed but not yet committed. Without locks, users can never be sure that the data they are viewing is correct. When using locks, no transaction other than your own can modify data that is being used by your transaction. While data is being modified by your transaction, an exclusive lock will hold the data. We will talk more about the different types of locking later in this chapter.

You can view the types of locks on your system by running *sp_lock* or *sp_processinfo*. Exercise 8-1 will show you how to observe the locks on your SQL Server.

EXERCISE 8-1

Observing Locks by Running sp_lock

1. Click Start | Programs | SQL Server 7.0 | Query Analyzer.

2. You should see the Connect to SQL Server dialog box. Select your SQL Server and log in.

3. In the Query window, type the following statement:

```
Exec sp_loc
Go
```

4. Click the Query menu and select Execute Query. You should see something like Figure 8-1.

As you can see from Figure 8-1, it is very difficult to interpret the results on the sp_lock query. Table 8-1 will show you what each of the columns stand for.

FIGURE 8-1

It is difficult to interpret the results of the sp_lock query just by viewing the Microsoft SQL Server Query Analyzer

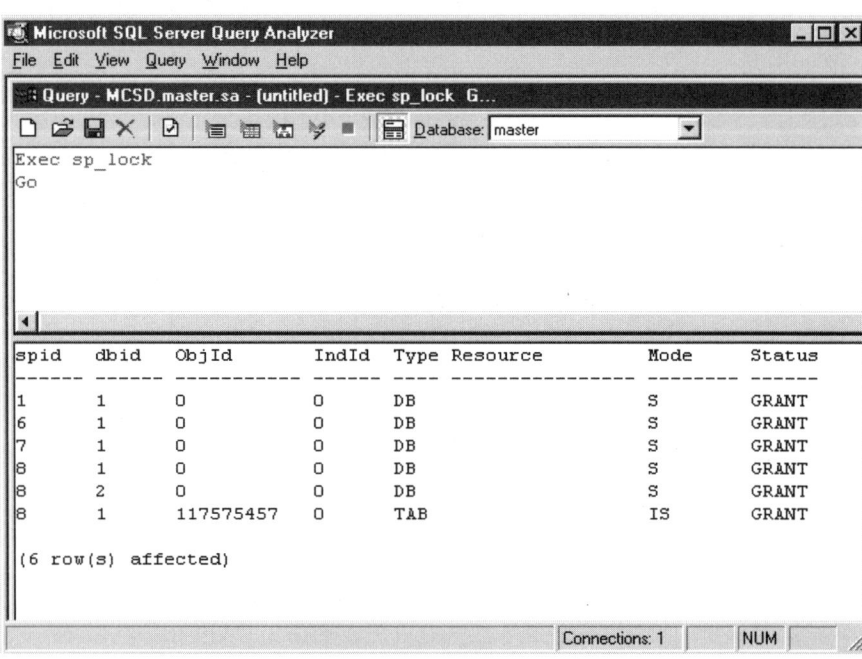

TABLE 8-1

Description of the Column Names of sp_lock

Column Name	Description
spid	The SQL Server process ID number
dbid	The database identification number requesting a lock
ObjId	The object identification number of the object requesting a lock
IndId	The index identification number
Type	The lock type: DB = Database FIL = File IDX = Index PG = PAGE KEY = Key TAB = Table EXT = Extent RID = Row identifier.

	Column Name	Description
TABLE 8-1	Resource	The lock resource
Description of the Column Names of sp_lock (continued)	Mode	The lock requester's lock mode (S for shared, X for exclusive, I for Intent)
	Status	The lock request status: GRANT (Lock is currently being used.) WAIT (Waiting because the lock can't be taken.) CNVRT (Lock is being converted, i.e., lock is being escalated.)

You can also observe the locks in SQL Server Enterprise Manager. Exercise 8-2 will show you how to access the lock information in SQL Server Enterprise Manager.

EXERCISE 8-2

Observing Locks by Using SQL Server Enterprise Manager

1. Click Start | Programs | SQL Server 7.0 | SQL Server Enterprise Manager.
2. Expand the SQL Server group and your own server.
3. Right click your server and select Task | Current Activity.
4. You will now see the Current Activity dialog box. Click the Object Locks tab, as shown in Figure 8-2.

CERTIFICATION OBJECTIVE 8.02

Managing Transactions

As a SQL Server developer, you are in charge of designing the applications that work with transactions. One of the most important parts of the database application is controlling and managing transactions. By using Transact-SQL statements or SQL Server API, you can start and end transactions.

FIGURE 8-2

Use the Object Locks tab to access the lock information in the SQL Server Enterprise Manager

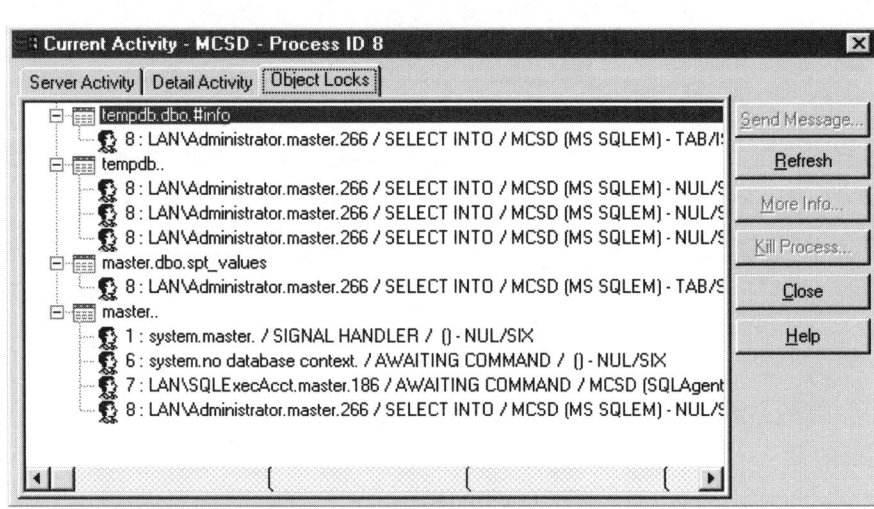

Explicit, Implicit, and Autocommit Transactions

Three types of transactions can be started in SQL Server 7.0: explicit, implicit, and autocommit. Using transactions increases performance. With transactions, multiple statements are seen as one entity. Transaction logs are written less often and this increases the efficiency of the hard disk.

Each transaction is separate from the connections. If a transaction changes modes, the same connection will be used.

Explicit Transactions

Explicit transactions are manually configured transactions in which you define the beginning and the end of the transaction. Earlier versions of SQL Server referred to explicit transactions as user-defined transactions. You need to use specific Transact-SQL statements, called *reserved words*, to specify the beginning and end of the transactions. The reserved words are

- BEGIN TRANSACTION
- COMMIT TRANSACTION
- COMMIT WORK

- ROLLBACK TRANSACTION
- ROLLBACK WORK

To start an explicit transaction, type the **BEGIN TRAN** or **BEGIN TRANSACTION** statement. To end the transaction, type the **COMMIT TRAN** or **COMMIT TRANSACTION** statement. To cancel a transaction, type **ROLLBACK WORK** or **ROLLBACK TRANSACTION**. All work done before the ROLLBACK WORK or ROLLBACK TRANSACTION will be canceled, or rolled back. Before you perform any explicit transaction, you need to be aware of some statements that are not supported, such as these:

- ALTER DATABASE
- DROP DATABASE
- RECONFIGURE
- BACKUP LOG
- RESTORE DATABASE
- CREATE DATABASE
- RESTORE LOG
- UPDATE STATISTICS
- DISK INIT
- LOAD DATABASE
- LOAD TRANSACTION
- DUMP TRANSACTION

Explicit transactions last only for the duration of the transaction. Once the transaction ends, connection returns to the previous transaction mode. Exercise 8-3 shows you how to create and manage explicit transactions to ensure data consistency and recoverability.

EXERCISE 8-3

Creating and Managing Explicit Transactions to Ensure Data Consistency and Recoverability

1. Click Start | Programs | SQL Server 7.0 | Query Analyzer.

2. You should see the Connect to SQL Server dialog box. Select your SQL Server and log in.

3. Select the pubs database from the database pull-down menu.

4. In the Query window, type the following statement:

```
BEGIN TRANSACTION
      UPDATE authors
      SET city='San Jose' WHERE au_lname='Smith'
      INSERT titles
VALUES ('BU1122', 'Teach yourself SQL
Server','business','9998',$39.99,$1000.00,10,4501,'A great book','8/1/1998')
      SELECT * from titleauthor
COMMIT TRANSACTION
```

5. Click the Query menu and select Execute Query.

Implicit Transactions

Implicit transactions are an ANSI-compliant feature of SQL Server 7.0. This type of transaction is enabled with the statement SET IMPLICIT_TRANSACTIONS ON. This type of transaction is different from the explicit transaction in that the server starts the implicit transaction, whereas the developer starts the explicit transaction. Once you turn on implicit transactions, SQL Server will start a transaction whenever it sees the following keywords:

- ALTER TABLE
- FETCH
- REVOKE
- CREATE
- GRANT
- SELECT
- DELETE
- INSERT
- TRUNCATE TABLE
- DROP
- OPEN UPDATE

Once the implicit transaction starts, SQL Server will generate a continuous chain of implicit transactions until you turn off implicit transactions. To turn off implicit transactions, you run SET IMPLICIT_TRANSACTIONS OFF. If any transaction in the chain of implicit transactions fails, the entire chain is automatically aborted and all successful transactions within the chain are rolled back to their original states. This type of transaction does not need BEGIN TRAN or BEGIN TRANSACTION. Implicit transactions runs automatically. Exercise 8-4 will show you how to create and manage implicit transactions to ensure data consistency and recoverability.

EXERCISE 8-4

Creating and Managing Implicit Transactions to Ensure Data Consistency and Recoverability

1. Click Start | Programs | SQL Server 7.0 | Query Analyzer.

2. You should see the Connect to SQL Server dialog box. Select your SQL Server and log in.

3. Select the pubs database from the database pull-down menu.

4. In the Query window, type the following statement:

```
SET IMPLICIT_TRANSACTIONS ON
INSERT INTO AUTHORS (au_id, au_lname, au_fname, phone, address, city, state,
zip, contract)
VALUES ('111-11-1111','Woo','Derrick','310-876-5213','987 Microsoft Way','Los
Angeles','CA','64114',1)
SELECT @@trancount
COMMIT TRAN
```

5. Click the Query menu and select Execute Query. Your screen should look similar to Figure 8-3.

on the
ⓙob

You must be cautious about running implicit transactions since you are required to commit or roll back every transaction. If you forget, the transaction can be locked longer than you anticipate, thus slowing down access to your data.

Autocommit Transactions

Autocommit is SQL Server's default transaction mode. Each *batch* is broken up into smaller statements, making it like a batch file. If any transaction within a batch statement fails, the other statements are not affected.

FIGURE 8-3

Running an implicit
transaction on Microsoft
SQL Server Query
Analyzer

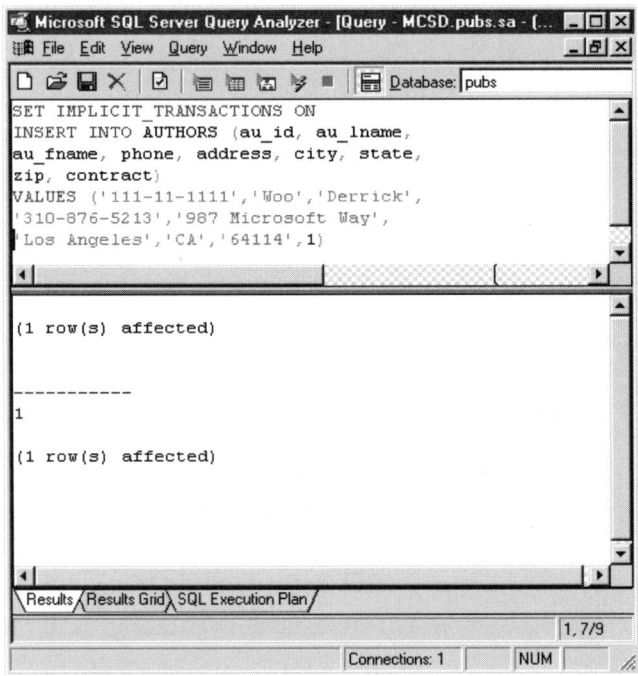

Exercise 8-5 will show you how to create and manage autocommit
transactions to ensure data consistency and recoverability.

EXERCISE 8-5

Creating and Managing Autocommit Transactions to Ensure Data Consistency and Recoverability

1. Click Start | Programs | SQL Server 7.0 | Query Analyzer.

2. You should see the Connect to SQL Server dialog box. Select your SQL Server and log in.

3. Select the pubs database from the database pull-down menu.

4. In the Query window, type the following statement:

```
INSERT INTO AUTHORS (au_id, au_lname, au_fname, phone, address, city, state,
zip, contract)
VALUES ('111-11-1111','Woo','Derrick','310-876-5213','987 Microsoft Way','Los
Angeles','CA','64114',1)
GO
```

5. Click the Query menu and select Execute Query.

Define the Transaction Isolation Level

Setting transaction isolation levels is a balance between concurrency and data integrity. Choosing the correct transaction isolation level can dramatically improve performance. There are four transaction isolation levels to choose from:

- **Read Committed** This is the SQL Server default. Data can be changed before the transaction is over.

- **Read Uncommitted** This is the least restrictive isolation level. There are no shared locks and no exclusive locks. Data can be changed and rows can be deleted and added before the transaction is over.

- **Repeatable Read** Locks are held so that no data can be updated but rows can be added.

- **Serializable** The serializable isolation level ensures integrity, but is the least concurrent. The entire data set is locked so that no rows can be added or updated. In previous versions of SQL Server, the Repeatable Read and Serializable isolation level are the same.

The syntax for setting the transaction isolation level is

```
SET TRANSACTION ISOLATION LEVEL {READ COMMITTED|READ UNCOMMITTED|REPEATABLE READ
|SERIALIZABLE}
```

Exercise 8-6 will show you how to define the transaction isolation level.

| EXERCISE 8-6 |

Defining the Transaction Isolation Level

1. Click Start | Programs | SQL Server 7.0 | Query Analyzer.

2. You should see the Connect to SQL Server dialog box. Select your SQL Server and log in.

3. In the Query window, type the following statement:

```
SET TRANSACTION ISOLATION LEVEL READ UNCOMMITTED
GO
DBCC USEROPTIONS
GO
```

4. Click the Query menu and select Execute Query. You should see the following display:

```
Set Option                    Value
---------------------------   ----------------
textsize                      64512
language                      us_english
dataformat                    mdy
datefirst                     7
ansi_null_dft_on              SET
isolation level               read uncommitted
(6 row(s) affected)
DBCC execution completed. If DBCC printed error messages,
Contact your system administrator.
```

Design Transactions of Appropriate Length

When you start designing transactions, remember to minimize transaction duration. The shorter the transaction, the quicker the locks are released. When locks are quickly released from the row or table, other transactions can access the data. There are many ways to shorten the length of a transaction.

Transaction Execution

One way to shorten the life span of the transaction is to break up the large batch jobs, such as the monthly summary calculation, into smaller steps. After every completed step, changes will be committed. Committing changes as quickly as possible translates into locks being released more quickly.

Another way to shrink the time for the transaction is to utilize the SQL Server *statement batches*. Statement batches are used to send multiple Transact-SQL statements to SQL Server at once with the same connection, thus saving time it would take to open another network connection. If a statement batch contains more than one SELECT statement, the server will return the sets of results in one single stream.

Parameter arrays are shortcuts for repeated operations. The SQLParamOptions ODBC function allows multiple parameter sets for a single Transact-SQL statement to be sent to the server in a batch.

Coding Efficient Transactions

When you code transactions, it is important to minimize the duration of these transactions. Systems with a few users might not notice long-running transactions; but, when the system grows to several hundred or several thousand users, transaction execution times will be intolerable.

One way to minimize the duration of these transactions is to minimize the input from users. Humans deciding what choices to make take more time for those decisions than a computer takes to execute the command. Resources are held up while users are deciding what to choose.

Start transactions only when all of the data analysis is done. Do not start any execution until it is required.

Understand and choose the best transaction isolation level and cursor concurrency option. Not all transactions require the high, serializable transaction isolation level. Some applications can function correctly with the lower, read-committed transaction isolation level.

One of the best ways to speed up transactions is to return only the least amount of required data. The smaller the amount of data in a transaction, the quicker the transaction can be executed.

CERTIFICATION OBJECTIVE 8.03

Distributed Transactions

With the Microsoft Distributed Transaction Coordinator (MSDTC) service, SQL Server can support transactions spanning multiple servers. With distributed transactions, data being queried does not have to be on one server. There are three ways to use distributed transactions:

- You can program your own distributed transactions with DB-Lib, ODBC, or OLE DB.

- You can use the BEGIN DISTRIBUTED TRANSACTION Transact-SQL statement.

■ You can set the SET REMOTE_PROC_TRANSACTIONS option to enable distributed transactions for that session.

Distributed transactions allow you to connect to two types of remote databases: *remote servers* and *linked servers*. The remote server is provided for backward compatibility with previous versions of SQL Server. The linked server is a new option in SQL Server 7.0.

Remote Servers

Remote servers enable a client to execute stored procedures on another SQL Server using the same connection. The connected server accepts the client's request and passes it on to the remote server. The remote server processes the request and sends it back to the original server, which passes it on to the client. To set up a remote server, you must use *sp_addserver*, *sp_addremotelogin*, and *sp_remoteoption*.

The syntax for sp_addserver is

```
sp_addserver [@server =] 'server'
[,[@local =] 'local']
[,[@duplicate_ok =] 'duplicate_OK']
```

The following table shows the arguments of sp_addserver:

Arguments	Function
Server	Name of the server
Local	Specifies whether the server that is being added is a local or remote server
Duplicate_ok	Specifies whether or not a duplicate server name is allowed

The syntax for sp_addremotelogin is

```
sp_addremotelogin [@remoteserver =] 'remoteserver' [,[@loginame =] 'login']
[,[@remotename =] 'remote_name']
```

The following table shows the arguments of sp_addremotelogin:

Arguments	Function
Remoteserver	Name of the remote server that the remote login applies to
Login	Login ID of the user on the local SQL Server
Remote_name	Login ID of the user on the remote server

The syntax for sp_remoteoption is

```
sp_remoteoption [[@remoteserver =] 'remoteserver'] [,[@loginame =] 'loginame']
[,[@remotename =] 'remotename'] [,[@optname =] 'optname'] [,[@optvalue =]
'optvalue']
```

The following table shows the arguments of sp_addremoteoption:

Arguments	Function
Remoteserver	Name of the remote server that the remote login applies to
Loginame	Login ID of the user on the local SQL Server
Remotename	Login ID of the user on *remoteserver*
Optname	Option to set or turn off
Optvalue	Value for *optname*

Exercise 8-7 will show you how to set up a remote server to do distributed transactions.

EXERCISE 8-7

Set Up a Remote Server

1. Click Start | Programs | SQL Server 7.0 | Query Analyzer.
2. You should see the Connect to SQL Server dialog box. Select your SQL Server and log in.

3. Add the name of the remote server to the Sysservers system table on SQL Server, by running

```
EXEC sp_addserver <remote server>
```

4. Repeat the same procedure on the remote server.

5. Go back to your original server and type

```
EXEC sp_addremotelogin <remote server>, sa, sa
EXEC sp_remoteoption <remote server>, sa, sa, trusted,
true
```

6. Repeat the same thing on the remote server except reference the <remote server> to your server.

Once you have set up the remote servers, you can access the remote stored procedures by executing the <servername>.<database name>.<owner>.<stored procedure name>. For example, if you wanted to access the chkauthors stored procedure in the Pubs database on server MCSD, you would run

```
Exec mcsd.pubs.dbo.chkauthors 10
```

Linked Servers

Linked servers are a new addition to SQL Server 7.0. A linked server is similar to a remote server but it also has the ability to harness the power and flexibility of OLE DB. Linked servers allow you to also access an OLE DB rowset from any OLE DB data source, such as Microsoft Access and Oracle; join remote tables; and execute remote stored procedures. To set up a linked server, use sp_addlinkedserver and sp_addlinkedsrvlogin system-stored procedures.

The syntax for sp_addlinkedserver is

```
sp_addlinkedserver [@server =] 'server' [, [@srvproduct =] 'product_name']
[, [@provider =] 'provider_name'] [, [@datasrc =] 'data_source']
[, [@location =] 'location'] [, [@provstr =] 'provider_string']
[, [@catalog =] 'catalog'
```

The following table shows the arguments of sp_addlinkedserver:

Arguments	Function
Server	Name of the linked server to create
Product_name	Product name of the OLE DB data source to add as a linked server
Provider_name	Unique programmatic identifier (PROGID) of the OLE DB provider corresponding to this data source
Data_source	Name of the data source as interpreted by the OLE DB provider
Location	Location of the database as interpreted by the OLE DB provider
Provider_string	OLE DB provider-specific connection string that identifies a unique data source
Catalog	Catalog to be used when making a connection to the OLE DB provider

The syntax for sp_addlinkedsrvlogin is

```
sp_addlinkedsrvlogin [@rmtsrvname =] 'rmtsrvname' [,[@useself =] 'useself']
[,[@locallogin =] 'locallogin'] [,[@rmtuser =] 'rmtuser'] [,[@rmtpassword =]
'rmtpassword'
```

The following table shows the arguments of sp_addlinkedsrvlogin:

Arguments	Function
Rmtsrvname	Name of the linked server
Useself	Name of the login used to connect to the linked server
Locallogin	Name of the login for the local server
Rmtuser	The backup name of the login to connect to the linked server to be used *if useself* cannot log in. Default is NULL
Rmtpassword	The password for *rmtuser*. Default is NULL

You must run the instcat.sql script against any SQL Server 6.5 servers if you want to run distributed transactions with the linked server options.

Exercise 8-8 shows you how to set up a linked server.

EXERCISE 8-8

Set Up a Linked Server

1. Click Start | Programs | SQL Server 7.0 | Query Analyzer.

2. You should see the Connect to SQL Server dialog box. Select your SQL Server and log in.

3. Type the following:

   ```
   Exec sp_addlinked server 'remoteserver', 'SQL Server'
   Exec sp_addlinkedsrvlogin 'remoteserver', 'TRUE'
   ```

4. Click the Query menu and select Execute Query.

CERTIFICATION OBJECTIVE 8.04

Microsoft SQL Server Locking

New to Microsoft SQL Server 7.0 is *dynamic locking*. SQL Server will determine the appropriate locking when a query is executed. This helps simplify database administration and increases performance, since the server determines the appropriate locks. Though Microsoft SQL Server 7.0 enforces locking automatically through dynamic locking, you can still configure locking in applications by configuring deadlocks, time outs, and transaction isolation levels; locking granularity for an index; and using table-level hints with SELECT, INSERT, UPDATE, and DELETE statements.

Though SQL Server 7.0 has dynamic locking, it is still very important that you can differentiate between the four main locks. You can differentiate between the lock types by their use of each of the main SQL statements and their compatibility with each other.

Lock Types

SQL Server 7.0 has four lock types: *shared locks, update locks, exclusive locks, and intent locks.*

Shared Locks

Shared locks allow connections to read data. Since concurrent reads do not affect the integrity of the data, shared locks can be used concurrently with other shared locks. When the data is locked, no data-modifying transactions can access the data until the shared lock is released.

Update Locks

Update locks are used for update transactions. In an update, data is first locked using a shared lock. Once the data is found, the shared lock is upgraded to an exclusive lock to modify the data. A problem can arise when one of two sessions, having shared locks on the same resource, wants to change to an exclusive lock to modify data, but cannot do that because the exclusive lock is not compatible with the shared lock. To avoid this potential deadlock problem, update locks are used. Only one session can obtain an update lock to a resource at a time. If a transaction modifies a resource, the update lock is converted to an exclusive lock. Otherwise, the lock is converted to a shared-mode lock.

Exclusive Locks

Exclusive locks are used for an insert or delete statement. Exclusive locks are held until the transaction commits or rolls back. Since exclusive locks are used for writes, it is used to prevent access to the data so that integrity is maintained. No other transactions can access data locked with an exclusive lock.

Intent Locks

Intent locks are used to lock low-level resources in a hierarchy. This improves performance since only the higher-level intent lock is compared instead of having SQL Server checking the locks in all the resources lower in the hierarchy.

Now that you know the differences between the lock types, here is a quick reference for possible scenario questions.

QUESTIONS AND ANSWERS

Pseudo Code	Lock Selected
I need to select * from table...	Use Shared locks. They are used for reads.
I need to update a row...	This is a tough one. Should we use Update lock or Exclusive lock? Update lock. Exclusive lock is only for Insert or Delete.
I need to delete a row...	I mentioned this earlier. Delete and Insert use Exclusive lock.
I have a lot of transactions and I need to update my row...	Use Intent locks. Intent locks put locks on upper hierarchies and only those locks are compared instead of comparing all locks in the lower level.

Lock Compatibility

Not all locks are compatible with each other. The following table shows the compatibility matrix for the different locks:

Lock Type	IS	S	U	IX	SIX	X
Intent Shared (IS)	Yes	Yes	Yes	Yes	Yes	No
Shared (S)	Yes	Yes	Yes	No	No	No
Update (U)	Yes	Yes	No	No	No	No
Intent Exclusive (IX)	Yes	No	No	Yes	No	No
Shared with Intent Exclusive (SIX)	Yes	No	No	No	No	No
Exclusive (X)	No	No	No	No	No	No

Exclusive locks aren't compatible with anything. This is because when a transaction has an exclusive lock on a row, no other transaction can access it. Shared locks are different because they only involve reading data. That's why shared locks are compatible with many other locks.

Lock Levels

You can lock different types of objects or levels in SQL Server 7.0. The different levels that you can lock are

- **RID**   Row identifier. Used to individually lock a single row within a table.
- **Key**   A row lock taken within an index. Used to protect key ranges in serializable transactions.
- **Page**   8KB data page or index page.
- **Extent**   Contiguous group of eight data pages or index pages.
- **Table**   Entire table, including all data and indexes.
- **DB**   Database
- **Intent**   Shows that page or row locks within the table are locked.

CERTIFICATION OBJECTIVE 8.05

Managing Locks

Although SQL Server automatically sets the optimum table-level locking hints, there may be instances in which manual settings are more fitting. For example, if SQL Server uses a coarse locking hint, you may prefer a finer lock. You can specify a range of table-level locking hints using the SELECT, INSERT, UPDATE, or DELETE statement, which overrides the current transaction isolation level for that session.

You set the locking hint by running a query such as this one:

```
SELECT * FROM AUTHORS (<HINT>)
```

You can choose from various locking hints to replace the <HINT> from the preceeding example:

- **HOLDLOCK and READ COMMITTED** Hold a shared lock until completion of the transaction instead of releasing the lock as soon as the required table, row, or data page is no longer required.

- **NOLOCK** Does not issue shared locks and does not honor exclusive locks.

- **PAGELOCK** Uses page locks when a single table lock would usually be taken.

- **READCOMMITTED** Performs a scan but data can be edited before the scan is complete.

- **READPAST** Skips locked rows.

- **REPEATABLEREAD** Performs a scan but rows can be added before the transaction is complete.

- **ROWLOCK** Uses row-level locks rather than page- and table-level locks.

- **SERIALIZABLE** Performs a scan when no other transaction can access the data.

- **TABLOCK** Uses a table lock that is held until the end of the statement.

- **TABLOCKX** Uses an exclusive lock on a table.

- **UPDLOCK** Uses update locks instead of shared locks while reading a table, and holds locks until the end of the transaction.

Avoiding or Handling Deadlocks

Deadlock occurs when two applications, which already have locks on separate objects, want a lock on the other's object. This causes a stalemate, because neither application can release its locks and finish its sessions unless the other application releases its locks. SQL Server automatically fixes this by choosing one application and forcing it to release its lock, while allowing the other session to continue. By setting the *SET DEADLOCK PRIORITY*, you can decide which session is more likely to be SQL Server's next victim.

SQL Server releases the lock of the session that has the lower priority. The syntax is

```
SET DEADLOCK_PRIORITY {LOW | NORMAL}
```

The best fix for a deadlock is to avoid it. Whenever a deadlock occurs, time and resources are wasted. One way to prevent deadlocks is to run transactions so that they don't run simultaneously. If transactions run serially, and if they try to access the same data, the latter one will wait for the earlier one to complete.

EXERCISE 8-9

Avoiding Deadlocks with SET DEADLOCK_PRIORITY

1. Click Start | Programs | SQL Server 7.0 | Query Analyzer.
2. You should see the Connect to SQL Server dialog box. Select your SQL Server and log in.
3. Select the pubs database from the database pull-down menu.
4. In the Query window, type the following statement:

```
SET DEADLOCK_PRIORITY LOW
INSERT INTO AUTHORS (au_id, au_lname, au_fname, phone, address, city, state,
zip, contract)
VALUES ('111-11-1111','Woo','Derrick','310-876-5213','987 Microsoft Way','Los
Angeles','CA','64114',1)
```

5. Click the Query menu and select Execute Query.

Using Optimistic Locking Appropriately

Though locks are crucial to the integrity of the database, there are times when you can minimize the use of locks. This is called *optimistic locking* or *optimistic concurrency* and is used to speed up transactions. There are two types of optimistic locking: optimistic with values or optimistic with row versioning.

Optimistic with Values

Optimistic locking with values is used when there is a small chance that another user will update a row between the time that a cursor is opened and the row is updated. When the cursor is first opened, no locks are held. However, if the user attempts to modify the row, the current value in the row is compared with the values retrieved when the row was last fetched. If any of the values have changed, it returns an error. If the values are the same, the server performs the modification. Usually when this happens, the cursor is refreshed and the user will attempt to perform the modification again.

exam
ⓦatch

Transact-SQL cursors do not support the optimistic with values concurrency option.

Optimistic with Row Versioning

Optimistic locking with row versioning is similar to optimistic locking with values. However with row versioning, the value of the row is not compared. They compare the @@DBTS, a global current timestamp value. Each time a row with a *timestamp* column is modified, the current @@DBTS value is stored and incremented in the timestamp column. Whenever a modification is about to take place, the server can compare the current timestamp value of a row with the timestamp value that was stored when the row was last fetched. The OPTIMISTIC keyword on the DECLARE CURSOR Transact-SQL statement specifies optimistic with row versioning.

exam
ⓦatch

If an application requests optimistic concurrency with row versioning on a table that does not have a timestamp column, the cursor reverts back to optimistic locking with values.

EXERCISE 8-10

Declare Cursor with Optimistic Locking

1. Click Start | Programs | SQL Server 7.0 | Query Analyzer.
2. You should see the Connect to SQL Server dialog box. Select your SQL Server and log in.
3. Select the pubs database from the database pull-down menu.
4. Type the following:

```
DECLARE OPCURSOR CURSOR
OPTIMISTIC FOR
Select * FROM AUTHORS
```

Implementing Error Handling by Using @@trancount

@@trancount is a Transact-SQL global variable used to return the number of active connections for the current connection. Whenever you run the BEGIN TRANSACTION statement, @@trancount is increased to one. When you run the ROLLBACK TRANSACTION statement and you don't specify the last transaction name, @@trancount is reset to zero. COMMIT TRANSACTION or COMMIT WORK decreases @@trancount by 1. Exercise 8-11 will show you how to implement error handling by using @@trancount.

EXERCISE 8-11

Implementing Error Handling by Using @@trancount

1. Click Start | Programs | SQL Server 7.0 | Query Analyzer.
2. You should see the Connect to SQL Server dialog box. Select your SQL Server and log in.
3. In the Query window, type the following statement, as shown in Figure 8-4:

```
BEGIN TRANSACTION
UPDATE authors SET state = upper(state)
IF @@ROWCOUNT = 2
COMMIT TRAN
IF @@TRANCOUNT > 0
BEGIN
PRINT 'Must roll back transaction'
ROLLBACK TRAN
END
```

4. Click the Query menu and select Execute Query.

Diagnose and Resolve Locking Problems

The LOCK_TIMEOUT setting sets a time limit on how long a statement will wait for a blocked resource. When a statement has waited longer than the LOCK_TIMEOUT setting, the statement is canceled, and the error message "Lock request time-out period exceeded" is returned. Exercise 8-12 shows you how to diagnose and resolve locking problems.

FIGURE 8-4

Implementing error
handling by using
@@trancount on
Microsoft SQL Server
Query Analyzer

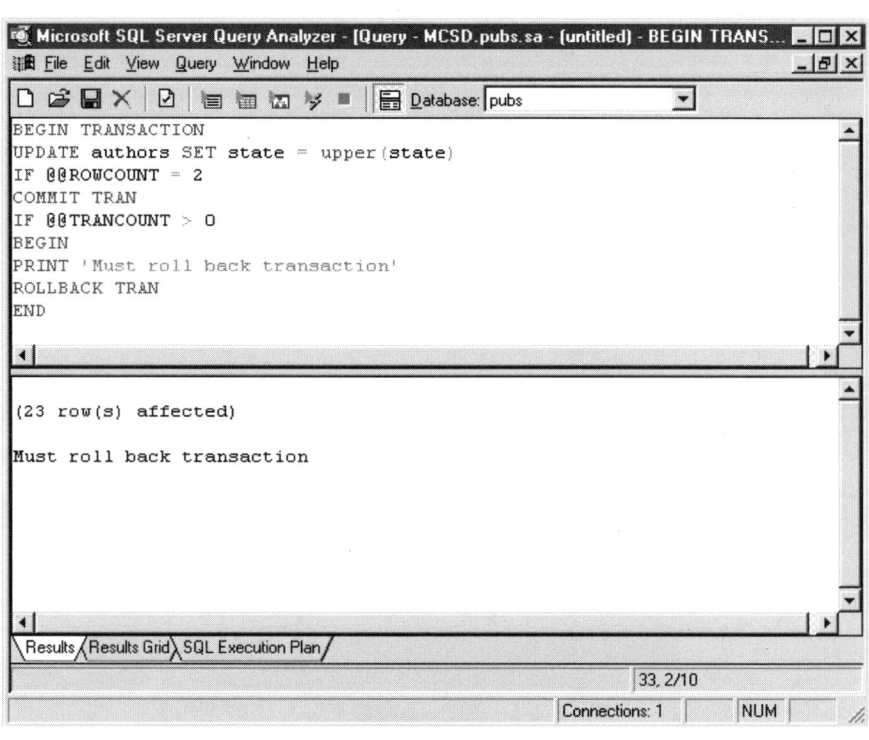

```
BEGIN TRANSACTION
UPDATE authors SET state = upper(state)
IF @@ROWCOUNT = 2
COMMIT TRAN
IF @@TRANCOUNT > 0
BEGIN
PRINT 'Must roll back transaction'
ROLLBACK TRAN
END
```

```
(23 row(s) affected)

Must roll back transaction
```

EXERCISE 8-12

Diagnosing and Resolving Locking Problems

1. Click Start | Programs | SQL Server 7.0 | Query Analyzer.

2. You should see the Connect to SQL Server dialog box. Select your SQL Server and log in.

3. Select the pubs database from the database pull-down menu.

4. In the Query window, type the following statement:

```
SET LOCKOUT_TIMEOUT 1800
INSERT INTO AUTHORS (au_id, au_lname, au_fname, phone, address, city, state,
zip, contract)
VALUES ('111-11-1111','Woo','Derrick','310-876-5213','987 Microsoft Way','Los
Angeles','CA','64114',1)
```

5. Click the Query menu and select Execute Query.

CERTIFICATION SUMMARY

Since the SQL Server database developer's job involves designing databases, one of the most important areas of the database that he or she must be familiar with is transactions and locks. By being familiar with the options that are available in programming the transactions and configuring the options, the database developer will increase the efficiency of the database.

Transactions are made up of four ACID properties: atomicity, consistency, isolation, and durability. These four properties ensure that the work performed will either completely succeed or completely fail. There are three types of transactions: explicit, implicit, and autocommit. Transactions increase the efficiency of the database because fewer things are required to be written in the transaction logs.

One of the major features included in SQL Server 7.0 is distributed transactions. Distributed transactions allow you to run stored procedures on remote servers, access data on OLE DB datasources, and join remote tables. SQL Server 7.0 allows you to join two types of remote databases: remote servers and linked servers. Remote servers allow you to execute stored procedures on remote SQL Server databases, whereas the linked servers allow you to access OLE DB datasources and join remote tables. The movement toward distributed transactions gives the user more freedom in accessing data.

When there are transactions, there must be locks. Locks prevent multiple users from accessing the same data. There are four types of locks in SQL Server: shared, exclusive, update, and intent. The different locks can lock distinct levels of the database, from the page to the database itself. Though SQL Server 7.0 introduces dynamic locking, you are still able to configure locks by means of locking hints. You can observe the different locks on your system by running the sp_lock or sp_processinfo stored procedure, or the SQL Server Enterprise Manager. A big problem with locks is that two locks can occur at the same time and the transactions can interfere with each other. A way to prevent this from happening is to set the transaction isolation levels.

This chapter discussed the importance of locks and transactions. Only by being aware of the options available can the database developer be successful in improving the performance of his or her applications.

✓ TWO-MINUTE DRILL

❑ The most basic unit of work in Microsoft SQL Server 7.0 is a transaction.

❑ It is imperative that you know how to properly set up transactions so they preserve data integrity.

❑ One of the most important parts of a database's design is to ensure that the data on the SQL Server is logically consistent.

❑ A transaction is the smallest logical unit of work for the database.

❑ All actions that occur on the database break down to one or more transactions. Transactions consist of four properties, called the *ACID* properties.

❑ The four ACID properties are Atomicity, Consistency, Isolation, and Durability.

❑ Aggressively designing data modifications, retrievals, or updates with the mindset of transactions can provide numerous benefits in a scaled-up environment down the road. Being thrifty with locking needs and the batching up of data commands can yield increasingly large dividends as usage increases.

❑ Transactions that are partially complete can upset the consistency of the data.

❑ By using Transact-SQL statements or SQL Server API, you can start and end transactions.

❑ Three types of transactions can be started in SQL Server 7.0: explicit, implicit, and autocommit.

❑ Each transaction is separate from the connections. If a transaction changes modes, the same connection will be used.

❑ Explicit transactions are manually configured transactions in which you define the beginning and the end of the transaction. You need to use specific Transact-SQL statements, called *reserved words*, to specify the beginning and end of the transactions.

❑ You must be cautious about running implicit transactions since you are required to commit or roll back every transaction. If you forget, the transaction can be locked longer than you anticipate, thus slowing down access to your data.

❑ Autocommit is SQL Server's default transaction mode. Each *batch* is broken up into smaller statements, making it like a batch file.

❑ Setting transaction isolation levels is a balance between concurrency and data integrity. Choosing the correct transaction isolation level can dramatically improve performance.

❑ There are four transaction isolation levels to choose from: Read Committed, Read Uncommitted, Repeatable Read, and Serializable.

❑ When you start designing transactions, remember to minimize transaction duration. The shorter the transaction, the quicker the locks are released.

❑ With the Microsoft Distributed Transaction Coordinator (MSDTC) service, SQL Server can support transactions spanning multiple servers. With distributed transactions, data being queried does not have to be on one server.

❑ Distributed transactions allow you to connect to two types of remote databases: *remote servers* and *linked servers*.

❑ Remote servers enable a client to execute stored procedures on another SQL Server using the same connection. The connected server accepts the client's request and passes it on to the remote server.

❑ A linked server is similar to a remote server but it also has the ability to harness the power and flexibility of OLE DB. Linked servers allow you to also access an OLE DB rowset from any OLE DB data source, such as Microsoft Access and Oracle; join remote tables; and execute remote stored procedures.

❑ You must run the instcat.sql script against any SQL Server 6.5 servers if you want to run distributed transactions with the linked server options.

❑ New to Microsoft SQL Server 7.0 is *dynamic locking*. SQL Server will determine the appropriate locking when a query is executed. This helps simplify database administration and increases performance, since the server determines the appropriate locks.

❑ SQL Server 7.0 has four lock types: shared locks, update locks, exclusive locks, and intent locks.

❑ Shared locks allow connections to read data. Since concurrent reads do not affect the integrity of the data, shared locks can be used concurrently with other shared locks.

❑ Exclusive locks aren't compatible with anything. This is because when a transaction has an exclusive lock on a row, no other transaction can access it.

❑ Although SQL Server automatically sets the optimum table-level locking hints, there may be instances when manual settings are more fitting. For example, if SQL Server uses a coarse locking hint, you may prefer a finer lock.

❑ Deadlock occurs when two applications, which already have locks on separate objects, want a lock on the other's object. SQL Server automatically fixes this by choosing one application and forcing it to release its lock, while allowing the other session to continue.

❑ Though locks are crucial to the integrity of the database, there are times when you can minimize the use of locks. This is called *optimistic locking* or *optimistic concurrency* and is used to speed up transactions.

❑ Transact-SQL cursors do not support the optimistic with values concurrency option.

❑ If an application requests optimistic concurrency with row versioning on a table that does not have a timestamp column, the cursor reverts back to optimistic locking with values.

❑ @@trancount is a Transact-SQL global variable used to return the number of active connections for the current connection.

❑ The LOCK_TIMEOUT setting sets a time limit on how long a statement will wait for a blocked resource.

SELF TEST

The following Self Test questions will help you measure your understanding of the material presented in this chapter. Read all the choices carefully, as there may be more than one correct answer. Choose all correct answers for each question.

1. What properties do transactions consist of? (Choose all that apply.)

   A. Atomicity
   B. Consistency
   C. Isolation
   D. Durability

2. What do you use to prevent concurrent users from reading data that has been changed but not yet committed?

   A. Keys
   B. Locks
   C. Switches
   D. Holds

3. What stored procedures can you use to display locking information? (Choose all that apply.)

   A. sp_lock
   B. sp_indexes
   C. sp_processinfo
   D. sp_monitor

4. What are the types of transactions? (Choose all that apply.)

   A. Explicit
   B. Implicit
   C. Default

   D. Autocommit

5. How do you end an explicit transaction? (Choose all that apply.)

   A. BEGIN TRAN
   B. COMMIT TRANSACTION
   C. BEGIN TRANSACTION
   D. COMMIT TRAN

6. How do you cancel a transaction? (Choose all that apply.)

   A. BEGIN TRAN
   B. ROLLBACK WORK
   C. ROLLBACK TRANSACTION
   D. COMMIT TRAN

7. How do you enable implicit transactions?

   A. BEGIN TRAN
   B. BEGIN TRANSACTION
   C. SET IMPLICIT_TRANSACTIONS ON
   D. SET IMPLICIT_TRANSACTIONS OFF

8. How do you start an explicit transaction? (Choose all that apply.)

   A. BEGIN TRAN
   B. COMMIT TRANSACTION
   C. BEGIN TRANSACTION
   D. COMMIT TRAN

9. What is the least concurrent transaction isolation level?

   A. Read committed
   B. Read uncommitted

C. Repeatable read

D. Serializable

10. What are the different transaction isolation levels available on SQL Server 7.0? (Choose all that apply.)

A. Read committed

B. Read uncommitted

C. Repeatable read

D. Serializable

11. How do you minimize the transaction duration? (Choose all that apply.)

A. Use exclusive locks

B. Committing changes quicker

C. Use parameter arrays

D. Use statement batches

12. What option do you set to enable distributed transactions for a session?

A. BEGIN TRANSACTION

B. SET REMOTE_PROC_ TRANSACTIONS

C. BEGIN DISTRIBUTED TRANSACTIONS

D. SET IMPLICIT_TRANSACTIONS ON

13. What type of server allows you to access data from any OLE DB data source, such as Microsoft Access and Oracle?

A. Remote servers

B. Dynamic servers

C. Linked servers

D. Resident servers

14. What are the lock types? (Choose all that apply.)

A. Shared locks

B. Update locks

C. Exclusive locks

D. Intent locks

15. What are most locks incompatible with?

A. Shared locks

B. Update locks

C. Exclusive locks

D. Intent Exclusive locks

16. What are the types of optimistic locking available on SQL Server 7.0? (Choose all that apply.)

A. Optimistic with error checking

B. Optimistic with values

C. Optimistic with row versioning

D. Optimistic with table versioning

17. What is the SQL Server global variable that is used to return the number of active connections for the current connection?

A. @@IDENTITY

B. @@CONNECTIONS

C. @@TRANCOUNT

D. @@MAX_CONNECTIONS

18. What setting sets a time limit on how long a statement will wait for a blocked resource?

A. LOCK_TIMEOUT

B. LOCK_REQUEST

C. LOCK_TIME

D. LOCK_RELEASE

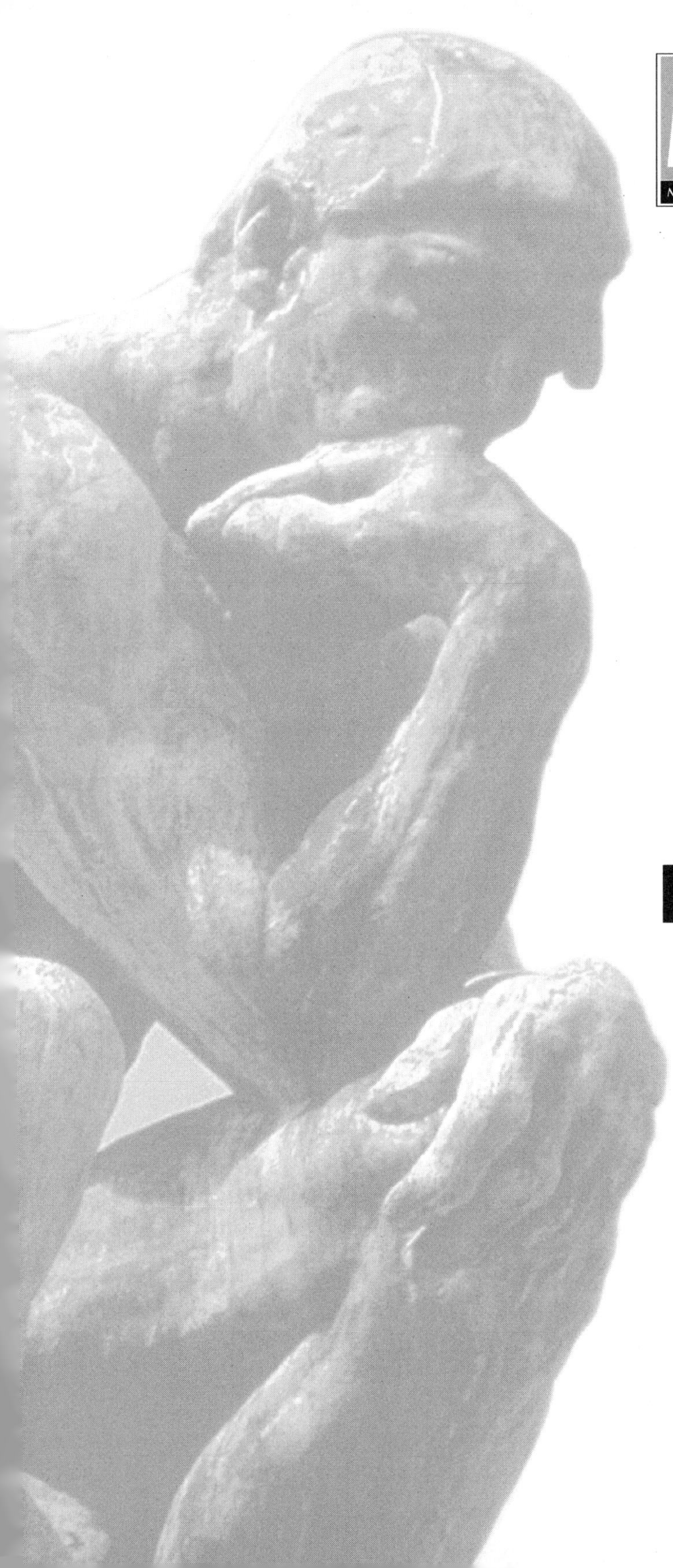

9

Implementing Views

CERTIFICATION OBJECTIVES

9.01	Definition of a View
9.02	Advantages of Views
9.03	Defining Views
9.04	Modifying Data Through Views
9.05	Querying Data Through Views
9.06	Performance Considerations

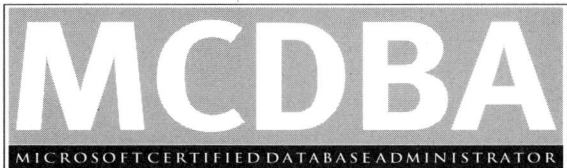

Instead of querying and directly manipulating the data in tables, Microsoft SQL Server 7.0 supports the use of simulated tables that present existing table data in new ways. These simulated tables support almost all of the same functionality as physical tables: you can read data in them, you can add to or update content in them, and you can delete records from them. These simulated tables are called *views*, and in this chapter we will demonstrate their creation and use.

FROM THE CLASSROOM

A View to Your Data

The use of views can provide numerous benefits to the SQL developer. Views are simulated tables that allow WHERE clause restrictions, constraints, JOIN syntax, and other complex data-retrieval SQL commands to be masked by or integrated into a view definition, thereby greatly simplifying data-retrieval complexity. You can benefit from being aware of these additional facts about views:

- Consistent naming conventions for views are recommended to assist in distinguishing them from physical tables.

- Views can be created with the granting of execute permission in the CREATE VIEW statement, although not having the necessary permissions on the underlying base tables results in return results that are empty.

- The use of joins in a view definition should be limited to inner joins. Outer joins can be used in defining a view, but may result in unexpected output.

- The ALTER VIEW SQL statement supported by T-SQL in SQL Server 7.0 is not supported as a part of the ANSI SQL-92 standard.

- The options gained by using the WITH ENCRYPTION or WITH CHECK OPTION in creating a view will only be retained after using the ALTER VIEW if these are included in the alteration command syntax.

- No functional limit exists for the maximum number of levels of nested views (views used in view definitions), but nesting views should be limited to three levels for simplicity.

—Michael Lane Thomas,
MCSE+I, MCSD, MCP+SB, MSS, MCT, A+

Definition of a View

When an end user looks at a view, he or she may assume to be looking directly at a table. However, when you look at a view, you should see a resource that can reduce development time, simplify data access, and help distribute the right content to the right audience.

A view is a simulated table that can include up to 1,024 columns that are retrieved from a table, from a combination of tables, or even from other views. You can use views for a variety of actions, including

- To replace a query used for a frequently generated report
- As the source for a common bulk copy program (bcp) export
- As the source for a scrollable cursor used to update fields
- Almost anywhere else a table could be used

One way to understand the advantages provided by views is to compare the use of views to another technique used to create ad hoc data sets: temporary tables. For example, imagine that you wanted to compare current employee job levels with the recommended maximum job level for that employee, and you wanted to have this result set available for subsequent analysis.

One way to do this would be to create a temporary table. After executing the following code, you could retrieve that content by using SELECT * FROM #JobLevelComparison:

```
SELECT employee.pub_id, employee.fname, employee.lname,
    employee.job_lvl, jobs.max_lvl,
    jobs.max_lvl - employee.job_lvl AS Difference
INTO #JobLevelComparison
FROM jobs INNER JOIN
    employee ON jobs.job_id = employee.job_id
```

Alternatively, you could create a view. After executing the following code, you could retrieve that content by using SELECT * FROM JobLevelComparison. (The syntax of the CREATE VIEW command will be discussed in more detail later in the chapter; but, for now, simply observe how similar the SQL is to the previous example.)

```
CREATE VIEW JobLevelComparison AS
SELECT employee.pub_id, employee.fname, employee.lname,
    employee.job_lvl, jobs.max_lvl,
    jobs.max_lvl - employee.job_lvl AS Difference
FROM jobs INNER JOIN
    employee ON jobs.job_id = employee.job_id
```

Both of these SELECT statements (SELECT * from #JobLevelComparison and SELECT * FROM JobLevelComparison return the result set displayed in Figure 9-1.

Although the result set is the same, the use of views has some distinct advantages over the use of temporary tables, as Table 9-1 illustrates.

Result set from a query executed on a view

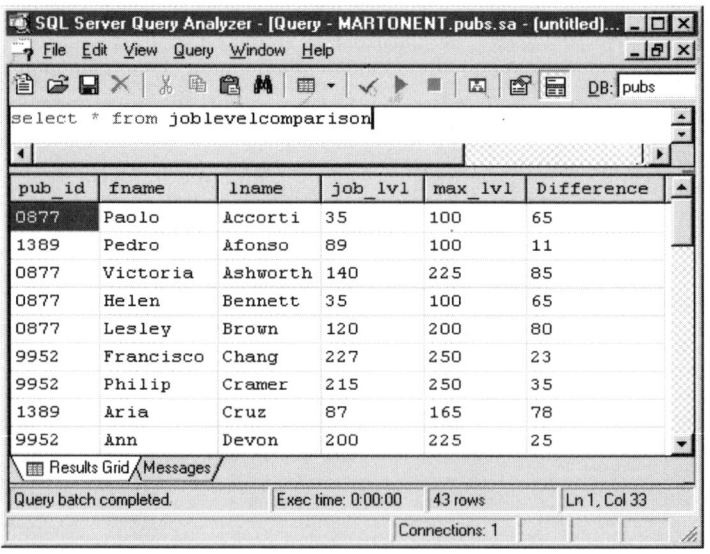

TABLE 9-1

Comparison Between
Temporary Tables
and Views

Attribute	Temporary Tables	Views
Can include only desired columns?	Yes	Yes
Can include only desired rows?	Yes	Yes
Can include content from multiple tables?	Yes	Yes
Are updates saved back into source tables?	No	Yes
Must be initialized before use?	Yes	No
Takes up system resources when not being used?	Yes	No

As you can see, views offer the same advantages as temporary tables, but they also can provide much more flexibility in how the data is deployed and used.

Although views appear to be tables to the user, they take up almost no system resources when they are not being used. Furthermore, it is not necessary (or even possible) to define indexes or defaults for views, because they inherit the constraints associated with their underlying tables.

Another way to gain an appreciation for views is to compare them to subqueries (originally presented in Chapter 6). As we learned, it is possible to use subqueries to nest multiple SELECT statements, providing some very sophisticated data analysis. Unfortunately, the SQL statements required to create these can quickly grow incomprehensible, and it can become difficult for other users to understand the intentions of the original developer.

However, if these complicated subqueries are defined as a view, and the parent view is referenced in this view, instead of the subquery, then the system can become much more self-documenting. This example illustrates one of the primary reasons why views are so popular: views can make database development more modular, and thus easier to maintain. To make an analogy, if you think of SQL statements as programs, then the use of views can make these programs more object oriented.

CERTIFICATION OBJECTIVE 9.02

Advantages of Views

The use of views offers numerous potential advantages for users (Table 9-2), for developers (Table 9-3), and for database administrators (Table 9-4).

TABLE 9-2

Advantages of Views for the End User

Advantage for the User	Explanation
Easier to understand results	When you use views, you can rename the columns so that they are clear to the users. For example, a user may think that a field named *EmpID* is confusing, and may want the field name read *Employee Identification* instead. By renaming the column in a view instead of in the table, you can avoid having a negative impact upon other processes that depend upon the column names.
Easier to obtain data	A lot of people know a little SQL. Most people would rather find a way to get the data they need by themselves, rather than ask for support from a database administrator. If you can deploy some of the more complicated queries they would need, encapsulated in views to reduce user confusion, you can increase their ability to do the job they need to do, while reducing their dependence upon you. (Of course, this also could be a negative, depending upon how paranoid you are.)
Result sets are more consistent	If your users develop resources that depend upon consistent table definitions, they will be frustrated if these definitions change. However, if your users are using views that you've developed, instead of using the base tables, you have much greater flexibility in changing the definition of these tables without their protest (or even their knowledge). You can even use this technique to wean the users from the tables themselves.

on the
!
()ob

Sometimes a column needs to be removed from a table (perhaps because of new normalization opportunities, or perhaps because the responsibility for updating content has shifted to a new source). By renaming the table and creating a new view with the same name as the original table, you can make these adjustments without inconveniencing your users. They will not even notice that they used to use a table, but now use a view.

TABLE 9-3	Advantages for the Developer	Explanation
Advantages of Views for the Developer	Easier to restrict data retrieval	Often you will want to expose content in a table, but conceal the information in certain columns or rows. By using views, you can still give users flexible access to the data they need, while maintaining appropriate security on other data in the same tables. For example, suppose you were the MIS director for a research hospital. The researchers at the hospital might want access to the raw medical data for statistical analysis, but due to your legal restrictions, you should not give them access to any data that can identify individuals. To do this, you could set up views that excluded the columns that identified personal users, and only allow researchers to see the rows describing diseases they are authorized to investigate. By granting rights on the view instead of on the table, you can do a much better job of avoiding data redundancy.
	Easier to restrict data entry	Using a view makes it easy to permit different groups of users to enter different ranges of valid data into the same table. For example, one group of users could enter salaries of up to $60,000, but a different group of users with access to a different view could enter salaries greater than that amount. (This is done using WITH CHECK OPTION, described in the table in the CREATE VIEW Syntax section later in the chapter)

Advantages for the Developer	Explanation
Applications are easier to maintain	It can be easier to debug views than it is to debug complex queries. If you have views built upon views, it is easier to check each step of the process to see if the results are correct. (Although it is relatively easy to break a query into components for testing, this may not be the case for users linking to SQL Server.) The use of modular views can also make development more consistent and easier to manage. Suppose that you have business rules that define a benefit class based upon salary, but this definition changes at irregular intervals. By building a base view that incorporates the current definition, and by joining other tables to it, you can easily cascade this change through a series of other views.
Easier to understand legacy development	The use of views can make development more legible and self-documenting. As queries grow in sophistication, it can become difficult to understand how the content flows through all the joins and subqueries. Using views instead of subqueries can make it easier for other developers to understand legacy development. (Again though, this could be a disadvantage if you're really, really paranoid.)

exam
ⓦatch

It is possible for a user to have access to the data in a view, even if the user doesn't have access to the underlying table.

Advantages for the Administrator	Explanation
Easier to deploy variable result sets	Views are not the only way you can assign rights to a group on a per-column basis. Column-based security provides much of the same functionality. However, when you use column-based security, the user must know what fields are accessible before querying, because *SELECT* * will fail if any fields are restricted from the user. By contrast, when using views, users can easily see what columns are available by using SELECT *.

	Advantages for the Administrator	Explanation
TABLE 9-4 Advantages of Views for the Administrator *(continued)*	Partitioned data can be combined for presentation	When all users across a WAN need to make updates to the tables, they often need servers that are physically nearby to provide acceptable performance. This can make it inconvenient to present the data in a unified report. However, you can create views that join the content from these partitioned tables into what appears to be a single table, combining local and remote content. However, it is not possible to update a query directly; you must modify the underlying tables.
	Fewer server resources are required	Organizations often develop redundant data, importing and exporting data unnecessarily as the content moves from business unit to business unit. Not only does this make it harder to keep data synchronized, it also requires more storage space and server processing to manage redundant indexes and user connections. By fostering the use of views to draw upon common data sources for different organizational needs, you can reduce the workload on the server, and provide better performance for all users.
	Easier to migrate data	When migrating data from SQL Server to another source using bcp, it is sometimes necessary to denormalize the content in the tables. By creating a view that incorporates this denormalization, it can be easier to port this data.

CERTIFICATION OBJECTIVE 9.03

Defining Views

In previous versions of SQL Server Enterprise Manager, there was only one way to define a view, and that was with the CREATE VIEW statement. Because this required the developer to manually type SQL statements, there was significant potential for error, and it was time-consuming to analyze existing views.

Fortunately, Microsoft has created a new visual tool in SQL Server 7.0, which allows the user to create and edit views using an interface that is very user friendly, especially for users familiar with using Microsoft Access to create queries.

You may end up using this visual editor much more than you use the CREATE VIEW command, but you should still be familiar with both approaches. Not only are there some commands that are not supported by the visual editor, but the use of CREATE VIEW also will give you an appreciation for your rugged forebears, who debugged their queries by hand and killed bears for food.

exam
ⓦatch

Most of the answers on Microsoft multiple-choice exams are expressed using text. Because of this, there is a bias on the exams toward solutions that can be expressed without using pictures. Even if you find that the visual tools more than meet your needs, for the test, you will need to make sure that you are familiar with the dynamic SQL-based approaches to the administrative tools.

It is also possible to combine these two techniques. A query originally created with CREATE VIEW can be edited visually, and a query created visually can be modified with ALTER VIEW.

Regardless of which technique you use, the results are the same. The syntax of the statement is verified, and if it is correct, the definition of the view is stored in the system tables. This information is stored in multiple tables, including sysobjects, sysprocedures, syscolumns, sysdepends, and syscomments. The text used to create the view is visible in syscomments using the *sp_helptext* stored procedure, unless WITH ENCRYPTION OPTION is used. This option is discussed in more detail in a later section.

We will examine the creation of these views using the visual designer, and then we will see how to perform the same actions using Transact-SQL.

Designing Views

Even in the demonstration databases, pubs and Northwind, there aren't many user demonstration views. (There are several system views, but you will almost never want to modify a system view; and, unless you are extraordinarily cautious, you will not even want to open them.) Therefore, rather than observing an existing view, we will see how easy it is to create your own.

When you open up the Views node in the pubs database, you see a list of views similar to Figure 9-2.

When you click Design View from the right-click shortcut menu, the screen expands into a four-pane interface for editing views, as shown in Figure 9-3. Using this screen, you can view a visual model of your query, the SQL required to build it, and the data that it returns.

Existing views in the pubs database

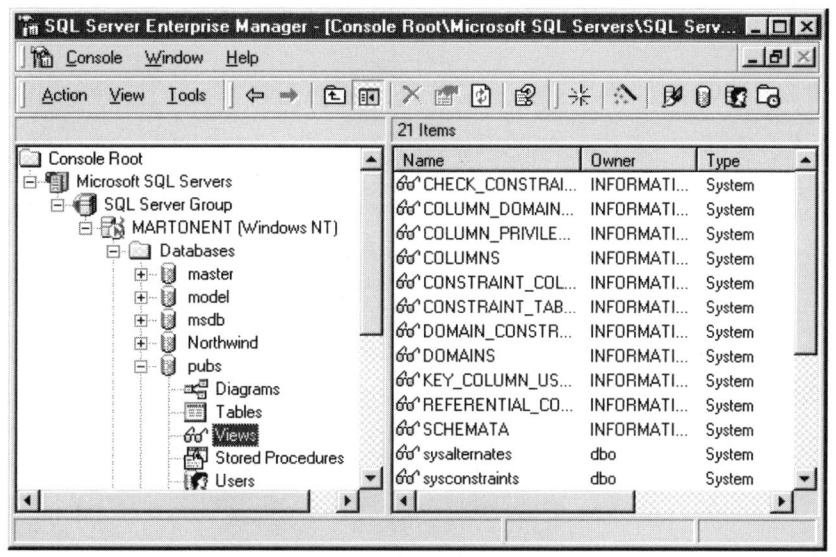

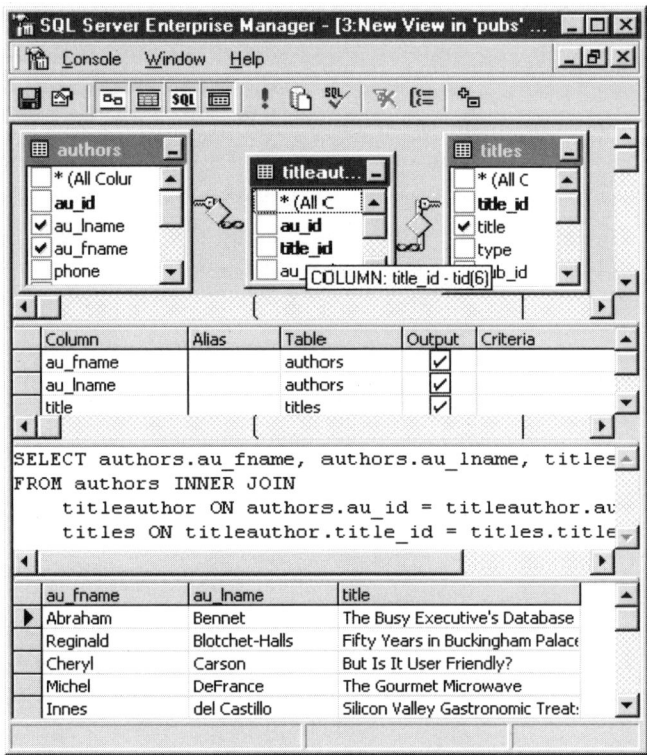

Most of the actions performed in the designer are performed with the
buttons on the tool bar, not with the menu commands. From left to right,
the buttons are as follows:

Button	Description
Save	Saves design changes to the current view
Properties	Allows definition of view name, GROUP BY extensions when applicable, and other view-wide options
Show/Hide Diagram pane	Toggles visibility of pane used to add and relate tables

Button	Description
Show/Hide Grid pane	Toggles visibility of pane used to define column details
Show/Hide SQL pane	Toggles visibility of SQL statements generated by modifying Diagram or Grid pane
Show/Hide Results pane	Toggles visibility of output generated by the query
Run Query	Executes the query, and displays output in the Results pane
Cancel Execution and Clear Results	Frees the connection used to execute the query
Verify SQL	Checks syntax of SQL (only needed when editing directly into SQL pane)
Remove Filter	Removes filter from a query
Use "Group By"	Adds Group By column to grid pane to allow selection of aggregate functions
Add Table	Adds a table (or a view) to the diagram pane

In most cases, you can enter your design changes either visually or directly in the SQL pane. After you make your changes, they are propagated to the other panes. When you enter changes into the SQL pane, sometimes the changes do not propagate to the other panes until a syntax check is performed upon the query, or until the query is executed for the first time. If you are experienced with SQL, but new to this visual tool, the easiest way to learn this tool may be to just type (or copy) your SQL into the third pane. Then execute the query, and observe how the first two panes adjust to display what you created.

A more complete walk-through of the capabilities of this tool is presented in Exercise 9-2.

The CREATE VIEW Statement

Although the preceding technique is the easiest for developing new views from scratch, if the SQL for the view is already known, you may want to implement it using the CREATE VIEW command.

CREATE VIEW Syntax

The syntax of the CREATE VIEW statement is as follows:

```
CREATE VIEW view_name [column names]
[WITH ENCRYPTION]
AS
SQLstatement
[WITH CHECK OPTION]
```

The sections of this statement are described in detail in this table:

Syntax	Description
View_name	Defines the name to be used for the new view.
[column names]	Provides the names of the columns defined by the view. (When left blank, as this parameter often is, the names of the columns are inherited from the SELECT statement.)
WITH ENCRYPTION	Determines whether the definition of the view can be displayed using sp_helptext.
SQLstatement	Provides the SQL statement that selects the columns to be returned in the view.
WITH CHECK OPTION	Determines whether the user will be allowed to enter data that is valid for the table but invalid for the view.

Note the following about these options:

- **column names** Although you can create a normal query that has multiple fields with the same name, every field in a view must have a unique name. Therefore, if you are pulling from multiple tables and have two fields with the same name, you must rename at least one of them. This can be performed in the column name parameter, or in the SQL statement itself.

- **SQL statement** This statement is validated when the query is created. However, if the query later becomes invalid (for example, if a table that it was referencing is renamed), the view is not updated to reflect this change.

■ **WITH ENCRYPTION** The definition of the view is stored in the syscomments table, so normally the logic used to create the view would be accessible to users with SELECT rights on that table. However, if you select WITH ENCRYPTION, the definition of this view is encrypted within the table. (One situation in which this might be useful is if you were developing a commercial SQL Server add-on and you wanted to protect your ideas.)

Applying Security to Views

Just as it is when creating a table, after creating a view it is necessary to assign the appropriate rights to it by using the GRANT, DENY, and REVOKE commands. For example, the following command would provide the user, JohnDoe, with the rights to modify the content defined by the view, JobLevelComparison.

```
GRANT INSERT, UPDATE, DELETE ON JobLevelComparison TO JohnDoe
```

The rights for views are managed independently from the rights for the tables upon which the views are based. This means that it is possible to have rights to a view based upon a table, even if you don't have rights to see that table itself. This is one of the primary advantages of using views, but there is an administrative side effect.

It is easy to forget that when you revoke a user's rights to select content in a table, they still may be able to see the content in that table. If you want users to no longer see content in a table, you need to identify all of the objects that reference that table.

Restrictions Applied to Creating Views

Although there is great flexibility in creating views, there are considerations that apply to views that should be kept in mind:

■ There are some commands that are legal in SELECT statements but are not allowed when creating a view. These commands include ORDER BY, COMPUTE, COMPUTE BY, and INTO. (It is possible to use these commands *on* a view, just not *in* one.)

- You cannot reference a temporary table (local or global) in a view, and there is no such thing as a temporary view.

- It is not possible to create views in databases other than the current one. (This is in contrast to the CREATE TABLE command, in which the database name is an optional parameter, defining where the table should be created.)

Altering Views

Much of the time, when you are modifying a view, you may want to use the visual tools to manage the process. However, it is much more likely that the use of Transact-SQL will be covered on the certification test. To prepare yourself most thoroughly both for the test and for development, you should familiarize yourself with all three techniques for altering views: the flexible way, the fast way, and the way that will be on the test.

The Flexible Way to Modify Views

If you right-click on a view and then select a view, you are brought into the visual query editor. This provides the entire set of design tools that you are provided when you initially create a view.

This will often be the easiest way to implement changes. However, there are some disadvantages to this approach. When you make visual changes to the query, Enterprise Manager recompiles the entire SQL string. If you have made changes that cannot be processed by the visual editor, then some of your changes may be lost.

The Fast Way to Modify Views

If you are experienced with hand-coding SQL statements, but you'd still like some visual assistance in maintaining your views, you may want to use *View Properties*. If you right-click a view and select Properties from the shortcut menu, you will see a screen similar to that shown in Figure 9-4.

This screen not only displays the existing SQL used to define a view, but it also allows the user to make changes directly in the Text window. This interface can be very useful if you are making minor changes to a query, for

FIGURE 9-4

Editing a view directly from
the Enterprise Manager

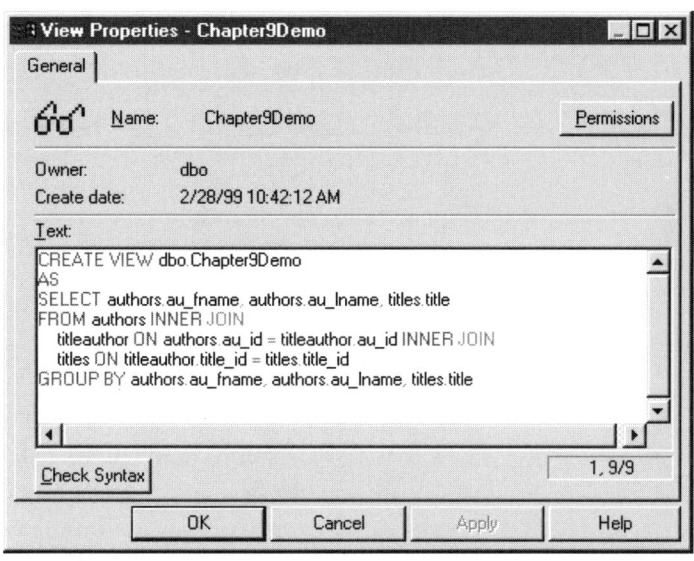

example, if you are changing filter criteria. In addition to supporting these
direct edits, the Properties window provides color coding of keywords to
help provide content, and a syntax check to assure that the changes made
are valid.

Of course, because this interface involves direct editing of the SQL
statement, it is easy to make typos or logic errors that result in invalid
statements. Fortunately, Enterprise Manager allows you to save views that
are syntactically invalid (for example, if you misspelled SELECT), but if
you have a semantic error (for example, if you used the % wildcard when
you meant to use _), you will not discover it until you execute the query.

The Way Most Likely to Be Tested

Because of the bias on Microsoft exams toward Transact-SQL, you will
want to make sure you are familiar with using ALTER VIEW to modify
views. Of course, there are some other good reasons to know this approach.
For example, you could modify a view with a stored procedure using this
approach, but not using the other two approaches.

You can use the ALTER VIEW statement to change any attribute of a view, except for its name or permissions. The syntax of the ALTER VIEW statement is as follows:

```
ALTER VIEW view_name [columns]
[WITH ENCRYPTION]
AS
SQLstatement
[WITH CHECK OPTION]
```

Because the syntax is identical to that of CREATE VIEW, it is not necessary to identify the meaning of each part of the statement—just refer to the definition of CREATE VIEW. In fact, this may look so similar to CREATE VIEW, that you may wonder why anybody would bother with ALTER VIEW. If you have to redefine all the parameters anyway, why not just discard the old view and create a new one?

Some developers share this opinion, and they modify a view by dropping the view and re-creating it. While this technique can be used successfully, the permissions on the view will be lost; so ALTER VIEW should be used instead of this technique when possible.

exam
ⓦatch

For all objects (not just views), deleting the object and re-creating it destroys any user rights that had been applied to that object.

Exercise 9-1 demonstrates how to create a view, observe the data it returns, and make modifications to it using the view editor.

EXERCISE 9-1

Designing, Creating, Using, and Altering Views

1. Load Enterprise Manager, and open the pubs database on the current server.

2. Click Views. Observe that the right pane fills with the default views for this database.

3. Select New View from the Action menu. Observe the four panes, stacked vertically, each with no content.

4. Click the rightmost button on the toolbar (it should have a ToolTip of Add Table. Note that you can add tables or previously defined views.

5. Add the tables *Sales* and *Stores* by double-clicking those table names, and then click the Close button.

6. Note that now the first pane has a visual representation of the two tables you added, while the third pane includes a new SQL statement. These actions have provided the initial definition for the FROM clause and a representation of the join. (As a default, SQL Server assumes you want to have the relationships that are defined by the foreign keys, but this can be overridden.)

   If you accidentally add a table twice, it will appear twice in the Diagram pane, and in the SQL pane it will link to itself. Although this may be useful for a self-join, it would be an error in this query. To get rid of it, click the second copy of the table and press the DELETE key.

7. In the Stores table, click the check box next to state. Then, in the Sales table, click the check boxes next to the ord_num and qty fields. Observe that as you add the fields, the name of the field is added to the third pane, and the field is entered into the table in the second pane.

8. You now have provided enough definition to execute the query. The button on the tool bar with an exclamation point is the Run button. Click this button, and observe that the fourth pane is now filled with the data returned from this query. The screen should look similar to Figure 9-5.

9. On the toolbar, observe the four consecutive buttons that each begin with a ToolTip of *Show/Hide*... Practice toggling these buttons to make the four panes appear and disappear.

10. In the Grid pane (the second pane from the top), click inside the ord_num field. See that a combo-box indicator appears. Click the indicator, and change the field to read **ord_date**. Observe that the first and third panes are updated to reflect this change. Click the Run button to see this change in the Results pane.

11. In the SQL pane (the third pane from the top), select the text, ord_date, and replace it with **ord_num**. Note there is no immediate change in the first or second panes. Now click the Verify SQL button on the tool bar (appearing like a check mark). You should receive the message, "The SQL Syntax has been verified against the data source," and you should see your design change reflected in the first and second panes.

FIGURE 9-5

Editing views in
Enterprise Manager

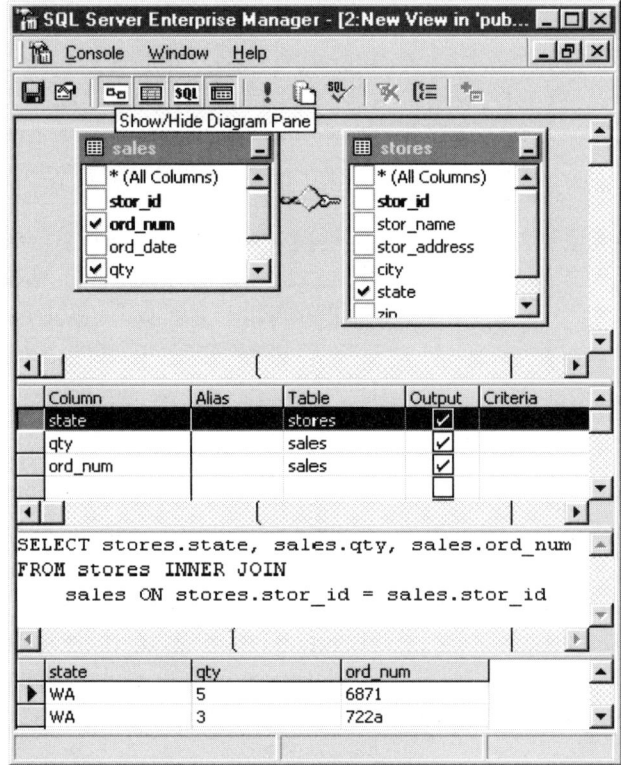

12. In the SQL pane, where you typed ord_num, replace it with the intentional mistake **ord_numb**, and click the Verify SQL button. You should receive a message indicating (among other things) that you have an invalid column name. Remove the extraneous *b* from the field name and click the Verify SQL button again. Observe that you can enter design changes in the Diagram pane, the Grid pane, or the SQL pane; but, when you enter changes in the SQL pane, it is easier to make typos.

13. From the tool bar, click the Save button. Save the view with the name **testview**.

14. In the SQL pane, type **SELECT * FROM testview** and run the query. Observe that the view that you just created is now available from this pane, just as the original tables were.

Modifying Data Through Views

With minor exceptions, the process of modifying data through a view is identical to the process of modifying the underlying tables. Though it is not possible to add constraints upon the view itself, the user still has to obey the same constraint, type, uniqueness, and foreign key limits that would otherwise be needed. As long as these are obeyed, the modification should execute properly.

However, because views can draw from multiple tables, and because they can exclude critical fields, there are some additional complications that may arise during development (or, just as importantly, on the exam!). These are detailed as follows:

Can I Modify Records from a View with Computed Columns?

You can modify records from a view with computed columns. The following view will illustrate this:

```
CREATE VIEW RoyDoub AS SELECT title_id, title, pub_id, royalty *
        2 AS DoubleRoyalty FROM titles
```

You would be able to insert, update, and delete records from this view with computed fields. However, if you attempt to edit the computed column itself, you will receive an error.

Can I Modify Records from a View That References Multiple Tables?

You can modify records from a view that references multiple tables. It is possible to use the DELETE, INSERT, or UPDATE queries on views if it is possible for the query to identify unambiguously the unique rows being referenced, and if only one table in the view is actually being updated. In Exercise 9-3, we will observe an attempt to modify multiple tables at the same time using a single view.

Can I Modify Records from a View When Excluded Fields Are Required in the Underlying Table?

You can modify records from a view when excluded fields are required in the underlying table, but only when the excluded required fields have default values.

When you create a new record using a view that doesn't include all the columns in a table, it is similar to using the INSERT statement on the underlying table and selecting only a subset of columns to enter. As you remember from Chapter 6, when you omit columns from the INSERT statement, the default values are used for all other columns for which defaults are defined, and a NULL is used for columns for which no default is defined. If a column is defined using NOT NULL and there is no default available for that column, it is not possible to insert a new record using a view that excludes that column.

Can I Modify Records from a View When the Key Is Not Available in the View?

You can modify records from a view when the key is not available in the view, but the content in the view can only be modified when the required omitted field is populated with an Identity or Timestamp.

This issue is similar to the preceding issue, in which a required field was omitted from the view. However, if the key had to be unique, it obviously would not be appropriate to assign a default value to it.

This will not be a problem if the key field is an Identity. In this case, the field will populate correctly without any assistance from the user. However, a unique identifier field is not automatically populated when a new row is completed; so, if this field is used as the key, it cannot be excluded from the view if the view is required to add new records.

How Does WITH CHECK OPTION Affect Updates to a View?

The use of WITH CHECK OPTION restricts users from entering data through a view that could not be read from that view.

Suppose that you created the following view:

```
CREATE VIEW dbo.PsychologyBooks AS
SELECT type, title_id, title, pubdate FROM titles WHERE (type = 'psychology')
```

This view would only return Psychology books, but it is possible to add other types of books using this view, as follows:

```
INSERT INTO PsychologyBooks (type, title_id, title, pubdate)
VALUES ('chemistry', 'PS0001', 'Sample chemistry title', '9-10-99')
```

Because the record could be inserted from this view, but not selected from it, this could cause confusion to users who wonder why their records "disappear."

This can be solved by using the WITH CHECK OPTION when defining the view, as follows:

```
CREATE VIEW dbo.PsychologyBooks AS
SELECT type, title_id, title, pubdate FROM titles WHERE
          (type ='psychology')
WITH CHECK OPTION
```

When the view is defined in this way, the INSERT statement defined previously is unsuccessful.

There are two main reasons why this feature is used. One is to confirm that data entered in a view would continue to be visible from within that same view. The second is to provide an easy mechanism for restricting the values that a user could enter.

Regardless of how WITH CHECK OPTION is used, any data populated into a table from a view must not violate any existing constraints required by a table. If a value is supported by the view but prohibited by the table, then the value could not be accepted into the table.

Exercise 9-2 demonstrates how to modify content through a view, and under what circumstances it is not possible to do so.

EXERCISE 9-2

Modifying Data Through Views

1. From the pubs database in Enterprise Manager, select New View from the Action menu. (The Action menu is context sensitive; so, if you don't see this option, confirm that you have the collection of views selected.)

2. Add the table, Stores.

3. Add the fields, stor_name, city, and state in the Stores table.

4. Execute the query. There should be six records returned in the bottom pane.

5. In the bottom pane, attempt to enter a new record with a stor_name of **My New Store**, a city of **Cleveland**, and a state of **OH**. After you press ENTER, you should receive an error, indicating that the stor_id field is required. Press ESC to abort the attempt to enter this data.

6. Without closing the view window, return to Enterprise Manager, select the Stores table, and select Properties. Observe that the only field in which nulls are not allowed is the stor_id field, and that this field is the key for this table.

7. Return to the view window. Observe that the stor_id field is displayed in bold. Add this field to the query, and execute the query.

8. In the bottom pane, attempt to enter a new record with a stor_name of **My New Store**, a city of **Cleveland**, a state of **OH**, and a stor_id of **12344**. After you press ENTER, the new record should be accepted.

9. In the second (Grid) pane, enter a new field with a column definition of **city + ', ' + state** and an alias of **Location**. Then, delete the city and state columns, and execute the query. Your results should look like Figure 9-6.

10. In the bottom pane, try to enter a new store with a stor_name of **My Other Store**, a stor_id of **4321**, and a Location of **Dayton, OH**. You should receive an error as soon as you attempt to edit the Location field. Press ESC to abort the edit.

11. Repeat step 10; but, instead of attempting to populate the Location field, leave it blank and press ENTER. Your new record should be accepted. Execute the query and you should see your new entry, sorted in order, and with a <NULL> for a Location field.

12. Select the new record that you just created (My Other Store) and press the DELETE key. When prompted to confirm that you want to delete the record, select Yes.

13. Add the city and state fields back into the view, and save this view as **Exercise9_2**. (It will be required for the next exercise.)

FIGURE 9-6

Updating views with a
calculated field

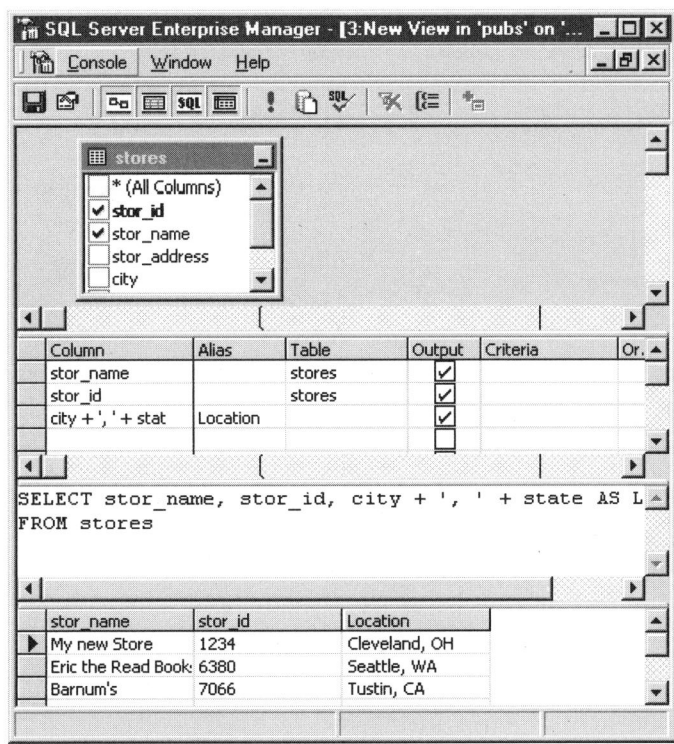

From this, it should be clear that you can insert and delete records that
have a computed field, but that it is not possible to modify the content in
the computed fields themselves. In the next exercise, we will learn more
about how modifications affect multitable views.

exam
ⓦatch

*Sometimes, the same structures used in the demonstration tables
(pubs, and now Northwind as well) can show up on the exam. When
they do, the table definitions are provided in the question; but, if you
already have a rough understanding of what the tables do, you may
save some time on the exam. Because of this, it is helpful to
familiarize yourself with the relationships among the tables in the
demonstration databases.*

CERTIFICATION OBJECTIVE 9.05

Querying Data Through Views

As we have observed, views can be enormously useful in managing your data. It can be tempting to think of a view as a table, and forget about the underlying complexity. However, because the changes made in one view can affect the content in other views and tables, it is important to understand the relationships among these objects, and to keep these relationships in mind when developing your applications.

Exercise 9-3 demonstrates how a view can reference a view, in the same way it would reference a table. It then shows how changes made to a view can have an impact in other locations.

EXERCISE 9-3

Querying Data Through a View

1. From the Enterprise Manager, create a new view.

2. Add the table Sales and the view from Exercise9_2 (created earlier in this chapter in Exercise 9-2). Note that Enterprise Manager assumes a join between these two objects on the stor_id field. We could override that default, but we will preserve it in this example.

3. In the Sales table, add the * field (which selects all columns). In the Exercise9_2 view, add the Location field. Execute the query.

4. Add a new record in the Results pane for the new bookstore you just created, with the following values: **1234**, **xyz**, **9/10/99**, **10**, **Net 30**, and **PC1035**. (Leave the final field blank—remember that you can't update calculated fields.)

5. Execute the query. You should now see your new record, with the Location populated with the city and state.

6. Enter three more records, keeping all fields the same, except selecting unique values for the order name. (You may vary the qty field if you choose, so you can more easily distinguish among the rows you've added.)

7. Add the field city from the view in Exercise9_2 and execute the query. You should now see content that appears similar to Figure 9-7.

FIGURE 9-7

Updating a view using
multiple tables

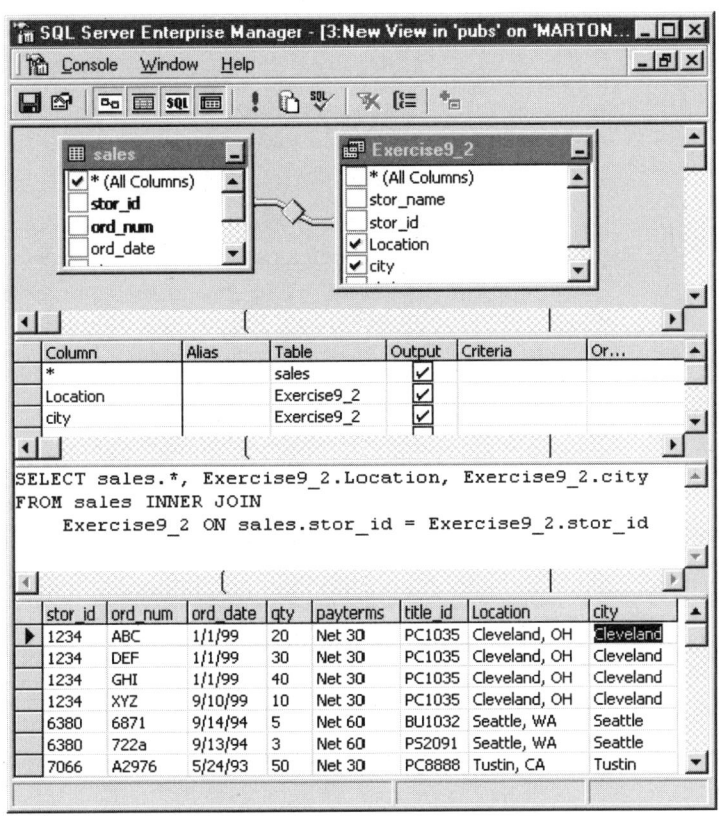

8. In the first of your four rows, select the city name Cleveland and
change it to **Lakewood**. (The field to modify is the field selected in
Figure 9-7.) Execute the query. Observe that the location of the
order has been changed, both in the city field and the Location field,
in all four records that you've entered.

9. In the view, Exercise9_2, add the field, stor_id and execute the query.

10. Attempt to add a new record with the following values: **1234**,
ABCD, **9/14/99**, **50**, **Net 30**, **PC1035**, and **1234**. (Skip the final two
fields.) You should receive an error stating that SQL Server cannot
create a new store, 1234, because this would violate an index.

11. Attempt to add a new record with the same values as in the previous example; but, instead of using 1234 in the final field, try **2345**. Press ENTER to submit the data.

12. Execute the query. You shouldn't be able to find the record you just entered in the view.

13. Replace the entire contents of the SQL pane with **SELECT * FROM Stores** and execute the query. (It is not necessary to add the Stores table; it is automatically added when the query is executed.) You should see the new store that you tried to create, 2345. Delete all the records that you added.

14. Replace the entire contents of the SQL pane with **SELECT * FROM Sales**. If you scroll through the results, you should see the new record that was added in step 11. However, because the store is identified as 1234 in the Sales table and as 2345 in the Stores table, it will not be possible to join the results of these tables. Delete all the records that you added.

From these exercises, we can observe that there is a great deal of power available when using views to update content. Because the changes made to a row in a table can reflect in other rows in the table when a join forces the same record in the table to be referenced in several records in the view, it is possible to do a lot of damage very quickly, and to make changes you did not intend.

CERTIFICATION OBJECTIVE 9.06

Performance Considerations

Despite the flexibility that views offer, they are not the right solution for every problem. One issue that arises when using views is that they are executed when they are needed. Normally, this would be an advantage. This assures that the data is always up-to-date and doesn't take up unnecessary storage space.

However, this may not always be the best option. If you have views that take a very long time to execute, you may want to consider replacing the view with a scheduled process to update a table. For example, if you are combining local data with data on a remote server, and you do not have replication established, you may want to compile local copies of summary reports during an overnight batch process.

There also can be new challenges introduced when managing the rights associated with views. The rights to content are defined when a view is created, and they are not updated as the rights on the underlying tables are modified. Therefore, when you change the rights on a table, make sure that you also change the rights on the views that reference that table. (This is in contrast to the constraints on a table, which are honored by the view even if they were created after the view was created.)

Some of the issues associated with views, and approaches that can be used to address them, are summarized in the following scenario questions.

QUESTIONS AND ANSWERS

A user wants me to create a view for him, but he requires summary statistics.	Most of the time when views are not permitted, it is still possible to use views to generate most of the intermediate steps. Create a view to aggregate the data you need and then instruct the user to use the COMPUTE statement on that view.
I have created a view that UNIONs two tables: one residing locally, and one on a remote server in Vilnius, Lithuania. I am disappointed by the performance of this view.	You may want to consider replicating or importing some of the remote data locally.
The number of views is constantly growing. I have no idea where they are coming from.	You may have accidentally granted to users the rights not only to create new views, but also to grant the rights to create new views to other users. Both of these rights can be easily revoked.
I thought I removed access rights for a user on a table, but I just found out that this user has been continuing to modify the content in the table anyway.	Confirm that this user does not have rights to any views that have access to this table.
I understand I can't use SELECT INTO in a view, but I still need to distribute the rights to execute this command.	This is a task better suited to stored procedures than to views. Stored procedures are discussed in Chapter 10.

However, you should not let any of these issues dissuade you from using views. When used appropriately, they will cure many more headaches than they cause. If you come up with an appropriate strategy for using them in your organization, you will increase user satisfaction and make your own life much easier.

CERTIFICATION SUMMARY

Instead of exposing tables directly to the user, you can create *views* that expose exactly the content you want to provide, in the format in which you want to provide it. With a few exceptions, if a record set can be expressed in a SQL query, it can be encapsulated in a view. These views can draw content from one table, many tables, or other views. By selecting only the needed columns and using the WHERE or HAVING clauses appropriately, views can be used to restrict the data that is visible to the users.

Views can be created and modified by using the CREATE VIEW and ALTER VIEW statements, or by using the visual tools provided by Enterprise Manager. While the visual tools are easier to use, the Transact-SQL statements can provide more flexibility.

Updating content in a view is very similar to updating content in a table, and it is subject to the same restrictions. If a table requires a field and the field has no usable default, then the field must be included in a view if the view is used to update records. It is possible to enter data into a view that would not be visible from the view, unless WITH CHECK OPTION is included in the view definition.

 # TWO-MINUTE DRILL

- ❏ Instead of querying and directly manipulating the data in tables, Microsoft SQL Server 7.0 supports the use of simulated tables that present existing table data in new ways.

- ❏ These simulated tables support almost all of the same functionality as physical tables: you can read data in them, you can add to or update content in them, and you can delete records from them.

❑ A view is a simulated table that can include up to 1,024 columns that are retrieved from a table, from a combination of tables, or even from other views.

❑ Although views appear to be tables to the user, they take up almost no system resources when they are not being used. Furthermore, it is not necessary (or even possible) to define indexes or defaults for queries, because they inherit the constraints associated with their underlying tables.

❑ When you use views, you can rename the columns so that they are clear to the users. For example, a user may think that a field named *EmpID* is confusing, and may want the field name to read *Employee Identification* instead.

❑ By using views, you can still give users flexible access to the data they need, while maintaining appropriate security on other data in the same tables.

❑ Using a view makes it easy to permit different groups of users to enter different ranges of valid data into the same table.

❑ It can be easier to debug views than it is to debug complex queries. If you have views built upon views, it is easier to check each step of the process to see if the results are correct.

❑ Using views instead of subqueries can make it easier for other developers to understand legacy development.

❑ It is possible for a user to have access to the data in a view, even if the user doesn't have access to the underlying table.

❑ In previous versions of SQL Server Enterprise Manager, there was only one way to define a view, and that was with the CREATE VIEW statement. Because this required the developer to manually type SQL statements, there was significant potential for error, and it was time-consuming to analyze existing views.

❑ Microsoft has created a new visual tool in SQL Server 7.0, which allows the user to create and edit views using an interface that is very user friendly, especially for users familiar with using Microsoft Access to create queries.

❑ Most of the answers on Microsoft multiple-choice exams are expressed using text. Because of this, there is a bias on the exams toward solutions that can be expressed without using pictures. Even if you find that the visual tools more than meet your needs, for the test you will need to make sure that you are familiar with the dynamic SQL-based approaches to the administrative tools.

❑ When you click Design View from the right-click shortcut menu, the screen expands into a four-pane interface for editing views. Using this screen, you can view a visual model of your query, the SQL required to build it, and the data that it returns.

❑ If the SQL for the view is already known, you may want to implement it using the CREATE VIEW command.

❑ Much of the time, when you are modifying a view, you may want to use the visual tools to manage the process. However, it is much more likely that the use of Transact-SQL will be covered on the certification test. To prepare yourself most thoroughly both for the test and for development, you should familiarize yourself with all three techniques for altering views: the flexible way, the fast way, and the way that will be on the test.

❑ Because of the bias on Microsoft exams toward Transact-SQL, you will want to make sure you are familiar with using ALTER VIEW to modify views.

❑ You can use the ALTER VIEW statement to change any attribute of a view, except for its name or permissions.

❑ For all objects (not just views), deleting the object and re-creating it destroys any user rights that had been applied to that object.

❑ With minor exceptions, the process of modifying data through a view is identical to the process of modifying the underlying tables. Though it is not possible to add constraints upon the view itself, the user still has to obey the same constraint, type, uniqueness, and foreign key limits that would otherwise be needed.

❑ You can modify records from a view with computed columns.

❑ You can modify records from a view that references multiple tables. It is possible to use the DELETE, INSERT, or UPDATE queries on views if it is possible for the query to identify unambiguously the unique rows being referenced, and if only one table in the view is actually being updated.

❑ You can modify records from a view when excluded fields are required in the underlying table, but only when the excluded required fields have default values.

❑ You can modify records from a view when the key is not available in the view, but the content in the view can only be modified when the required omitted field is populated with an Identity or Timestamp.

❑ The use of WITH CHECK OPTION restricts users from entering data through a view that could not be read from that view.

❑ Sometimes, the same structures used in the demonstration tables (pubs, and now Northwind as well) can show up on the exam. When they do, the table definitions are provided in the question; but, if you already have a rough understanding of what the tables do, you may save some time on the exam. Because of this, it is helpful to familiarize yourself with the relationships among the tables in the demonstration databases.

❑ It can be tempting to think of a view as a table, and forget about the underlying complexity. However, because the changes made in one view can affect the content in other views and tables, it is important to understand the relationships among these objects, and to keep these relationships in mind when developing your applications.

❑ If you have views that take a very long time to execute, you may want to consider replacing the view with a scheduled process to update a table.

❑ There also can be new challenges introduced when managing the rights associated with views. The rights to content are defined when a view is created, and they are not updated as the rights on the underlying tables are modified.

SELF TEST

The following questions will help you measure your understanding of the material presented in this chapter. Read all of the choices carefully, as there may be more than one correct answer. Choose all correct answers for each question.

1. Which of the following definitions best describes a view?

    A. A copy in the database of existing data

    B. A simulated table that presents existing table data in a new way

    C. A group of users that have permissions on a table

    D. A group of precompiled Transact-SQL statements

2. How many columns can a view have?

    A. 1,024

    B. 520

    C. Limited only by memory and storage constraints

    D. Defined using the sp_maxcolumns stored procedure

3. Which of the following are advantages of using views? (Choose all that apply.)

    A. To exclude certain rows from certain users

    B. To combine partitioned data into a single view for UPDATE queries, when all of the data resides on a local server

    C. To provide a data definition that can be used by bcp

    D. To combine partitioned data into a single view for SELECT queries when some of the data resides on a remote server

4. In which table is the entire definition of the view stored?

    A. syscolumns

    B. sysdepends

    C. syscomments

    D. sysobjects

5. When assigning security, what do views support that column-based security doesn't? (Choose all that apply.)

    A. Renaming of columns to be more readable

    B. Assignment of groups

    C. Support of the SELECT * command

    D. Creation of user-based legal field ranges

6. Which of the following could be the first line of a View definition? (Choose all that apply.)

    A. SELECT Employees.EmployeeID, Employees.LastName, EmployeeTerritories.EmployeeID, EmployeeTerritories.TerritoryID

    B. SELECT Employees.EmployeeID, Employees.LastName, EmployeeTerritories.EmployeeID as EmpID, EmployeeTerritories.TerritoryID

C. SELECT Employees.EmployeeID as EmpID, Employees.LastName, EmployeeTerritories.EmployeeID as TerID, EmployeeTerritories. TerritoryID

D. SELECT INTO Employees.EmployeeID, Employees.LastName, EmployeeTerritories.EmployeeID as EmpID, EmployeeTerritories. TerritoryID

7. Which of the following best describes the function of the WITH ENCRYPTION option?

   A. The data in the view will be encrypted so it can't be intercepted over the network.

   B. The definition of the view will be encrypted as it is stored in the system tables.

   C. The view will only be available to users with an encrypted connection.

   D. The specified column in the view will be encrypted so it can't be intercepted over the network.

8. What happens when you attempt to create the following view?

   create view ViewWithATypo as select * fromm sales

   A. An error will be generated when the view is created, but the view will be created.

   B. No error will be generated when the view is created, but an error will be generated when the view is executed.

   C. An error will be generated when the view is created, and the view will not be created.

   D. No error will be generated when the view is created, and no error will be generated when the view is executed, but the view will return no records.

9. Which of the following can be used when creating a view? (Choose all that apply.)

   A. Subqueries

   B. COMPUTE

   C. INTO

   D. UNION

10. A user can use a view that draws content from which of the following? (Choose all that apply.)

    A. Tables that the user has permission to view

    B. Tables that the user does not have permission to view

    C. Views that the user has permission to view

    D. Views that the user does not have permission to view

    E. Temporary tables that the user has permission to view

    F. Temporary tables that the user does not have permission to view

11. Which aspects of a view can you change using the ALTER VIEW statement? (Choose all that apply.)

    A. The permissions for the view

    B. The *Check Option* flag for the view

C. The name of the view

D. The Encryption flag for the view

12. What happens when you try to add the same table multiple times in the Design pane?

   A. Your request is ignored.

   B. Another copy of the table is displayed.

   C. In the SQL pane an alias for the second copy of the table is created.

   D. B and C

13. When creating a view, in which panes can you enter design changes to the view? (Choose all that apply.)

   A. Diagram pane

   B. Grid pane

   C. SQL pane

   D. Results pane

14. Which actions are permissible on a calculated field in a view? (Choose all that apply.)

   A. You can SELECT the content in a field.

   B. You can INSERT a new value into that field.

   C. You can DELETE the field by deleting the entire row.

   D. You can UPDATE a value in that field.

15. In SQL Server 7.0, which of the following can be used on views that reference multiple tables? (Choose all that apply.)

   A. SELECT

   B. DELETE

   C. INSERT

   D. UPDATE

16. If you have a view that references a single table, and includes the key fields, but excludes the primary key (which is an IDENTITY), and a required field, which of the following is true?

   A. You cannot modify an existing row, and you cannot create a new row.

   B. You can modify an existing row, and you can create a new row.

   C. You can modify an existing row, but you can create a new row only if the NOT NULL field has an assigned default value.

   D. You cannot modify an existing row, but you can create a new row.

17. How do you prevent the users from entering invalid data into a view?

   A. Use the WITH CHECK OPTION to validate that the content meets input the same criteria as the view.

   B. Add a rule onto a column of the view.

   C. Create a new rule, and bind it to a column of the view.

   D. Create a new rule on the underlying table, and use the WITH VIEW OPTION to make the rule apply to views.

18. A view is defined using WITH CHECK OPTION and a WHERE SALARY < 80000 AND SALARY > 60000. However, there is a constraint on the table prohibiting salaries of more than 50,000. What would happen if a user tried to enter a salary of 70,000?

    A. The user could enter the data, but could never possibly view existing records.

    B. The user could not enter the data, but could possibly view existing records.

    C. The user could not enter the data, and could never possibly view existing records.

    D. The user could enter the data, and could also possibly view existing records.

19. You have an Actors table and a Movies table, and the Actors table has a foreign key into the Movies table. You create a view referencing the Names column of the Actors table and the Titles column of the Movies table. What happens if you attempt to edit the Titles column in the view?

    A. The Titles field cannot be updated.

    B. The Titles field will be updated only in the record in which it was entered.

    C. The Titles field will be updated in every record in which it was referenced.

    D. The Titles field can only be updated when the Names column is updated at the same time.

20. You have created a table, and another user with access to your table has created a view based upon this table. It was a mistake for that user to see the content in that table, and you ask the system administrator to prevent that user from seeing the content in your table. Which actions will accomplish this?

    A. Removing their rights to the table

    B. Removing their rights to the table and to the view

    C. Removing their rights to the view

    D. Removing their rights to create new views

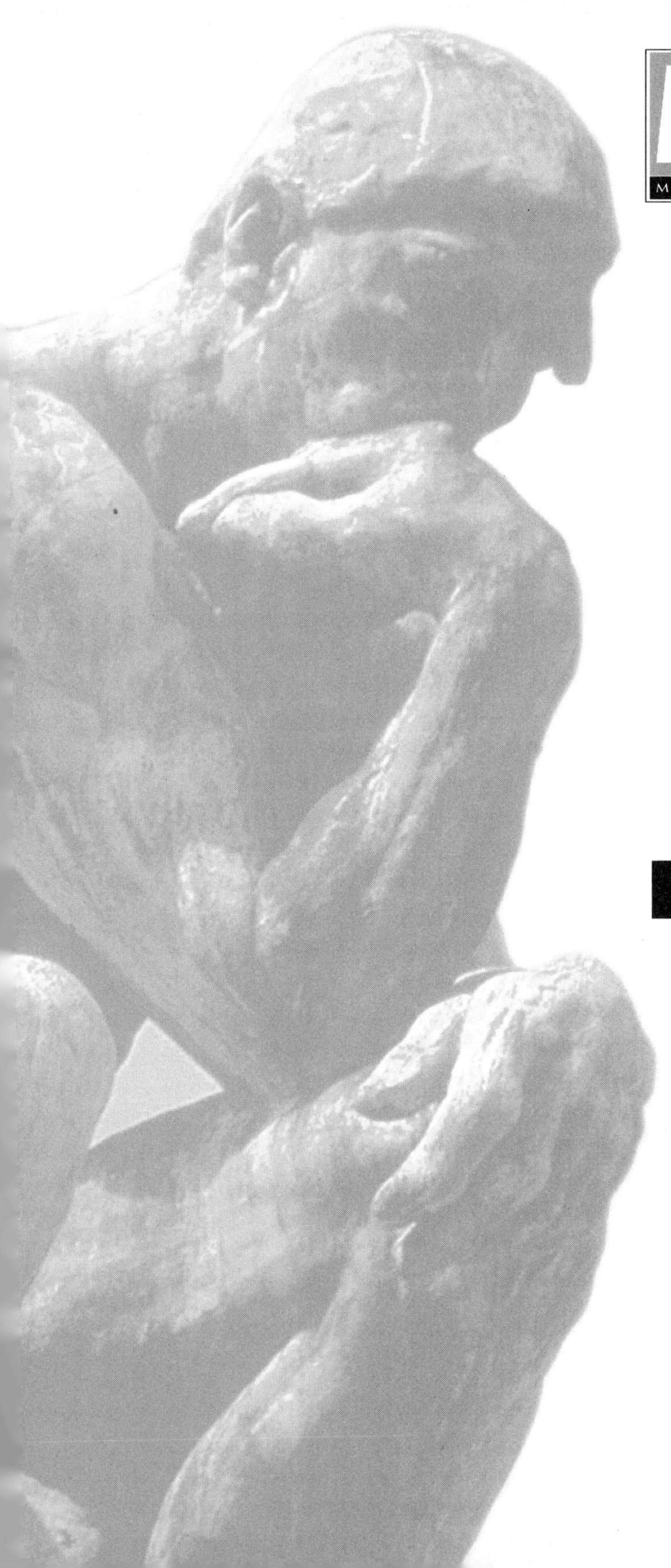

MCDBA

MICROSOFT CERTIFIED DATABASE ADMINISTRATOR

10

Implementing Stored Procedures

CERTIFICATION OBJECTIVES

10.01	Introduction to Stored Procedures
10.02	Creating, Executing, and Modifying Stored Procedures
10.03	Using Parameters in Stored Procedures
10.04	Executing Extended Stored Procedures
10.05	Handling Error Messages
10.06	Performance Considerations

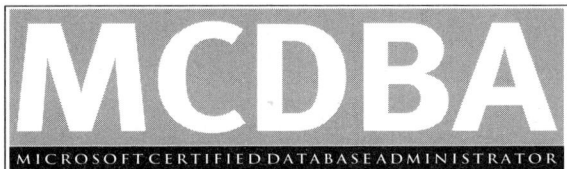

S tored procedures are vital to any database scheme. Database developers, as well as database administrators, often write their own stored procedures to run commonly performed administrative tasks or to apply a complex business rule. These types of procedures can contain control-of-flow structures, data modifications or data retrieval statements, cursors, and error-handling statements. This chapter describes stored procedures and the options available in utilizing them.

Introduction to Stored Procedures

Stored procedures can be as simple as a single SELECT statement or as complex as a series of SQL statements using control-of-flow statements. These *control-of-flow* statements allow you to perform tasks using techniques such as loops or conditional processing on variables that are found in programming languages like Visual Basic or C++. By using stored procedures, you do not have to write programs to perform operations on the database and its tables. This can speed up the deployment and design of the database by reducing the amount of time spent in developing applications. Besides deploying the database, using stored procedures has many other benefits.

One of the biggest benefits of using stored procedures is the speed. Stored procedures are optimized the first time they are compiled, which allows them to run with much less overhead than a normal Transact-SQL statement. Stored procedures have been optimized for the best execution path to the data that they require. This greatly enhances the performance because SQL Server does not have to choose the best route to execute SQL statements and access data after it is compiled. When you execute the stored procedure, the query plan will be read into the procedure plan and run. In executing normal Transact-SQL statements, SQL Server must reparse, resolve, and compile a query tree every time it is executed.

Another benefit associated with stored procedures is being able to share application logic. A large stored procedure can be broken down into many smaller stored procedures. These smaller stored procedures can be shared between many larger stored procedures. This greatly decreases the time in designing and implementing stored procedures. These individual parts can be easily managed and debugged. Stored procedures are proven to work, and utilizing them enforces consistency because the users do not have to use their own Transact-SQL statements.

Using stored procedures to enforce security is another major benefit. If you do not want the users to access the data directly, you can revoke all access to the underlying tables and create your own stored procedure. You can give EXECUTE rights to this stored procedure, and it will perform the required tasks for the user. This creates a more controlled environment because fewer people have direct access to the underlying data.

Stored procedures are the database version of batch files, and they are classified as follows:

- System procedures (execute only)
- Extended stored procedures (create and execute only)
- User-defined procedures (create and execute only)

System procedures come with SQL Server and perform many of the informational and administrative activities. They are usually denoted with a prefix of *sp_*. The benefit of using system procedures is that the users do not have to interact with the system tables. The system procedures are grouped into the following categories:

- **Catalog procedures**   Implement ODBC to obtain information to access information from the SQL Server system catalog
- **Cursor procedures**   Implement the functionality of the cursor variable
- **Distributed queries procedures**   Used for distributed queries implementation and management
- **SQL Server Agent procedures**   Used for SQL Server Agent's event-driven and scheduled activities management
- **Replication procedures**   Used for replication management

- **Security procedures**   Used for security management
- **System procedures**   Used to maintain the general system
- **Web Assistant procedures**   Generate HTML files through the Web Assistant Wizard
- **General extended procedures**   Interface SQL Server to external programs for maintenance activities
- **SQL Mail extended procedures**   Perform e-mail operations within SQL Server
- **SQL Server Profiler extended procedures**   SQL Server Profiler procedures
- **OLE automation procedures**   Enable you to use OLE automation from within standard Transact-SQL batch statements

Extended stored procedures are similar to user-defined and system stored procedures except that they are not native to SQL Server. They work outside of SQL Server and are stored in DLLs (dynamic linked libraries) that SQL Server can dynamically load and execute. Extended stored procedures are usually denoted by the *xp_* prefix. We will talk more about extended stored procedures later in this chapter.

exam
Ⓦatch

Only members of the sysadmin fixed server role can register and grant permission to access extended procedures.

Utilizing stored procedures has many benefits, including:

- Faster execution due to precompiled code.
- Encapsulated business rules.
- They are explicitly started and can be set to run automatically when SQL Server starts.
- Increased security.
- Greater modularity.

Exercise 10-1 shows you how to display available system procedures.

| EXERCISE 10-1 | Displaying Available System Procedures |

1. Click Start | Programs | SQL Server 7.0 | Enterprise Manager.
2. Expand the SQL Server Group, your desired server, and the desired database on it.
3. Click Stored Procedures, as shown in Figure 10-1.

CERTIFICATION OBJECTIVE 10.02

Creating, Executing, and Modifying Stored Procedures

To create stored procedures, you use the CREATE PROCEDURE or CREATE PROC statement. All stored procedures are created in the current database, except when you create them in TempDB. In order for you to create the stored procedure, you must have permission to run CREATE

| FIGURE 10-1 |

Stored procedures on SQL Server 7.0 Enterprise Manager

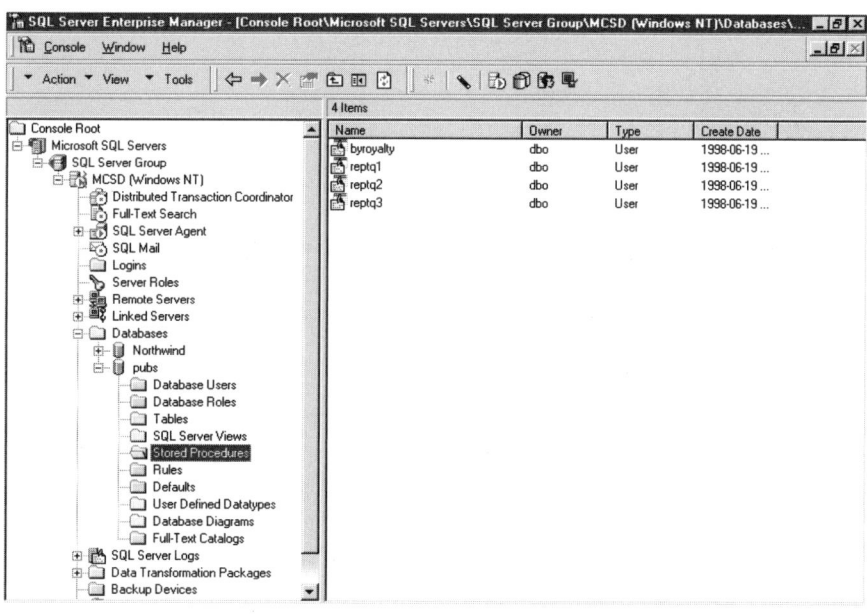

PROCEDURE. This permission defaults to the database owner, but the owner can transfer it to other users. There are a few rules you must adhere to when you create stored procedures:

- You must choose a name that follows the rules for identifiers.

- Objects that you reference must exist when you execute the stored procedure. SQL Server uses delayed name resolution, which enables you to reference objects that don't exist at compile time.

- You can't re-create objects with the same name in the same procedure, even after you drop the procedure.

- You can have up to 1024 parameters.

- You can nest procedures, but only up to 32 levels deep.

In addition to the preceding rules for implementing stored procedures, SQL Server includes a list of Transact-SQL commands that cannot be used within a stored procedure: CREATE DEFAULT, CREATE PROCEDURE, CREATE RULE, CREATE TRIGGER, and CREATE VIEW.

The syntax for CREATE PROCEDURE is

```
CREATE PROC[EDURE] procedure_name [;number]
[{@parameter data_type} [VARYING] [= default] [OUTPUT]]
[,...n][WITH {RECOMPILE | ENCRYPTION | RECOMPILE, ENCRYPTION}]
[FOR REPLICATION] AS sql_statement [...n]
```

Table 10-1 shows you each argument of CREATE PROCEDURE and its function.

Exercise 10-2 shows you how to create stored procedures.

EXERCISE 10-2

Creating Stored Procedures

1. Click Start | Programs | SQL Server 7.0 | Query Analyzer.

2. You should see the Connect to SQL Server dialog box. Select your SQL Server and log in.

TABLE 10-1		
	Argument	**Function**
Arguments of CREATE PROECEDURE	Procedure_name	Name of the procedure.
	;number	Optional integer used to drop group procedures with one DROP PROCEDURE statement.
	@parameter	The parameter in the procedure.
	Data_type	The data type for the parameter.
	VARYING	Specifies the result set supported as an output parameter. Used for cursor parameters only.
	Default	The default value of the parameter.
	OUTPUT	States the parameter is a return parameter.
	,...N	Indicates the number of parameters.
	RECOMPILE | ENCRYPTION | RECOMPILE, ENCRYPTION	RECOMPILE will force the stored procedure to recompile every time this is run. ENCRYPTION encrypts the syscomments table containing the text of this procedure.
	FOR REPLICATION	Used with RECOMPILE option. Won't allow stored procedure to execute on subscribing server.
	AS	Specifies the action of the procedure.
	Sql_statement	Number and type of SQL statements included in this stored procedure.
	N	Indicates that multiple Transact-SQL statements can be included.

3. In the Query window, type the following statement:

```
CREATE PROCEDURE spshwAuthors
AS SELECT au_lname, au_fname
FROM AUTHORS
```

4. Click the Query menu and select Execute Query.

To execute stored procedures, you can just type the name of the procedure. You must, however, use the EXECUTE statement if you want to access the return value for error reporting and checking.

When a stored procedure terminates, it returns a value that you can store for future use or utilize for error checking. The syntax for the EXECUTE statement is:

```
[[EXEC[UTE]] {[@return_status =]{procedure_name [;number] |
procedure_name_var}[[@parameter =] {value | @variable [OUTPUT] | [DEFAULT]]
[,...n][WITH RECOMPILE]
```

Table 10-2 shows you the arguments and their functions.

Exercise 10-3 shows you how to execute a stored procedure with the EXECUTE statement.

EXERCISE 10-3

Executing Stored Procedures with the EXECUTE Statement

1. Click Start | Programs | SQL Server 7.0 | Query Analyzer.

TABLE 10-2

Arguments and Functions for the EXECUTE Statement

Argument	Function
@return_status	Integer that outputs the return value of the procedure.
Procedure_name	Name of the procedure.
;number	Optional integer used to drop group procedures with one DROP PROCEDURE statement.
Procedure_name_var	Name of a locally defined variable that represents a stored procedure.
@parameter	Is the parameter for a procedure.
Value	Is the value of the parameter to the procedure.
@variable	Is the variable that stores a parameter or a return parameter.
OUTPUT	Specifies that the stored procedure returns a parameter.
DEFAULT	Supplies the default value of the parameter.
N	Indicates that the preceding items can be repeated multiple times.
WITH RECOMPILE	Forces the plan to be recompiled.

2. You should see the Connect to SQL Server dialog box. Select your SQL Server and log in.

3. In the Query window, type the following statement:

    `EXEC spshwAuthors`

4. Click the Query menu and select Execute Query.

In earlier versions of SQL Server, you must query system tables to show all the system procedures available. With SQL Server 7.0, you can use the Enterprise Manager to find out which procedures are available. Exercise 10-4 shows you how to view and modify stored procedures.

EXERCISE 10-4

Viewing and Modifying Stored Procedures

1. Click Start | Programs | SQL Server 7.0 | SQL Server Enterprise Manager.

2. Expand the SQL Server group and your own server.

3. Expand the pub database and click Stored Procedures.

4. Right click spshwAuthors and click Properties. You should see a screen similar to the one shown next.

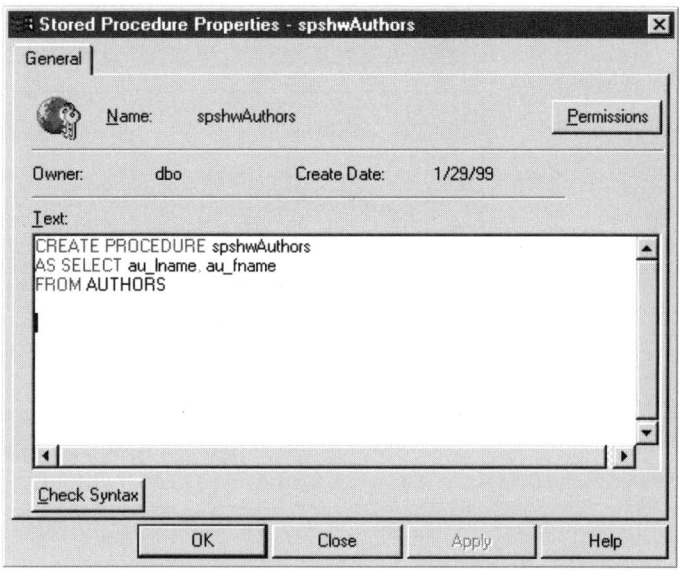

5. In the Text box, change the query to

```
CREATE PROCEDURE spshwAuthors
AS SELECT au_lname, au_fname
FROM AUTHORS
ORDER BY au_lname
```

6. Click Check Syntax to make sure the syntax is correct.

7. Click OK.

You can use the sp_depends system procedure to get a list of the objects that the stored procedure depends on. Exercise 10-5 shows you how to use the sp_depends system procedure.

Getting Information About Stored Procedures

1. Click Start | Programs | SQL Server 7.0 | Query Analyzer.

2. You should see the Connect to SQL Server dialog box. Select your SQL Server and log in.

3. In the Query window, type the following statement:

```
sp_depends spshwAuthors
```

The resulting Query window should look similar to the one shown next.

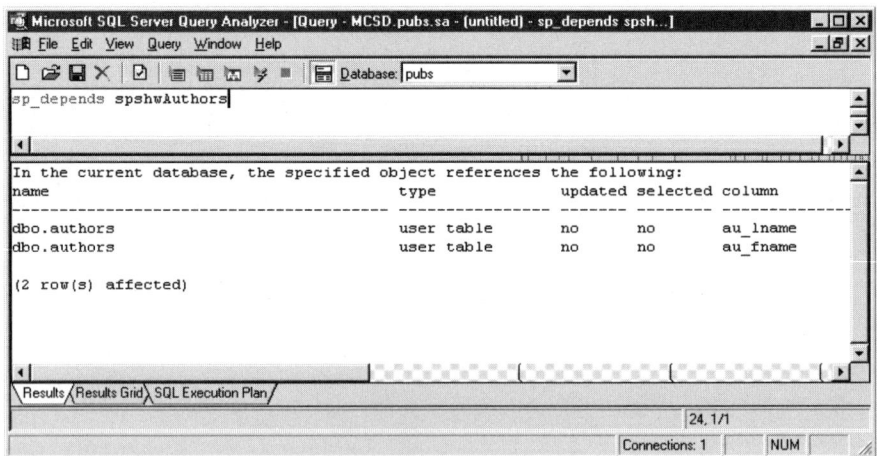

Performing Calculations

Stored procedures can be used to perform calculations. They can perform the following mathematical operations or functions:

- Addition(+)
- Multiplication(*)
- Subtraction(−)
- Division(/)

Exercise 10-6 shows you how to perform calculations using stored procedures.

EXERCISE 10-6

Performing Calculations Using Stored Procedures

1. Click Start | Programs | SQL Server 7.0 | Query Analyzer.
2. You should see the Connect to SQL Server dialog box. Select your SQL Server and log in.
3. Type the following:

```
CREATE PROCEDURE newavg
@avg1 smallint,
@avg2 smallint,
@avg3 smallint,
@avg4 smallint,
@myavg smallint OUTPUT
AS SELECT @myavg=
(@avg1+@avg2+@avg3+@avg4)/4
```

4. Type the following:

```
DECLARE @showAvg smallint
EXEC newavg 2, 4, 6, 8, @showAvg OUTPUT
SELECT 'The sum of these numbers is: ', @showAvg
GO
```

Choosing Appropriate Recompile Options

The WITH RECOMPILE and sp_recompile statements affect how the stored procedure is processed and executed. Recompiling stored procedures is rarely done because it will usually slow down the procedure. Usually it's done when the data within the indexes has changed significantly enough to warrant more optimization. There are three ways to use recompile statements: WITH RECOMPILE in either the CREATE PROCEDURE or EXEC statements, or by executing the sp_recompile stored procedure.

Using WITH RECOMPILE with CREATE PROCEDURE

Use WITH RECOMPILE with the CREATE PROCEDURE statement with care because the execution plan will not be saved in the procedure cache. The entire stored procedure is recompiled every time this is run. This should only be done when the database is changed so often that execution performance of the stored procedure is very poor.

Using WITH RECOMPILE with EXEC

Using WITH RECOMPILE with EXEC is the most used recompile option. It compiles the stored procedure the first time it is run and it saves the optimal path in the procedure cache for subsequent executions of the stored procedure.

Using sp_recompile

With sp_recompile, you can force all of the stored procedures that reference a table to recompile the next time that they run. The syntax for sp_recompile is

```
sp_recompile 'object'
```

'Object' can be the name of either a referenced table or a stored procedure. If it is a referenced table, all stored procedures and triggers referencing it are recompiled at the next run time. If it is a stored procedure, then that stored procedure will be recompiled the next time it is run.

exam
ⓌatchWatch

If an object within a stored procedure is deleted, the recompiled stored procedure will return an error. Recompilation does not check for such errors.

Using Parameters in Stored Procedures

Parameters allow you to pass variables into stored procedures. The syntax for the parameter portion of the CREATE PROCEDURE statement is

```
@parameter_name data_type [=default|name] [VARYING]
[OUTPUT]
```

The following table lists the arguments and their functions.

Arguments	Definition
Parameter_name	Name of the parameter
Data_type	The data type of the parameter
Default	Default value of the parameter
VARYING	Specifies the result set supported as an output parameter, used for cursor parameters only
OUTPUT	Return parameter

Input and Output Parameters

When you use parameters, you can choose to allow the input or output of values from the stored procedures. You can declare up to 1024 parameters within a stored procedure. The OUTPUT argument allows you to pass values out of the procedure to the calling procedure. Exercise 10-7 shows you how to create a stored procedure that uses input and output parameters.

EXERCISE 10-7

Creating and Executing a Stored Procedure That Uses Input and Output Parameters

1. Click Start | Programs | SQL Server 7.0 | Query Analyzer.
2. You should see the Connect to SQL Server dialog box. Select your SQL Server and log in.

3. Type the following:

```
CREATE PROCEDURE newsum
@sum1 smallint,
@sum2 smallint,
@sum3 smallint,
@sum4 smallint,
@mysum smallint OUTPUT
AS SELECT @mysum
(@sum1+@sum2+@sum3+@sum4)
```

4. Type the following:

```
DECLARE @showSum smallint
EXEC newsum 2, 4, 6, 8, @showSum OUTPUT
SELECT 'The sum of these numbers is: ', @showSum
GO
```

Your screen should look like this:

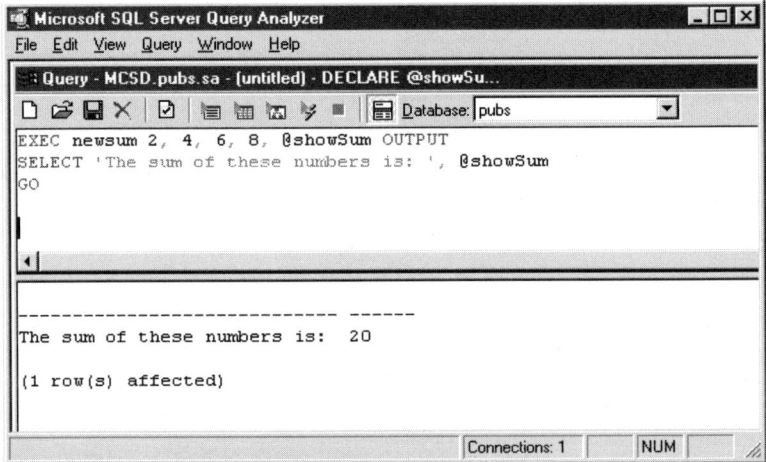

CERTIFICATION OBJECTIVE 10.04

Executing Extended Stored Procedures

You can execute an extended stored procedure like a normal stored procedure. The extended stored procedure has a prefix of *xp_*. Exercise 10-8 shows you how to execute an extended stored procedure.

EXERCISE 10-8

Executing an Extended Stored Procedure

1. Click Start | Programs | SQL Server 7.0 | Query Analyzer.

2. You should see the Connect to SQL Server dialog box. Select your SQL Server and log in.

3. Type the following:

   ```
   xp_enumgroups
   ```

4. Click Query | Execute with Grid. Your screen should be similar to the one shown next. This extended stored procedure lists local and global groups in a Windows NT domain.

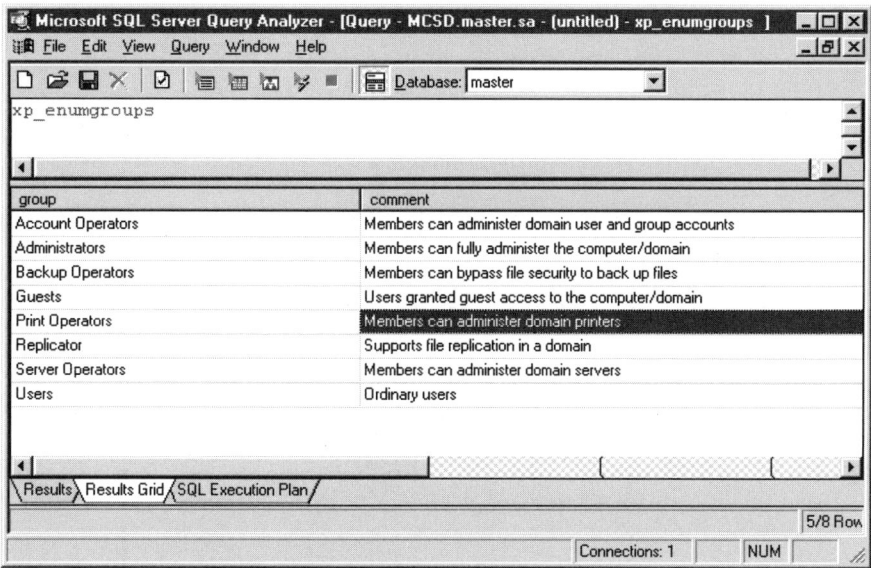

CERTIFICATION OBJECTIVE 10.05

Handling Error Messages

As your stored procedures get more complex, it becomes necessary to design error checking into your stored procedures. To inform the user of errors, you can use a return code or the RAISERROR statement.

FROM THE CLASSROOM

Extended Stored Procedures

The extended stored procedure is a unique form of stored procedure that can greatly expand the capabilities of Microsoft SQL Server. Extended stored procedure is somewhat of a misnomer, in that the procedures are not actually stored within the database as are standard system or user-defined stored procedures. Information regarding the location, use, and parameters of the extended stored procedures is stored in the database, but the actual code that is executed when the procedure is called is found in an external dynamic link library (DLL) file that is dynamically loaded by SQL Server when it is needed. These external routines are written in full-featured languages like C++, and can expand the capabilities of SQL Server far beyond normal database management system functionality. Loaded extended stored procedures run within the address space of

SQL Server and are developed using the SQL ODS API.

Extended stored procedures are extremely useful. They perform valuable functions such as sending query results, or other information, out through a valid MAPI mail client via assorted extended stored procedures that are provided with a SQL Server installation. Certain characteristics of extended stored procedures should be noted:

■ Extended stored procedures run under the security context of SQL Server.

■ The DLL remains loaded in memory until the server is stopped or the DLL is explicitly unloaded.

■ The Win32 thread used for the procedure is the same one used for the SQL client connection executing the extended stored procedure.

—*Michael Lane Thomas, MCSE+I, MCSD, MCP+SB, MSS, MCT, A+*

Return Codes

Return codes in stored procedures only return integer values. In order for you to output return codes, you must declare the variable, execute the stored procedure, and output the status. Exercise 10-9 shows you how to display the return codes of a stored procedure.

EXERCISE 10-9

Display Return Codes of a Stored Procedure

1. Click Start | Programs | SQL Server 7.0 | Query Analyzer.

2. You should see the Connect to SQL Server dialog box. Select your SQL Server and log in.

3. Type the following:

```
DECLARE @status int
EXEC @status=xp_enumgroups
SELECT @status As 'Status'
```

4. You should see a screen similar to the one shown next.

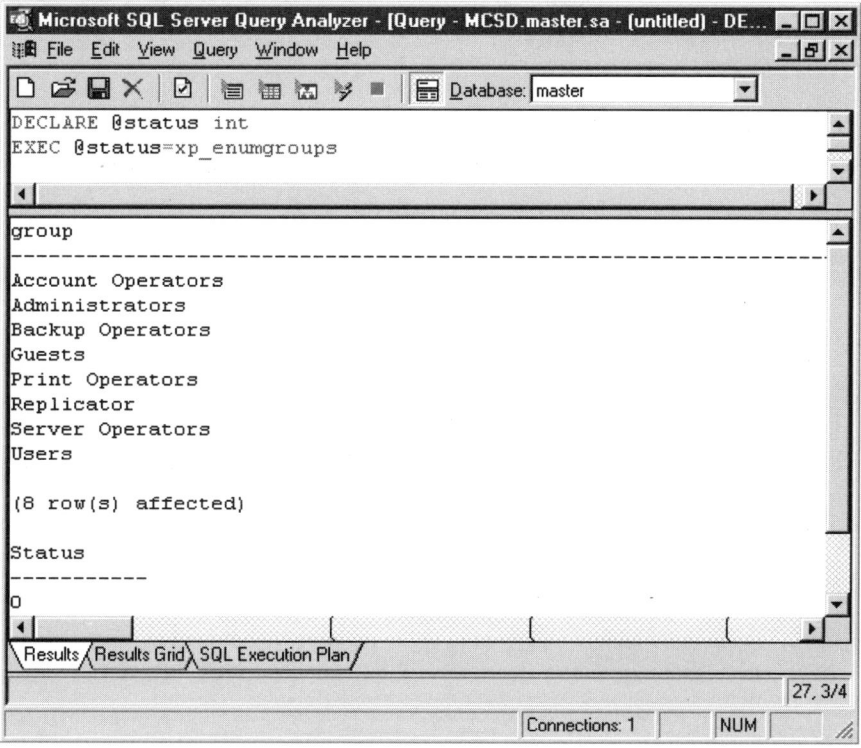

The **RAISERROR** Statement

With return codes, SQL Server informs the user only of SQL Server errors. With the RAISERROR statement, you can inform users of non-SQL Server errors. RAISERROR statements can be used to return user-defined error messages. The syntax for RAISERROR is

```
RAISERROR ({msg_id | msg_str}{, severity, state}
[, argument
[,...n]] )
[WITH option[,...n]]
```

Table 10-3 shows the arguments and the definitions of the RAISERROR statement.

TABLE 10-3	Arguments	Definition
	Msg_id	A user-defined error message specified in the sysmessages table.
RAISERROR Arguments and Definitions	Msg_str	An ad hoc message.
	Severity	A user-defined severity level associated with the ad hoc message. Levels 1–10 are informational. Levels 11–16 are reserved. Levels 17–19 are hardware or software errors. Levels 20–25 are severe errors that restrict future processing.
	State	A value from 1 through 127 that represents the state of the error.
	Argument	Specifies the parameter used when the variable is substituted. Defined in the *msg_str*.
	Option	Indicates that the error is going to be logged in the server error log.

The *msg_str* can contain a maximum of 255 characters, and ad hoc error messages have a standard ID of 14000. The *msg_str* format is:

```
% [[flag] [width] [precision] [{h|l}]] type
```

The following table shows the *msg_str* options.

Options	Description
Flag	Sets the spacing and justification
Width	Sets the maximum width
Precision	Sets the maximum number of characters or integers displayed
{h|l} type	Creates a value of a certain type

Exercise 10-10 shows you how to implement error checking by using the RAISERROR statement.

EXERCISE 10-10

Implementing Error Checking by Using the RAISERROR Statement

1. Click Start |Programs | SQL Server 7.0 | Query Analyzer.

2. You should see the Connect to SQL Server dialog box. Select your SQL Server and log in.

3. Type the following:

```
RAISERROR('Exercise Test',10,2).
```

Your screen should look similar to the one shown next.

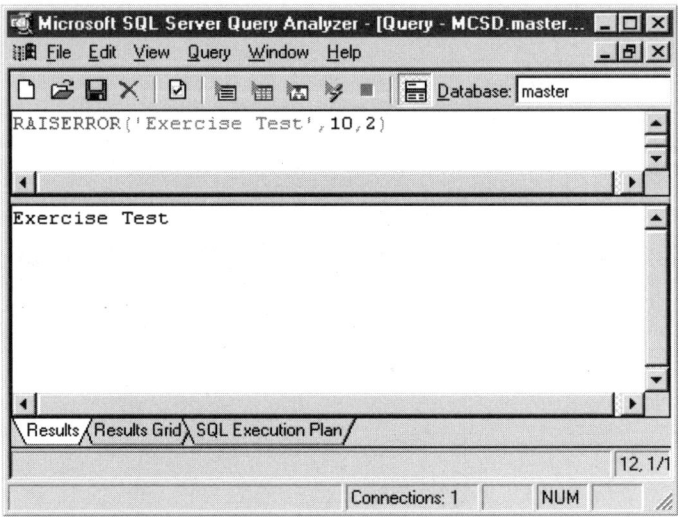

Performance Considerations

Because stored procedures are preoptimized, stored procedures run at the optimal path. However, as data changes, the optimal path for the stored procedure might change. In order for you to ensure that your stored procedure is running optimally, you should run sp_monitor as a maintenance measure. Sp_monitor is a Transact-SQL stored procedure that displays 13 columns of statistics on SQL Server. They are

- **Last run**   Time sp_monitor was last run
- **Current run**   Time sp_monitor is being run
- **Seconds**   Time in seconds since sp_monitor was run
- **Cpu_busy**   Time that the CPU has spent doing SQL Server work
- **Io_busy**   Time, in seconds, that SQL Server has been doing input and output operations

- **Idle**   Idle time in seconds
- **Packets_received**   Number of input packets that SQL Server has read
- **Packets_sent**   Number of output packets that SQL Server has read
- **Packet_errors**   Number of errors encountered while reading and writing packets
- **Total_read**   Number of reads
- **Total_write**   Number of writes
- **Total_errors**   Number of errors while reading and writing
- **Connections**   Number of logins or attempted logins to SQL Server

You should make a habit of running sp_monitor regularly to make sure your stored procedures are running optimally. Figure 10-2 shows the results you should see when you run sp_monitor.

FIGURE 10-2

Use sp_monitor to check stored procedure performance

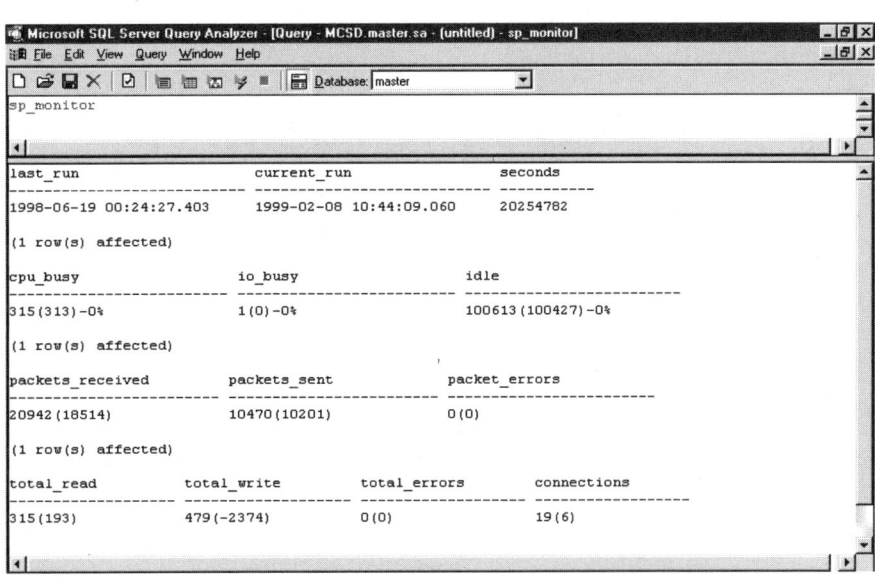

CERTIFICATION SUMMARY

Stored procedures are vital to the database scheme. They are precompiled and optimized Transact-SQL statements. The benefits of using stored procedures are speed, increased security, and sharing application logic.

The first step in becoming familiar with stored procedures is to create them. You create stored procedures with CREATE PROCEDURE. You execute the stored procedure by using EXECUTE or by typing the name of the stored procedure. By running EXECUTE, you have access to the return values of the procedure. Stored procedures can also change data in different tables, perform calculations, and utilize input and output parameters.

As your stored procedures become more complex, it is important that you display error messages. The two main ways to check for errors are return codes and the RAISERROR statement. Return codes are used to output messages on SQL Server errors, while the RAISERROR statement is used to output messages on non-SQL Server error messages.

It is important to understand and maximize the use of stored procedures in your SQL Server environment. The use of stored procedures will enhance performance and increase consistency.

 **TWO-MINUTE DRILL**

❑ Stored procedures are vital to any database scheme. Database developers, as well as database administrators, often write their own stored procedures to run commonly performed administrative tasks or to apply a complex business rule.

❑ Control-of-flow statements allow you to perform tasks using techniques such as loops or conditional processing on variables that are found in programming languages like Visual Basic or C++.

❑ By using stored procedures, you do not have to write programs to perform operations on the database and its tables. This can speed up the deployment and design of the database by reducing the amount of time spent in developing applications.

❑ Stored procedures are optimized the first time they are compiled, which allows them to run with much less overhead than a normal Transact-SQL statement.

❑ A large stored procedure can be broken down into many smaller stored procedures. This greatly decreases the time in designing and implementing stored procedures. These individual parts can be easily managed and debugged.

❑ Stored procedures are the database version of batch files. They are classified as system procedures (execute only), extended stored procedures (create and execute only), and user-defined procedures (create and execute only)

❑ System procedures come with SQL Server and perform many of the informational and administrative activities. They are usually denoted with a prefix of *sp_*.

❑ The benefit of using system procedures is that the users do not have to interact with the system tables.

❑ Extended stored procedures are similar to user-defined and system stored procedures except that they are not native to SQL Server.

❑ Only members of the sysadmin fixed server role can register and grant permission to access extended procedures.

❑ To create stored procedures, you use the CREATE PROCEDURE or CREATE PROC statement. All stored procedures are created in the current database, except when you create them in TempDB.

❑ SQL Server includes a list of Transact-SQL commands that cannot be used within a stored procedure: CREATE DEFAULT, CREATE PROCEDURE, CREATE RULE, CREATE TRIGGER, and CREATE VIEW.

❑ To execute stored procedures, you can just type the name of the procedure. You must, however, use the EXECUTE statement if you want to access the return value for error reporting and checking.

❑ In earlier versions of SQL Server, you must query system tables to show all the system procedures available. With SQL Server 7.0, you can use the Enterprise Manager to find out which procedures are available.

❑ Stored procedures can be used to perform mathematical calculations.

❑ There are three ways to use recompile statements: WITH RECOMPILE in either the CREATE PROCEDURE or EXEC statements, or by executing the sp_recompile stored procedure.

❑ Parameters allow you to pass variables into stored procedures.

❑ You can declare up to 1024 parameters within a stored procedure. The OUTPUT argument allows you to pass values out of the procedure to the calling procedure.

❑ You can execute an extended stored procedure like a normal stored procedure. The extended stored procedure has a prefix of *xp_*.

❑ Extended stored procedures are extremely useful. They perform valuable functions such as sending query results, or other information, out through a valid MAPI mail client via assorted extended stored procedures that are provided with a SQL Server installation.

❑ As your stored procedures get more complex, it becomes necessary to design error checking into your stored procedures. To inform the user of errors, you can use a return code or the RAISERROR statement.

❑ Return codes in stored procedures only return integer values. In order for you to output return codes, you must declare the variable, execute the stored procedure, and output the status.

❑ With the RAISERROR statement, you can inform users of non-SQL Server errors. RAISERROR statements can be used to return user-defined error messages.

❑ Because stored procedures are preoptimized, stored procedures run at the optimal path. However, as data changes, the optimal path for the stored procedure might change. In order for you to ensure that your stored procedure is running optimally, you should run sp_monitor as a maintenance measure.

SELF TEST

The following Self Test questions will help you measure your understanding of the material presented in this chapter. Read all the choices carefully, as there may be more than one correct answer. Choose all correct answers for each question.

1. What are the three types of stored procedures? (Choose all that apply.)

    A. System procedures

    B. Localized procedures

    C. User-defined procedures

    D. Extended stored procedures

2. What is the only type of stored procedure you cannot create?

    A. System

    B. User-defined

    C. Extended

    D. New

3. What are extended stored procedures stored as?

    A. Executables

    B. DLLs

    C. Batch files

    D. Script files

4. The permission to run CREATE PROCEDURE defaults to which user?

    A. Table owner

    B. Database owner

    C. Data owner

    D. Row owner

5. How deep can you nest stored procedures?

    A. 4

    B. 16

    C. 32

    D. 64

6. How many parameters can you pass into a stored procedure?

    A. 256

    B. 512

    C. 1024

    D. 2048

7. How do you run stored procedures? (Choose all that apply.)

    A. EXECUTE *procedure_name*

    B. RUN

    C. Type the name of the stored procedure

    D. ACCESS

8. What system procedure do you use to get a list of the objects that the stored procedure depends on?

    A. sp_who

    B. sp_configure

    C. sp_help

    D. sp_depends

9. What recompile option does not save the execution plan in the procedure cache?

    A. sp_recompile

B. WITH RECOMPILE with EXEC

C. WITH RECOMPILE with CREATE PROCEDURE

D. WITH RECOMPILE

10. What recompile option forces all of the stored procedures that reference a table to recompile the next time they run?

A. sp_recompile

B. WITH RECOMPILE with EXEC

C. WITH RECOMPILE with CREATE PROCEDURE

D. WITH RECOMPILE

11. What recompile option will compile the stored procedure the first time it is run and will save the optimal path in the procedure cache for subsequent executions of the stored procedure?

A. WITH RECOMPILE with CREATE PROCEDURE

B. WITH RECOMPILE with EXEC

C. sp_recompile

D. CREATE PROCEDURE

12. What create procedure argument allows you to pass values out of the procedure and into the calling procedure?

A. INPUT

B. OUTPUT

C. PASS

D. ARG

13. What statement do you use to inform users of non-SQL Server errors?

A. RAISERROR

B. ERRORCHECK

C. CHECKPROC

D. OUTPUT

14. What type of values do return codes return?

A. INTEGER

B. DOUBLE

C. CHAR

D. FLOAT

15. What stored procedure do you run to check for performance degradation?

A. sp_who

B. sp_monitor

C. sp_perfmon

D. sp_perf

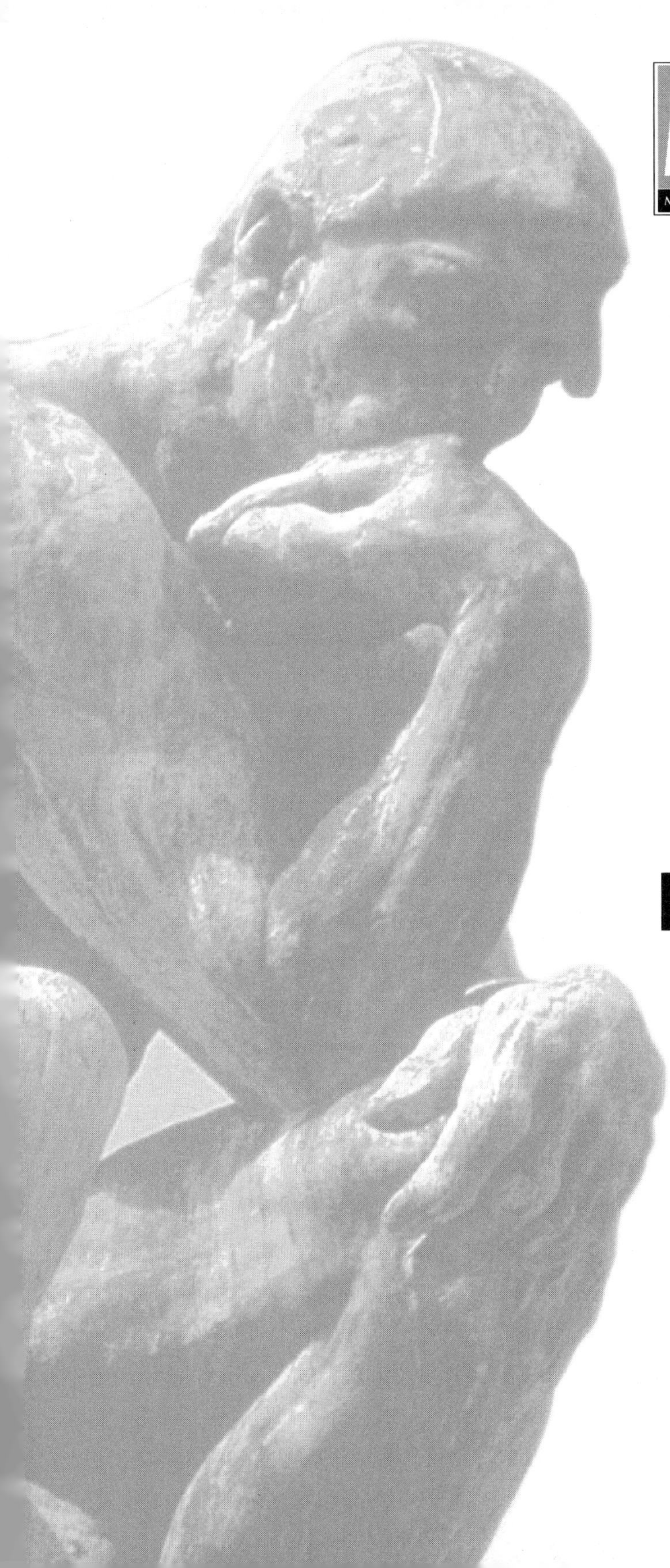

MCDBA
MICROSOFT CERTIFIED DATABASE ADMINISTRATOR

11

Implementing Triggers

CERTIFICATION OBJECTIVES

11.01 Defining Triggers

11.02 Examples of Triggers

11.03 Uses of Triggers

11.04 Performance Considerations

11.05 Transactional Error Handling

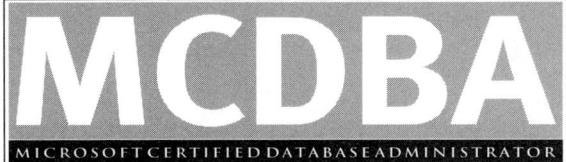

T riggers are special stored procedures that SQL Server automatically invokes in response to data modification Transact-SQL statements, such as INSERT, UPDATE, or DELETE. You can use triggers to help enforce business rules as well as to prevent unauthorized changes to the data and guarantee data integrity and consistency. This chapter explains how to implement triggers and the benefits associated with using them.

CERTIFICATION OBJECTIVE 11.01

Defining Triggers

Triggers are special stored procedures that respond when an UPDATE, INSERT, or DELETE statement occurs. Triggers are a part of the transaction. Any error in the transaction or in the trigger will roll back the entire transaction. Unlike regular stored procedures, triggers are used to protect data modifications by enforcing business rules so that rogue changes don't occur. Triggers can check data before and after a transaction has been made. Because triggers are fired after all the filters such as rules and defaults have been used, they give the final approval of a data modification.

Creating Triggers

There are three types of triggers that use inserted and deleted tables: the insert trigger, the update trigger, and the delete trigger. You create triggers with the CREATE TRIGGER statement, and you must be the owner of the database to do so. The syntax for the CREATE TRIGGER is

```
CREATE TRIGGER trigger_name
ON table
FOR { [DELETE] [,] [INSERT] [,] [UPDATE] }
[WITH ENCRYPTION]
As sql_statement
```

The following table details the arguments for the CREATE TRIGGER statement:

Arguments	Description
Trigger_name	Name of the trigger.
Table	Name of the table in which the trigger is to be executed.
WITH ENCRYPTION	Encrypts the entry in syscomments that contains the text for CREATE TRIGGER. This is used to prevent other users from seeing the text of the trigger after it has been loaded into SQL Server.
[DELETE] [,] [INSERT] [,] [UPDATE]	Keywords that specify which statements will activate the trigger.
AS	Trigger's action.
Sql_statement	Transact-SQL statement that is executed when a trigger is run.

on the **Job**

Be careful not to use the same name as an existing trigger when you create a trigger. If you do, the new trigger will overwrite the existing one.

Displaying Trigger Information

To get a list of the triggers on the database server, type

```
SELECT name
'INSERT'=object_name(instrig),
'UPDATE'=object_name(updtrig)
'DELETE'=object_name(deltrig)
FROM sysobjects
WHERE type ='U'
AND (instrig <> 0 OR updtrig <> 0 OR deltrig <> 0)
```

Besides seeing the list of the triggers available in the system, it is also important to view information about a trigger. Exercise 11-1 shows you how to view information about a trigger by using the SQL Server Enterprise Manager.

Viewing Trigger Information

1. Click Start | Programs | Microsoft SQL Server 7.0 | SQL Server Enterprise Manager.

2. Log in.

3. Expand the SQL Server group and desired server.

4. Expand the desired table, database, and table.

5. Select the desired table. Click the Action menu | All Tasks | Manage Triggers. You should see a screen similar to Figure 11-1.

FIGURE 11-1

Viewing trigger information
in the SQL Server
Enterprise Manager

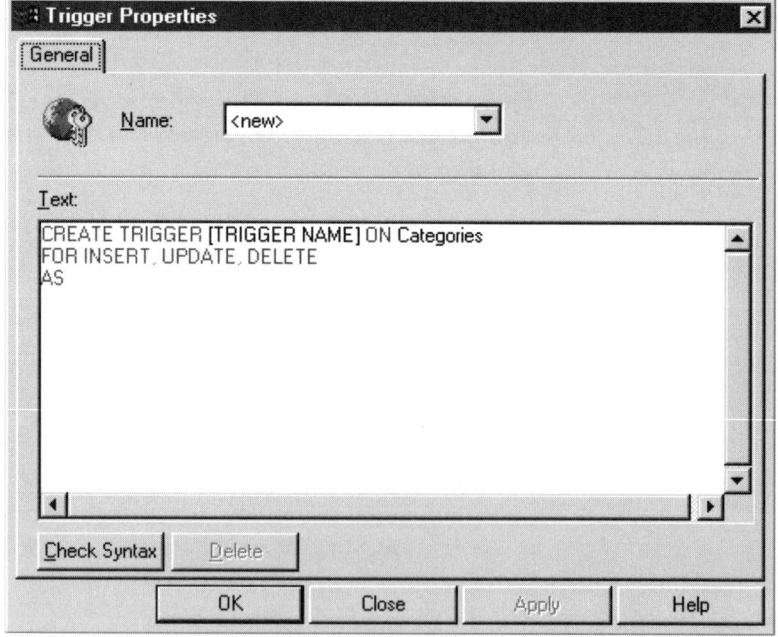

The other way to view information about triggers is to use the sp_help and the sp_helptext stored procedures. With the sp_help stored procedure, you can view the owner of the trigger and when it was created. The syntax of sp_help is

```
sp_help 'trigger_name'
```

Figure 11-2 shows you an example of sp_help.

Another stored procedure that you can utilize to view trigger information is sp_helptext. With sp_helptext, you can obtain the text of the stored procedure that is stored in the syscomments system catalog table. If you enable encryption on the trigger, you will not be able to read the text.

The syntax of sp_helptext is

```
Sp_helptext 'trigger_name'
```

Figure 11-3 shows you an example using sp_helptext to view the text of the sp_grantlogin trigger.

FIGURE 11-2

Using sp_help to view trigger information

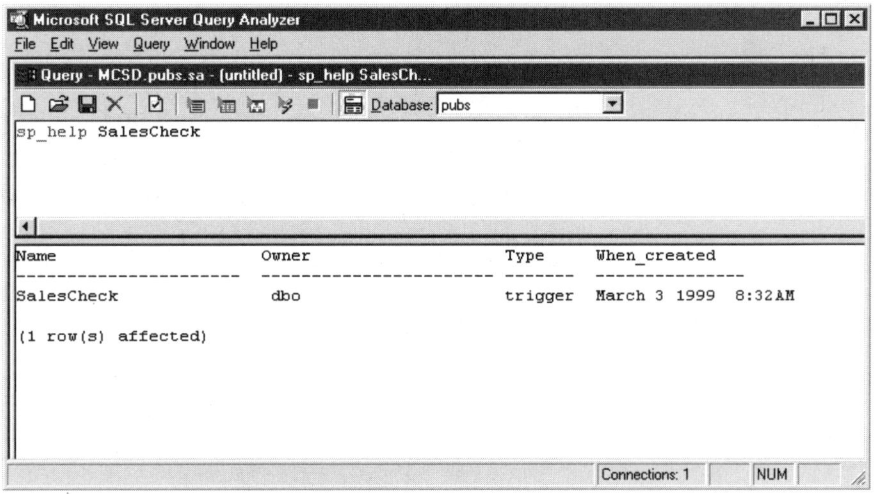

FIGURE 11-3

Using sp_helptext to view
the text of a trigger

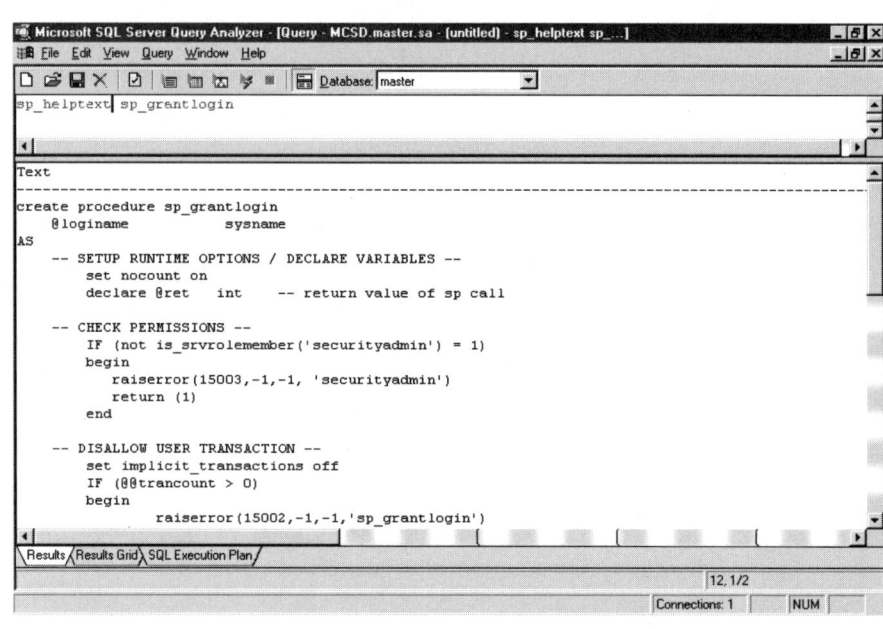

Limitations

Before you can use triggers, you must be aware of the limitations on creating the trigger, as well as the limitations of the Transact-SQL statements that can be executed in the body of a trigger.

- Triggers can only be created on tables. Although they can be used to reference temporary tables, triggers cannot be created on temporary tables and views.

- Triggers cannot be used to output result sets from the SQL statements that lie within the trigger.

- Triggers cannot contain object creation statements, such as CREATE DATABASE, CREATE TABLE, CREATE INDEX, CREATE PROCEDURE, CREATE DEFAULT, CREATE RULE, CREATE TRIGGER, and CREATE VIEW.

- Triggers cannot contain any DROP statements, such as DROP DATABASE, DROP DEFAULT, DROP INDEX, DROP PROCEDURE, DROP RULE, DROP TABLE, DROP TRIGGER, and DROP VIEW.

- Triggers cannot use the database object modification statement, such as ALTER TABLE, ALTER DATABASE, and TRUNCATE TABLE.

- Triggers cannot utilize the SQL statements related to object permissions: GRANT and REVOKE.

- Triggers cannot use the database load operations, such as LOAD DATABASE and LOAD TRANSACTION.

- Triggers cannot use any physical disk modification statements. They are defined by DISK.

- Triggers cannot use the UPDATE STATISTICS and RECONFIGURE statements.

The following shows you all of the Transact-SQL statements that cannot be used to create triggers:

ALTER DATABASE	DROP DATABASE
ALTER PROCEDURE	DROP DEFAULT
ALTER TABLE	DROP INDEX
ALTER TRIGGER	DROP PROCEDURE
ALTER VIEW	DROP RULE
CREATE DATABASE	DROP TABLE
CREATE DEFAULT	DROP TRIGGER
CREATE INDEX	DROP VIEW
CREATE PROCEDURE	GRANT
CREATE RULE	LOAD DATABASE
CREATE SCHEMA	LOAD LOG
CREATE TABLE	RESTORE DATABASE

CREATE TRIGGER	RESTORE LOG
CREATE VIEW	REVOKE
DENY	RECONFIGURE
DISK INIT	TRUNCATE TABLE
DISK RESIZE	UPDATE STATISTICS

There are quite a few commands that cannot be executed from a trigger. You have to know you cannot use any of the DROP, CREATE, GRANT, REVOKE, or DISK statements.

Dropping Triggers

In the future, when rules change, you may decide to delete some triggers. Triggers are removed from the database with the DROP TRIGGER statement. The syntax for the DROP TRIGGER statement is:

```
DROP TRIGGER {trigger_name}
```

If you drop a table, all associated triggers will be dropped as well.

CERTIFICATION OBJECTIVE 11.02

Examples of Triggers

Triggers use the inserted and deleted tables to hold changes to data that haven't been committed yet. Since these tables are created dynamically in RAM and do not use any persistent storage, they are called logical tables. When you add a new record to the table, it is recorded in the base table as well as in the inserted table. When you delete a record, it is recorded in the deleted table. In an update, both the inserted table and the deleted table are used. When you update a record, the original data is moved to the deleted table, and the new data is recorded in the base and the inserted table. Triggers query these tables to determine whether further action is needed. If the changes are not satisfactory, they are rolled back. There are three types of triggers that use the inserted table and the deleted table: the insert trigger, the update trigger, and the delete trigger.

Insert Triggers

Insert triggers are used to ensure that the data being inserted into a table is valid. When an INSERT transaction is detected by the database, the insert trigger is executed. Once the insert trigger is run, inserted data is held in the logical inserted table and then added to the trigger table. A copy of the new row stays in the inserted table until the trigger decides how to implement the new data insert. The following is an example of an insert trigger:

```
CREATE TRIGGER SalesCheck
ON sales
FOR INSERT
AS
IF (SELECT qty FROM inserted) > 50
BEGIN
        PRINT 'SalesCheck: Quantity cannot exceed 50'
        ROLLBACK TRANSACTION
END
```

The SalesCheck trigger checks to ensure that the quantity in the sales table does not exceed 50. If it exceeds 50, it will output an error message and then rollback the transaction.

Update Triggers

When an update trigger is executed, the original data is moved to the logical deleted table. The new rows are then moved to the inserted table and the trigger table. Once the data has been successfully moved, the trigger will check to see if the data can be verified. Unlike the insert and delete triggers, an update trigger can occur at both the table level and the column level.

Table Level

The update trigger that occurs at the table level fires when any field in the row is updated. The following is an example of the update trigger occurring at the table level:

```
CREATE TRIGGER Nohiqty
ON sales
FOR UPDATE
AS
IF (SELECT qty FROM inserted) > 50
BEGIN
        PRINT 'Quantity cannot exceed 50'
        ROLLBACK TRANSACTION
END
```

Column Level

The update trigger that occurs at the column level uses the IF UPDATE (*column_name*) clause, which binds the update trigger to a column. It executes when data in a particular column is altered. The following is an example of the update trigger occurring at the column level:

```
CREATE TRIGGER NoBDay
ON employees
FOR UPDATE
AS
IF UPDATE (bday)
BEGIN
        PRINT 'You cannot update the birth day of the
employee'
        ROLLBACK TRANSACTION
END
```

In this example, the trigger checks for updates that are to the bday column in the employees table. If there are changes, the trigger will output a message informing you that you cannot change the bday column. It will then rollback the transaction.

Delete Triggers

Delete triggers are executed when a DELETE statement is issued against rows in a table. When you attempt to delete rows from a table that is protected by a delete trigger, the deleted rows are moved from the target table to the logical deleted table. Since no data is being updated, the inserted table is not used. Delete triggers are used for two reasons: enforcing data integrity and cascading deletes. Delete triggers can prevent the deletion of crucial data, such as foreign keys. Without delete triggers, there is no way to maintain the integrity of the data on the table outside of the methods native to SQL Server, such as PRIMARY KEY constraints. The other reason to use delete triggers is for the option of cascading delete triggers. An example of a cascading delete is when the deletion of the master record prompts an automatic deletion of all the children records. We will explore cascading triggers in greater detail in the next section. An example of a delete trigger is as follows:

```
CREATE TRIGGER NoDeleteQty
ON sales
FOR DELETE
AS
IF (SELECT sale_id FROM deleted) < 50
BEGIN
        PRINT 'You must maintain at least the first 50
sales'
        ROLLBACK TRANSACTION
END
```

This example ensures that the original 50 sales in the Sales table are not deleted. If a delete is detected in one of the rows, the transaction will be rolled back.

on the Job

Although a delete trigger is executed when you attempt to delete rows of data from a table, a delete trigger will not fire when you run the TRUNCATE TABLE statement. The TRUNCATE TABLE statement deletes all rows from a table.

Uses of Triggers

Now that you know how to use triggers, you have to learn when to use them. Triggers are very useful and are often used to encapsulate business rules, enforce referential integrity, and perform cascading updates and deletes. First, let's consider some possible scenario questions and their answers.

Encapsulating Business Rules

SQL Server 7.0 uses many options to enforce business rules, such as user-defined data types, defaults, and triggers. In many cases, the lower-level options, such as constraints, are the logical choice for enforcing business rules. There are other times, however, in which the use of triggers is more prudent. Triggers have many advantages that do not exist in the other options. Triggers allow you to use the programming-type structures such as loops, complex error checking, comparisons, and access to values in other columns. For simple business decisions, it is better to use the other options. For example, using a trigger to ensure that a value in a column is not NULL would be wasteful when a constraint is available. For the complex business rules, triggers are usually the best choice.

Enforcing Referential Integrity

Enforcing referential integrity involves ensuring that corresponding data values in the foreign key-to-primary key relationship between tables are accurate and consistent. Although you can use constraints to enforce referential integrity, which we will talk about later in the chapter, there are some instances in which triggers are the better or only option.

One feature that constraints do not have is nesting. In an instance where you must have cascading updates and deletes, a trigger is the only option. If

QUESTIONS AND ANSWERS

I need my updates and deletes to affect other tables.	Use triggers. Unlike the other options to enforce referential integrity, triggers support cascading updates and deletes.
I need to validate data from columns within the same table.	Use constraints. Lower-level options such as constraints always perform better than the higher-level options such as triggers. Always choose the lower-level option unless you gain more with the higher-level options.
I need to validate data but it's in a different table.	Use triggers. You cannot use constraints because you cannot compare data in a column in another table.
I just need standard error messages.	Use constraints. Constraints offer minimal error handling and standard error messages.
I need complex error handling.	Use triggers. Triggers are the only referential integrity option that can produce complex error handling.

your application requires that an update or delete must cascade to one or more other tables, then you must use triggers.

Another feature that makes triggers better than constraints is that they can compare columns in multiple tables. A constraint can only validate data from columns within the same table. A big improvement in the validation feature of triggers is that they can verify data that is not exactly the same as the data in the other column. A constraint's verification process requires that the data you are validating be an exact match to the data in the other column.

Triggers support the customizable messages and complex error handling that do not exist in constraints. You should choose triggers over constraints when you have an application that requires more than the constraint's standardized error messages and would greatly benefit from the complex error handling that is native to triggers. The following exercise shows you how to use a trigger to enforce referential integrity.

Creating Triggers That Enforce Referential Integrity

    1. Click Start | Programs | Microsoft SQL Server 7.0 | Query Analyzer.

    2. Log in.

    3. Type

```
CREATE TRIGGER check_author
ON books
FOR INSERT
AS
DECLARE @rows int
SELECT @rows=@@rowcount
IF (SELECT count(*)
FROM inserted I, authors a
Where i.au_name=a.name) <> @rows
BEGIN
PRINT "Author does not exists. Please insert into
authors table first."
ROLLBACK TRANSACTION
END
```

    4. Click Query | Execute Query.

This exercise ensures that the inserted row in the books table has the corresponding author in the authors table. This ensures that the author is properly referenced.

Performing Cascading Updates and Deletes

The nested triggers option allows triggers to cascade updates and deletes. A nested trigger is a trigger that executes within another trigger. To enable nested triggers, go to the Query Analyzer and type

```
Sp_configure 'nested_triggers',1
```

To disable nested triggers, type

```
Sp_configure 'nested triggers',0
```

You must be aware that a trigger cannot recurse, or fire another instance of itself. For example if a trigger on TableX causes a row to be inserted in itself, the row would be inserted without another instance of the trigger being fired. You can use the @@NESTLEVEL global variable to check the nesting levels of your trigger. It returns a value from 0 to 16. Exercise 11-3 shows you how to perform cascading updates and deletes.

SQL Server 7.0 does not support a recursive trigger that calls itself.

EXERCISE 11-3

Creating Triggers That Perform Cascading Updates and Deletes

1. Click Start | Programs | Microsoft SQL Server 7.0 | Query Analyzer.

2. Log in.

3. Type

```
Create Trigger Del_Sales
On Sales
For Delete
As
Declare @Storedeleted char(6)
Select @Storedeleted=stor_id
FROM DELETED
Delete stores
Where Storedeleted=@storID
Go
```

The preceding delete trigger is created on the Sales table. This trigger deletes all related rows in the Stores table.

```
Create Trigger Del_Stores
On Stores
For Delete
As
Declare
@Storedeleted char(6)
Select @Storedeleted=stor_id
FROM DELETED
Delete discounts
Where Storedeleted=@storID
Go
```

The preceding trigger is created on the Stores table. When this is executed, it will also delete orphaned related rows in the Discounts table.

4. In order for this to work, ensure that nesting triggers are enabled by typing

```
sp_configure 'nested triggers', 1
```

5. Click Query | Execute Query.

Performance Considerations

One major performance consideration for triggers is that they are not performed by the system, as are PRIMARY KEY constraints and defaults. By having to run a trigger every time data is modified, performance is slightly degraded. If possible, use the lower-level option of constraints to enforce business rules. Another performance disadvantage of triggers is the potential for deadlocking. Other processes can block a trigger if the same row or table is being used. Although triggers do not add significant stress to the SQL Server, they do pose problems with locking issues. If possible, use the other business rule enforcement options. If you must use a trigger, you can speed up its execution time by having one trigger apply to more than one user action.

To function, triggers use logical tables such as the inserted and deleted tables, as well as referenced tables. Access to logical tables adds very little overhead because these tables are created in memory and the majority of the execution table is used to access referenced target tables. For example, if you create a delete trigger for the Customer tables that deletes corresponding rows in the Sales table, most of the trigger's run time is used to access the data in the Sales table. You can increase performance of the trigger, by having one trigger apply to more than one user action, such as UPDATE or INSERT. By having more than one action apply to the same trigger, execution speed improves because the target table does not have to be referenced numerous times.

Transactional Error Handling

Like stored procedures, triggers have complex error handling and checking. In order for you to inform users of transactional errors, you must use RAISERROR. RAISERROR returns user-defined error messages in the same style and form as SQL Server errors. The syntax for RAISERROR is in Chapter 10. Exercise 11-4 shows you how to use RAISERROR in outputting error messages for triggers.

EXERCISE 11-4

Implementing Transactional Error Handling

1. Click Start | Programs | Microsoft SQL Server 7.0 | Query Analyzer.

2. Log in.

3. Type

```
CREATE TRIGGER TrgDeleteQty
ON sales
FOR DELETE
AS
Declare @qtycount=COUNT(*) FROM sales  /* count the
number of sales on hand */
IF @qtycount > 15   /*If the quantity is greater than
15, error 50001 which is the */
BEGIN                /* user defined error message. The
user defined error message */
RAISERROR(50001,16,-1) /* will send an alert to the
operator */
END                  /* The RAISERROR parameters are 16
for the severity level  */
/* and "1 for the error state */
```

In addition to using the RAISERROR statement for errors in SQL Server, you can also work with the ROLLBACK TRANSACTION option. The ROLLBACK TRANSACTION statement is a self-destruct statement. When this statement is run, the execution of the trigger is halted, and all data modification is reverted to the state it was in before the trigger was run. Be aware that when you run the ROLLBACK TRANSACTION in a batch statement, only the present statement will fail.

The syntax for ROLLBACK TRANSACTION is

```
ROLLBACK [TRAN[SACTION] [transaction_name |
@tran_name_variable | savepoint_name |
@savepoint_variable] ]
```

The arguments and their definitions are shown in the following table:

Arguments	Definitions
Transaction_name	Name of the transaction to rollback.
@tran_name_variable	User defined variable. The variable must contain a working transaction name.
Savepoint_name	The name from the SAVE_TRANSACTION statement under the same name.
@savepoint_variable	User-defined variable. This must contain a working savepoint transaction name.

CERTIFICATION SUMMARY

Triggers are special stored procedures that are executed whenever data is modified in a table. They respond to the DELETE, INSERT, and UPDATE data modification Transact-SQL statements. Because triggers execute before a change has been made, they help enforce business rules and enforce referential integrity.

There are three main types of triggers: update triggers, insert triggers, and delete triggers. Each one responds to a different modification statement. All of the triggers occur at the table level except for update triggers. Update triggers occur at both the table level and the column level.

Triggers are created mainly to encapsulate business rules, enforce referential integrity, and cascade inserts and deletes. Although triggers execute in a higher level in SQL Server compared to the other options, such as defaults and constraints, there are many benefits of triggers that are not available in the other options. The main benefits are loops, complex error checking, comparisons, and access to values in other columns. For applications that can benefit from these features, triggers are the preferred choice.

✓ TWO-MINUTE DRILL

❑ Triggers are special stored procedures that SQL Server automatically invokes in response to data modification Transact-SQL statements, such as INSERT, UPDATE, or DELETE.

❑ Because triggers are fired after all the filters such as rules and defaults have been used, they give the final approval of a data modification.

❑ You create triggers with the CREATE TRIGGER statement, and you must be the owner of the database to do so.

❑ Be careful not to use the same name as an existing trigger when you create a trigger. If you do, the new trigger will overwrite the existing one.

❑ Besides seeing the list of the triggers available in the system, it is also important to view information about a trigger.

❑ With the sp_help stored procedure, you can view the owner of the trigger and when it was created.

❑ With sp_helptext, you can obtain the text of the stored procedure that is stored in the syscomments system catalog table. If you enable encryption on the trigger, you will not be able to read the text.

❑ Before you can use triggers, you must be aware of the limitations on creating the trigger, as well as the limitations of the Transact-SQL statements that can be executed in the body of a trigger.

❑ There are quite a few commands that cannot be executed from a trigger. You have to know you cannot use any of the DROP, CREATE, GRANT, REVOKE, or DISK statements.

❑ Triggers are removed from the database with the DROP TRIGGER statement.

❑ If you drop a table, all associated triggers will be dropped as well.

❑ When you add a new record to the table, it is recorded in the base table, as well as in the inserted table. When you delete a record, it is recorded in the deleted table.

❑ There are three types of triggers that use the inserted table and the deleted table: the insert trigger, the update trigger, and the delete trigger.

❑ Insert triggers are used to ensure that the data being inserted into a table is valid. When an INSERT transaction is detected by the database, the insert trigger is executed.

❑ When an update trigger is executed, the original data is moved to the logical deleted table. The new rows are then moved to the inserted table and the trigger table.

❑ Delete triggers are executed when a DELETE statement is issued against rows in a table. When you attempt to delete rows from a table that is protected by a delete trigger, the deleted rows are moved from the target table to the logical deleted table.

❑ Although a delete trigger is executed when you attempt to delete rows of data from a table, a delete trigger will not fire when you run the TRUNCATE TABLE statement. The TRUNCATE TABLE statement deletes all rows from a table.

❑ Triggers are often used to encapsulate business rules, enforce referential integrity, and perform cascading updates and deletes.

❑ SQL Server 7.0 uses many options to enforce business rules, such as user-defined data types, defaults, as well as triggers. In many cases, the lower-level options, such as constraints, are the logical choice for enforcing business rules.

❑ Enforcing referential integrity involves ensuring that corresponding data values in the foreign key-to-primary key relationship between tables are accurate and consistent.

❑ One feature that constraints do not have is nesting. In an instance where you must have cascading updates and deletes, a trigger is the only option. If your application requires that an update or delete must cascade to one or more other tables, then you must use triggers.

❑ Another feature that makes triggers better than constraints is that they can compare columns in multiple tables. A constraint can only validate data from columns within the same table.

❑ The nested triggers option allows triggers to cascade updates and deletes. A nested trigger is a trigger that executes within another trigger.

❑ One major performance consideration for triggers is that they are not performed by the system, as are PRIMARY KEY constraints and defaults. By having to run a trigger every time data is modified, performance is slightly degraded.

❑ Another performance disadvantage of triggers is the potential for deadlocking.

❑ Like stored procedures, triggers have complex error handling and checking. In order for you to inform users of transactional errors, you must use RAISERROR.

❑ RAISERROR returns user-defined error messages in the same style and form as SQL Server errors.

❑ In addition to using the RAISERROR statement for errors in SQL Server, you can also work with the ROLLBACK TRANSACTION option.

SELF TEST

The following questions will help you measure your understanding of the material presented in this chapter. Read all of the choices carefully, as there may be more than one correct answer. Choose all correct answers for each question.

1. What Transact-SQL statement does a trigger respond to? (Choose all that apply.)

   A. UPDATE

   B. INSERT

   C. DELETE

   D. REMOVE

2. What does the WITH ENCRYPTION argument in the CREATE TRIGGER statement do?

   A. Encrypts the entry in syscomments that contains the text for CREATE TRIGGER

   B. Encrypts the database where the trigger is defined

   C. Encrypts the data in the database where the trigger is defined

   D. Encrypts the trigger

3. Who can create and delete triggers in a table?

   A. DBA

   B. Database owner

   C. Database owner and anyone to whom the owner transfers the permissions

   D. NT network administrator

4. Which stored procedure do you execute to view the text of the trigger stored in the syscomments table?

   A. sp_help

   B. sp_depends

   C. sp_helptext

   D. sp_owner

5. What stored procedure do you execute to view the owner of the trigger and when the trigger was created?

   A. sp_help

   B. sp_depends

   C. sp_helptext

   D. sp_owner

6. Which of the following Transact-SQL statements is allowed in triggers?

   A. GRANT

   B. DENY

   C. UPDATE

   D. CREATE TRIGGER

7. How do you delete triggers?

   A. DELETE 'trigger_name'

   B. CLEAR 'trigger_name'

C. REMOVE 'trigger_name'

D. DROP 'trigger_name'

8. What is the name of the logical tables that hold changes that haven't yet been committed? (Choose all that apply.)

A. Temp

B. Deleted

C. Inserted

D. Commit

9. In which of these items can the update trigger check for changes? (Choose all that apply.)

A. A column

B. A database

C. A table

D. A row

10. What do triggers support that do not exist in constraints? (Choose all that apply.)

A. Customizable error messages

B. Static error messages

C. Complex error handling

D. Constraint denial

11. What Transact-SQL statement do you use to enable nested triggers?

A. Sp_configure 'nested triggers',0

B. Sp_configure 'nested triggers',1

C. Sp_configure 'cascaded triggers',0

D. Sp_configure 'cascaded triggers',0

12. Which one of these numbers would not be stored in the @@NESTLEVEL global variable?

A. 5

B. 10

C. 15

D. 20

13. What determines the majority of the time it takes for a trigger to execute?

A. The type of trigger

B. The length of the trigger

C. The location of the target table

D. The location of the trigger

14. What statement returns user-defined error messages in the same style and form as SQL Server errors?

A. SHOWERROR

B. RAISERROR

C. OUTPUTERROR

D. DISPLAYERR

15. What trigger option forces the entire trigger to halt and all modifications to reset?

A. HALT TRANSACTION

B. CLOSE TRANSACTION

C. ROLLBACK TRANSACTION

D. END TRANSACTION

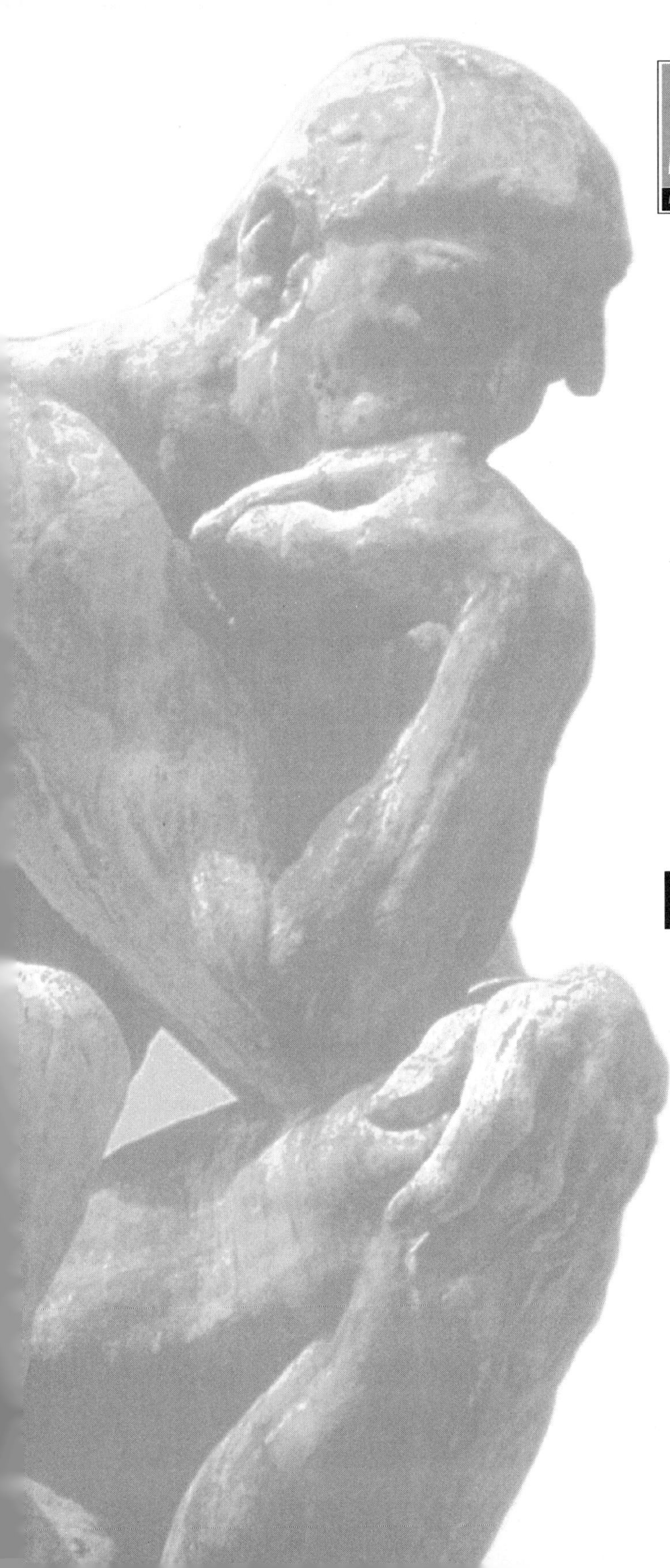

MCDBA
MICROSOFT CERTIFIED DATABASE ADMINISTRATOR

12

Working with Distributed and External Data

CERTIFICATION OBJECTIVES

12.01 Setting Up a Distributed Environment

12.02 Querying a Linked Server

12.03 Accessing Data from Static or Dynamic Sources

12.04 Populating the Database with External Data

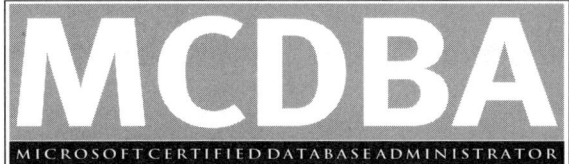

With companies shifting to an enterprise environment, it is becoming crucial for a database developer to be familiar with distributed transactions. Distributed transactions are transactions that span more than one server. By distributing your data, you can allow a single transaction to access data from more than one source. With more databases spanning multiple servers, it would be helpful to examine transferring data in a distributed environment.

SQL Server provides many tools and utilities—such as Data Transformation Services (DTS), bulk copy program, and BULK INSERT —to transfer data into and out of SQL Server. Choosing the right tools is crucial to importing and exporting data because it often involves transferring data between SQL Server and a non-Microsoft SQL Server database such as Oracle or IBM DB2. This happens often with distributed data sources. This chapter will review and compare the many tools available on SQL Server 7.0 to demystify data transfer as well as distributed transactions.

CERTIFICATION OBJECTIVE 12.01

Setting Up a Distributed Environment

SQL Server, starting with version 6.5, has facilitated distributed transactions with the Microsoft Distributed Transaction Coordinator (MS DTC). The MS DTC utilizes Object Linking and Embedding (OLE) to allow applications to modify data in multiple SQL Server databases through one transaction. Like a normal transaction, distributed transactions guarantee each data modification is complete or else the transaction rolls back.

Configuring Remote Servers

When you call remote stored procedures in a distributed transaction, you must specify the name of the remote server in the transaction's execution statement. In order for you to reference these names, you must define the

FROM THE CLASSROOM

Expand Your Horizons by Distributing Your Data

Without argument, the ability to distribute your company or business data among multiple database servers can provide numerous benefits. With the benefits of distributing data assumed to be without question, the mechanism for implementing distributed data should become the focal point of analysis. Any DBA or student with experience in SQL Server 6.5 may decide to pose the question of differentiation between using remote servers versus linked servers. The ability to configure and designate another Microsoft SQL Server as a remote server was available in version 6.5 of SQL Server. This allowed the execution of stored procedures on properly configured remote servers. The execution of these stored procedures remotely could open the door to manipulating distributed data, albeit within limitations.

The ability to create or establish linked servers eliminates certain restrictions or constraints that using remote servers inherently created. With a properly configured and linked SQL Server, SQL queries themselves can be executed on the remote, distributed data. Furthermore, these SQL queries can be constructed dynamically, and run either locally or remotely. In the arena of security, a more flexible model exists with linked servers, allowing either a one-to-one mapping to identical usernames on the linked server, or mapping local SQL Server accounts and Windows NT groups to the linked server.

Although the benefits of using linked servers are numerous, the ability to continue to configure and use remote servers is still available and supported. This backward-compatibility issue allows the continued use of existing SQL code.

—Michael Lane Thomas,
MCSE+I, MCSD, MCP+SB, MSS, MCT, A+

names. You can set up and configure the remote server by going to the Remote Server Properties in the Enterprise Manager. You can access this by clicking Start | Programs | SQL Server 7.0 | Enterprise Manager. Expand the SQL Server group and the server you are presently in. Right-click Remote Servers and select New Remote Server from the pop-up menu. Figure 12-1 shows you the same dialog box that you should be seeing.

Remote server properties
in Enterprise Manager

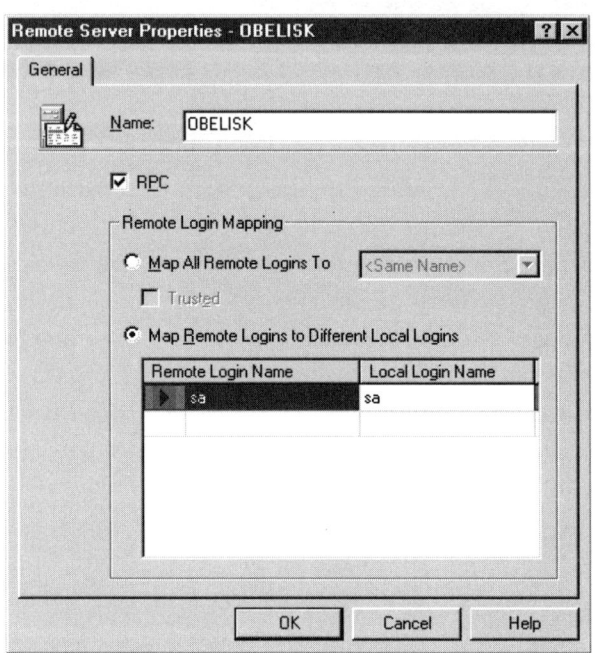

Be sure to specify the name of server and check RPC (remote procedure
call), because MS DTC uses RPC to communicate with remote servers. To
ensure RPC is installed on your computer, check Services in the Control
Panel to determine if the RPC Locator and RPC Service is running on your
server. If it is not, you may want to install the RPC Configuration Service
in Network under the Control Panel. Under Remote Login Mapping, you
will specify the login information. The first, and easiest, option is to Map
All Remote Logins To <Same Name>. This uses the current login as the
login to the remote system. In order to use this option, make sure that the
same user is also a valid user in the remote system. The second option is to

map the remote login to different local logins. In using this option, you map your local login to another login name. This is useful when you wish to use a different login in the remote server or if your local login does not exist in the remote server.

If you can't connect to remote servers via RPC, check the network protocols and ensure the RPC service is loaded and started.

Installing and Configuring the Distributed Transaction Coordinator

When you install SQL Server, the Microsoft Distributed Transaction Coordinator should be automatically installed. However, after you install it, it must be manually started because it is not an automatically started service. In order to start the service, go to the Control Panel and select Services. Find the MS DTC service and manually start it or have it start automatically. This illustration shows you the MS DTC service in the Control Panel:

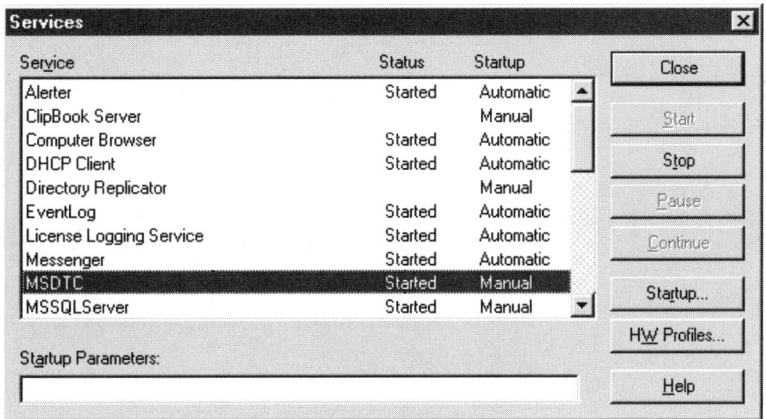

If you are going to be using the MS DTC service often, you should consider having the service run automatically. To set that up, click the Startup button and you should see a screen similar to this one:

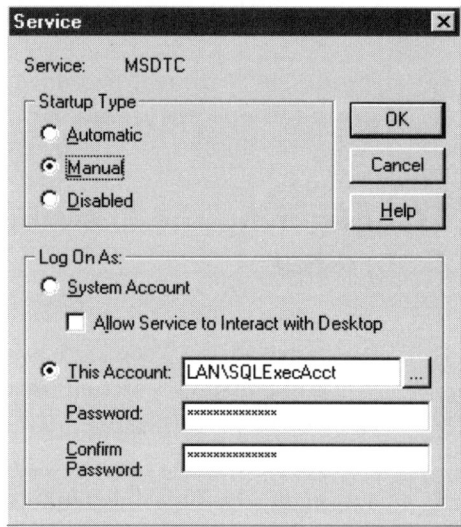

The Service startup dialog box allows you to specify the

- **Startup Type**   If you want the service to be started every time the server is restarted, select Automatic. If you want the service to be started at will, select Manual. If the service is already started and you want to disable it, select Disabled.

- **Log On As**   You can use this option to indicate the type of account that the MS DTC service uses when the server starts up.

If you are running distributed transactions, the startup type should be set to Automatic.

The main way that you can work with the MC DTC is through the MS DTC Administrative Console. You can access this by clicking Start | Programs | Microsoft SQL Server 7.0 | MS DTC Administrative Console. The MS DTC Administrative Console is shown here:

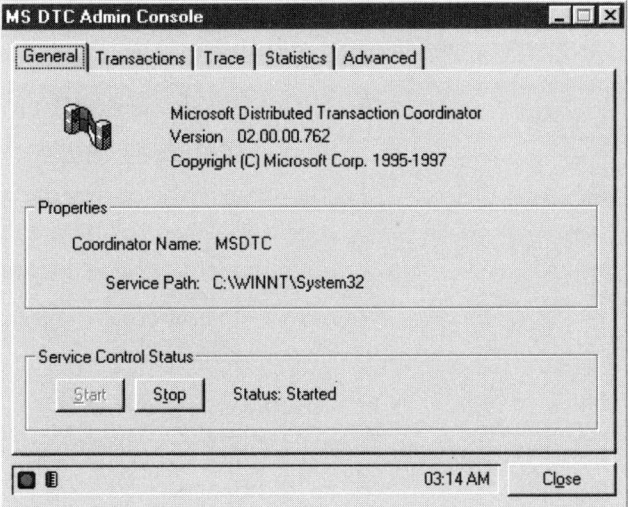

The MS DTC Administrative Console consists of the following five tabs:

■ **General**   You can use this to start or stop the MS DTC service.

■ **Transactions**   Allows you to display any open transactions, as well as show trace information for each transaction.

■ **Trace**   This tab will provide a table and information about the transactions that you are monitoring. Traces produce four different types of severity levels:

   ■ **Error**   Indicates a fatal error. When this happens, be sure to check the error.log in the LOG directory and restart the MS DTC service.

   ■ **Information**   This is not a serious error. This is usually used to assist in debugging or in a trace.

   ■ **Trace**   Normal information from a trace.

   ■ **Warning**   This is a fatal error, but not as fatal as Error because it won't take down the server. Always review warnings and do not allow a system with this severity level to be put in production.

Along with the severity levels, the Trace tab also shows the different status states for each transaction:

■ **Aborted** Shows that the transaction has been aborted and that the MS DTC has notified all the participating systems.

■ **Aborting** Shows that the transaction is in the process of aborting. When the transaction is in this status, the MS DTC is notifying all the participating systems.

■ **Active** Shows that the transaction is active, but has not yet been committed.

■ **Committed** Shows that the transaction is completely successful and has been committed.

■ **Forced Commit** This status occurs with a forced transaction that was previously In-Doubt. When the transaction succeeds, it is marked as a Forced Commit.

■ **Forced Abort** This status occurs with a forced transaction that was previously In-Doubt. When the transaction fails, it is marked as a Forced Abort.

■ **In-Doubt** This status is displayed when the coordinating system in a distributed transaction is unavailable.

■ **Notifying Committed** Shows that the coordinating MS DTC is notifying all the participating systems that the transaction is being committed.

■ **Only Fail Remain to Notify** Shows that one or more participating servers have not been able to notify the coordinating server that the transaction has been properly committed.

■ **Prepared** Shows that the participating systems are ready to commit the transactions.

■ **Preparing** Shows that the participating systems are being checked to see if they can commit the transaction.

■ **Statistics** Shows you the number and type of transactions that are being processed by the MS DTC, as shown here:

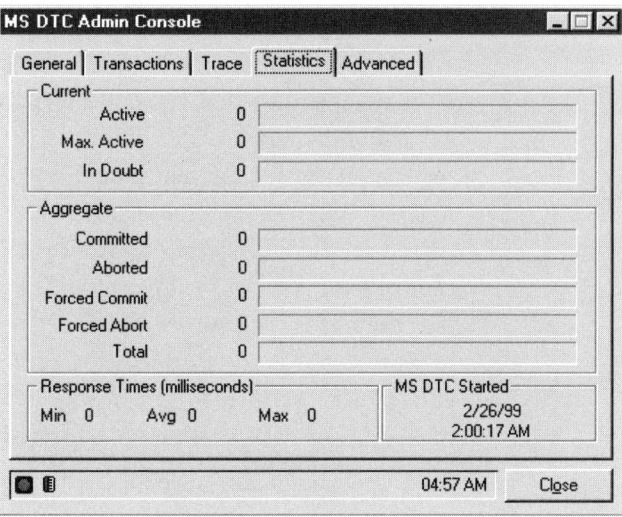

■ **Advanced**   This tab allows you to access the advanced options available in the MS DTC Admin Console. The following shows an example of the configuration dialog box:

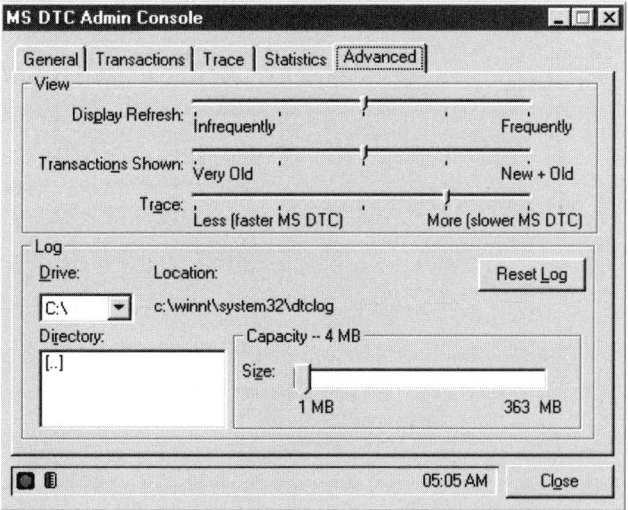

The Display Refresh option ranges from infrequently to frequently. The more frequently it occurs, the more it impacts server performance. This option lets you determine how frequently statistical and trace information is sent to the different graphical interfaces available in SQL Server. You might want to set this so that you can see transactions sooner, because it is very helpful in debugging. The Transactions Shown option controls the age of the transactions displayed. Under normal conditions, you should only need to see transactions several seconds only. You might want to lengthen the time if you are debugging transactions. The Trace option allows you to change from a faster to slower MS DTC, because it sets the length of time that the transaction must be active before it gets displayed. You might want to set it to less if you find that the action of tracing transactions is impacting your server's performance. The log options allow you to control the size of the log file, as well as where it is located. Reset Log clears the log file.

CERTIFICATION OBJECTIVE 12.02

Querying a Linked Server

Linked servers are a new feature in SQL Server 7.0. Using linked servers, you can open an OLE DB rowset on a remote server. This feature is much different than the remote servers available in previous versions of SQL Server in that it also allows you to access data from non-SQL Server data sources. Because you use OLE DB to access these data sources, you can access data sources from Oracle, Microsoft Excel, or any other OLE DB data source. To set up a linked server, you first have to use the sp_addlinkedserver and sp_addlinkedsrvlogin system stored procedures:

```
Exec sp_addlinkedserver <remoteserver>,<type of OLE DB data source>
Exec sp_addlinkedsrvlogin <remoteserver>.'TRUE'
```

The preceding statements add a remote server to your SQL Server and tell it to connect with the credentials that you are using in the local server.

OPENQUERY

OPENQUERY is a Transact-SQL statement that executes a query on a linked server. You can reference OPENQUERY as the target table on an INSERT, UPDATE, or DELETE statement. The syntax of OPENQUERY is

```
OPENQUERY(<linked_server_name>, <query>)
```

Exercise 12-1 shows you how to use OPENQUERY.

EXERCISE 12-1

Evaluating Where Processing Occurs by Using OPENQUERY

1. Click Start | Programs | Microsoft SQL Server 7.0 | Query Analyzer.

2. Type

```
EXEC sp_addlinkedserver 'NewSQLSvr',
'SQL Server',
'SQLOLEDB',
GO
SELECT *
FROM OPENQUERY(NewSQLSvr, 'SELECT name, id FROM pub.titles')
GO
```

The preceding lines create a linked server called NewSQLSvr against a SQL Server database using the SQL Server OLE DB provider. It uses a pass-through query against this linked server.

CERTIFICATION OBJECTIVE 12.03

Accessing Data from Static or Dynamic Sources

With distributed transactions, it is crucial that you are able to access data from static or dynamic data sources. There are two ways to access data: by using remote stored procedures or by using OPENROWSET to execute a query.

Remote Stored Procedures

With the addition of remote servers, you can now run stored procedures on remote databases. In order to allow remote stored procedures to run, you must follow these steps:

1. Add the name of the remote server to the sysservers system table on your SQL Server by running

   ```
   exec sp_addserver <remoteserver>
   ```

2. Do the same to the remote SQL Server by running

   ```
   exec sp_addserver <localserver>
   ```

3. On your server, run

   ```
   EXEC sp_addremotelogin <remoteserver>, sa, sa
   EXEC sp_remoteoption <remoteserver>,sa, sa, trusted, true
   ```

4. On the remote server, run

   ```
   EXEC sp_addremotelogin <localserver>, sa, sa
   EXEC sp_remoteoption <localserver>,sa, sa, trusted, true
   ```

With the preceding statements, you can run remote stored procedures while logged in as sa. The first two statements define the remote servers. The last two statements insert a remote login ID on the local server, allowing the remote servers to access and execute remote stored procedures. You can also do this with other logins. Just substitute the desired login name in the statements. To run a remote stored procedure, you have to refer to the stored procedure by its four-part name in the execute statement, as in the following example:

```
Exec servername.dbname.owner.storedprocedure_name
```

Exercise 12-2 demonstrates how to access data using remote stored procedures.

EXERCISE 12-2

Accessing Data Using Remote Stored Procedures

1. Click Start | Programs | Microsoft SQL Server 7.0 | Query Analyzer.

2. Execute

```
sp_addserver <remoteserver>
```

3. Go to the remote server and execute

```
sp_addserver <localserver>
```

4. Go back to the local server and execute

```
EXEC sp_addremotelogin <remoteserver>, sa, sa
EXEC sp_remoteoption <remoteserver>,sa, sa, trusted, true
```

5. Go to the remote server and execute

```
EXEC sp_addremotelogin <localserver>, sa, sa
EXEC sp_remoteoption <localserver>,sa, sa, trusted, true
```

6. Go to the local server and run this statement:

```
Exec <remoteserver>.pub.dbo. spshwAuthors.
```

This statement executes the spshwAuthors stored procedure that we made in Chapter 10.

OPENROWSET

OPENROWSET accesses remote data using OLE DB. It is a one-time, ad hoc method. You can reference OPENROWSET as the target table in the FROM clause of a query, or as the target table of an INSERT, UPDATE, or DELETE statement. The syntax for OPENROWSET is

```
OPENROWSET('provider_name'
{
'datasource';'user_id';'password'
| 'provider_string'
},
{
[catalog.][schema.]object
| 'query'
})
```

The following table shows you the arguments and functions of OPENROWSET. Exercise 12-3 will demonstrates accessing data using linked servers and OPENROWSET.

Arguments	Functions
provider_name	The name of the OLE DB provider
datasource	The name of the OLE DB data source
user_id	The username that is passed to the OLE DB provider
password	The password that is passed to the OLE DB provider
provider_string	The connection string needed to initialize the OLE DB provider
catalog	The name of the catalog or database in which the specified object resides
schema	The name of the schema or object owner for the specified object
object	The name of the object
query	The query that is going to be executed by the provider

EXERCISE 12-3

Accessing Data Using Linked Servers and OPENROWSET

1. Click Start | Programs | Microsoft SQL Server 7.0 | Query Analyzer.

2. Type

```
USE pubs
GO
SELECT a.*
FROM OPENROWSET('SQLOLEDB','NewSQLAvr';'sa';'password',
'SELECT * FROM pubs.dbo.authors ORDER BY au_fname, au_lname')
AS a
GO
```

CERTIFICATION OBJECTIVE 12.04

Populating the Database with External Data

Transferring external data to the database is called *importing*. The process of importing data and objects can either be a one-time migration or a constant updating of data. When a company is migrating from one database management system, such as Oracle or Access, to SQL Server, it must import the data and the other objects, such as schema and security. Because SQL Server will replace the older database, data is imported so that SQL Server can be used for all data-related tasks immediately. You perform a one-time import so that use of the old database management system is eliminated and use of the SQL Server can start right away.

Another reason for importing data is to manually upgrade the SQL Server data. For example, if you have a database that needs weekly updates of data from a coexisting non-SQL Server database system that is updated with many client applications, you need to do weekly imports of the data. This is different from the one-time import, but it is a requirement for many companies.

Using Data Transformation Services (DTS)

Data Transformation Services (DTS), as shown in Figure 12-2, is a powerful new tool introduced in SQL Server 7.0. DTS is used to transfer data across heterogeneous sources using OLE DB. This gives SQL Server access to a variety of database sources from Microsoft Excel to Oracle. Because all database sources do not have access to an OLE DB provider, Microsoft implements the OLE DB Provider for Open Database Connectivity (ODBC) driver to make any ODBC data source an OLE DB provider.

You can use the Data Transformation Service Import and Export wizards to transfer objects such as indexes, stored procedures, and referential integrity constraints across SQL Server 7.0 computers. One of the most helpful features in the DTS Import and Export wizards allows you to map a destination column to a source column. This allows you to specify where you want an entire column to copy to and allows you to change the destination column's data type.

The DTS wizards allow you to specify how to transform the data when you are copying to a destination table. You can use Visual Basic Scripting Edition (VBScript), Java Script (JScript), or the ActiveX scripting engine to write the data transformation scripts.

Once you have access to the data, you can create a DTS package to import and export data over ODBC and OLE DB. The DTS package is an

FIGURE 12-2

The DTS Import wizard allows you to customize data transfers

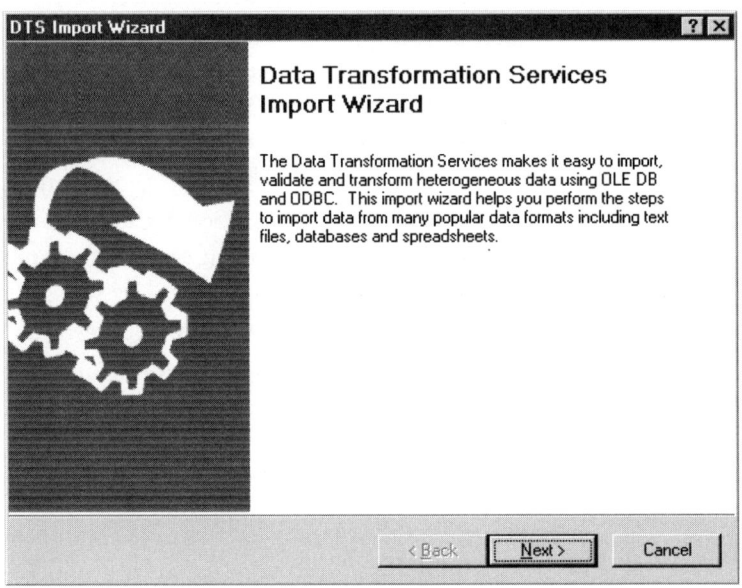

object within DTS that saves the entire set of commands that you specify so that the package can be run again without having to go through the DTS wizard prompts. Programmers can also edit the DTS package interface through an OLE Automation interface implemented in Dtspkg.dll by using development languages that support Object Linking and Embedding (OLE).

Another feature of the Data Transformation Services is the advanced transformation properties. They are used to define how data can be converted between the source and destination database. Before the copy, the DTS Data Pump checks to see if the copy is valid according to the transformation flags that you define in the advanced transformation properties. If any of the columns fail the check, the copy operation is aborted. This ensures that the copy is done to your specification.

Using the Import and Export Wizards

DTS requires you to first use the Export wizard to export the data and then use the Import wizard to import the data. Exercise 12-4 and Exercise 12-5 show you how to transfer data with Data Transformation Services Import and Export wizards. To perform these exercises, you need to have Microsoft Access installed, as well as all of the sample databases.

EXERCISE 12-4

Populating a Database with External Data Using DTS

1. Select Start | Programs | SQL Server 7.0 | SQL Enterprise Manager.

2. Expand the SQL Server group and then expand the tree of the SQL Server from which you want to export your data.

3. Expand Database and click your desired database. For this exercise, choose pubs. Select Action | Task | Export Wizard to start the Data Transformation Export wizard.

4. Click Next after you read the introduction screen.

5. You should see the Choose a Data Source dialog box similar to the one shown next. Next to Source, you can select the data format. In this exercise, choose the default, which is Microsoft SQL Server 7.0 Only (OLE DB Provider). Next to Server, you can select the server that contains the database from which you will import. By default, your local server should be already selected. While choosing your source, you can choose the type of authentication you wish to use when logging in to SQL Server to perform the import. For this exercise, choose Use SQL Server authentication. Next to User Name, type **sa**. Next to Password, type *your password* for sa if any. Next to Database, you can select the databases available on the server you selected. For this exercise, choose the pubs database. Click Next.

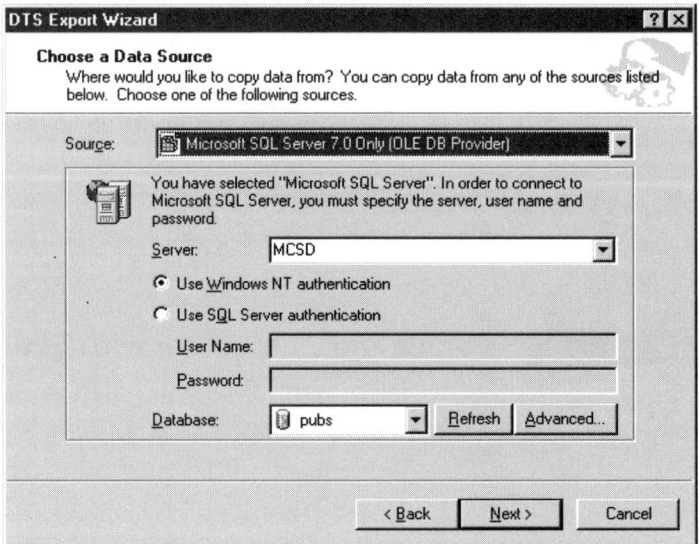

6. The next screen is the Choose a Destination dialog box, as shown
   next. This is similar to the Choose a Data Source dialog box in the
   DTS Import wizard. In Destination, we will choose Text File. Once
   you select this, a subscreen prompting you for the destination of the
   text file will appear. In this example, type **C:\temp.txt**. Click Next.

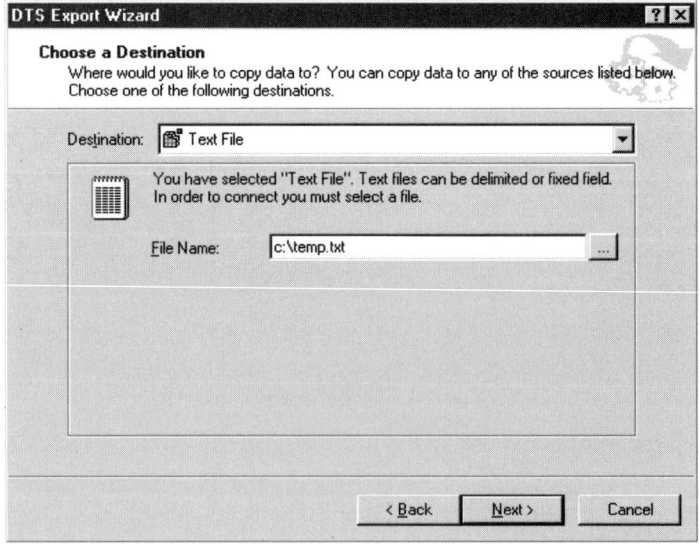

7. You should now see the Specify Table Copy or Query screen. You can specify whether to copy all the records from one or more tables or use a query to filter the data to a specific subset. In this exercise, choose Copy table(s) from the source database. Click Next.

8. You should see the Select Destination File Format dialog box, as shown in Figure 12-3. This dialog box prompts you for the format of the text file that you want to export. This dialog box has nine fields for you to set:

   ■ **Source** Choose the table used for the export. In this exercise, ensure [pubs].[dbo].[authors] is selected.

   ■ **Delimited** Choose this option if you want every field in your text file to be separated by a specified character such as a comma. In this exercise, select Delimited.

   ■ **Fixed Field** Choose this option if you want every field in your text file to be the same number of characters.

   ■ **File Type** You can choose the type of file that you want your destination file to be saved as. You can choose from Unicode or ANSI. The difference between ANSI and Unicode is that Unicode uses twice as much storage space because it allows you to use characters that can cross multiple character sets. ANSI is a standard in one character set. In this exercise, choose ANSI.

   ■ **Row Delimiter** You can choose the character to indicate the end of a row. The default is {CR}{LF}, which is a carriage return and a line feed. In the exercise, leave the option at its default.

   ■ **Column Delimiter** You can choose the character to separate the columns. The default is comma. In the exercise, leave the option at its default.

   ■ **Text Qualifier** You can choose how to indicate that a field is a text field. The default is double quote(" "). It's important that you indicate that a field is a text field when a field that appears to be numeric is going to be input as a character. If this happens, the import will fail. In the exercise, leave the option at its default.

   ■ **First row has column names** Check this setting if you want the first row to contain the name of the fields instead of a record. In this exercise, leave the option at its default, which is unchecked.

■ **Transform** This allows you to specify the column mappings and transformations.

9. Click Next.

10. The next screen you should see is the Save, Schedule and Replicate Package dialog box. This dialog box is asking whether you want to save the DTS package. In this exercise, make sure that Run Immediately is the only option checked and click Next.

11. The next screen is the Completing the DTS Wizard dialog box. This dialog box shows you a summary of the choices you made. If this is not correct, you can click Back to change the settings. If it is correct, click Finish.

FIGURE 12-3

Allows you to specify
whether the file is
Delimited or Fixed Field

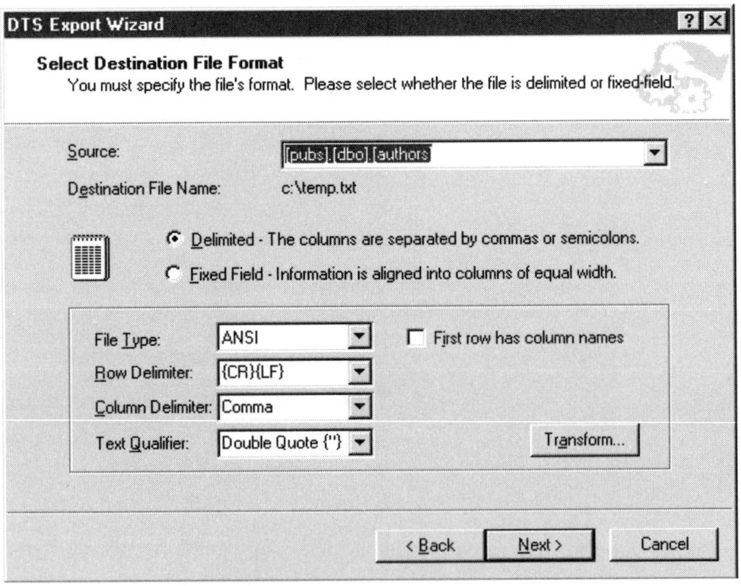

Using DTS to Import Data

1. Select Start | Programs | SQL Server 7.0 | SQL Enterprise Manager.

2. Expand the SQL Server group and then expand the tree of the SQL Server into which you want to import your data.

3. Expand Database and click your desired database. For this exercise, choose pubs. Select Action | Task | Import Wizard to start the Data Transformation Import wizard.

4. Click Next after you read the introduction screen.

5. You should now see the Choose a Data Source screen, as shown next.

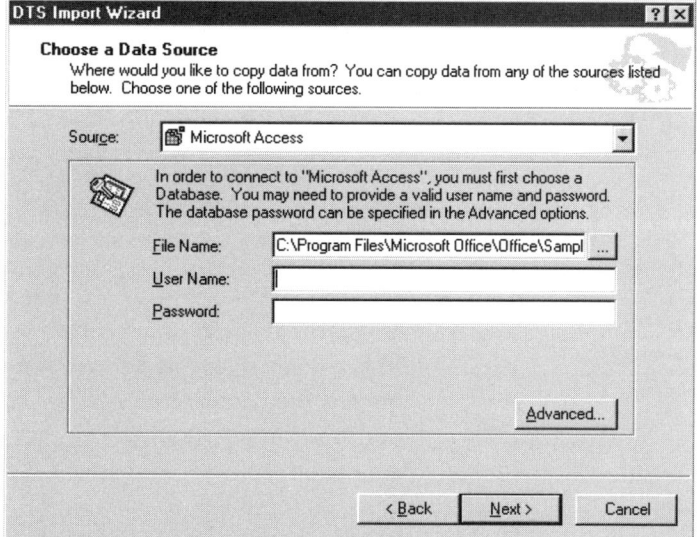

6. Next to Source, you are able to choose the different file types from which you can import data. In this exercise, choose Microsoft Access. Next to File Name, you must specify the path of the database. If you installed Microsoft Access to its default path, it should be C:\Program Files\Microsoft Office\Office\Samples\ NORTHWIND.MDB. If your database uses security, you can specify the User Name and Password in their corresponding boxes. For this exercise, you should leave both fields blank. Click Next.

7. You should now see the Choose a Destination dialog box, as shown next. This dialog box prompts you for the destination of your imported data.

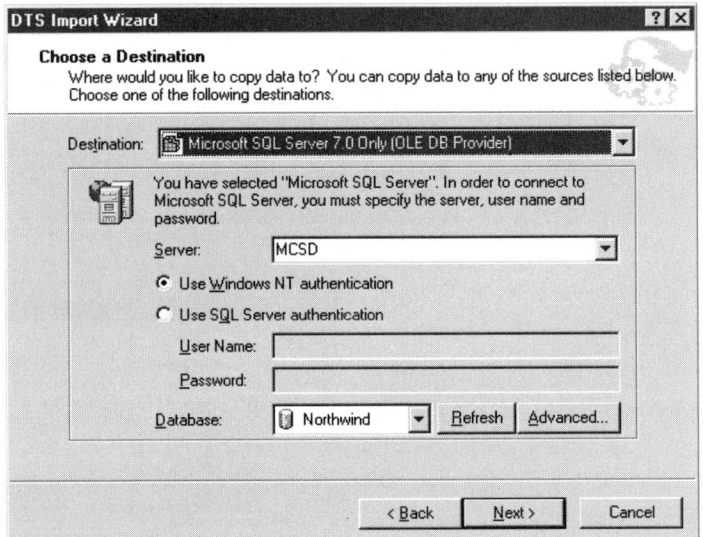

8. Next to Destination, you can select the data format. In this exercise, choose the default, which is Microsoft SQL Server 7.0 Only (OLE DB Provider). Next to Server, you can select the server that contains the database to which you will import the data. By default, your local server should be already selected. While choosing your destination, you can choose the type of authentication you wish to use when logging in to SQL Server to perform the import. For this exercise, choose Use SQL Server authentication. Next to User Name, type **sa**. Next to Password, type *your password* for sa, if any. Next to Database, you can select the databases available on the server you selected. For this exercise, choose the pubs database. Click Next.

9. You should now see the Specify Table Copy or Query screen. You can specify whether to copy all the records from one or more tables or use a query to filter the data to a specific subset. In this exercise, choose Copy table(s) from the source database. Click Next.

10. You should now see the Select Source Tables dialog box as shown in Figure 12-4. In this dialog box, you are presented with a three-column grid. The three columns are

■ **Source Table**   Check the source tables to import data from them.

■ **Destination Table**   If the source table is checked, you can specify the destination table for the imported data. By default, the destination table name is the same as the source table name. If the table already exists, all imported data will be appended so existing data will not be overwritten. If the table does not exist, SQL Server will create it.

■ **Transform**   Allows you to specify the column mappings and transformations.

FIGURE 12-4

Select the source
of your data

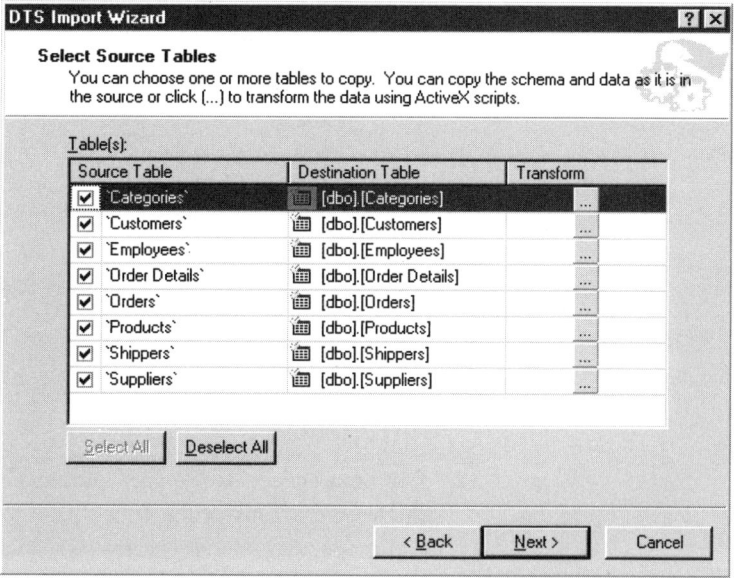

11. In this exercise, select all the Source Tables, leave the Destination Table to the default, and set Transform to the default setting. Click Next.

12. The next screen that you should see is the Save, Schedule and Replicate Package dialog box, shown next. This dialog box is asking whether you want to save the DTS package. A DTS package is the entire set of instructions that you set for this import session. If you save this, you don't have to run it all again. Check Save Package on SQL Server, if you will do this again at a later time. Uncheck it if this is a one-time import. If this will be done later, you can schedule the import times by clicking Schedule DTS Package for later execution. In this exercise, make sure Save Package on SQL Server is not checked. For this exercise, make sure Run Immediately is the only option checked and click Next.

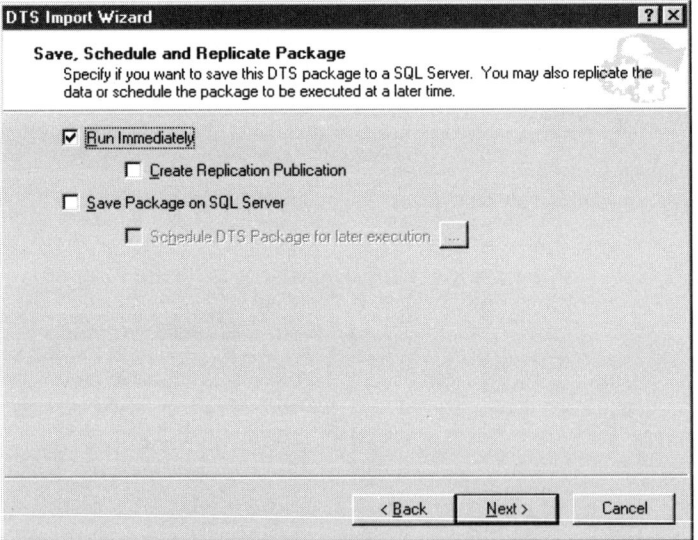

13. The next screen is the Completing the DTS Wizard dialog box, shown next. This dialog box shows you a summary of the choices you made. If this is not correct, you can click Back to change the settings. If it is correct, click Finish.

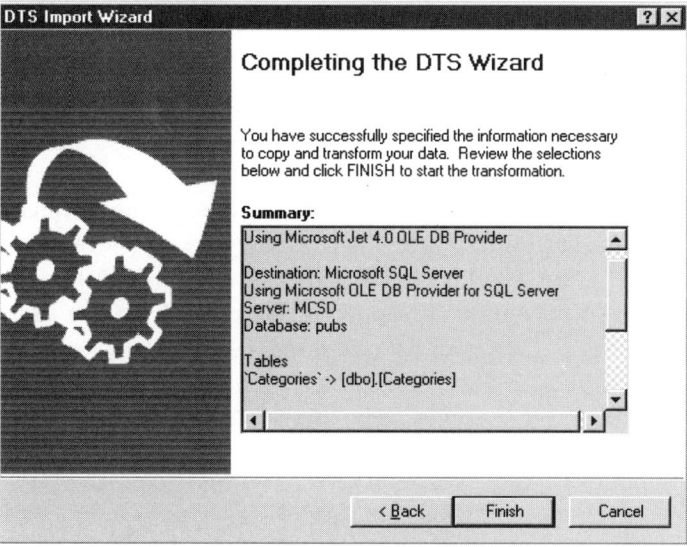

Using the Bulk Copy Program

SQL Server's bulk copy program utility (bcp) is a command-line based program that is used to copy data into and out of SQL Server. A database administrator would usually use this to transfer large amounts of data to SQL Server from another database management system. To use bcp, you must first export the SQL Server data to a data file. bcp then imports the data file into SQL Server.

In order for you to use bcp, you must have the appropriate permission to access the data in the table:

- You must have INSERT and SELECT permissions on the destination table.

- You must have SELECT permissions on the source table.

- You must have appropriate operating system permissions on the files you wish to modify or create.

- You must have SELECT permissions on the syscolumns, sysobjects, and sysindexes tables.

The bcp Command

The bulk copy utility (bcp) is a program that must be run from a DOS prompt. BCP.EXE can be found in the BINN subdirectory under the SQL Server installation directory. The syntax is

```
bcp {[[database_name.][owner].]{table_name | view_name} | "query"}
{in | out | queryout | format} data_file [-m max_errors] [-f format_file] [-e err_file]
[-F first_row] [-L last_row] [-b batch_size] [-n] [-c] [-w] [-N] [-6] [-q] [-C code_page]
[-t field_term] [-r row_term] [-i input_file] [-o output_file] [-a packet_size]
[-S server_name] [-U login_id] [-P password] [-T] [-v] [-R] [-k] [-E] [-h "hint [,...n]"]
```

The following table lists the arguments and switches that allow you to control the way bcp executes.

Arguments and Switches	Function
Database_name	Name of the database. Required if source database is not the current database.
Owner	Name of the owner. Optional if you own the source table or view. Required if you do not own the table.
Table_name	Name of the table being copied.
View_name	Name of the view being copied.
Query	Transact-SQL statement that returns a result set.
in | out | queryout | format	Specified in for import, out for export, and the format creates a format file.
Data_file	The full path of the data file used in the copy operation.
-m max_errors	The maximum number of errors that can occur before copy operation is aborted. Default is 10.
-f format_file	The full path of the optional format file.
-e err_file	The full path of the optional error file in which bcp stores the rows that were not copied.

Arguments and Switches	Function
-F first_row	The number of the first row to copy.
-L last_row	The number of the last row to copy.
-b batch_size	The number of rows copied in a batch. Default is all rows.
-n	Sets the data's data type as native. This is best used when transferring data from one SQL Server to another. Since data is native, no conversions are required. Transferring data with the native format is the fastest way to copy since there is no need for conversion of data types and character formats.
-c	Sets the data's data type as character. The character format is best used with non-SQL Server database transfers such as Excel or Oracle. This format uses tabs between fields and a newline character at the end of every row. This is a universal format since data is output into a text file format.
-w	This is the same as the character format except it uses Unicode data types so that transfers between two code pages will not result in a loss of character data. This should only be used on transfers between two heterogeneous databases with different code pages.
-N	This is the same as the native format (-n) when applied to noncharacter data, but it uses the character data format for character data types so that transfers between two code pages will not result in a loss of character data. This should only be used on transfers between two heterogeneous databases with different code pages.
-6	Performs the bulk copy operation using SQL Server 6.x data types.

Arguments and Switches	Function
-q	Requires quoted identifiers.
-C code_page	Sets the code page of the data in the data file. Can be set to ACP, OEM, RAW, or a specific code page number.
-t field_term	Sets the field terminator.
-r row_term	Sets the row terminator.
-i input_file	Specifies the name of the file where all responses to the prompts during a bcp interactive mode.
-o output_file	Specifies the name of the file in which output is redirected during a bcp session.
-a packet_size	Sets the size of network packets sent during bcp in bytes.
-S server_name	Specifies the SQL Server to connect to.
-U login_id	Supplies the Login ID to connect to SQL Server.
-P password	Supplies the password to connect to SQL Server.
-T	Specifies that bcp connect via a trusted connection.
-v	Reports the bcp version number.
-R	Specifies currency, date, and time are copied in a regional format.
-k	Specifies that blank columns should be set to NULL.
-E	Specifies identity columns must contain values.
-h "hint [,...n]"	Specifies hints are to be used during bulk copy operations.

Applying bcp

In Exercise 12-6, we will bulk copy data from one table to another.

Populating a Database with External Data Using bcp

1. Click Start | Run. Next to Open, type

   command

   Click OK.

2. At the command prompt, type

   BCP pubs..employee out exercise.dat -T -n

   Your screen should look similar to the one shown next. This command exports the contents of the Employee table in the pubs database to the EXERCISE.DAT file. The contents are stored in their native format.

   ```
   C:\WINNT\System32\cmd.exe                                          _ □ ×
   Microsoft(R) Windows NT(TM)
   (C) Copyright 1985-1996 Microsoft Corp.

   C:\>BCP pubs..employee out exercise.dat -T -n

   Starting copy...

   43 rows copied.
   Network packet size (bytes): 4096
   Clock Time (ms.): total        31 Avg          0 (1387.10 rows per sec.)

   C:\>
   ```

3. Now type

   BCP pubs..employee out exercise.txt -T -c

This command exports the contents of the Employee table in the pubs database to the EXERCISE.TXT file. The contents of the file are stored as a text format.

Loading Data Using Other Methods

Though the two main ways to copy data to and from SQL Server are with Data Transformation Services and bcp, you are still able to use other methods such as the INSERT, SELECT INTO, and BULK INSERT statements. There are different reasons why you should choose each and you should carefully assess which tool you can use to effectively transfer data in the specification deemed appropriate.

Transfer Manager

In SQL Server version 6.0 and earlier, SQL Server came with a separate tool called SQL Transfer Manager. This graphical user interface tool enabled you to transfer data easily and quickly. In version 6.5, SQL Server added this functionality to SQL Server Enterprise Manager. Unlike bcp, the SQL Transfer Manager was able to transfer both data and objects, such as triggers and stored procedures, between databases. With version 7.0, SQL Server introduces the new Data Transformation Services Import and Export wizards, which replace the functionality of the SQL Transfer Manager. DTS now allows storing commands in packages, scripting capabilities with JScript and VBScript, and access to OLE DB providers. Although SQL Transfer Manager no longer exists in SQL Server 7.0, it is important that you are aware of the history of the SQL Transfer Manager and its relationship with DTS and bcp.

INSERT Statement

Like bcp, you can use the INSERT statement to add data from an external OLE DB provider to SQL Server in one or more rows. In order for you to run the INSERT command, you must be the table owner or you must have the privilege transferred to you. The syntax for an INSERT statement is

INSERT [INTO] {*table_name*| *view_name*} [(*column_list*)] {*DEFAULT VALUES*|*values*|*derived_table*|*execute_statement*}

The following table lists the keywords and switches for the INSERT statement.

Keyword or Switch	Function
INTO	Optional word.
Table_name| view_name	Specifies the table name or the view name where the data will be inserted.

Keyword or Switch	Function
Column_list	The list of columns in which data will be inserted.
DEFAULT VALUES	Inserts the default values for all of the columns.
Values	The values going to be added to the columns.
Derived_table	A SELECT statement used to retrieve values to be added to an existing table.
Execute_statement	An EXECUTE statement that returns data with SELECT or READTEXT statements.

SELECT INTO Statement

The SELECT INTO statement creates a table and retrieves data for the table by pulling data from other rows in another table.

> SELECT [*select_list*] INTO {*:hvar* [,...]} *select_options*

The following table lists the keywords and switches for the SELECT INTO statement.

Keyword or Switch	Function
Select_list	The list of table columns or expressions from which the data is retrieved.
:hvar	The host variables to receive the *select_list* items.
Select_options	One or more Transact-SQL SELECT statements. GROUP BY, HAVING, COMPUTE, CUBE, and ROLLUP clauses are not supported.

on the
job

Before you execute the SELECT INTO statement, make sure the user has CREATE TABLE permissions in the destination database.

BULK INSERT

BULK INSERT is used to copy data into SQL Server using the functionality of the bcp utility with a Transact-SQL statement rather than from the command prompt. This is the fastest way to transfer data from a text file to SQL Server. Because BULK INSERT cannot transform data, you should only use BULK INSERT to copy only data and when speed is the most crucial factor.

The syntax for the BULK INSERT statement is

```
BULK INSERT [['database_name'.]['owner']].]{'table_name' FROM data_file}
[WITH
(
[ BATCHSIZE [= batch_size]]
[[,] CHECK_CONSTRAINTS]
[[,] CODEPAGE [= 'ACP' | 'OEM' | 'RAW' | 'code_page']]
[[,] DATAFILETYPE [=
{'char' | 'native'| 'widechar' | 'widenative'}]]
[[,] FIELDTERMINATOR [= 'field_terminator']]
[[,] FIRSTROW [= first_row]]
[[,] FORMATFILE [= 'format_file_path']]
[[,] KEEPIDENTITY]
[[,] KEEPNULLS]
[[,] KILOBYTES_PER_BATCH [= kilobytes_per_batch]]
[[,] LASTROW [= last_row]]
[[,] MAXERRORS [= max_errors]]
[[,] ORDER ({column [ASC | DESC]} [,...n])]
[[,] ROWS_PER_BATCH [= rows_per_batch]]
[[,] ROWTERMINATOR [= 'row_terminator']]
[[,] TABLOCK]
)
]
```

The following table lists the arguments for the BULK INSERT statement.

Arguments	Function
database_name	Name of the database. If not specified, BULK INSERT will use current database.
owner	Table or view owner. If user is owner, this argument is optional.
table_name	Name of the table or view to bulk insert into.
data_file	Full path of the data file that BULK INSERT will copy data from.

Arguments	Function
BATCHSIZE [= batch_size]	Sets the number of rows in the batch. Each batch counts as a single transaction. By default, all data will be copied as one batch.
CHECK_CONSTRAINTS	Enables that all constraints are checked during the bulk insert.
CODEPAGE [= 'ACP' | 'OEM' | 'RAW' | 'code_page']	Sets the type of code page of the data in the data file. The code page value of *ACP* will convert columns of char, varchar, or text data type from ANSI/Microsoft Windows code page to the SQL Server code page. The code page value of *OEM*, which is also the default, will convert columns of char, varchar, or text data type from the system OEM code page to the SQL Server code page. The code page value of *RAW* is the fastest option because it will not perform any conversions. The *code page* specifies the code page number.
DATAFILETYPE [= {'char' | 'native' | 'widechar' | 'widenative'}]	Tells BULK INSERT to perform the bulk copy with the *char, native, widechar,* or *widenative* data file types.
FIELDTERMINATOR [= 'field_terminator']	Sets the field terminator for use with *char* or Unicode char (*widechar*) data files. The default is the tab character (\t).
FIRSTROW [= first_row]	Sets the first row for the BULK INSERT operation to copy. The default is 1, which is the first row.
FORMATFILE [= 'format_file_path']	Sets the full path of the format file. The format file is a file that describes the data file that contains the responses created using bcp. This argument should be used when the data file is different than the table or view, such as a different number of columns, different ordered columns, or different column delimiters.
KEEPIDENTITY	This argument is used to tell BULK INSERT that the identity values are present in the file being imported. If this is not specified, SQL Server will automatically use seed and increment values to set the values for the rows.

Arguments	Function
KEEPNULLS	Sets the columns with no values to contain a NULL value instead of having default values inserted.
KILOBYTES_PER_BATCH [= kilobytes_per_batch]	Sets the size of data per batch in kilobytes.
LASTROW [= last_row]	Sets the last row for the BULK INSERT operation to copy. The default is 0, which is the last row.
MAXERRORS [= max_errors]	Sets the maximum number of errors that can occur before the bulk insert operation is aborted.
ORDER ({column [ASC | DESC]} [,...n])	Sets how the data in the data file is sorted. You can improve the performance of the bulk insert if the data is sorted the same as the clustered index on the table. By default, no ordering is assumed.
ROWS_PER_BATCH [= rows_per_batch]	Sets the number of rows per batch. ROWS_PER_BATCH cannot be used at the same time as BATCHSIZE.
ROWTERMINATOR [= 'row_terminator']	Sets the row terminator used for *widechar* and *char* data files. The default is newline character (\n).
TABLOCK	Sets a table-level lock for the BULK INSERT operation. By setting the table level only for the duration of the BULK INSERT operation increases the performance of the operation by only having the table locked when necessary.

exam
Ⓦatch

In order to run the BULK INSERT statement, you must be a member of the sysadmin fixed server role.

Here are some possible scenario questions about transferring data, along with the correct answers.

QUESTIONS AND ANSWERS

I want to copy data from an existing table to a new table I haven't created yet.	Use SELECT INTO. SELECT INTO allows you to create a table based on an existing table.
I need to transfer data from a data file into a table very quickly.	Use BULK INSERT. When speed is at the utmost priority, BULK INSERT is the only way to go. Please note that you can only retrieve information from the data file. If you want to put data into a flat file, you have to use bcp.
I need to transfer data to and from SQL Server, but I need the database schema too.	Use DTS. DTS is your choice to transfer data AND database schema.
I need to transfer data between SQL Server and a flat file.	Use bcp. Bulk copy is the best option to transfer data when it involves a flat file.
I need to transfer data from an external OLE DB provider.	Use INSERT. INSERT is the best option when you need data from an OLE DB provider.

CERTIFICATION SUMMARY

Distributed transactions are transactions that span more than one server. By distributing your data, you can allow a single transaction to access data from more than one source. In order for you to have access to distributed transactions, you must first install and configure the Microsoft Distributed Transaction Coordinator.

There are many different ways to access data in distributed transactions. You can use OPENROWSET or OPENQUERY, or you can execute remote stored procedures. OPENROWSET is used to access tables with a one-time, ad hoc method using OLE DB. Remote stored procedures are stored procedures that you can run on remote databases. OPENQUERY is a Transact-SQL statement that executes a query on a linked server.

The main ways to populate the database with external data are with Data Transformation Services (DTS) and the bulk copy program utility (bcp). However, you are still able to use other methods such as the INSERT,

SELECT INTO, and BULK INSERT statements. You can use the INSERT statement to add data from an external OLE DB provider to SQL Server in one or more rows. The SELECT INTO statement is used to retrieve one row of data and assign the value to another row. BULK INSERT is used to copy data into SQL Server using the functionality of the bcp utility with a Transact-SQL statement rather than from the command prompt.

With the new enterprise environment, it becomes more essential for queries and data to span more than one server. SQL Server 7.0 introduces many new features and improves older ones to allow us to take advantage of the distributed architecture. By being aware of these features, you will greatly improve your success as a database developer.

TWO-MINUTE DRILL

- ❑ Distributed transactions are transactions that span more than one server. By distributing your data, you can allow a single transaction to access data from more than one source.

- ❑ With a properly configured and linked SQL Server, SQL queries themselves can be executed on the remote, distributed data. Furthermore, these SQL queries can be constructed dynamically, and can be run either locally or remotely.

- ❑ SQL Server, starting with version 6.5, has facilitated distributed transactions with the Microsoft Distributed Transaction Coordinator (MS DTC). The MS DTC utilizes Object Linking and Embedding (OLE) to allow applications to modify data in multiple SQL Server databases through one transaction.

- ❑ When you call remote stored procedures in a distributed transaction, you must specify the name of the remote server in the transaction's execution statement.

- ❑ You can set up and configure the remote server by going to the Remote Server Properties in the Enterprise Manager.

- ❑ If you can't connect to remote servers via RPC, check the network protocols and ensure the RPC service is loaded and started.

- ❑ When you install SQL Server, the Microsoft Distributed Transaction Coordinator should be automatically installed.

However after you install it, it must be manually started because it is not an automatically started service.

❑ If you are running distributed transactions, the startup type should be set to Automatic.

❑ Using linked servers, you can open an OLE DB rowset on a remote server. This feature is much different than the remote servers available in previous versions of SQL Server in that it also allows you to access data from non-SQL Server data sources.

❑ OPENQUERY is a Transact-SQL statement that executes a query on a linked server. You can reference OPENQUERY as the target table on an INSERT, UPDATE, or DELETE statement.

❑ With distributed transactions, it is crucial that you are able to access data from static or dynamic data sources.

❑ There are two ways to access data: by using remote stored procedures or by using OPENROWSET to execute a query.

❑ With the addition of remote servers, you can now run stored procedures on remote databases.

❑ OPENROWSET accesses remote data using OLE DB. It is a one-time, ad hoc method. You can reference OPENROWSET as the target table in the FROM clause of a query, or as the target table of an INSERT, UPDATE, or DELETE statement.

❑ Transferring external data to the database is called *importing*. The process of importing data and objects can either be a one-time migration or a constant updating of data.

❑ Data Transformation Services (DTS) is used to transfer data across heterogeneous sources using OLE DB. This gives SQL Server access to a variety of database sources from Microsoft Excel to Oracle.

❑ Because all database sources do not have access to an OLE DB provider, Microsoft implements the OLE DB Provider for Open Database Connectivity (ODBC) driver to make any ODBC data source an OLE DB provider.

❑ The DTS wizards allow you to specify how to transform the data when you are copying to a destination table. You can use Visual Basic Scripting Edition (VBScript), Java Script (JScript), or the ActiveX scripting engine to write the data transformation scripts.

❏ DTS requires you first to use the Export wizard to export the data, and then to use the Import wizard to import the data.

❏ SQL Server's bulk copy program utility (bcp) is a command-line based program that is used to copy data into and out of SQL Server. A database administrator would usually use this to transfer large amounts of data to SQL Server from another database management system.

❏ Though the two main ways to copy data to and from SQL Server are with Data Transformation Services and bcp, you are still able to use other methods such as the INSERT, SELECT INTO, and BULK INSERT statements.

❏ Before you execute the SELECT INTO statement, make sure the user has CREATE TABLE permissions in the destination database.

❏ In order to run the BULK INSERT statement, you must be a member of the sysadmin fixed server role.

SELF TEST

The following questions will help you measure your understanding of the material presented in this chapter. Read all of the choices carefully, as there may be more than one correct answer. Choose all correct answers for each question.

1. What must be installed in order for distributed transactions to work?

   A. Microsoft Distributed Transaction Coordinator

   B. Query Analyzer

   C. Enterprise Manager

   D. Performance Monitor

2. What status occurs with a forced transaction that was previously In-Doubt? (Choose all that apply.)

   A. Prepared

   B. Forced Commit

   C. Forced Abort

   D. Preparing

3. To set up a linked server, what system stored procedures would you first have to run? (Choose all that apply.)

   A. sp_addlinkedserver

   B. sp_addalert

   C. sp_addlogin

   D. sp_addlinkedsrvlogin

4. What is the Transact-SQL statement that executes a query on a linked server? (Choose all that apply.)

   A. bcp

   B. SELECT

   C. OPENQUERY

   D. OPENROWSET

5. What checks to see if the copy can be done validly according to the transformation flags that you define in the advanced transformation properties?

   A. DTS Packager

   B. DTS Export wizard

   C. DTS Data Pump

   D. DTS Import wizard

6. What command-line–based program is used to copy data into and out of SQL Server?

   A. Data Transformation Services

   B. Bulk copy program

   C. Bulk Insert

   D. Insert Statement

7. Where is the BCP.EXE found?

   A. \WINNT

   B. The SQL Server 7.0 installation directory

   C. The BINN subdirectory in the SQL Server 7.0 installation directory

   D. The BIN subdirectory in the SQL Server 7.0 installation directory

8. In what format can bcp create and access data? (Choose all that apply.)

   A. Native
   B. Character
   C. Unicode native
   D. Unicode character

9. When should you use Unicode native and character data formats when you are using bcp?

   A. When you have a single code page
   B. When you have different code pages
   C. Any time
   D. Never

10. What tool in SQL Server 7.0 allows scripting in JScript and VBScript?

    A. SQL Transfer Manager
    B. Bulk copy program
    C. SQL Enterprise Manager
    D. Data Transformation Services

11. Which of the following is used to check whether a copy is valid according to the transformation flags that you define in the advanced transformation properties?

    A. DTS Data Pump
    B. DTS Export wizard
    C. DTS Import wizard
    D. SQL Transfer Manager

12. What statement do you use to copy data from an external OLE DB provider to SQL Server?

    A. INSERT statement
    B. UPDATE statement
    C. SELECT statement
    D. SELECT INTO statement

13. What statement do you use to create a new table based on an existing table?

    A. INSERT statement
    B. UPDATE statement
    C. SELECT INTO statement
    D. BULK INSERT

14. What tool is used to copy data into SQL Server using the functionality of the bcp utility with a Transact-SQL statement rather than from the command prompt?

    A. INSERT statement
    B. UPDATE statement
    C. SELECT INTO statement
    D. BULK INSERT

15. What tool do you use to quickly transfer data from a text file to SQL Server?

    A. BULK INSERT
    B. SQL Transfer Manager
    C. SQL Enterprise Manager
    D. Bulk copy program

A

Self Test
Answers

Chapter 1 Answers

1. What company first developed SQL?

    A. Microsoft

    B. Oracle

    C. Ingres

    D. IBM

    E. Sybase

    D. IBM first developed SQL in the 1970s.

2. With which operating systems is Microsoft SQL Server 7.0 compatible? (Choose all that apply.)

    A. Windows 95

    B. Windows 98

    C. Windows NT Workstation 4.0

    D. Windows NT Server 4.0

    E. TCP/IP

    A, B, C, D. SQL Server is compatible with all these operating systems; TCP/IP is a networking protocol, not an operating system. Note that only Windows NT Workstation 4.0 can run the full version of SQL Server; Windows NT Workstation 4.0 and Windows 95/98 can run client versions or the Desktop/Management tools.

3. How many CPUs can Microsoft SQL Server 7.0 run on without any vendor added support?

    A. 1

    B. 2

    C. 4

    D. 8

    E. 32

    D. SQL Server 7.0 can run with 4 CPUs straight out of the box.

4. With which protocols is SQL Server 7.0 compatible? (Choose all that apply.)

    A. NW Link

    B. Windows 95/98

    C. NetBEUI

    D. UNIX

    E. TCP/IP

    A, C, E. NW Link, NetBEUI, and TCP/IP are protocols, whereas Windows 95/98 and UNIX are operating systems. Remember, AppleTalk and Banyan VINES are supported as well.

5. The term used to describe the ability of SQL Server to support additional processors is:

    A. Multiprotocol support

    B. RAID

    C. SMP

    D. NW Link

    E. C2-level compliant

    C. Microsoft NT Server 4.0 supports SMP, and applications can be multithreaded. SQL Server is a multithreaded application.

6. Which form of data replication allows each site to change replicated data?

    A. Transactional

B. Snapshot

C. Picture

D. Merge

E. Duplicated Transactional Replication (DTR)

D. Merge replication enables individual sites to make changes to replicated data.

7. What is the minimum CPU required to install SQL Server? (Choose all that apply.)

A. Intel 16-bit

B. Intel 32-bit

C. DEC Alpha AXP

D. Intel 80386

E. DEC Beta BXP with 32-bit enhanced mode

B, C. Intel 32-bit and DEC Alpha AXP meet the minimum requirements to install SQL Server. The other CPUs are incompatible.

8. How can you test the SQL Server connection between a client and a server?

A. Use RAID 3.

B. Add additional CPUs.

C. Run MAKEPIPE and READPIPE commands.

D. Run Windows Diagnostics

C. The READPIPE and MAKEPIPE commands test the connection.

9. In order to execute a T-SQL command, what type of permissions are used?

A. REFERENCES

B. Statement

C. Implied

D. Object

B. Statement permissions allow you to execute a T-SQL statement.

10. What type of permission enables you to view data in a table?

A. DELETE

B. EXECUTE

C. CREATE VIEW

D. SELECT

D. SELECT permission allows you to search for and view data in a table.

11. What role allows complete control over SQL Server?

A. Syscreator

B. Sysadmin

C. Administrator

D. Domain admins

B. Sysadmin gives you total control over SQL Server.

12. What role gives the user the ability to create a database?

A. Db_creator

B. Db_owner

C. Administrator

D. Domain admins

A. The db_creator role gives the user the ability to create a database.

13. A single data element, such as Social Security Number, is considered a:

A. Row

B. Column

C. Rule

D. Cluster
   B. SSN is an example of a column.

14. The type of index that sorts pointers to the columns in a table is called:

    A. Clustered

    B. Nonclustered

    C. Triggers

    D. Sorted
       B. Nonclustered indexes sort pointers to the data stored in columns.

15. A set of precompiled programs that can be executed to make a DBA's job easier is called a:

    A. Trigger

    B. Clustered index

    C. Stored procedure

    D. Rule
       C. A stored procedure is a precompiled program that the DBA can use.

Chapter 2 Answers

1. What is the name of the column that uniquely identifies a row?

   A. Primary key

   B. Foreign key

   C. DUPLICATED KEY

   D. DEFAULT
      A. The primary key of the table uniquely identifies each row in the table.

2. What is used to make a cursor reflect modified table data?

   A. INSENSITIVE

   B. Omitting INSENSITIVE

   C. Global variable

   D. Local variable
      B. By omitting the INSENSITIVE option, a cursor will reflect table data changes.

3. What is used to make a variable local?

   A. @@

   B. @@@

   C. /*

   D. @
      D. The @ symbol is used to make a variable local.

4. To display all the rows, what would you use?

   A. SELECT emp_name

   B. SELECT ONLY

   C. DELETE *

   D. SELECT *
      D. SELECT * displays all the columns in a table. The star (*) symbol implies all columns.

5. What is used to test whether a condition is true or false?

   A. RAISERROR

   B. IF...ELSE

   C. SET

D.   DECLARE
  B. IF...ELSE is the DCL construct to test conditions.

6.   What symbols identify a comment?

A.   ??

B.   @@

C.   @

D.   /* and */
  D. A /* at the beginning, and a */ at the end, identify comments in SQL query code. Double hyphens, - - , will also work.

7.   Identify the two types of variables.

A.   Global and local

B.   Insensitive and sensitive

C.   IF and ELSE

D.   WHILE
  A. There are both global and local variables.

8.   What command removes a row?

A.   INSERT

B.   SELECT

C.   DELETE

D.   MOVE
  C. DELETE will remove a row in a table.

9.   What command will put data into a row?

A.   INSERT

B.   SELECT

C.   DELETE

D.   MOVE
  A. INSERT will put data in a row.

10.   What is used to assign a variable?

A.   MOVE

B.   INSERT

C.   DELETE

D.   SET
  D. SET assigns a variable.

11.   What is the looping construct?

A.   IF...ELSE

B.   WHILE

C.   CASE

D.   SELECT
  B. The WHILE statement causes looping.

12.   What will allow you to export and import data? (Choose all that apply.)

A.   DTS

B.   Enterprise Manager

C.   Query Analyzer

D.   SELECT
  A, B, C. DTS will export and import data. Enterprise Manager and Query Analyzer are also technically correct.

13.   What command line utility will copy data from and to a table?

A.   DTS

B.   bcp

C.   Query Analyzer

D.   INSERT
  B. bcp will copy data from and to a table.

14.   How can you get the next row in a cursor?

A. FETCH NEXT

B. FETCH LAST

C. FETCH PREVIOUS

D. FETCH ALL
   A. FETCH NEXT will get the next row in a cursor.

15. How can you get the first row in a cursor?

   A. FETCH FIRST

   B. FETCH NEXT

   C. FETCH PRIOR

   D. FETCH LAST
      A. FETCH FIRST will get the first row in a cursor.

Chapter 3 Answers

1. What syntax can you use to change the format that SQL Server presents dates to your session without impacting other users?

   A. SET DATEFORMAT

   B. CHANGE DATETIME

   C. DBCC FORMATDATE

   D. UPDATE DATESTAT
      A. SET DATEFORMAT. The SET command is used for all session-specific configuration changes.

2. What command would you execute if you wanted determine how many logical and physical reads SQL Server is performing to resolve your query?

   A. SET SHOWPLAN ON

B. SET SHOWTEXT ON

C. SET STATISTICS_IO ON

D. SET DATA ON
   C. SET STATISTICS_IO ON. The SET STATISTICS_IO ON command impacts a single session and tells SQL Server to return details about data input and output. The other commands are not valid SQL Server syntax.

3. Which of the following is not a valid SQL Server file type?

   A. Primary data file

   B. Secondary data file

   C. Primary log file

   D. Log file
      C. Primary log file. Although data is stored in primary and secondary data files, there are no primary and secondary log files.

4. How large are the data pages in SQL Server 7.0?

   A. 2KB

   B. 4KB

   C. 6KB

   D. 8KB
      D. 8KB. All earlier versions of SQL Server have used 2KB pages, but SQL Server 7.0 now uses 8KB pages.

5. Which of the following were added to SQL Server in version 7.0?

   A. 8KB pages

   B. Mixed extents

C. Native operating system file support

D. All of the above.

D. All of the above. In SQL Server 7.0 Microsoft increased the standard page size from 2KB to 8KB. One impact of this was that extents became 64KB in size. Allocating those to a single table proved inefficient so mixed extents were added as well. Microsoft also eliminated the need for disk devices by providing support for native operating system files for database objects.

6. Which of the following is the correct term for groups of data files that can be used to strategically locate database objects?

A. Filegroups

B. Datagroups

C. Clusters

D. SMP support

A. Filegroups. Filegroups are groups of SQL Server data files that can be used to distribute database objects for best efficiency. Clusters refer to a grouping of servers. SMP support refers to support for multiple processors on a server and there are no datagroups within SQL Server.

7. Which of the following is *not* a performance trend within SQL Server 7.0?

A. Transaction log writes are sequential and thus benefit from being on an isolated device to minimize physical movement of read and write heads.

B. Data files benefit from being spread across multiple physical disks.

C. RAID 5 provides the most efficient fault tolerance for transaction logs.

D. RAID 5 provides the most efficient fault tolerance for data files.

C. RAID 5 provides the most efficient fault tolerance for transaction logs. Transaction log writes are sequential and benefit from minimizing the movement of the read and write heads. For fault tolerance, transaction logs function best using disk mirroring (RAID 1), whereas RAID 5 is best for the remainder of the database.

8. How many fixed-length fields are in the following table?

```
CREATE TABLE testtable
(
lname        varchar(25),
fname        char(15) NULL,
ssnum        char(15) NOT NULL,
score int
)
```

A. 1

B. 2

C. 3

D. 4

B. 2. The score column is always 4 bytes in length as an integer data type and the ssnum column is always 15 bytes in length. The lname column is defined as variable character, so it will vary in size. The fname column allows NULLS, which by default makes it variable length.

9. Which of the following is the correct syntax for creating a user-defined data type?

   A. Create Type

   B. Create Data type

   C. sp_addtype

   D. sp_addatatype
      C. sp_addtype. The sp_addtype command is used to create a user-defined data type that is based upon system-defined data types.

10. Which of the following is the correct syntax for creating a new table?

    A. CREATE TABLE

    B. Disk Init

    C. sp_createtable

    D. sp_addtable
       A. CREATE TABLE. The CREATE TABLE command is used to create a new table. You must define the columns and placement for the table.

11. What command would you execute to determine if the SQL Server database engine was using the index that you created?

    A. SET SHOWPLAN_TEXT ON

    B. SET SHOWINDEX ON

    C. SET SHOWPLAN_TEXT OFF

    D. SET INDEXUSAGE
       A. SET SHOWPLAN_TEXT ON. By executing this command, your session will no longer execute your SQL commands. It will instead return the plan that SQL would use to perform the stated task.

12. What tool would you use if you want to see a graphical representation of what indexes SQL Server would use to resolve a query?

    A. SQL Server Profiler

    B. SQL Server Query Analyzer

    C. Enterprise Manager

    D. Client Network Utility
       B. SQL Server Query Analyzer. By using the graphical showplan portion of the SQL Query Analyzer, you have the ability to see a graphical diagram of what indexes are being used to execute a SQL command.

13. What command would you execute to determine if your database is suffering from excessive disk fragmentation?

    A. SET SHOWPLAN_TEXT ON

    B. SET SHOWFRAGMENTATION ON

    C. DBCC SHOWCONTIG

    D. DBCC SHOWFRAGMENTS
       C. DBCC SHOWCONTIG. The DBCC SHOWCONTIG command returns information such as the number of pages and extent reads required and the scan density of these reads.

14. What command can you issue to update information about the distribution of key

values for one or more indexes in the specified table?

A. DBCC SHOWINDEX

B. DBCC REINDEX

C. UPDATE INDEX

D. UPDATE STATISTICS
   D. UPDATE STATISTICS. The UPDATE STATISTICS command will rebuild the statistics page for one or more indexes. By default, SQL Server 7.0 will automatically update these pages if the UPDATE STATISTICS command is run with a NORECOMPUTE command.

15. What tool would you use to trap the activity between clients and a SQL Server database to flat files?

A. SQL Server Profiler

B. SQL Server Query Analyzer

C. Enterprise Manager

D. Client Network Utility
   A. SQL Server Profiler. By using the SQL Server Profiler, all client activity can be trapped to a flat file or a to a SQL Server database. These files can be processed against the database for testing purposes, if desired.

Chapter 4 Answers

1. Which normal form requires that a query be able to reassemble a table that was divided into multiple tables for normalization purposes?

A. First normal form

B. Second normal form

C. Third normal form

D. Fourth normal form

E. Fifth normal form
   E. Fifth normal form. The fifth normal form requires that a table that has been divided into multiple tables must be capable of being reconstructed to its exact original structure by one or more joins.

2. Which normal form specifies that non-key fields in a table must relate to the key field(s) in the table?

A. First normal form

B. Second normal form

C. Third normal form

D. Fourth normal form

E. Fifth normal form
   B. Second normal form. The second normal form requires all non-key fields in a table must be related to the key field. The table cannot contain information that is not related to the key fields.

3. Which normal form specifies that tables must be flat and that each row must contain only one set of values?

A. First normal form

B. Second normal form

C. Third normal form

D. Fourth normal form

E.   Fifth normal form
A. First normal form. The first normal form dictates that tables must be flat. This means that each row of the table can contain only one set of data values. Each data value must be stored in its own column, rather than an item in the database containing a list of values for a specific piece of information.

4.   Which normal form requires related data entities to be included in one table?

A.   First normal form

B.   Second normal form

C.   Third normal form

D.   Fourth normal form

E.   Fifth normal form
D. Fourth normal form. The fourth normal form requires that only related data entities be included in a single table and that tables may not contain data related to more than one data entity when many to one relationships exist among the entities.

5.   Which form dictates that no column in a normalized table can be dependent upon a non-key column in the table?

A.   First normal form

B.   Second normal form

C.   Third normal form

D.   Fourth normal form

E.   Fifth normal form
C. Third normal form. The third normal form dictates that that any column that is not a key column can not be dependent upon another non-key column.

6.   Which of the following is not a benefit of narrow normalized tables?

A.   Reduces the amount of data returned for simple queries

B.   Improved performance of range searches due to clustered indexes

C.   Improved performance from multitable joins

D.   Lower overhead by reducing the number of indexes in each table
C. Improved performance from multitable joins. Narrow tables improve performance by reducing the number of nonclustered indexes per table while benefiting from the clustered indexes that physically sort the data in the most logical manner for returning ranges of data. By returning fewer columns for simple queries, database performance is improved.

7.   Which of the following is not a good reason to denormalize your database schema?

A.   To reduce the number of joins required to satisfy frequent queries

B.   To benefit a decision support database with standard queries

C.   To store the results of frequently performed arithmetic calculations

D. To reduce overhead by decreasing the number of tables

D. To reduce overhead by decreasing the number of tables. Generally SQL Server performs better with a larger number of narrow tables. Combining tables to reduce overhead does not work unless it is designed to meet one of the options in A, B, or C.

8. When designing your table, you specify a PRIMARY KEY constraint on the empl_id column. Which of the following is this an example of?

A. Entity integrity

B. Domain integrity

C. Referential integrity

D. User-defined integrity

A. Entity integrity. By specifying the empl_id column as the primary key, you have assured that each row can be uniquely identified in the database, and thus is an identifiable entity.

9. When designing the schedule table, you specify the empl_id column as a foreign key related to the employee table. What type of integrity are you building into your database?

A. Entity integrity

B. Domain integrity

C. Referential integrity

D. User-defined integrity

C. Referential integrity. By setting the foreign key constraint and relating it to the employee table you have made

sure that an ID that doesn't match an employee cannot be entered. In addition, an employee cannot be removed from the system if they are currently scheduled to work.

10. When designing our database, we set a trigger to make sure that if the country code is set to US, the Zip1 column contains five numeric characters. What type of integrity have you created?

A. Entity integrity

B. Domain integrity

C. Referential integrity

D. User-defined integrity

D. User-defined integrity. You have applied a business rule to your database design. This is an example of user-defined integrity.

11. When designing a table, you add a check constraint to verify that the employee ID contains nine characters and has valid characters in each position. What type of integrity are you enforcing?

A. Entity integrity

B. Domain integrity

C. Referential integrity

D. User-defined integrity

B. Domain integrity. Your table is forcing users to put valid information in the employee ID column.

12. What is the best method to enforce uniqueness for values being placed into a non-key column?

A. Create a Unique Index on the field

B. Set a UNIQUE constraint

C. Set a PRIMARY KEY constraint

D. Set a FOREIGN KEY constraint

B. Set a UNIQUE constraint. A FOREIGN KEY constraint would not enforce uniqueness. A PRIMARY KEY constraint enforces uniqueness but can only be used on one column or group of columns that have been identified as the key. A unique index should only be used on records that have uniqueness as a characteristic, not to enforce it.

13. You are migrating your application from Microsoft Access to SQL Server 7.0. The Access database has a column with a *counter* data type that automatically assigns a member number (by adding one to the member number of the last row added) when records are added to the member table. What data type and property can accomplish the same function in SQL Server?

A. Varchar(10) with the count property

B. Varchar(10) with the IDENTITY property

C. Int with the count property

D. Int with the IDENTITY property

D. Int with the IDENTITY property. There is not a count property in SQL Server. The IDENTITY property can be applied to a variety of numeric data types. When the table is created or altered, you can specify the value for the first record, as well as the value to add for each successive record.

14. You are creating a database to support a Human Resources application. Your users explain that when the support staff first enters records, they do not have a way to enter the starting salary. You know that you don't want NULLs in this field and decide that because it is a money data type, you will enter 0 if a value is not specified. What is the recommended method to implement this solution?

A. Modify the application to enter a 0 if the user doesn't set a value

B. Create a Default object and bind it to the money data type

C. Set a DEFAULT definition of 0 for the column

D. Do nothing, the money data type defaults to 0

C. Set a DEFAULT definition of 0 for the column. There is not a default for the money data type. A Default object can only be bound to a column or a user-defined data type, not a system-defined data type like money. Modifying the application only works if no other app is ever used to add records to the table.

15. Which of the following is not a good use of a trigger?

A. Verify that the data in the state column matches the data in the area code column.

B. Verify that the data entered for starting salary falls within the range stored in another table for this job class.

C. Roll back the deletion of a customer record if a search of the orders table shows they have placed an order in the past 90 days.

D. Roll back an update to the salary field if it is increasing by more than 20 percent
A. Verify that the data in the state column matches the data in the area code column. A CHECK constraint will compare columns in a table more efficiently. Triggers should be used if another table needs to be referenced or if there is a need to compare the new information to the old information in a row.

Chapter 5 Answers

1. What is the term for SQL Server accessing data if it does not use an index?

   A. Direct read

   B. Page scan

   C. Table scan

   D. Page read
   C. Table scan. When SQL Server performs a table scan, it reads sequentially from the beginning of the data to the end.

2. What option under All Tasks on the shortcut menu in the Enterprise Manager

can you use to determine what indexes exist on a table?

   A. View Indexes

   B. Manage Indexes

   C. Table Properties

   D. Index Properties
   B. Manage Indexes is the option that you can use to determine what indexes exist on a table.

3. Which of the following wizards does SQL Server 7.0 offer to help you identify changes to your indexes that might help performance?

   A. Create Index Wizard

   B. Delete Index Wizard

   C. Database Maintenance Plan Wizard

   D. Index Tuning Wizard
   D. Index Tuning Wizard. There is no Delete Index Wizard. The Database Maintenance Plan Wizard is used to create a maintenance schedule for backups, DBCC, and commands. The Create Index Wizard is used for developing new indexes. Only the Index Tuning Wizard analyzes user activity and recommends changes.

4. Which of the following SQL Server 7.0 tools provides an input file to the SQL Server Index Tuning Wizard?

   A. SQL Query Analyzer

   B. Enterprise Manager

   C. SQL Server Profiler

D. SQL Server Service Manager
C. SQL Server Profiler. The SQL
Server Profiler creates a script that
tracks user activity. The Index Tuning
Wizard uses this file to determine
what indexes are needed most.

5. Which of the following types of indexes
always sort the data rows?

A. Clustered indexes

B. Nonclustered indexes

C. Composite indexes

D. Unique indexes
A. Clustered indexes. Nonclustered
indexes never sort the data. Unique
and composite indexes can be
clustered or nonclustered (sorted or
not sorted).

6. Which of the following are included in the
leaf pages of a clustered index?

A. Pointers to disk location

B. Pointers to the clustered key

C. Data rows

D. All of the above
C. Data rows. The leaf pages of a
clustered index are the data rows.
There are no pointers in the leaf page
of a clustered index.

7. How many clustered indexes are allowed
on a table?

A. One

B. 249

C. 250

D. There is no limit
A. One. When a clustered index is
created, the data is physically sorted. It
can only be sorted in one order.

8. Which of the following columns is a good
candidate for a clustered index?

A. A column that must contain 1 of 50
valid values

B. A column that is frequently queried
for a serial range of values

C. A column that is frequently used in
the order by portion of a query

D. All of the above
D. All of the above. Each of these
columns could be a very good
candidate for a clustered index.

9. How much additional space is needed to
create a clustered index on a table?

A. None, the clustered index merely
rearranges data.

B. 10 percent more space than the
current space consumed by the data.

C. 50 percent more space than the
current space consumed by the data.

D. 120 percent more space than the
current space consumed by the data.
D. 120 percent. During the process of
creating a clustered index, SQL Server
creates a duplicate copy of the table.
There is additional overhead during
the process.

10. Which of the following is found in the
row locator of a nonclustered index if the
table has a clustered index?

A. The data row

B. A pointer to the data row

C. The clustered index key

D. None of the above
   C. The clustered index key. If a clustered index exists on the table, the index includes the nonclustered index key and the clustered index key.

11. Which of the following is found in the row locator of a nonclustered index if the table does not have a clustered index?

   A. The data row

   B. A pointer to the data row

   C. The clustered index key

   D. None of the above
      B. A pointer to the data row. If a clustered index does not exist on the table, the nonclustered index includes the nonclustered key value and a pointer to the data row.

12. What is the maximum number of columns that can be included in a composite index?

   A. 2

   B. 4

   C. 8

   D. 16
      D. 16. A composite index includes between 2 and 16 columns.

13. Which of the following is not one of the types of nodes in a SQL Server index?

   A. Home node

B. Root node

C. Intermediate node

D. Leaf node
   A. Home node. SQL Server indexes have three types of nodes. The top node is called the root node, the bottom nodes are called leaf nodes, and all other node levels are called intermediate nodes.

14. What is the maximum size allowed for the key in a SQL Server index?

   A. 100 bytes

   B. 300 bytes

   C. 900 bytes

   D. None of the above
      C. 900 bytes. SQL Server 7.0 limits the size of keys to 900 bytes, no matter how many or how few columns are included in the key.

15. If you execute the CREATE INDEX command with the UNIQUE parameter, what happens if rows with duplicate keys exist?

   A. The command terminates.

   B. Nothing, if the IGNORE_DUP_KEY parameter is included.

   C. The command executes and returns a list of duplicate rows.

   D. The command executes.
      A. The command terminates. A unique index cannot be created if rows with duplicate keys exist.

16. Which of the following is not true if the CREATE INDEX command is run with a FILLFACTOR of 100 percent?

    A. Inserts and updates are slowed down.

    B. The index consumes less space.

    C. Database queries run faster.

    D. None of the above
       D. None of the above. If the FILLFACTOR is set to 100, the index consumes the minimum number of pages possible. This setting helps query performance, but hurts inserts and updates (due to page splits).

17. Which of the following is true when the IGNORE_DUP_KEY parameter is applied to an index ?

    A. If duplicate rows exist when the index is created, they are ignored.

    B. If a transaction inserts rows that would duplicate an existing key, the rows are inserted.

    C. If a transaction inserts rows that would duplicate an existing key, those rows are rejected but the transaction completes.

    D. None of the above
       C. If a transaction inserts rows that would duplicate an existing key, those rows are rejected, but the transaction completes. A unique index cannot be created if duplicate keys exist. If a unique index exists, rows that would duplicate an existing key cannot be inserted.

Chapter 6 Answers

1. Which of the following could have an impact upon the query execution plan determined by SQL Server? (Choose all that apply.)

    A. Removing a clustered index

    B. Querying the table from an administrative account

    C. Adding 10,000 records to a 100 record table

    D. Reducing the number of unique values in a column while keeping the number of rows constant
       A, C, D. Removing a clustered index; Adding 10,000 records to a 100 record table; Reducing the number of unique values in a column while keeping the number of rows constant. Even an administrator cannot directly define the query execution plan.

2. When using the Query Analyzer, you get a warning that the statistics are out of date. Which of the following could fix this? (Choose all that apply.)

    A. DBCC SHOW_STATISTICS

    B. DROP STATISTICS on the table, then CREATE STATISTICS

    C. Drop the index, then create the index

    D. UPDATE STATISTICS
       B, C, D. DROP STATISTICS on the table; then CREATE STATISTICS; Drop the index; then create the index; UPDATE STATISTICS. Using

SHOW_STATITICS you can report on statistics, but not update them. Statistics are automatically created when an index is created.

3. You execute the following query:
SELECT *table1.name, table2.number*
FROM table1 INNER JOIN table2 ON
table1.keyfield = table2.keyfield ORDER BY
name.
Which of the following joins would SQL Server most likely use if both tables had 5,000,000 rows, and *keyfield* was indexed in both tables?

A. Nested loop

B. Hash

C. Build input

D. Merge
D. Merge. Nested loop and hash joins are both inefficient choices when neither table is relatively small.

4. What is an advantage of using JOIN (the new syntax) instead of WHERE (the old syntax) to define your joins? (Choose all that apply.)

A. The WHERE syntax may not be supported in future versions of SQL Server.

B. More database vendors support the JOIN syntax.

C. It is not possible to represent a right outer join using the WHERE syntax.

D. It is easier to distinguish between joins and filter criteria.
A, B, D. The WHERE syntax may

not be supported in future versions of SQL Server; More database vendors support the JOIN syntax; It is easier to distinguish between joins and filter criteria. The right outer join can be represented in the WHERE statement by using =*.

5. Using the pubs database, you want to view all the authors and titles. You use the following query:
SELECT *authors.au_lname,*
authors.au_fname, titleauthor.title_id
FROM authors, titleauthor
You receive far too many rows. What went wrong?

A. No join was specified, so a cross join was implied.

B. You didn't include the primary keys in the SELECT clause.

C. A foreign key needs to be created for the titleauthor table.

D. There is nothing wrong with the query.
A. No join was specified, so a cross join was implied. When no join is specified, you get a cross join, or Cartesian product, which returns every possible match between the two tables, whether they match or not.

6. Can two fields with different data types be joined?

A. They cannot be joined with any join.

B. They can only be joined with a cross join.

C. If the field can be implicitly converted, they can be joined.

D. The fields will not be implicitly converted, but if the developer CASTs or CONVERTs one of the fields, they can be joined.

C. If the field can be implicitly converted, they can be joined. It is not necessary for the developer to convert these fields, as long as SQL Server can perform a conversion between the field types.

7. What would be the caption of the second field in the following UNION query: *SELECT CompanyName, ShipperID, Phone FROM Shippers UNION SELECT CompanyName, SupplierID AS ID, Phone.*

A. Suppliers

B. ShipperID

C. SupplierID

D. ID

B. ShipperID. When using the UNION operator, the names of all of the fields are as defined in the first SELECT statement, no matter how they are defined in subsequent SELECT statements.

8. How do you define local and global temporary tables when using SELECT INTO?

A. One dollar sign for a local temporary table, two number signs for a dollar temporary table

B. One dollar sign for a global temporary table, two number signs for a dollar temporary table

C. One number sign for a local temporary table, two number signs for a global temporary table

D. One number sign for a global temporary table, two number signs for a local temporary table

C. One number sign for a local temporary table, two number signs for a global temporary table. It is not legal to define a table name starting with a dollar sign.

9. Assuming that the select into/bulkcopy option is set, which of the following must also be true for a SELECT INTO statement to successfully create a new permanent table? (Choose all that apply.)

A. The source and destination tables must have the same number of fields.

B. In the database, the user must have the permission CREATE TABLE.

C. There can be no computed fields in the SELECT list.

D. All fields in the SELECT list must be unique.

B, D. In the database, the user must have the permission CREATE TABLE. All fields in the SELECT list must be unique. Computed fields in the SELECT list are resolved and populated into the new table as values.

10. If you look at a query and see a < as the join operator, which of the following is most likely?

    A. The developer was using a right outer join.

    B. The developer was using a self-join.

    C. The developer was using a cross join.

    D. The developer was using a full outer join.
    B. The developer was using a self-join. Inequalities are most frequently used with self-joins. This is because when you join a table to itself, the content would often be inadvertently retrieved twice if you used an equals operator.

11. Which clauses can have a subquery? (Choose all that apply.)

    A. HAVING

    B. GROUP BY

    C. SUMMARIZE

    D. WHERE
    A, D. HAVING, WHERE. Although you can include the subquery in the HAVING or WHERE clause, if you have a choice between these two options, you should use the WHERE clause.

12. How many rows can be returned by a subquery without generating an error?

    A. Only one

    B. Only one, unless preceded by the ANY, ALL, EXISTS, or IN operators

    C. Unlimited

    D. Unlimited, unless preceded by the ANY, ALL, EXISTS, or IN operators
    B. Only one, unless preceded by the ANY, ALL, EXISTS or IN operators. Unless you are using one of these operators, the subquery should retrieve a single value to be evaluated in the parent query.

13. How many levels deep can subqueries be nested?

    A. Up to 32, memory permitting

    B. Up to 16, memory permitting

    C. Up to 8, memory permitting

    D. Up to 4, memory permitting

    E. Up to 2, memory permitting
    A. Up to 32, memory permitting. Although subqueries nested this level would be difficult to debug, they are supported according to Microsoft's specifications.

14. Which of the following is true for a correlated subquery? (Choose all that apply.)

    A. The subquery is evaluated once.

    B. The subquery is evaluated multiple times.

    C. The subquery can refer to a field in the parent query.

    D. The subquery cannot refer to a field in the parent query.
    B, C. The subquery is evaluated multiple times. The subquery can refer to a field in the parent query. Not only can a correlated subquery refer to a field in the parent query, it is

this act of referring to the parent which makes it a correlated subquery.

15. How many fields can be returned by a subquery?

    A. One, always

    B. One, unless preceded by the EXISTS clause

    C. The same number of fields as the outer query, always

    D. The same number of fields as the outer query, unless preceded by the EXISTS clause

    B. One, unless preceded by the EXISTS clause. The EXISTS operator doesn't care how many fields are returned, because it only reports the presence or absence of entire rows.

16. Which of the following can be successfully excluded from an INSERT statement? (Choose all that apply.)

    A. An identity column that is a primary key

    B. A uniqueidentifier column that is a primary key

    C. A NOT NULL field with no default

    D. A NOT NULL field with a default

    A, D. An identity column that is a primary key; A NOT NULL field with a default. Unlike identity columns, uniqueidentifiers are not automatically populated when a row is created.

17. If you run the query, DELETE FROM Director, when the Name field of the Director table is used as a foreign key constraint by the Films table, what would happen?

    A. All rows would be deleted from Director and no rows would be deleted from Films.

    B. All rows would be deleted from Director and all referenced rows would be deleted from Films.

    C. No rows would be deleted from Director or from Films.

    D. The rows in Director that were not referenced by Films would be deleted.

    C. No rows would be deleted from Director or from Films. When a DELETE operation would violate a constraint or a trigger, an error is generated, and the entire DELETE operation is cancelled.

18. Which of the following is guaranteed to modify, at most, one record?

    A. UPDATE...WHERE

    B. UPDATE...WHERE CURRENT OF

    C. UPDATE FIRST...WHERE

    D. UPDATE...WHERE ROWCOUNT=1

    B. UPDATE...WHERE CURRENT OF. The CURRENT OF command is used with a cursor to modify a single record. Option A will modify all records that meet the WHERE criteria, while the constructs in Options C and D are fictional.

19. You have confirmed that the Microsoft Search service is running, and you have used the Full-Text Indexing Wizard to create a full-text index. However, you have not yet scheduled the population of this full-text index. What will you get when you run a query using CONTAINS?

   A. You will receive the following warning: "Cannot use a CONTAINS or FREETEXT predicate on table 'Categories' because it is not full-text indexed."

   B. The query will execute, automatically creating the indexes on an as-needed basis.

   C. The CONTAINS operator will automatically be converted to a LIKE command.

   D. The query will execute, but return no data.
   D. The query will execute, but return no data. If you attempt to use CONTAINS or FREETEXT on a table without creating the index, you will receive an error similar to that in answer B.

20. What is an advantage of FREETEXTTABLE over CONTAINSTABLE?

   A. FREETEXTTABLE be used to rank the results by how well they match.

   B. FREETEXTTABLE can automatically parse the search parameter into words and phrases to be found in the destination table.

   C. FREETEXTTABLE doesn't require Microsoft Search service to be running.

   D. FREETEXTTABLE allows you to search for tense variants of nouns and verbs.
   B. FREETEXTTABLE can automatically parse the search parameter into words and phrases to be found in the destination table. Both commands return a MATCH column, and they both require the search service to be active.

Chapter 7 Answers

1. What type of aggregate function produces a single value for each column found in the select list?

   A. Scalar

   B. Vector

   C. Singular

   D. Modular
   A. Scalar. Scalar aggregates are aggregate functions that provide a single value per column.

2. Which data type is not valid for SUM and AVG?

   A. Int

   B. Smallint

   C. Text

   D. Tinyint
   C. Text. Text data is not valid for

SUM and AVG, but can be used with COUNT, MAX, and MIN.

3. What is the safest and easiest way to return a full row count from a table without having to worry about null values?

A. COUNT ALL

B. COUNT(*)

C. COUNT (NOT NULL)

D. COUNT(ALL)
B. COUNT(*). COUNT(*) eliminates worrying about null values because it counts all rows, including those with null values.

4. What operator can be used with a column in order to eliminate duplicate values?

A. UNIQUE

B. NOMATCH

C. ALL UNIQUE

D. DISTINCT
D. DISTINCT. DISTINCT is used to eliminate duplicate values within the results set.

5. Which clause can you use to refer to the rows that are being returned by the GROUP BY clause?

A. WHERE

B. GROUP WHERE

C. HAVING

D. You can't refer to the GROUP BY rows
C. HAVING. The HAVING clause can be used to filter the rows that are being returned by the GROUP BY clause.

6. How many columns or expressions can be used in the GROUP BY clause if you plan to use CUBE or ROLLUP?

A. 10

B. 20

C. 15

D. No limit.
A. 10. Only 10 expressions are allowed.

7. What is the purpose of the ALL statement that contains a GROUP BY clause?

A. ALL nullifies the use of a WHERE clause.

B. ALL by passes the HAVING statement

C. ALL returns the number of rows in a table.

D. ALL returns all rows produced by the GROUP BY, ignoring the WHERE clause.
D. ALL returns all rows produced by the GROUP BY, ignoring the WHERE clause.

8. Jennifer is trying to group date values by the month; however, the value she has to work with is a whole date value. What function can Jennifer use to pull out the month?

A. DateMonth( )

B. Month( )

C. ReturnMonth( )

D. GetMonth( )
   B. Month( ). Use the Month function to group the dates based on the month.

9. How many conditions does HAVING support?

   A. 256

   B. 10

   C. 128

   D. 15
      C. 128. You can use 128 conditions in a HAVING clause.

10. Which aggregate can be used to produce super-aggregate rows that summarize the data being returned by the GROUP BY clause?

   A. CUBED

   B. ROLLED

   C. SUMMARIZE

   D. CUBE
      D. CUBE. CUBE produces super-aggregate rows, which are summaries of the information returned by the GROUP BY clause.

11. Which aggregate functions are supported by COMPUTE BY?

   A. AVG, MIN, MAX, and SUM

   B. COUNT, MIN, MAX, and SUM

   C. AVG, COUNT, MIN, MAX

   D. AVG, COUNT, MIN, MAX, and SUM
      D. AVG, COUNT, MIN, MAX, and SUM are supported by COMPUTE BY.

12. Which statement best explains the rules about the field list in the COMPUTE BY clause?

   A. You must start with the same expression as the SELECT clause.

   B. You must start with the same expression as the SELECT clause, the remaining columns maybe in any order you desire.

   C. You must start with the same expression as the SELECT clause, and the remaining columns must be identical to or a subset of the columns found in the SELECT list.

   D. You must start with the same expression as the SELECT clause, and must include all columns found in the SELECT list.
      C. You must start with the same expression as the SELECT clause, and the remaining columns must be identical to or a subset of the columns found in the select list.

13. When you add or average integer data in SQL Server, what type of value is returned?

   A. Int

   B. Tinyint

   C. LargeInt

   D. Smallint
      A. Int. Any integer value will be returned as int.

14. Which clause can be used to limit the number of rows being returned in a results set?

    A. TOP *n*

    B. COUNT *n*

    C. RETURN *n*

    D. SELECT *n*

    A. TOP *n*. Use TOP *n* to return a specified number of rows.

15. Tiffany has written the following SQL statement:

    SELECT Customers.CustomerID, Customers.Country, Customers.Region
    FROM Customers
    GROUP BY Customers.Region, Customers.Country
    ORDER BY Region, Country

    Why will this statement return an error?

    A. The ORDER BY clause doesn't specify the table names for the Region and Country columns.

    B. Her use of the CustomerID column will generate an error. CustomerID must either have an aggregate function applied to it in the SELECT clause, or the CustomerID must be part of the column list in the GROUP BY clause.

    C. The GROUP BY clause will generate an error because you cannot group by more than one column.

    D. The GROUP BY clause will generate an error because the order of fields or expressions in the GROUP BY must match the order used in the SELECT clause.

    B. Her use of the CustomerID column will generate an error. CustomerID must either have an aggregate function applied to it in the SELECT clause, or the CustomerID must be part of the column list in the GROUP BY clause.

Chapter 8 Answers

1. What properties do transactions consist of? (Choose all that apply.)

   A. Atomicity

   B. Consistency

   C. Isolation

   D. Durability

   A, B, C, D. Transactions consist of the atomicity, consistency, isolation, and durability properties. These properties are known as the ACID properties.

2. What do you use to prevent concurrent users from reading data that has been changed but not yet committed?

   A. Keys

   B. Locks

   C. Switches

   D. Holds

   B. You use locks to prevent concurrent users from reading data that has been changed but not yet committed. Locks are used to enforce logical consistency.

3. What stored procedures can you use to display locking information? (Choose all that apply.)

   A. sp_lock

   B. sp_indexes

   C. sp_processinfo

   D. sp_monitor
   A, C. You can use sp_lock and sp_processinfo to display locking information.

4. What are the types of transactions? (Choose all that apply.)

   A. Explicit

   B. Implicit

   C. Default

   D. Autocommit
   A, B, D. Explicit, implicit, and autocommit are types of transactions.

5. How do you end an explicit transaction? (Choose all that apply.)

   A. BEGIN TRAN

   B. COMMIT TRANSACTION

   C. BEGIN TRANSACTION

   D. COMMIT TRAN
   B, D. You use COMMIT TRAN or COMMIT TRANSACTION to end an explicit transaction. COMMIT TRAN and COMMIT TRANSACTION are also used to end any transaction.

6. How do you cancel a transaction? (Choose all that apply.)

   A. BEGIN TRAN

   B. ROLLBACK WORK

   C. ROLLBACK TRANSACTION

   D. COMMIT TRAN
   B, C. You use ROLLBACK WORK or ROLLBACK TRANSACTION to cancel a transaction.

7. How do you enable implicit transactions?

   A. BEGIN TRAN

   B. BEGIN TRANSACTION

   C. SET IMPLICIT_TRANSACTIONS ON

   D. SET IMPLICIT_TRANSACTIONS OFF
   C. You use SET IMPLICIT_TRANSACTIONS ON to enable implicit transactions.

8. How do you start an explicit transaction? (Choose all that apply.)

   A. BEGIN TRAN

   B. COMMIT TRANSACTION

   C. BEGIN TRANSACTION

   D. COMMIT TRAN
   A, C. You use BEGIN TRAN or BEGIN TRANSACTION to start an explicit transaction. BEGIN TRAN and BEGIN TRANSACTION are also used to start any transaction.

9. What is the least concurrent transaction isolation level?

   A. Read committed

   B. Read uncommitted

C. Repeatable read

D. Serializable
D. Serializable is the least concurrent transaction isolation level.

10. What are the different transaction isolation levels available on SQL Server 7.0? (Choose all that apply.)

A. Read committed

B. Read uncommitted

C. Repeatable read

D. Serializable
A, B, C, D. Read committed, read uncommitted, repeatable read, and serializable are the different transaction levels available on SQL Server 7.0.

11. How do you minimize the transaction duration? (Choose all that apply.)

A. Use exclusive locks

B. Committing changes quicker

C. Use parameter arrays

D. Use statement batches
B, C, D. Committing changes quicker, using parameter arrays, and using statement batches help you minimize the transaction duration.

12. What option do you set to enable distributed transactions for a session?

A. BEGIN TRANSACTION

B. SET REMOTE_PROC_ TRANSACTIONS

C. BEGIN DISTRIBUTED TRANSACTIONS

D. SET IMPLICIT_TRANSACTIONS ON
B. You set the SET REMOTE_PROC_TRANSACTION option to enable distributed transactions for a session.

13. What type of server allows you to access data from any OLE DB data source, such as Microsoft Access and Oracle?

A. Remote servers

B. Dynamic servers

C. Linked servers

D. Resident servers
C. Linked servers allow you to access data from any OLE DB data source, such as Microsoft Access and Oracle.

14. What are the lock types? (Choose all that apply.)

A. Shared locks

B. Update locks

C. Exclusive locks

D. Intent locks
A, B, C, D. Shared, update, exclusive, and intent locks are the different types of locks available on SQL Server 7.0.

15. What are most locks incompatible with?

A. Shared locks

B. Update locks

C. Exclusive locks

D. Intent Exclusive locks
C. Most locks are incompatible with exclusive locks.

16. What are the types of optimistic locking available on SQL Server 7.0? (Choose all that apply.)

    A. Optimistic with error checking

    B. Optimistic with values

    C. Optimistic with row versioning

    D. Optimistic with table versioning
       B, C. Optimistic with values and optimistic with row versioning are the types of optimistic locking available on SQL Server 7.0.

17. What is the SQL Server global variable that is used to return the number of active connections for the current connection?

    A. @@IDENTITY

    B. @@CONNECTIONS

    C. @@TRANCOUNT

    D. @@MAX_CONNECTIONS
       C. @@TRANCOUNT is the SQL Server global variable that is used to return the number of active connections for the current connection.

18. What setting sets a time limit on how long a statement will wait for a blocked resource?

    A. LOCK_TIMEOUT

    B. LOCK_REQUEST

    C. LOCK_TIME

    D. LOCK_RELEASE
       A. LOCK_TIMEOUT is the setting that sets a time limit on how long a statement will wait for a blocked resource.

Chapter 9 Answers

1. Which of the following definitions best describes a view?

    A. A copy in the database of existing data

    B. A simulated table that presents existing table data in a new way

    C. A group of users that have permissions on a table

    D. A group of precompiled Transact-SQL statements
       B. A simulated table that presents existing table data in a new way. "A group of precompiled Transact-SQL statements" describes a stored procedure, which is discussed in a later chapter.

2. How many columns can a view have?

    A. 1024

    B. 520

    C. Limited only by memory and storage constraints

    D. Defined using the sp_maxcolumns stored procedure
       A. 1024. A view can have up to 1024 columns. Previous versions of SQL server had a limit of 520 columns.

3. Which of the following are advantages of using views? (Choose all that apply.)

A. To exclude certain rows from certain users

B. To combine partitioned data into a single view for UPDATE queries, when all of the data resides on a local server

C. To provide a data definition that can be used by bcp

D. To combine partitioned data into a single view for SELECT queries when some of the data resides on a remote server

A, C, D. With a view, you can exclude certain rows from certain users, provide a data definition that can be used by bcp, and combine partitioned data into a single view for SELECT queries when some of the data resides on a remote server. You can use a view with a union to combine locally partitioned data with remote data, but this data could only be updated through the base tables themselves.

4. In which table is the entire definition of the view stored?

A. syscolumns

B. sysdepends

C. syscomments

D. sysobjects

C. syscomments. However, if WITH ENCRYPTION is used, then the definition of the view can not be retrieved, even by the creator of the object.

5. When assigning security, what do views support that column-based security doesn't? (Choose all that apply.)

A. Renaming of columns to be more readable

B. Assignment of groups

C. Support of the SELECT * command

D. Creation of user-based legal field ranges

A, C, D. Views support renaming of columns to be more readable, the SELECT * command, and creation of user-based legal field ranges. Groups are supported when using column-based security. (You can define different default values based upon the user at the table level, but by using rules, not column-based security.)

6. Which of the following could be the first line of a View definition? (Choose all that apply.)

A. SELECT Employees.EmployeeID, Employees.LastName, EmployeeTerritories.EmployeeID, EmployeeTerritories.TerritoryID

B. SELECT Employees.EmployeeID, Employees.LastName, EmployeeTerritories.EmployeeID as EmpID, EmployeeTerritories.TerritoryID

C. SELECT Employees.EmployeeID as EmpID , Employees.LastName, EmployeeTerritories.EmployeeID as TerID, EmployeeTerritories.TerritoryID

D. SELECT INTO
Employees.EmployeeID,
Employees.LastName,
EmployeeTerritories.EmployeeID as
EmpID,
EmployeeTerritories.TerritoryID
B, C. When there are two fields with
the same name, one of them must be
provided with an alias. The INTO
command is never permitted in views.

7. Which of the following best describes the
function of the WITH ENCRYPTION
option?

A. The data in the view will be encrypted
so it can't be intercepted over the
network.

B. The definition of the view will be
encrypted as it is stored in the system
tables.

C. The view will only be available to
users with an encrypted connection.

D. The specified column in the view will
be encrypted so it can't be intercepted
over the network.
B. The definition of the view will be
encrypted as it is stored in the system
tables. Use of the WITH
ENCRYPTION option can be used
by commercial developers to protect
their work from reverse engineering.
SQL Server does not encrypt the data
as it is passed over the network, and
there is not an "encrypted connection"
associated with views in SQL Server.

8. What happens when you attempt to create
the following view?
create view ViewWithATypo as select *
fromm sales

A. An error will be generated when the
view is created, but the view will be
created.

B. No error will be generated when the
view is created, but an error will be
generated when the view is executed.

C. An error will be generated when the
view is created, and the view will not
be created.

D. No error will be generated when the
view is created, and no error will be
generated when the view is executed,
but the view will return no records.
C. An error will be generated when
the view is created, and the view will
not be created. The validity of the
SQL statement is evaluated when
CREATE VIEW executes. Because
the word "from" is misspelled in the
SELECT statement, the view would
not be created.

9. Which of the following can be used when
creating a view? (Choose all that apply.)

A. Subqueries

B. COMPUTE

C. INTO

D. UNION
A, D. Subqueries and UNION can be
used to create a view. COMPUTE
creates extra rows at the end of the
data set. Temporary tables will not be

consistently available, and the INTO statement will perform an action, instead of providing the data set required.

10. A user can use a view that draws content from which of the following? (Choose all that apply.)

A. Tables that the user has permission to view

B. Tables that the user does not have permission to view

C. Views that the user has permission to view

D. Views that the user does not have permission to view

E. Temporary tables that the user has permission to view

F. Temporary tables that the user does not have permission to view
A, B, C, D. Views can be built upon other views, nesting to several levels deep. A user can use the data from a view without having access to the underlying data, which makes views a great technique for distributing data. However, under no circumstances can a view reference a temporary table.

11. Which aspects of a view can you change using the ALTER VIEW statement?(Choose all that apply.)

A. The permissions for the view

B. The *Check Option* flag for the view

C. The name of the view

D. The Encryption flag for the view
B, D. You can change the *Check Option* flag for the view and the Encryption flag for the view. You can rename the view using the Enterprise Manager, or the sp_rename stored procedure.

12. What happens when you try to add the same table multiple times in the Design pane?

A. Your request is ignored.

B. Another copy of the table is displayed.

C. In the SQL pane an alias for the second copy of the table is created.

D. B and C
D. When you try to add the same table multiple times in the Design pane, another copy of the table is displayed, and an alias for the second copy of the table is created in the SQL pane. The new table may also join to the other instance of itself.

13. When creating a view, in which panes can you enter design changes to the view? (Choose all that apply.)

A. Diagram pane

B. Grid pane

C. SQL pane

D. Results pane
A, B, C. You can enter design changes to the view in the Diagram pane, the Grid pane, and the SQL pane. Although you cannot edit the view

in the Results pane, you can directly edit the underlying data.

14. Which actions are permissible on a calculated field in a view? (Choose all that apply.)

    A. You can SELECT the content in a field.

    B. You can INSERT a new value into that field.

    C. You can DELETE the field by deleting the entire row.

    D. You can UPDATE a value in that field.

    A, C. You can SELECT the content in a field and you can DELETE the field by deleting the entire row. You can insert or update rows containing calculated fields, but it is not possible to modify the calculated fields themselves.

15. In SQL Server 7.0, which of the following can be used on views that reference multiple tables? (Choose all that apply.)

    A. SELECT

    B. DELETE

    C. INSERT

    D. UPDATE

    A, B, C, D. SELECT, DELETE, INSERT, and UPDATE are used on views that reference multiple tables. When modifying content in such a view, however, it is best to make changes to the fields in one source table at a time.

16. If you have a view that references a single table and includes the key fields, but excludes the primary key (which is an IDENTITY), and a required field, which of the following is true?

    A. You cannot modify an existing row, and you cannot create a new row.

    B. You can modify an existing row, and you can create a new row.

    C. You can modify an existing row, but you can create a new row only if the NOT NULL field has an assigned default value.

    D. You cannot modify an existing row, but you can create a new row.

    C. You can modify an existing row, but you can create a new row only if the NOT NULL field has an assigned default value. Because the IDENTITY field will populate by itself, it is not necessary to include it in the view. If there is a default available for the required field, it is also not necessary to include that field in the view.

17. How do you prevent the users from entering invalid data into a view?

    A. Use the WITH CHECK OPTION to validate that the content meets input the same criteria as the view.

    B. Add a rule onto a column of the view.

    C. Create a new rule, and bind it to a column of the view.

    D. Create a new rule on the underlying table, and use the WITH VIEW OPTION to make the rule apply to views.

A. Use the WITH CHECK OPTION to validate that the content meets input the same criteria as the view. Using WITH CHECK OPTION will make sure that you cannot enter content into a view that could not be displayed in that view. You cannot bind a rule to a view, and there is no WITH VIEW OPTION.

18. A view is defined using WITH CHECK OPTION and a WHERE SALARY < 80000 AND SALARY > 60000. However, there is a constraint on the table prohibiting salaries of more than 50000. What would happen if a user tried to enter a salary of 70000?

   A. The user could enter the data, but could never possibly view existing records.

   B. The user could not enter the data, but could possibly view existing records.

   C. The user could not enter the data, and could never possibly view existing records.

   D. The user could enter the data, and could also possibly view existing records.

   B. The user could not enter the data, but could possibly view existing records. No matter how the view is defined, the constraints in the table are still in effect. Therefore, because there are no salaries that are legal for both the table and the view, new records can not be entered through

the view. However, if the constraint was applied after the table was created but not enforced on existing data, it may be possible to retrieve records through this view.

19. You have an Actors table and a Movies table, and the Actors table has a foreign key into the Movies table. You create a view referencing the Names column of the Actors table and the Titles column of the Movies table. What happens if you attempt to edit the Titles column in the view?

   A. The Titles field cannot be updated.

   B. The Titles field will be updated only in the record where it was entered.

   C. The Titles field will be updated in every record where it was referenced.

   D. The Titles field can only be updated when the Names column is updated at the same time.

   C. The Titles field will be updated in every record where it was referenced. Modifying the single record in the view modifies only a single record in the Movies table, but because this record was referenced in several records in the view, the change is propagated onto several lines of the view.

20. You have created a table, and another user with access to your table has created a view based upon this table. It was a mistake for that user to see the content in that table, and you ask the system administrator to prevent that user from

seeing the content in your table. Which actions will accomplish this?

A. Removing their rights to the table

B. Removing their rights to the table and to the view

C. Removing their rights to the view

D. Removing their rights to create new views
B. Removing their rights to the table and to the view. You need rights to a table to create a view based upon that table, but after it is created, you can still access the view even after permission to the table is gone.

Chapter 10 Answers

1. What are the three types of stored procedures? (Choose all that apply.)

   A. System procedures

   B. Localized procedures

   C. User-defined procedures

   D. Extended stored procedures
   A, C, D. System procedures, user-defined procedures, and extended stored procedures are the three types of stored procedures.

2. What is the only type of stored procedure you cannot create?

   A. System

   B. User-defined

   C. Extended

   D. New
   A. You cannot create system procedures.

3. What are extended stored procedures stored as?

   A. Executables

   B. DLLs

   C. Batch files

   D. Script files
   B. Extended stored procedures are stored as DLLs.

4. The permission to run CREATE PROCEDURE defaults to which user?

   A. Table owner

   B. Database owner

   C. Data owner

   D. Row owner
   B. The permission to run CREATE PROCEDURE defaults to the database owner.

5. How deep can you nest stored procedures?

   A. 4

   B. 16

   C. 32

   D. 64
   D. You can nest procedures up to 32 levels deep.

6. How many parameters can you pass into a stored procedure?

   A. 256

   B. 512

   C. 1024

D. 2048
C. You can pass up to 1024 parameters into a stored procedure.

7. How do you run stored procedures? (Choose all that apply.)

A. EXECUTE *procedure_name*
B. RUN
C. Type the name of the stored procedure
D. ACCESS
A, C. You run a stored procedure by using EXECUTE or by typing the name of the stored procedure.

8. What system procedure do you use to get a list of the objects that the stored procedure depends on?

A. sp_who
B. sp_configure
C. sp_help
D. sp_depends
D. You use the sp_depends system procedure to get a list of the objects that the stored procedure depends on.

9. What recompile option does not save the execution plan in the procedure cache?

A. sp_recompile
B. WITH RECOMPILE with EXEC
C. WITH RECOMPILE with CREATE PROCEDURE
D. WITH RECOMPILE
C. The WITH RECOMPILE with CREATE PROCEDURE recompile option does not save the execution plan in the procedure cache.

10. What recompile option forces all of the stored procedures that reference a table to recompile the next time they run?

A. sp_recompile
B. WITH RECOMPILE with EXEC
C. WITH RECOMPILE with CREATE PROCEDURE
D. WITH RECOMPILE
A. The sp_recompile recompile option forces all of the stored procedures that reference a table to recompile the next time they run.

11. What recompile option will compile the stored procedure the first time it is run and will save the optimal path in the procedure cache for subsequent executions of the stored procedure?

A. WITH RECOMPILE with CREATE PROCEDURE
B. WITH RECOMPILE with EXEC
C. sp_recompile
D. CREATE PROCEDURE
B. The WITH RECOMPILE with EXEC option will compile the stored procedure the first time it is run and will save the optimal path in the procedure cache for subsequent executions of the stored procedure.

12. What create procedure argument allows you to pass values out of the procedure and into the calling procedure?

A. INPUT
B. OUTPUT

C. PASS

D. ARG

B. The OUTPUT argument allows you to pass values out of the procedure and into the calling procedure.

13. What statement do you use to inform users of non-SQL Server errors?

A. RAISERROR

B. ERRORCHECK

C. CHECKPROC

D. OUTPUT

A. You can use the RAISERROR statement to inform users of non-SQL Server errors.

14. What type of values do return codes return?

A. integer

B. double

C. char

D. float

A. Return codes return integer values.

15. What stored procedure do you run to check for performance degradation?

A. sp_who

B. sp_monitor

C. sp_perfmon

D. sp_perf

B. You use the sp_monitor stored procedure to check for performance degradation.

Chapter 11 Answers

1. What Transact-SQL statement does a trigger respond to? (Choose all that apply.)

A. UPDATE

B. INSERT

C. DELETE

D. REMOVE

A, B, C. A trigger responds to the UPDATE, INSERT, and DELETE statements.

2. What does the WITH ENCRYPTION argument in the CREATE TRIGGER statement do?

A. Encrypts the entry in syscomments that contains the text for CREATE TRIGGER

B. Encrypts the database where the trigger is defined

C. Encrypts the data in the database where the trigger is defined

D. Encrypts the trigger

A. WITH ENCRYPTION encrypts the entry in syscomments that contains the text for CREATE TRIGGER.

3. Who can create and delete triggers in a table?

A. DBA

B. Database owner

C. Database owner and anyone to whom the owner transfers the permissions

D. NT network administrator
   B. Only the database owner can create and delete triggers in a table.

4. Which stored procedure do you execute to view the text of the trigger stored in the syscomments table?

   A. sp_help

   B. sp_depends

   C. sp_helptext

   D. sp_owner
      C. You use the sp_helptext stored procedure to view the text of the trigger stored in the syscomments table.

5. What stored procedure do you execute to view the owner of the trigger and when the trigger was created?

   A. sp_help

   B. sp_depends

   C. sp_helptext

   D. sp_owner
      A. You use the sp_help stored procedure to view the owner of the trigger and when the trigger was created.

6. Which of the following Transact-SQL statements is allowed in triggers?

   A. GRANT

   B. DENY

   C. UPDATE

   D. CREATE TRIGGER
      C. UPDATE is allowed in triggers.

7. How do you delete triggers?

A. DELETE '*trigger_name*'

B. CLEAR '*trigger_name*'

C. REMOVE '*trigger_name*'

D. DROP '*trigger_name*'
   D. You use DROP '*trigger_name*' to delete triggers.

8. What is the name of the logical tables that hold changes that haven't yet been committed? (Choose all that apply.)

   A. temp

   B. deleted

   C. inserted

   D. commit
      B, C. The deleted and inserted logical tables hold changes that haven't yet been committed.

9. In which of these items can the update trigger check for changes? (Choose all that apply.)

   A. A column

   B. A database

   C. A table

   D. A row
      A, C. The update trigger can check for changes in both a column and a table.

10. What do triggers support that do not exist in constraints? (Choose all that apply.)

   A. Customizable error messages

   B. Static error messages

   C. Complex error handling

   D. Constraint denial
      A, C. Triggers support the

customizable messages and complex error handling that do not exist in constraints.

11. What Transact-SQL statement do you use to enable nested triggers?

    A. Sp_configure 'nested triggers',0
    B. Sp_configure 'nested triggers',1
    C. Sp_configure 'cascaded triggers',0
    D. Sp_configure 'cascaded triggers',0
       B. You use the sp_configure 'nested triggers',0 Transact-SQL statement to enable nested triggers.

12. Which one of these numbers would not be stored in the @@NESTLEVEL global variable?

    A. 5
    B. 10
    C. 15
    D. 20
       D. @@NESTLEVEL global variable cannot store 20. It can only stored nest level numbers from 0 to 16.

13. What determines the majority of the time it takes for a trigger to execute?

    A. The type of trigger
    B. The length of the trigger
    C. The location of the target table
    D. The location of the trigger
       C. The location of the target table determines the majority of the time it takes for a trigger to execute.

14. What statement returns user-defined error messages in the same style and form as SQL Server errors?

    A. SHOWERROR
    B. RAISERROR
    C. OUTPUTERROR
    D. DISPLAYERR
       B. RAISERROR returns user-defined error messages in the same style and form as SQL Server errors.

15. What trigger option forces the entire trigger to halt and all modifications to reset?

    A. HALT TRANSACTION
    B. CLOSE TRANSACTION
    C. ROLLBACK TRANSACTION
    D. END TRANSACTION
       C. The ROLLBACK TRANSACTION option forces the entire trigger to halt and all modifications to reset.

Chapter 12 Answers

1. What must be installed in order for distributed transactions to work?

    A. Microsoft Distributed Transaction Coordinator
    B. Query Analyzer
    C. Enterprise Manager
    D. Performance Monitor
       A. The Microsoft Distributed Transaction Coordinator must be

installed for distributed transactions to work.

2. What status occurs with a forced transaction that was previously In-Doubt? (Choose all that apply.)

A. Prepared

B. Forced Commit

C. Forced Abort

D. Preparing

B, C. The Forced Commit and Forced Abort statuses occur with a forced transaction that was previously In-Doubt.

3. To set up a linked server, what system stored procedures would you first have to run? (Choose all that apply.)

A. sp_addlinkedserver

B. sp_addalert

C. sp_addlogin

D. sp_addlinkedsrvlogin

A, D. To set up a linked server, you would first have to run sp_addlinkedserver and sp_addlinkedsrvlogin.

4. What is the Transact-SQL statement that executes a query on a linked server? (Choose all that apply.)

A. bcp

B. SELECT

C. OPENQUERY

D. OPENROWSET

C, D. OPENQUERY and OPENROWSET are the Transact-SQL statements that execute a query on a linked server.

5. What checks to see if the copy can be done validly according to the transformation flags that you define in the advanced transformation properties?

A. DTS Packager

B. DTS Export Wizard

C. DTS Data Pump

D. DTS Import Wizard

C. DTS Data Pump checks to see if the copy can done validly according to the transformation flags that you define in the advanced transformation properties.

6. What command-line based program is used to copy data into and out of SQL Server?

A. Data Transformation Services

B. Bulk copy program

C. Bulk Insert

D. Insert Statement

B. The bulk copy program utility is a command-line based program used to copy data into and out of SQL Server.

7. Where is the BCP.EXE found?

A. \WINNT

B. The SQL Server 7.0 installation directory

C. The BINN subdirectory in the SQL Server 7.0 installation directory

D. The BIN subdirectory in the SQL Server 7.0 installation directory

C. The BCP.EXE is found in BINN subdirectory in the SQL Server 7.0 installation.

8. In what format can bcp create and access data? (Choose all that apply.)

    A. Native

    B. Character

    C. Unicode native

    D. Unicode character

    A, B, C, D. Bcp can create and access data in native, character, Unicode native, and Unicode character format.

9. When should you use Unicode native and character data formats when you are using bcp?

    A. When you have a single code page

    B. When you have different code pages

    C. Anytime

    D. Never

    B. You should use Unicode native and character data formats when you using bcp on different code pages.

10. What tool in SQL Server 7.0 allows scripting in JScript and VBScript?

    A. SQL Transfer Manager

    B. Bulk copy program

    C. SQL Enterprise Manager

    D. Data Transformation Services

    D. Data Transformation Services is the tool in SQL Server 7.0 that allows scripting in JScript and VBScript.

11. Which of the following is used to check if a copy is valid according to the transformation flags that you define in the advanced transformation properties?

    A. DTS Data Pump

    B. DTS Export Wizard

    C. DTS Import Wizard

    D. SQL Transfer Manager

    A. DTS Data Pump. Before the copy, the DTS Data Pump checks to see if the copy is valid according to the transformation flags that you define in the advanced transformation properties. If any of the columns fail the check, the copy operation is aborted. This ensures that the copy is done to your specification.

12. What statement do you use to copy data from an external OLE DB provider to SQL Server?

    A. INSERT statement

    B. UPDATE statement

    C. SELECT statement

    D. SELECT INTO statement

    A. You use the INSERT statement to copy data from an external OLE DB provider to SQL Server.

13. What statement do you use to create a new table based on an existing table?

    A. INSERT statement

    B. UPDATE statement

    C. SELECT INTO statement

D. BULK INSERT
   C. You use the SELECT INTO statement to create a new table based on an existing table.

14. What tool is used to copy data into SQL Server using the functionality of the bcp utility with a Transact-SQL statement rather than from the command prompt?

    A. INSERT statement
    B. UPDATE statement
    C. SELECT INTO statement
    D. BULK INSERT
       D. The BULK INSERT tool is used to copy data into SQL Server using the functionality of the bcp utility with a Transact-SQL statement rather than from the command prompt.

15. What tool do you use to transfer data from a text file to SQL Server quickly?

    A. BULK INSERT
    B. SQL Transfer Manager
    C. SQL Enterprise Manager
    D. Bulk copy program
       A. BULK INSERT is the tool you use to transfer data from a text file to SQL Server quickly.

B

About the CD

This CD-ROM contains a browser-based testing product, the *Personal Testing Center*. The *Personal Testing Center* is easy to install on any Windows 95/98/NT computer.

Installing the Personal Testing Center

Double-clicking on the Setup.html file on the CD will cycle you through an introductory page on the *Test Yourself* software. On the second page, you will have to read and accept the license agreement. Once you have read the agreement, click on the Agree icon and you will be brought to the *Personal Testing Center's* main page.

On the main page, you will find links onto the *Personal Testing Center*, to the electronic version of the book, and to other resources you may find helpful. Click on the first link to the *Personal Testing Center* and you will be brought to the Quick Start page. Here you can choose to run the Personal Testing Center from the CD or install it onto your hard drive.

Installing the *Personal Testing Center* onto your hard drive is an easy process. Click on the Install to Hard Drive icon and the procedure will start for you. An instructional box will appear, and walk you through the remainder of the installation. If installed to the hard drive, the "Personal Testing Center" program group will be created in the Start Programs folder.

Should you wish to run the software from the CD-ROM, the steps are the same as above until you reach the point where you would select the Install to Hard Drive icon. Here, select Run from CD icon and the exam will automatically begin.

To uninstall the program from your hard disk, use the add/remove programs feature in your Windows Control Panel. InstallShield will run uninstall.

Test Type Choices

With the *Personal Testing Center*, you have three options in which to run the program: Live, Practice, and Review. Each test type will draw from a pool of over 220 potential questions. Your choice of test type will depend on whether you would like to simulate an actual MCDBA exam, receive instant feedback on your answer choices, or review concepts using the testing simulator. Note that selecting the Full Screen icon on Internet Explorer's standard toolbar gives you the best display of the *Personal Testing Center.*

Live

The Live timed test type is meant to reflect the actual exam as closely as possible. You will have the option to skip questions and return to them later, move to the previous question, or end the exam. Once the timer has expired, you will automatically go to the scoring page to review your test results.

Managing Windows

The testing application runs inside an Internet Explorer 4.0 or 5.0 browser window. We recommend that you use the full-screen view to minimize the amount of text scrolling you need to do. However, the application will initiate a second iteration of the browser when you link to an Answer in Depth or a Review Graphic. If you are running in full-screen view, the second iteration of the browser will be covered by the first. You can toggle between the two windows with ALT-TAB, you can click your task bar to maximize the second window, or you can get out of full-screen mode and arrange the two windows so they are both visible on the screen at the same time. The application will not initiate more than two browser windows, so you aren't left with hundreds of open windows for each Answer in Depth or Review Graphic that you view.

Saving Scores as Cookies

Your exam score is stored as a browser cookie. If you've configured your browser to accept cookies, your score will be stored in a cookie named History. If you don't accept cookies, you cannot permanently save your scores. If you delete the History cookie, the scores will be deleted permanently.

Using the Browser Buttons

The test application runs inside the Internet Explorer browser. You should navigate from screen to screen by using the application's buttons, not the browser's buttons.

JavaScript Errors

If you encounter a JavaScript error, you should be able to proceed within the application. If you cannot, shut down your Internet Explorer browser session and re-launch the testing application.

Practice

When choosing the Practice exam type, you have the option of receiving instant feedback as to whether your selected answer is correct. The questions will be presented to you in numerical order, and you will see every question in the available question pool for each section you chose to be tested on.

As with the Live exam type, you have the option of continuing through the entire exam without seeing the correct answer for each question. The number of questions you answered correctly, along with the percentage of correct answers, will be displayed during the post-exam summary report. Once you have answered a question, click the Answer icon to display the correct answer.

You have the option of ending the Practice exam at any time, but your post-exam summary screen may reflect an incorrect percentage based on the number of questions you failed to answer. Questions that are skipped are counted as incorrect answers on the post-exam summary screen.

Review

During the Review exam type, you will be presented with questions similar to both the Live and Practice exam types. However, the Answer icon is not present, as every question will have the correct answer posted near the bottom of the screen. You have the option of answering the question without looking at the correct answer. In the Review exam type, you can also return to previous questions and skip to the next question, as well as end the exam by clicking the Stop icon.

The Review exam type is recommended when you have already completed the Live exam type once or twice, and would now like to determine which questions you answered correctly.

Questions with Answers

For the Practice and Review exam types, you will have the option of clicking a hyperlink titled Answers in Depth, which will present relevant study material aimed at exposing the logic behind the answer in a separate browser window. By having two browsers open (one for the test engine and one for the review information), you can quickly alternate between the two windows while keeping your place in the exam. You will find that additional windows are not generated as you follow hyperlinks throughout the test engine.

Scoring

The *Personal Testing Center* post-exam summary screen, called Benchmark Yourself, displays the results for each section you chose to be tested on, including a bar graph similar to the real exam, which displays the percentage of correct answers. You can compare your percentage to the actual passing percentage for each section. The percentage displayed on the post-exam summary screen is not the actual percentage required to pass the exam. You'll see the number of questions you answered correctly compared to the total number of questions you were tested on. If you choose to skip a question, it will be marked as incorrect. Ending the exam by clicking the End button with questions still unanswered lowers your percentage, as these questions will be marked as incorrect.

Clicking the End button and then the Home button allows you to choose another exam type, or test yourself on another section.

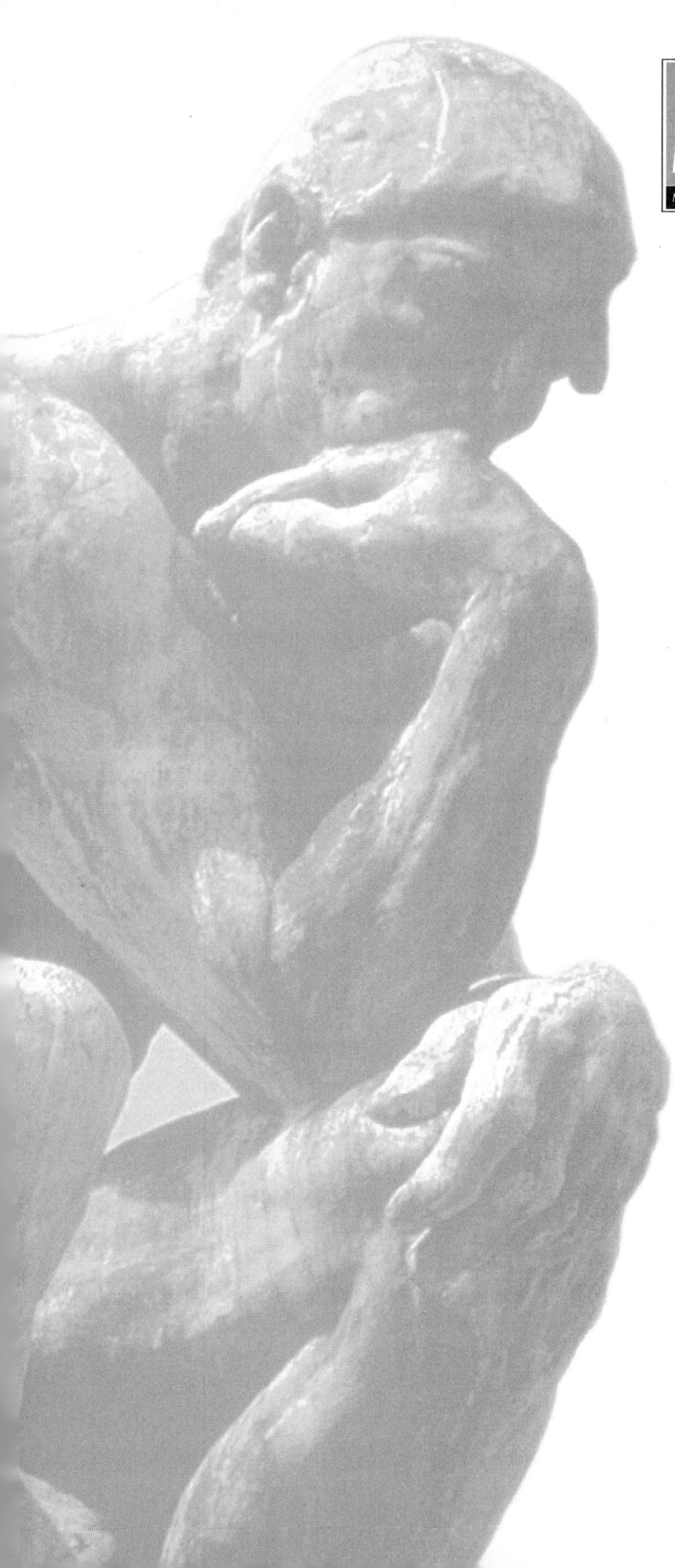

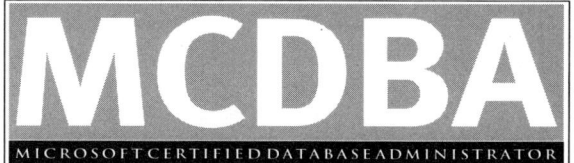

MCDBA
MICROSOFT CERTIFIED DATABASE ADMINISTRATOR

C

About the Web Site

Access Global Kowledge

As you know by now, Global Knowledge is the largest independent IT training company in the world. Just by purchasing this book, you have also secured a free subscription to the Global Knowledge Web site and its many resources. You can find it at

http://access.globalknowledge.com

You can log on directly at the Global Knowledge site, and you will be e-mailed a new, secure password immediately upon registering.

What You'll Find There. . .

The wealth of useful information at the Global Knowledge site falls into the following three categories:

Skills Gap Analysis

Global Knowledge offers several ways for you to analyze your networking skills and discover where they may be lacking. Using Global Knowledge's trademarked Competence Key Tool, you can do a skills gap analysis and get recommendations for where you may need to do some more studying. (Sorry, it just might not end with this book!)

Networking

You'll also gain valuable access to another asset, people. At the Access Global site, you'll find threaded discussions as well as live discussions. Talk to other MCDBA and MCSE candidates, get advice from folks who have already taken the exams, and get access to instructors and MCTs.

Product Offerings

Of course, Global Knowledge also offers its products here, and you may find some valuable items for purchase—CBTs, books, or courses. Browse freely and see if there's something that could help you take that next step in career enhancement.

MICROSOFT CERTIFIED DATABASE ADMINISTRATOR

D

SQL References
(Electronic and
Printed)

T here's a lot of information available on SQL, Transact-SQL (TSQL), and Microsoft SQL Server. The problem is trying to plow through it all. You could spend hours weeding through bookstores, surfing the Internet, and researching all the avenues available to you. To save you the time, this appendix has a number of printed and Internet resources dealing with these topics.

Table D-1 lists SQL references on the World Wide Web. To access SQL references on the Web, you'll need a connection to the Internet and a browser such as Microsoft Internet Explorer or Netscape® Communicator installed and configured on your computer. Depending on the type and version of browser you're using, you may need to type **http://** before the URLs listed below. Also, at the time of this writing, all of the sites and pages were up and running. If a particular site is no longer functioning, either move onto the next one in the list or attempt to access the site at a later time (remember, Web servers do go down occasionally).

TABLE D-1   SQL References on the World Wide Web

Site Name or Page Title	URL	Description
Microsoft SQL Server	www.microsoft.com/sql	Product information, downloads, support, and resources on the latest version of SQL Server.
Microsoft TechNet	technet.microsoft.com/cdonline /default.asp (Note this site requires a FREE registration process)	Provides technical information, reference material, backgrounders, and much more on SQL, SQL Server, and other languages and Microsoft products. If you want to order the information on this site to view offline, you can join TechNet for a fee.
MSDN (Microsoft Developer Network)	msdn.microsoft.com/developer/ sqlserver/default.htm	While MSDN provides technical information and reference material on numerous languages and products, this link takes you directly to the SQL Server portion of MSDN's site. Note that the MSDN and Site Builder Network sites are merging to form a single online entity, known as MSDN Online.

TABLE D-1	SQL References on the World Wide Web *(continued)*	
Site Name or Page Title	**URL**	**Description**
SQL Server Magazine Online	www.sqlmag.com	Online magazine focusing on Microsoft SQL Server. From the same publishers of *Windows NT Magazine*.
SQL Forum Online	www.sqlforum.com	Articles and reference material on SQL and SQL Server.
Syngress Media	www.syngress.com	Personal Testing Centers: certification products offering a powerful combination of exam simulation, reference material, and skills assessment. All of the questions in the Personal Testing Centers have been derived from the content of our best-selling series of study guides prepared by MCSEs and MCTs.
Training and Certification Resources for Microsoft SQL Server 7.0	microsoft.com/train_cert/ resource/sql7.htm	This site includes a broad range of information for learning about SQL Server 7.0, including information on Instructor-led training, Online training, and MCP certification.
Site Builder Network	www.microsoft.com/sitebuilder	Dedicated to creating Internet sites, this site carries information on using SQL Server with Internet sites. Note that the MSDN and Site Builder Network sites are merging to form a single online entity, known as MSDN Online.
Introduction to Structured Query Language Version 4.3	www.geocities.com/ ResearchTriangle/Node/9672 /sqltut.html	Online tutorial for SQL.
iCat Tech Support Doc Base	Teamserver.icat.com	Contains tutorials and reference material on SQL Server.
Database Unlimited	www.dbu.co.uk	Contains some articles, reference material, and source code samples on different database topics, including SQL Server.

TABLE D-I	SQL References on the World Wide Web *(continued)*

Site Name or Page Title	URL	Description
MS Intranet Strategy	Home.pacbell.net/amfritts/Choosing.htm	Microsoft white paper on choosing the appropriate database development tool. Covers a wide range of Microsoft database tools, including SQL Server.
SQL Server 7.0 Highlights	www.cunninghamconsulting.com/CC%20SQL%20SIG%208-12-98/index.htm	Tutorials with online slideshow. Provides an overview of SQL Server 7.0
CNET	www.cnet.com	Contains features and reviews on SQL Server, as well as product downloads. Content changes very frequently, so navigation through the site will be required to find the latest information.
Access-Office-VB Advisor	www.advisor.com/av.htm	This site provides articles on developing database and Web solutions. Includes limited information on SQL Server.

In addition to the WWW, we've also included a number of newsgroups (also referred to as *Usenet*) in Table D-2. Newsgroups are similar to bulletin boards, where people post a message that everyone else can read. To access these sites, you will need to have a news reader installed and configured on your machine, in addition to the aforementioned connection to the Net. If you have installed a recent copy of Outlook Express (which comes with Internet Explorer Suite) , you can access such sites through this application. Otherwise, download a copy of Forte Agent or other fine newsreaders to access these groups. Again, all of the newgroups and Web sites listed were functioning at the time of this writing.

Electronic and Printed References and Magazines

Electronic references are CDs and other media that allow you to view information offline. What is required to view such information depends on what the company providing this service deems necessary. For example, to

TABLE D-2	bit.listserv.sqlinfo	comp.databases.ms-sqlserver
	cz.comp.microsoft.sql	fido7.su.dbms.sql
SQL-Related Newsgroups Available on the Usenet	git.sql.help	relcom.fido.su.dbms.sql
	microsoft.public.de.sqlserver	microsoft.public.sqlserver.connect
	microsoft.public.sqlserver.odbc	microsoft.public.sqlserver.programming
	microsoft.public.sqlserver.replication	microsoft.public.sqlserver.server
	microsoft.public.sqlserver.workshop	

view information provided by Microsoft, it is highly recommended that you have Internet Explorer installed on your system. Other resources may require text readers or some other program. In subscribing to any of the resources listed in Table D-3, a fee may be charged.

In addition to electronic resources, we've also included some magazines in Table D-3 that may only be available in printed rather than electronic format. In the ordering information column of this section we've included contact information so you can inquire about formats available, and order the associated material.

TABLE D-3   Electronic References and Magazines

Name	Ordering Information	Description
Microsoft TechNet	www.microsoft.com/technet/subscription/ordernow.htm http://www.microsoft.com/technet/resource/technet/servers/sql/sql7.0.htm	*Microsoft TechNet* provides a subscription for CDs, which include technical information, backgrounders, tools, utilities, and other resources. Among the many products covered in TechNet is SQL Server.
MSDN (Microsoft Developer Network)	msdn.microsoft.com/subscriptions/prodinfo/purchase.asp	*MSDN* provides CDs containing technical information and reference material on numerous languages and products, including SQL Server.

TABLE D-3	Electronic References and Magazines *(continued)*

Name	Ordering Information	Description
The Advisor Magazines Line of Periodicals	www.advisor.com/whome.nsf/wpages/magazines	*Access-Office-VB Advisor* magazine focuses on Microsoft database and Web solutions, inclusive to SQL Server. This link takes you to a series of profiles on various magazines put out by Advisor.
MCP Magazine Resource Central	www.mcpmag.com/secure/rcentralsub/default99a.asp	Online, subscription-based resource for MCPs.
MCP Magazine	www.mcpmag.com/subs.asp	*Microsoft Certified Professional Magazine* provides information for subscribes MCPs on numerous topics, including SQL Server.
Windows NT Magazine	www.winntmag.com/Sub/Main.cfm?Action=Subscribe	Online version of the printed magazine. Through this site, you can read articles and other information, as well as order the printed magazine.

E

T-SQL Command Reference for Database Implementors

Data Control Language (DCL) Statements

Command	Description
DENY	Creates an entry that denies permissions from security accounts in the current database. Once an entry has been made in the security system, the security account is prevented from inheriting permissions from groups or role memberships.
GRANT	Used to assign permissions to users.
REVOKE	Removes permissions from a user in the current database.

Data Definition Language (DDL) Statements

Command	Description
ALTER DATABASE	Changes the amount of space that's allocated to a database by changing file definitions and size settings.
ALTER PROCEDURE	Changes procedures you've previously created, without affecting permissions, dependent stored procedures or triggers.
ALTER TABLE	Changes the table definition. Allows you to add or remove columns; add, remove enable or disable constraints.
ALTER TRIGGER	Changes the definition of a previously created trigger.
ALTER VIEW	Changes views you've previously created, without affecting permissions, dependent stored procedures, or triggers.
CREATE DATABASE	Creates a new database or attaches the files of a previously created database.
CREATE DEFAULT	Creates an object that's used to specify a value inserted into a (or all columns if a user-defined datatype is used), column when no value is explicitly supplied at the time of the insert.
CREATE INDEX	Creates an index of one or more columns.
CREATE PROCEDURE	Creates a stored procedure that can take and/or return one or more user-supplied parameters. A stored procedure is a collection of T-SQL statements that have been saved.
CREATE RULE	Creates an object that's used to specify values that can be inserted into a particular column, or any column of a user-defined data type.

Command	Description
CREATE SCHEMA	Creates a schema (conceptual container object), which is a database without any data inside of it.
CREATE TABLE	Creates a new table.
CREATE TRIGGER	Creates a trigger, which is a type of stored procedure. Triggers are usually used for enforcing integrity constraints, and are automatically executed when users attempt specified data modification statements on specified tables.
CREATE VIEW	Creates a new view, which is an alternate way of looking at data in one or more tables.
DROP DATABASE	Removes one or more databases from SQL Server.
DROP DEFAULT	Removes one or more default objects from the current database.
DROP INDEX	Removes one or more indices from the current database.
DROP PROCEDURE	Removes one or more procedures from the current database.
DROP RULE	Removes one or more rules from the current database.
DROP STATISTICS	Removes statistics from one or more columns in a specified table of the current database.
DROP TABLE	Removes one or more tables from the current database. When the table is removed, its data, indexes, triggers, and permission specifications are also removed.
DROP TRIGGER	Removes one or more triggers from the current database.
DROP VIEW	Removes one or more views from the current database.

Data Manipulation Language (DML) Statements

Command	Description
DELETE	Used to remove rows from a table.
INSERT	Used to add a new row to a table or view in a database.
SELECT	Used to retrieve rows from databases.
UPDATE	Used to change the existing data rows of the database by either adding or modifying the data.

Command	Description
UPDATETEXT	Used to update a text, ntext, or image field.
WRITETEXT	Permits a nonlogged, interactive updating of an existing text, ntext, or image column.

Additional TSQL Statements

Command	Description
BACKUP	Initiates a backup of a database, transaction log, or one or more files or filegroups.
BEGIN ... END	Encloses a group of T-SQL statements and causes them to be executed as a group.
BEGIN DISTRIBUTED TRANSACTION	Marks the start of a T-SQL distributed transaction that's managed by MS DTC (Microsoft Distributed Transaction Coordinator).
BEGIN TRANSACTION	Marks the start of a local transaction.
BREAK	Causes an exit from a WHILE loop.
BULK INSERT	Causes a data file to be inserted into a database table. The file is inserted in the format that the user specifies.
CAST	Converts an expression from one data type to another. This command performs the same action as CONVERT.
CHECKPOINT	Causes all of the database pages that have been updated but not saved (i.e., "dirty pages") to be saved to the database.
CLOSE	Closes an active cursor.
COMMIT TRANSACTION	Marks the end of a user-defined or implicit transaction.
COMMIT WORK	Marks the end of a transaction.
CONTINUE	Causes a WHILE loop to restart.
CONVERT	Converts an expression from one data type to another. This command performs the same action as CAST.
DBCC	Database Consistency Checker (DBCC) are statements used by administrators to check the logical and physical consistency of a database.

Command	Description
DEALLOCATE CURSOR	Used to make a cursor inaccessible. When the last cursor is made inaccessible, the data structures that committed to that cursor are released from memory by SQL Server.
DECLARE CURSOR	Used to define a T-SQL cursor.
DUMP DATABASE	Creates a backup copy of a database, in a form that can be read by SQL Server using the LOAD DATABASE command.
DUMP TRANSACTION	Creates a copy of the transaction log.
EXECUTE	Runs a system procedure, user defined stored procedure, or an extended stored procedure.
FETCH	Retrieves a row or set or rows from a T-SQL server cursor.
GO	Marks the end of a batch of T-SQL statements to SQL Server utilities.
GOTO	Used to alter the flow of execution, by causing execution to branch to a specific label. The syntax for this command is GOTO *label*
GROUP BY	Used in SELECT statements, this divides a table into groups. A groups can be comprised of column names, results, or computed columns.
HAVING	Used in SELECT statements, it sets restrictions on a the groups returned in a result set.
IDENTITY	Creates an identity column in a table.
IF ... ELSE	Used for conditional execution of T-SQL statements. The T-SQL statement following the IF keyword is executed if its condition is satisfied (it returns a Boolean value of TRUE), otherwise the optional ELSE keyword is executed (when the IF condition returns a Boolean value of FALSE).
LOAD DATABASE	Loads a backup copy of the user database.
LOAD TRANSACTION	Loads a backup copy of the transaction log.
LOAD HEADERONLY	Loads a backup copy of the header information about a DUMP.
OPEN	Opens a T-SQL server cursor for processing.
OPENQUERY	Runs a specified passthrough query.
OPENROWSET	Used to access remote data from an OLE DB data source.

Command	Description
ORDER BY	Used to return query results returned by a SELECT statement in a specific sorted order.
READTEXT	Used to read text and image values, starting at a specified offset and reading a specified number of characters or bytes.
RECONFIGURE	Used to implement a new configuration value in the config_value column of a sp_configure result set.
RESTORE DATABASE	Used to restore an entire database, or specific files or filegroups that have been backed up.
RESTORE LOG	Used to restore a transactional log from backup.
RESTORE FILELISTONLY	Used to return a list of database and log files contained in the backup set.
RESTORE HEADERONLY	Used to retrieve header information for all backups on a particular device.
RESTORE LABELONLY	Used to return information about the backup media.
RESTORE VERIFYONLY	Used to verify the backup without restoring it.
RETURN	Used to unconditionally exit from a query or procedure, so that statements following the RETURN statement aren't executed.
ROLLBACK TRANSACTION	Rolls back implicit or explicit transaction to the transaction's last savepoint, or to the beginning of the transaction.
ROLLBACK WORK	Rolls back a user-specified transaction to the beginning of the transaction.
SAVE TRANSACTION	Sets a savepoint in the transaction.
SET	Used to alter session handling of specified information, and sets query processing for the user's work session.
SETUSER	Not recommended, but included for backward compatibility, this command allows one database user (who is a member of sysadmin or db_owner) to impersonate another user.
TEXTVALID	Checks to see if a specific text pointer is valid.
TRUNICATE TABLE	Removes all of the rows from a table, but doesn't log the individual row deletions.

Command	Description
UNION	Used to return a result set made up of a combination of two or more queries. Duplicate rows in the combined result set are removed.
UNION ALL	Used to return a result set made up of a combination of two or more queries. Duplicate rows in the combined result set are not removed.
UPDATE STATISTICS	Used to update the distribution of key values in one or more indexes in a specified table.
USE	Specifies the database you wish to use.
WAITFOR	Used to specify the time, time interval, or event that will trigger execution of a block of statements, a stored procedure, or transaction.
WHERE	Used to specify conditions in SELECT, INSERT, UPDATE, and DELETE statements. This sets a condition that determines which rows to retrieve.
WHILE	Used to set a condition for a loop (the repeated execution of a statement or block of code). The statement or statement block will continue to execute over and over until the condition of the WHILE statement has a value of TRUE.

Device Commands

Command	Description
KILL	Used to terminate a process, based on the System Process ID (SPID).
PRINT	Returns a user-defined message to the user's message handler, and prints it on the user's screen.
RAISERROR	Returns a user-defined error message and sets a system flag to record that an error has occurred. The error message is printed on the user's screen.
SHUTDOWN	Stops SQL Server. Only the system administrator can use this command.

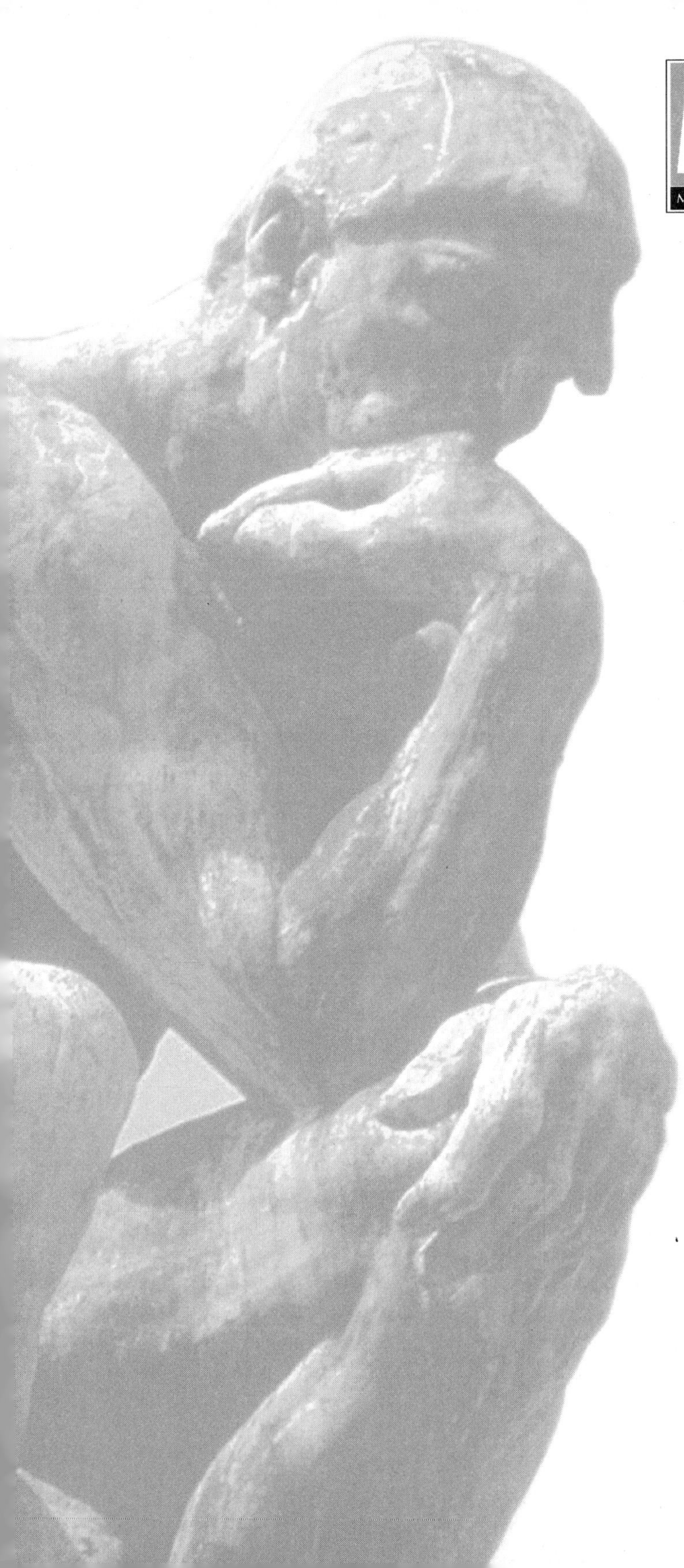

MCDBA

MICROSOFT CERTIFIED DATABASE ADMINISTRATOR

Glossary

ACID test   A transaction must have the ability to pass four primary tests: atomicity, consistency, isolation, and durability.

aggregate functions   Return summary values, such as averages and sums, from values in a particular column. The returned values represent a single value for each set of rows to which an aggregate function was applied. The aggregate functions are AVG, COUNT, COUNT(*), MAX, MIN, SUM, STDEV, STDEVP, VAR, and VARP.

alerts   Created using SQL Server Enterprise Manager, these are broadcasts to administrators of potential problems using benchmarks or parameters set by the administrator. SQL Server has two types of alerts: SQL Server Event Alert and SQL Server Performance Alert.

Alpha server   A generation of processors developed and marketed by Digital/Compaq Computer Corporation.

American National Standards Institute (ANSI)   An American organization of business and industry groups that develops communication and trade standards for the United States. These standards are coordinated with corresponding international standards. SQL Server is based on an ANSI-92 standard.

American Standard Code for Information Interchange (ASCII)   A character set built into every PC consisting of 96 uppercase and lowercase letters and 32 control characters. Note that ASCII does not include any formatting information such as font variances, bold face, or italics.

AppleTalk   The protocol designed for communicating with Macintosh computers. It is one of the protocols supported by SQL Server.

application database roles   Allows administrators to protect a database with a password. These types of roles do not contain any members (a user is associated with an application role only,) and application roles are by default inactive. They require a password to be activated.

application programming interfaces (API)   The set of routines in an application that are available to be used by programmers when they are designing an application interface. OLE DB, ODBC, and DB-Library are examples of APIs.

article   A grouping of data to be replicated. This may consist of an entire table, a subset of the columns of a table (via a vertical filter), or a subset of the rows of a table (via a horizontal filter).

atomicity   Part of the ACID test, this "all-or-nothing test" stipulates that a transaction must complete its run fully or be discontinued and completely rolled back and suspended by its process.

base data type   A system-supplied data type. User-defined data types are made from base data types. Examples of base data types include char, varchar, binary, and varbinary.

base table   The table on which a view is based. A view can have more than one base table.

batch   A group of SQL statements submitted and executed together.

Binary sort order   The simplest of sort methods, it uses ASCII values to distinguish characters based on a preset group of parameters.

Binn   The nerve center of the SQL Server directory (MSSQL7), it contains the executable files that run all SQL Server services, protocols, objects, data requests, and options.

Boolean search   A search method that allows the user to employ the use of Boolean operators: and, not, and or. Boolean operators are powerful search methods supported on most popular search engines such as AltaVista and InfoSeek. Microsoft SQL Server 7.0 also supports Boolean operators in its feature of full-text searching.

bulk copy program (bcp)   A command-line utility that allows external sources the ability to paste information into SQL Server. In previous versions of SQL Server, this was the only method to migrate data from earlier versions of SQL Server and from Sybase databases and text files. The ability to use this utility still exists in Microsoft SQL Server 7.0. *See also* **Data Transformation Services (DTS)**.

cache   A buffer that holds data during an input/output (I/O) transfer between a disk and the random access memory (RAM).

candidate key   A unique identifier for a row in a table. It can be made up of one or more columns. A table can have more than one candidate key, but every table must have at least one. If a table has only one candidate key, that key becomes the primary key.

cascading delete   Deletes all of the database rows or columns that are related.

cascading update   An update that updates all of the database rows or columns that are related.

character set   The collection of letters, numbers, and special characters that will define the values used in the char, varchar, and text character-based datatypes.

CHECK constraints   Acceptable data values for a column. A column can have multiple CHECK constraints, and you can apply CHECK constraints to many columns.

client A workstation accessing the resources in a client/server model. *See also* **client/server model**. (2) A program that runs on a computer, such as Microsoft Access, Microsoft Word, and Microsoft Excel.

client/server model A model in which multiple user workstations connect to one central server or many different servers with the intention of sharing information. The server manages a common resource, such as a database, and responds to client requests for data from this resource.

clustered index Determines the physical storage order of the data in a table. There can only be one clustered index in a table, but the index can be made up of multiple columns.

clustering A technology that allows for recovery from catastrophic network failure. Clustering is managed via the Microsoft Clustering Service (MSCS) which comes native in Windows NT Server Enterprise Edition. MSCS allows for the clustering of two servers and consists of a several options and features.

code page A database of 256 characters for all IBM PCs that stipulate a common character set.

column Contains an individual data item within a row; they are called *fields* in traditional programming.

component object model (COM) The programming model on which several SQL Server and database APIs are based, including SQL-DMO and OLE DB.

composite index An index using more than one column in a table.

computed column   A virtual column that is not physically stored in the table. It is computed using an expression that uses other columns in the same table.

computer-to-computer installation   Typically used when performing a hardware upgrade simultaneous to the installation of SQL Server. This method allows the administrator to specify a source and a destination system for the upgrade.

consistency   Part of the ACID test, this is the property of a transaction that defines how it manages the state of the database over time. There are three levels of consistency: immediate guaranteed, latent guaranteed, and convergence. *See also* **ACID test**.

constraint   A property that is placed on a column or a set of columns in a table. SQL Server uses CHECK, DEFAULT, FOREIGN KEY, PRIMARY KEY, REFERENCE, and UNIQUE constraints.

control-of-flow structures   A stored procedure that allows you to perform tasks using techniques such as loops or conditional processing on variables that are usually found in programming languages such as Visual Basic or C++.

cursors   Pointers to subsets within a result set. Types of cursors in Microsoft SQL Server are static, dynamic, forward-only, and keyset-driven.

database (DB)   An organization of alphanumeric information designed so that users may easily access and retrieve the information. Databases are organized into objects known as tables, which are groups of data that all have something in common.

database management system (DBMS)   A container for the collection of computerized data files that allow users to perform operations on the files, including appending, editing, generating reports, retrieving, and updating.

database owner (DBO)   Granted at the database level, this account allows for complete access to the database and all its objects. When a user creates a database he/she is automatically the DBO of that database.

database restore syntax   The command-line entries that are required in order to recover data from backups and return it to network ready status.

data bus   Connects the network interface card (NIC) to the processor. The data bus provides power, control information, and data to the card.

data definition language (DDL)   The SQL statements used to define all the objects (components), such as tables, queries, forms, and views in a SQL database.

data manipulation language (DML)   The SQL statements used to select, insert, update, and delete data in database objects.

data replication   *See* replication technology.

data type   Specifies what type of data can be stored in a column. Some of the data types include: tinyint, smallint, int, real, float, smalldatetime, datetime, smallmoney, money, and char.

Data Transformation Services (DTS)   A utility native to Microsoft SQL Server 7.0, it allows database administrators to migrate data from several other heterogeneous databases: Access, Excel, SQL, FoxPro, DBase, Paradox, Oracle, Site Server, Index Server, and any ODBC supported data source. Note that you can use VBScript, JScript, or the ActiveX scripting engine to write DTS scripts.

data warehouse   A database that is structured for query and analysis. It usually contains data that represents an organization's business history.

data warehousing   The idea that large amounts of information are stored on physical disks, typically measured in terabytes.

DB-Library   A group of high-level language libraries that provide the application programming interface (API) for the client in a client/server system.

deadlock   Occurs when two applications, which already have locks on separate objects, want a lock on the other's object. This option can be adjusted via the SET DEADLOCK PRIORITY.

default   A value that is automatically used for a column if a user does not insert a value for that column.

denormalize   The act of adding redundancy into a table in order to include data from another table. The other table can then be eliminated. This increases efficiency and performance by reducing complexity.

device   Preallocated storage space, stored in the form of a file or a partition. Microsoft SQL Server stores device information in the master database in the sysdevices system table.

differential backup   A backup method that only replicates data that has changed since the execution of the previous backup. This is considered a fast method of backing up of data and is commonly used in large enterprise environments.

direct memory access channel (DMA)   A hardware configuration that allows for bypassing the CPU of a PC and allows the operating system to transfer data from a given process directly to a peripheral device such as a hard disk controller, a network controller, or a tape backup. The device that controls this process is known as a DMA controller. While the process bypasses the CPU the transfer of data occurs at a speed one half the CPU's designated optimal running speed.

disk duplexing   Exactly like mirroring except that it uses two disk controller cards—one card for each drive in the mirror. This provides redundancy in case one of the controllers fails. *See also* **disk mirroring**.

disk mirroring   Used by RAID 1 to duplicate information to another hard disk. *See also* **Redundant Array of Inexpensive Disks (RAID)**.

disk striping   This technology allows for data to be placed over multiple physical disks. By allowing for multiple physical drives to maintain data integrity, data fault tolerance is increased. *See also* **Redundant Array of Inexpensive Disks (RAID)**.

Distribution Agent   Moves the transactions and snapshot jobs from the distribution database tables to the subscriber servers.

distributor   A server that contains the distribution database. It is the responsibility of the distributor to take publications from the publisher and distribute them to the subscriber servers.

domain controller   Installed with Windows NT 4.0, the domain consists of a mandatory Primary Domain Controller (PDC) and an optional Backup Domain Controller (BDC). Both can authenticate logins and distribute services as requested by workstations. In the event of a crash of the PDC, the BDC consistently replicates the domains user database and can be brought on line and "promoted" to PDC status. Each of the PDC and BDC are to installed on two physically different computers.

durability   Part of the ACID test, this property refers the to ability of the database to recover if the data is left in an inconsistent state. Once a database reports that a transaction has been committed to the database itself, the transaction is not able to be rolled back.

dynamic link library (DLL)   An executable routine that contains a specific set of functions stored in a DLL file. It can be loaded upon demand by the program that calls it.

dynamic locking   The process that SQL Server uses to find the most cost-effective locks at any one time.

dynamic memory allocation   The ability to adjust how much disk space is allocated for Microsoft SQL Server 7.0. These values can be adjusted by using the Memory tab in the SQL Server Properties.

dynamic self-management   An automated system new in SQL Server 7.0 that allows the system to monitor how much of its system resources are being consumed by running tasks. Microsoft SQL Server 7.0 can then automatically fit the size of the database to the amount of system resources available to it.

exclusive locks   Used to maintain data integrity during multiple database write attempts. This type of locks is used for INSERT, UPDATE, or DELETE statements.

extent   Consisting of 64KB, or eight contiguous pages, it is the smallest unit of space allocated to indexes and tables. As the need for more memory arises, more extents are allocated to the database.

fault tolerance   The ability of a computer to ensure that data and resources remain functional in the event of an emergency.

filegroup backup   Because some databases contain data from other systems, SQL Server allows for filegroups to be backed up. This backup process can be managed via the SQL Server Enterprise Manger interface.

filegroups   Collections of files sharing some common thread. In SQL Server there are three types of file groups: primary, which contains the data file; user-defined, containing any files the user wishes to create and place here; and, default, which contains the pages for all tables and indexes that did not have a filegroup specified when they were initially created by either the user or the administrator.

file types   Upon creation of a database using Microsoft SQL Server 7.0, three types of files are initially created: .MDF (primary files), .NDF (non-primary files), and .LDF (log files).

fixed database role   Defined at the database level, they exist within each database. In order to be added and granted access to a database, a user must have either an NT login account or a SQL login account. Users are typically added to this role via the SQL Server Enterprise Manager utility.

fixed memory allocation   The option in the Enterprise Manager that allows the administrator to set a consistent query memory size for Microsoft SQL Server 7.0. By using this option, it prevents the operating system from altering SQL Server memory pages.

foreign key   The column or columns whose values match the primary key in the same or another table. It does not have to be unique.

global temporary table   Prefaced by # #, these tables are available to every client and act as a temporary storage area for work tables and store procedures.

guest user account   A default account created by SQL that allows for logins to the database. The administrator can set the access rights to this account according to individual user needs.

GUID (globally unique identification number)   A GUID is a binary number that is guaranteed to be unique.

heaps   Tables that are created without a clustered index.

horizontal filtering   Used to restrict the rows that are replicated during the process of data replication. *See* **replication technology**.

implied permission   The ability to manipulate any object for which permission has already been granted. Owners of database objects are the only users capable of receiving implied permissions.

index   A database object that can speed up queries by looking up the data by key values instead of having to scan the entire table. Microsoft SQL Server 7.0 supports clustered and nonclustered indexes.

INSERT statement   Operates much like bcp. This statement can be used to add data from an external OLE DB provider to a SQL Server database in one or more rows. In order to run this command you must be the table owner.

intent locks   Locks resources in areas lower in the hierarchy of transactions.

Internet Information Services (IIS)   Provides FTP, Gopher, and Web services in Windows NT.

interprocess communication (IPC)   A method of communication between one program and another. Depending on the IPC method being used, this communication can even be across a network. IPC is often used in the client/server environment as a means of communication between the server and the client across the network.

IPX/SPX (Internetwork Packet Exchange/Sequenced Packet Exchange)   Protocol that is primarily used by Novell NetWare networks, but which can be used by other networks (such as Microsoft networks) as a routable protocol or to connect to Novell networks.

isolation   Part of the ACID test, this property defines the level of exposure that data modifications in the current transaction will have to other transactions.

jobs   Tasks that contain steps. Steps are run at intervals and can make certain administrative tasks much more manageable via their ability to automate the network processes.

join   A query that allows users to retrieve data from multiple tables based on logical relationships. Types of joins occurring in Microsoft SQL Server include inner, outer, and cross.

local temporary tables   Prefaced by #, these tables are available to the clients that created them.

locking granularity   Technology that allows Microsoft SQL Server 7.0 to differentiate the efficiency of various locking schemes.

locks As client applications access data simultaneously, Microsoft SQL Server 7.0 uses locks to prevent concurrent users from reading data that has been changed but not yet written to the database. There are four types of locks used by Microsoft SQL Server 7.0 to restrict access to a resource: shared, update, exclusive, and intent.

log file Holds all the transaction log information that is used to recover the database. The recommended file extension for all log files is .LDF.

Log Reader Agent Moves transactions that are marked for replication from the transaction log on the publisher sever to the distribution databases.

master server The server that processes and manages jobs. These jobs are then relayed via SQL Server to the receiving computers known as target servers.

Merge Agent Moves and reconciles incremental data changes that occurred after the initial snapshot was created. With this agent, data may move in both directions between subscriber and publisher severs.

merge replication This form of replication enables sites to make independent changes to replicated data. Later, changes are merged at all sites. However, this method does not ensure data consistency at each site.

Messaging Application Programming Interface (MAPI) A messaging structure that allows for a client graphical user interface in order to send and receive electronic mail. This messaging scheme allows for designing scheduling, calendars, and various personal information managers much like exist with Microsoft Exchange and Microsoft Outlook. MAPI also allows for more than one application program to exchange data with several other messaging sources over a wide range of different hardware and software operating platforms.

Microsoft Access   A database that operates as development tool, by using Visual Basic for Applications (VBA), and a database. It differs from Microsoft SQL 7.0 in that Microsoft SQL 7.0 is only a database.

Microsoft Distributed Transaction Controller   A service of Microsoft SQL Server that must run under Windows NT.

Microsoft Distributed Transaction Coordinator (MSDTC) Installed native with a typical SQL Server installation, this tool allows client (workstation) applications to receive data from multiple servers in a single transaction.

Microsoft English Query interface   Allows users to enter queries such as "What is the relationship of employees to vacation time?" without using Transact-SQL code.

Microsoft Management Console (MMC)   Included within the installation of SQL Server 7.0. This is Microsoft Corporation's strategy to normalize administrative tool interfaces across operating systems and the BackOffice server platform.

Microsoft SiteServer   Microsoft Corporation's internet/intranet commerce server software.

Microsoft System Management Server (SMS)   Part of Microsoft Corporations "zero administration strategy." SMS allows network engineers to manage software installations, network resource usability, workstation software installations, policies, and profiles, just to name a few. It is designed to exploit the Windows operating systems to their full potential in a network environment.

Microsoft SQL Server Roles   Ways in which SQL Server categorizes groups of users and assign permissions to group members. The four types of server roles are: fixed server, fixed database, public database, and user-defined.

Microsoft Transaction Server   A server used to store and distribute components. These components are developed using Microsoft's Component Object Model (COM).

Mixed Mode Authentication   Uses both Windows NT Server profile and Microsoft SQL Server authentication. If the user logs into Microsoft SQL Server without an NT login, Windows NT Server will allow its profiles to occur for the user, provided Microsoft SQL Server is set to Mixed Mode.

model database   A SQL Server database used as a template for all new databases created on the system.

multitier client/server architecture   Used for larger enterprises, this scheme of networking splits the logic of the network allowing the workstation to display data and the business logic or application program(s) to run on the server. Applications are then built and modified via ActiveX components or DLL files.

multiple backups   A data recovery in which it becomes necessary to restore the data from multiple sources. This method of operation in data recovery can be time-consuming, as pages of the database may be restore multiple times.

multipublisher   A condition when there are more than one publisher server providing data replication to one or more subscriber servers. As publisher server numbers increases, extra load is placed on the distributor.

multiserver capability   SQL Server allows for this, provided that all servers installed were installed using the same sort orders, Unicode collation, and code pages. During backup, if these parameters are not identical, then the back up will terminate.

multisubscriber   Exists when there are one or more publishers replicating data to more than one subscriber servers. When this occurs, database overhead increases as an extra load is put on the distributor.

multithreading   The capability of an application to start two or more threads of execution, which can then be concurrently processed. SQL Server is written as a multithreaded program.

NetBEUI   Originally written by IBM, NetBEUI runs on all Microsoft operating systems. It is a very fast, yet nonroutable protocol. It is ideally suited to an organization with few computers.

niladic functions   Functions that are built into SQL Server and do not retrieve information from SQL Server. These functions are often used to provide a default data value if one is not supplied during data insertion.

nonclustered index   An index in which the order of the index does not match the stored order of the physical table rows.

nonlogged operations   Used to prevent the transaction log from filling up and consuming large amounts of hard disk space.

Northwind database   A sample data set that accompanies many of Microsoft Corporation's database products such as Microsoft Access as well as Microsoft SQL Server 7.0

NWLink   Mircrosoft's implementation of Novell's IPX/SPX (Internetwork Packet Exchange/Sequenced Packet Exchange) protocol suite. NWLink is a routable transport protocol for Microsoft networks.

Object Linking and Imbedding (OLE)   A technology standard created by Microsoft Corporation, and adopted by Apple Computers, that allows for data to be shared and automatically updated between running applications. An object (picture, document) created with one client can be then placed within or called from another client.

object permission   Owners grant specific users the right to access particular objects that they own. Permission is granted at this level to tables, views, and stored procedures.

OLE DB   A set of initialization interfaces required for an OLE DB application to connect to an OLE DB data store. OLE DB is an application programming interface (API) that is based on the Component Object Model (COM).

onine transaction processing (OLTP)   A database management system that represents the state of a business function at one point in time. An OLTP database usually has large numbers of concurrent users modifying and adding data.

Open Database Connectivity (ODBC)   Originally conceived by Microsoft, it is now a universal standard to allow heterogeneous database access. Essentially, ODBC is a set of drivers that allow databases, such as Microsoft SQL 7.0 and Microsoft Access, to engage in relational database management. ODBC supports access to all databases for which ODBC drivers are available. *See also* **relational database management system.**

Open Data Services (ODS)   An application programming interface (API) for the server side of a client/server system. It acts as the liaison between the server applications and the network connection.

page   The smallest unit of storage space in Microsoft SQL Server. Consisting of 8KB of memory, there are six types of pages: date, text/image, global allocation map, page free space, index, and index allocation map.

performance baseline   The level at which the administrator determines the server is at its optimal level in terms of performance and efficiency. Factors affecting baseline performance include hardware (CPU speed, amount of RAM, cache, and so on); operating system upgrades (in terms of latest Microsoft service pack installed); design considerations on database front end interface; memory allocation via the setting of page faults; and the number of workstations and users attempting to write and read information from the database.

permissions   Authorization granted to users to access database resources. *See also* **object permission** and **statement permission**.

physical devices   Peripheral hardware machines, typically hard disks and tape drives, that allow for physical back up of mission-critical data.

physical security   The ability to control physical access to servers and peripheral equipment considered vital to the network and database.

point-of-failure   A critical point in data recovery. It is the point at which the network crashed. This is also the point to which adequate backup and restore procedures can quickly return a network to alleviate minimum down time and loss of data.

port number   The computer address for a specific service such as connection to the internet via a modem or other communications line.

primary data file   The starting point of the database. This file contains pointers to all other files in the database. The recommended naming conventions for SQL Server give this file a file extension of .MDF.

primary key   A column or columns that uniquely identifies one row from any other row in a table.

Priority-based merge replication   Replication based on custom Common Object Models specific to the network on which replication is set to run.

protocol   A set of standardized rules that multiple entities agree to abide by. Computers need a standard set of procedures in order to manage the data packets they send and receive. They must use the same compatible protocol or the communication will not work.

public database role   A special role to which all users belong by default. Users cannot be dropped from the public role as they may from fixed roles. Also, public roles capture all default permissions for users in a database.

Publication Wizard   An graphic user interface that steps the administrator through the procedure of setting up and designating the nature of a particular SQL Server. Through this wizard, an administrator can predetermine if a server is to operate as either a publisher server or a subscriber server.

publisher   The server that makes data available for replication to other servers, known as subscribers. This server is responsible for which data is to be replicated, as well as for which data has changed via late transactions.

pull subscription   A subscription in which the subscriber sever is set to request periodic updates of changes from the publisher server.

push subscription   A subscription in which the publisher server propagates the changes to the subscriber without a specific request from the subscriber server.

query   A request for the retrieval, deletion, or modification of specific data.

query governor   The option that allows administrators to conserve system resources by setting restrictions on the duration of a query.

query optimizer   The component that generates the optimum query execution plan.

Redundant Array of Inexpensive Disks (RAID)   A grouping of hard disks connected to a server with the intention of creating mirrored hard disks so that data exists in more than one place on a typical server. RAID levels run from 0 to 5, with 0 stipulating the lowest level of data security and level 5 stipulating complete data redundancy of the disk array.

relational database management system (RBDMS)   An organization of databases that share data, often across multiple networks. Data is sometimes entered into one database and another database can access this data and make it available to users or even to other databases. This system organizes data into related columns and rows.

remote procedure call (RPC)   Used extensively in distributed computing environments, a set of rules and methods for controlling and directing how a process is started and run on a network node foreign from the node/computer that initially requests the process.

remote server   A SQL sever on the network that can be accessed from a user's local server.

remote stored procedure   A collection of control-of-flow statements and SQL statements that are stored under a name on a remote server.

Replication Monitor   A graphical tool that can be used for viewing the status of replication agents and troubleshooting potential problems at the distributor. It is found in the SQL Server Enterprise Manager.

replication technology   The Microsoft technology that automatically copies data to multiple locations and can restore and/or move it to multiple locations. This provides a fast and inexpensive way of managing database housed on multiple servers. Note that data can also be replicated to/from other database used ODBC. Microsoft uses several elements to populate its database replication technology including publisher, subscriber, article, and distributor. *See also* **Open Database Connectivity (ODBC).**

restoration time   The time it takes in order to completely recover a database in the event of a catastrophic hard disk, server, or general network failure.

result set   The set of data returned from a SELECT statement.

roles   Database roles are ways in which users are added to databases and given permission to access those resources.

row   A data structure within a table that contains the complete set of columns. It is called a *record* in traditional programming.

row aggregate function   A function that displays detail and summary rows in one set of results. It does this by generating summary values that appear as additional rows in query results.

rule   A database object that is bound to a column, or a user-defined data type that specifies the types of data values that can be used for that column. For example, a rule can be made to make sure that the ZIP code in a record contains only numbers.

scalability   The capability to expand to meet future needs (in other words, to upgrade). It is a characteristic of both software and hardware.

scalar aggregate   A function that is applied to all of the rows in a table (which produces one value per function).

secondary data files   All data files other than primary data files and log files. Microsoft recommends these data files have an .NDF extension.

self-join   A join comparing rows within the same table.

select list   The expressions or keywords that define the attributes of the columns returned from the specified tables in a query.

server   A computer that provides shared resources to network users.

server back up   The complete copy and replication of all data that currently exists on the server.

server synchronization   The process by which servers in an NT domain, specifically PDC and BDC, are reconciled and brought current to contain identical user databases. In SQL Server, it is the synchronization of the primary and standby servers that allow for data replication and mirroring.

shared lock   A lock created by read operations. It allows concurrent database connections to read data. Because reading data does not affect database content, shared locks can be used concurrently with other lock types.

Showplan   A tool used for optimizing queries in Microsoft SQL Server 7.0. It displays the query execution plan for an SQL statement.

side-by-side installation   This method of installing Microsoft SQL Server 7.0 allows the latest version installed to run on the same machine as a previous version of SQL Server, such as Microsoft SQL Server version 6.0 or 6.5.

Simple Network Management Protocol (SNMP)   Part of the TCP/IP suite of protocols, this protocol allows for the management and monitoring of multiple nodes on a network. Two types of SNMP currently exist: SNMP1 and SNMP2.

single publisher   This replication involves a single publisher sever providing data information potentially to multiple subscriber servers.

single subscriber   A replication scenario in which there typically exists one publisher, one subscriber, and one distributor. This is the most common SQL Server database operating environment.

Snapshot Agent   Prepares the scheme and initial data files of published tables and store procedures. It then stores these snapshots on the distributor server and records information for data synchronization.

snapshot replication   This technique takes a snapshot of the current data on the publisher and replaces all of the data on the subscriber periodically. Snapshot replication provides guaranteed consistency among all servers marked for replication.

spin counter option   Specifies a limit on the attempts a process can make when trying to obtain access to a resource.

SQL Mail   A component of SQL Server that allows for the processing of queries about the status of the server via electronic mail. This service requires the installation of Windows Messaging Service or Microsoft Exchange, in addition to the appropriate Mail Application Programming Interface (MAPI) driver.

SQL Server Agent   Installed in a typical SQL Server installation, this tools allows for periodic scheduling of server jobs. It can be configured to respond on-demand to activities raised by alerts.

SQL Server Enterprise Manager   A graphical user interface used to manage and control users and processes on databases running under Microsoft SQL Server 7.0 and using system resources.

SQL Server Performance Monitor Integration   Provides up-to-the-minute performance and activity statistics. It is an integration of SQL Server with Windows NT Performance Monitor.

SQL Server Profiler   A graphical tool that allows system administrators to trace problems by monitoring events including deadlocking, server connects and disconnects, login attempts, and other vital server information. In order to achieve this type of information, data is captured in real time as processes run.

SQL Query Analyzer   A utility that allows you to enter stored procedures and Transact-SQL statements in a graphical user interface. It also provides the capability to analyze queries graphically.

standard database role   Allows the system administrator to set up the correct level of security needed within a database. These roles can contain

NT groups and users and other roles that simultaneously occur in other current databases.

standard security model Microsoft SQL Server maintains its own security log by requiring the user to authenticate to access the database. This is the most secure model.

statement permission Controls the use of Transact-SQL statements used to create objects within a database. Statement permission can be granted, denied, or revoked.

stored procedure A set of precompiled Transact-SQL statements that execute as an object. The benefit of using stored procedures is that they are precompiled, which translates into faster execution times. Security is more easily enforced because permissions can be set for the object only. Stored procedures that are supplied by SQL Server are called system stored procedures.

Structured Query Language (SQL) Developed by IBM in the 1970s, it is a language used to retrieve information from a database.

subscriber Servers that store data replicated from publishers. Microsoft SQL Server 7.0 allows subscriber servers to update data.

subscription database Database that receives data and tables that are replicated from a publication database.

subquery A SELECT query that returns one value and is nested inside another subquery or a SELECT, UPDATE, DELETE, or INSERT statement.

symmetric multiprocessing (SMP) SMP is the concept that a computer system can support multiple processors and the processors can balance the load between themselves. If your computer has four CPUs, then they would share the processing work load and each one could participate in executing parts of a single program. Having SMP leads to scalability. *See also* **scalability.**

system administrator   Similar to the DBO, but the system administrator has control over the entire server. A built-in feature of Microsoft SQL Server 7.0, this account automatically has control over all databases residing on the server. Note that when using Mixed Mode security, the system administrator account must be used for the first administrative login.

system catalog   A store of user account information in 13 system tables found in the master database. The user information includes security, ID, passwords, databases, environment tables, system error messages, and system stored procedures.

system stored procedures   A precompiled set of Transact-SQL statements supplied by SQL Server. System stored procedures provide shortcuts for retrieving information from system tables or for updating the tables. The names of system stored procedures begin with sp_.

system tables   Tables that are created when the database is created. They store SQL Server configuration information and definitions of the objects, permissions, and users in SQL databases. Initially they consume .5MB of disk space.

table   A collection of data that is stored in multiple rows and columns.

table scan   A scan in which SQL Server starts at the beginning of the table and reads every row to find the rows that meet the search criteria.

TCP/IP (Transmission Control Protocol/Internet Protocol)
An industry standard suite of protocols designed for local and wide area networking. Widely used for Internet communication.

TCP/IP sockets   A library native installed on SQL Server that communications with Windows 9x workstations. In order to run TCP/IP sockets, a port must be specified. The default number SQL Server uses is port 1433.

TerraServer   A one-terabyte database that is a collection of geographical information collected by Russian and United States satellites.

thread   The smallest unit of code in a process.

time slice option   Used by administrators of Microsoft SQL Server 7.0 to set a limit on the time that a process can be active.

timeoutoption   Sets a predetermined limit on the time that the system will wait for a resource that is currently busy or running.

tool   A SQL Server application with a graphical user interface used to perform common tasks.

Transact-SQL   The standard language used for communication between applications and SQL Server. It allows users to access the database and create and modify the data. In Microsoft SQL Server the four main statements to achieve this are: SELECT, UPDATE, DELETE, and INSERT. In SQL Server 7.0, Transact-SQL statements can be used to create a database.

transaction   A transaction is the smallest logical unit of work for the database. All actions that occur on the database break down into one or more transactions. Transactions consist of the four properties, called the ACID properties. Each level of work must contain all of these properties before they are considered transactions. *See also* **ACID test**.

transaction isolation levels   Settings that allow for various levels of data integrity. In Microsoft SQL Server 7.0 there are four different isolation levels: read committed, read uncommitted, repeatable read, and serializable.

transaction log   A serial record of all modifications that have occurred in the database. The log records the start of each transaction, the changes to the data, and enough information to undo the modifications.

transaction log backup   Server is only backed up to the point at which the network failed, according to the transaction log. *See also* **transaction log**.

transaction processing   A method in which transactions are executed as soon as the system receives them.

transactional replication   Uses the publisher's database transaction log to capture changes that were made to an article's data. The changes are transmitted to the subscribers as incremental changes. When using this method, SQL Server monitors all INSERT, UPDATE, and DELETE statements.

Transfer manager   Part of SQL Server Enterprise Manger in SQL 6.5, this utility allowed administrators to transfer data and objects (triggers, store procedures, etc) between databases. *See also* **Data Transformation Services (DTS)**.

trigger   A stored procedure that runs when data in a specific table is modified, such as with an update, delete, or insert. Triggers are often used to ensure consistency among related data in multiple tables.

Unicode   Defines a set of numbers, letters, and symbols that SQL Server recognizes in the nchar, nvarchar, and ntext data types. It includes characters for most languages and is related to but separate from character sets.

Unicode collation sequence   Removes language barriers by enabling a 16-bit multilingual character set. A sort order for Unicode data, this utility assists in the deployment of SQL Server using multiple languages within a single server.

UNIQUE constraints   Constraints that ensure a nonprimary key has data integrity.

unique index   An index in which no two rows can have the same index value. This prohibits duplicate key values.

update lock   A lock that is placed on resources, such as rows or tables, that can be updated. These locks are used to prevent deadlocks that occur when multiple sessions lock resources and update them later.

user connection option   A new feature in Microsoft SQL Server 7.0, this function allows for dynamic assignment of system resources as each user establishes a new connection with SQL Server. It is used to specify the maximum number of simultaneous user connections allowed on SQL Server; thus helping to avoid overloading the server with too many concurrent connections.

update statistics   A process of recalculating information about the key value distribution in specified indexes.

user-defined data type   A data type that is based on a SQL Server data type and is created by the user for data storage. User-defined data types can be bound by rules and defaults. *See also* **base data type**.

variable   A defined entity that has a value assigned to it. Users can define local variables. Global variables are predefined and maintained by the system.

vector aggregate   Functions that are applied to all rows with the same value in a specific column, using the GROUP BY clause. The HAVING clause can be used with the GROUP BY clause to produce a value for each group per function.

vertical filtering   Used to specify which rows are replicated during the process of data replication.

view   A display of a table that shows the table's data. A view is a virtual table that retrieves the data with queries, and can contain more than one table. Before the user is able to use the view, they must have permission on the view and on all dependent objects.

Visual InterDev   A suite of Microsoft development products including Visual Basic, Visual C++, Visual J++, and Visual FoxPro.

Windows New Technology (NT)   Microsoft's server operating system that is used as an operating platform for Microsoft SQL Server 7.0.

Windows NT Application Event Log   An applet running in Windows NT that tracks all occurrences on the network. SQL Sever writes all events including all SQL Server errors to the Windows NT Event Log.

Windows NT Authentication   Allows users with a Windows NT user account to connect to SQL Server.

wildcard characters   Characters used with the LIKE keyword for matching patterns. The percent (%), brackets ([]), and underscore (_) characters are examples of wildcard characters.

INDEX

A

B

E

F

L

M

P

U

V

Custom Corporate Network Training

Train on Cutting Edge Technology
We can bring the best in skill-based training to your facility to create a real-world hands-on training experience. Global Knowledge has invested millions of dollars in network hardware and software to train our students on the same equipment they will work with on the job. Our relationships with vendors allow us to incorporate the latest equipment and platforms into your on-site labs.

Maximize Your Training Budget
Global Knowledge provides experienced instructors, comprehensive course materials, and all the networking equipment needed to deliver high quality training. You provide the students; we provide the knowledge.

Avoid Travel Expenses
On-site courses allow you to schedule technical training at your convenience, saving time, expense, and the opportunity cost of travel away from the workplace.

Discuss Confidential Topics
Private on-site training permits the open discussion of sensitive issues such as security, access, and network design. We can work with your existing network's proprietary files while demonstrating the latest technologies.

Customize Course Content
Global Knowledge can tailor your courses to include the technologies and the topics which have the greatest impact on your business. We can complement your internal training efforts or provide a total solution to your training needs.

Corporate Pass
The Corporate Pass Discount Program rewards our best network training customers with preferred pricing on public courses, discounts on multimedia training packages, and an array of career planning services.

Global Knowledge Training Lifecycle
Supporting the Dynamic and Specialized Training Requirements of Information Technology Professionals

- Define Profile
- Assess Skills
- Design Training
- Deliver Training
- Test Knowledge
- Update Profile
- Use New Skills

College Credit Recommendation Program
The American Council on Education's CREDIT program recommends 53 Global Knowledge courses for college credit. Now our network training can help you earn your college degree while you learn the technical skills needed for your job. When you attend an ACE-certified Global Knowledge course and pass the associated exam, you earn college credit recommendations for that course. Global Knowledge can establish a transcript record for you with ACE, which you can use to gain credit at a college or as a written record of your professional training that you can attach to your resume.

Registration Information

COURSE FEE: The fee covers course tuition, refreshments, and all course materials. Any parking expenses that may be incurred are not included. Payment or government training form must be received six business days prior to the course date. We will also accept Visa/MasterCard and American Express. For non-U.S. credit card users, charges will be in U.S. funds and will be converted by your credit card company. Checks drawn on Canadian banks in Canadian funds are acceptable.

COURSE SCHEDULE: Registration is at 8:00 a.m. on the first day. The program begins at 8:30 a.m. and concludes at 4:30 p.m. each day.

CANCELLATION POLICY: Cancellation and full refund will be allowed if written cancellation is received in our office at least six business days prior to the course start date. Registrants who do not attend the course or do not cancel more than six business days in advance are responsible for the full registration fee; you may transfer to a later date provided the course fee has been paid in full. Substitutions may be made at any time. If Global Knowledge must cancel a course for any reason, liability is limited to the registration fee only.

GLOBAL KNOWLEDGE: Global Knowledge programs are developed and presented by industry professionals with "real-world" experience. Designed to help professionals meet today's interconnectivity and interoperability challenges, most of our programs feature hands-on labs that incorporate state-of-the-art communication components and equipment.

ON-SITE TEAM TRAINING: Bring Global Knowledge's powerful training programs to your company. At Global Knowledge, we will custom design courses to meet your specific network requirements. Call 1 (919) 461-8686 for more information.

YOUR GUARANTEE: Global Knowledge believes its courses offer the best possible training in this field. If during the first day you are not satisfied and wish to withdraw from the course, simply notify the instructor, return all course materials, and receive a 100% refund.

In the US:

CALL: 1 (888) 762-4442

FAX: 1 (919) 469-7070

VISIT OUR WEBSITE:

www.globalknowledge.com

MAIL CHECK AND THIS FORM TO:

Global Knowledge

Suite 200

114 Edinburgh South

P.O. Box 1187

Cary, NC 27512

In Canada:

CALL: 1 (800) 465-2226

FAX: 1 (613) 567-3899

VISIT OUR WEBSITE:

www.globalknowledge.com.ca

MAIL CHECK AND THIS FORM TO:

Global Knowledge

Suite 1601

393 University Ave.

Toronto, ON M5G 1E6

REGISTRATION INFORMATION:

Course title _____

Course location _____ Course date _____

Name/title _____ Company _____

Name/title _____ Company _____

Name/title _____ Company _____

Address _____ Telephone _____ Fax _____

City _____ State/Province _____ Zip/Postal Code _____

Credit card _____ Card # _____ Expiration date _____

Signature _____

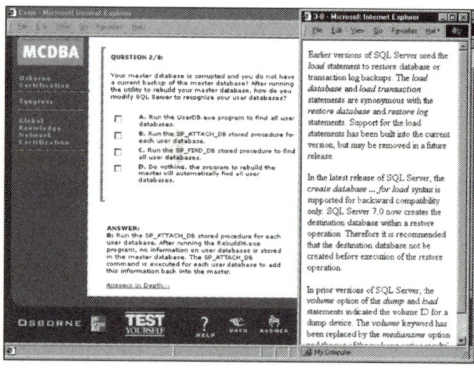
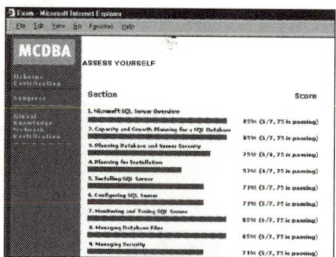
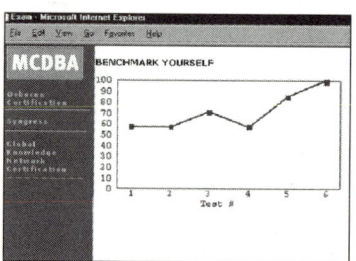